ASIAN VISIONS OF AUTHORITY

Sponsored by the

JOINT COMMITTEE ON SOUTHEAST ASIA

JOINT COMMITTEE ON KOREA

JOINT COMMITTEE ON JAPAN

of the SOCIAL SCIENCE RESEARCH COUNCIL

and the AMERICAN COUNCIL OF LEARNED SOCIETIES

Asian Visions of Authority

RELIGION AND THE MODERN
STATES OF EAST AND
SOUTHEAST ASIA

Edited by

Charles F. Keyes

Laurel Kendall

Helen Hardacre

UNIVERSITY OF HAWAII PRESS

HONOLULU

Asian visions of authority : religion and the modern states of East
   and Southeast Asia / edited by Charles F. Keyes, Laurel Kendall,
   Helen Hardacre.
      p. cm.
   Papers presented at a conference sponsored by the Social Science
Research Council and American Council of Learned Societies' Joint
Committees on Southeast Asia, on Korea, and on Japan.
   Includes bibliographical references and index.
   ISBN 0–8248–1471–1 (alk. paper)
   1. Religion and state—East Asia—Congresses.   2. Religion and
state—Asia, Southeastern—Congresses.   3. Authority (Religion)—
Congresses.   4. East Asia—Religion—Congresses.   5. Asia,
Southeastern—Religion—Congresses.   I. Keyes, Charles F.
II. Kendall, Laurel.   III. Hardacre, Helen, 1949– .   IV. Joint
Committee on Southeast Asia.   V. Joint Committee on Korea.
VI. Joint Committee on Japan.
BL1055.A87   1994
322'.1'095—dc20   93–37979
                                                     CIP

Designed by Paula Newcomb

CONTENTS

v

PREFACE

This book is the product of an unusual cooperative venture involving scholars specializing in both East and Southeast Asia. In the mid-1980s Charles Keyes, Laurel Kendall, and Helen Hardacre were each involved in separate investigations into the relationship between religious and social change in Southeast Asia, Korea, and Japan. The senior editor (Keyes) was also involved at the time in a project sponsored by the Joint Social Science Research Council/American Council of Learned Societies Committee on Southeast Asia to assess research on Buddhism, Christianity, and Islam in Southeast Asia. Toby Volkman, staff associate for the Committee on Southeast Asia at the Social Science Research Council, thought this project might be linked to similar ones being considered by the Joint Committees on Korea and Japan and through her encouragement we three editors came together.

When we first met in 1986 we thought a common theme might be the "new" religions of East and Southeast Asia. We sensed that some of the recently established religions in the region such as Kurozumikyō, Reiyū-kai, and Mahikari in Japan, Ch'ŏndogyo and the Unification Church (the so-called Moonies) in Korea, Cao Dai in Vietnam, Iglesia Ni Cristo in the Philippines, and the cult of the "Heavenly Valley" in Thailand might be profitably examined comparatively. Each of these religions offers its adherents a new authoritative sense of power with which to face personal or social crises. As we continued our discussions through correspondence and in subsequent meetings, it became clear to us that these religions were symptomatic of a more general phenomenon of religious resurgence in Asia. Older established religions have also sought to reassert and redefine their authority as political and economic conditions have undergone radical change. We then decided to propose a project to compare types of religious resurgence in East and Southeast Asia.

As a first step we organized a workshop with a small number of scholars specializing in the study of religion in Southeast Asia, Korea, Japan, and China. With support from the Joint SSRC/ACLS Committees on Southeast Asia, Korea, and Japan, the workshop was held in April 1987.

The position papers presented at the workshop, the discussion at the workshop itself, and some follow-up thoughts written by several of the participants led us to formulate a proposal for a conference at which participants would focus on the problematic nature of religious communities in Asian societies.

Support for the conference was obtained from a grant made to SSRC by the National Endowment for the Humanities. Some thirty people were invited to participate in a conference on "Communities in Question: Religion and Authority in East and Southeast Asia." Twenty-eight people actually attended the conference held in Hua Hin, Thailand, in May 1989.

We sought at the conference to stimulate discussion across the political and area studies boundaries within which the participants usually carry out their work. We were pleased that so many common issues emerged from the presentations and the discussions at Hua Hin.

Although the conference had a broad theme, it became apparent to us as we reflected on the results that most of the papers centered around the issue of the tension between religious authority and the authority of the modern states of Asia. While we were reluctant to exclude from this volume a number of excellent papers that explored other issues, we have chosen to emphasize thematic coherence in compiling this volume.

We have acquired many debts in seeing this project through to completion. We are especially grateful to Toby Volkman, who as staff associate at the Social Science Research Council for the Joint SSRC/ACLS Committee on Southeast Asia, prepared the proposals for submission to the Council and to the National Endowment for the Humanities for support of the project. Toby was also an active participant at both the conference and the workshop that preceded it. Raquel Orvyn Rivera, formerly also a staff associate at SSRC, served as a crucial link to the Joint SSRC/ACLS Committee on Korea.

We benefited greatly from the high level of discussion at the conference and thank for their stimulating contributions Nancy Abelman, Chungmoo Choi, Donald N. Clark, David Gosling, Inoue Nobutaka, Daniel L. Overmyer, Jennifer Robertson, Somboon Suksamran, Shimazono Susumu, Vivienne Wee, as well as those whose papers appear in this book. We are especially grateful for the reflections of the three main discussants —Benedict Anderson, Lawrence A. Babb, and Jean Comaroff. We wish also to thank Charnvit Kasetsiri, then vice-rector of Thammasat University in Bangkok, for the excellent arrangements he made for the conference.

Jane Atkinson read the manuscript of the book for the Joint Committee on Southeast Asia and provided us with a detailed and useful critique. We also benefitted from the comments of two anonymous reviewers for the University of Hawaii Press. The comments of many others also find acknowledgement in the papers that appear below.

The project would have faltered without the help of Jack David Elder, in 1987 a graduate student at Boston University, who prepared a report on the workshop that led up to the conference; Tom Miller, scientific assistant to Laurel Kendall at the American Museum of Natural History, who coordinated the editing and word processing of the book; Daniel Limawan, graduate student at the University of Washington, who spent many hours checking sources; and G. Carter Bentley, consulting editor in Seattle, who prepared the index. We were very fortunate in being assigned Joanne Sandstrom, senior editor at the Institute of East Asian Studies at the University of California at Berkeley, to be the copy editor for the manuscript.

Although the better part of a decade has elapsed between the conception of this project and its completion, each phase has led us to new insights into the processes of religious change in Asia. We now offer the results of this endeavor to readers and trust that they will also find in the essays that follow perspectives to stimulate new thoughts about a region that is not only economically but also religiously dynamic.

INTRODUCTION

Contested Visions of Community in East and Southeast Asia

CHARLES F. KEYES, HELEN HARDACRE,
AND LAUREL KENDALL

Religion and the Crisis of Authority in Asian Societies

The essays in this volume examine various religious facets of what we term a *crisis of authority* that has emerged as a consequence of the modernization and nation-building projects of Asian states. Over the past century the rulers of the various Asian states have sought to co-opt, reshape, marginalize, and, in some cases, suppress religious communities within the territories under their control to ensure that these communities do not promote visions that are in tension or conflict with their own. From the vantage point of the late twentieth century, it is now apparent that while the religious landscape in every Asian society has been significantly transformed since Japan's Meiji Restoration in 1868 initiated a new era in Asian history, the modernization and nation-building projects of Asian states have not only failed to subordinate religious authority to state authority but have generated what Chaiwat Satha-Anand (in this volume), following Jürgen Habermas, has termed a "deficit of legitimacy." As a result, many people in these countries have turned to religious visions of authority other than those sanctioned by their states.

The varieties of religious questioning of the social order discussed in this book are not limited to Asia, and Comaroff in her epilogue seeks to situate the cases examined in this book within a broad theoretical perspective. In our introduction we do, however, focus on Asia, looking at the commonalities that can be found through a comparison of East and Southeast Asian cases, since we think there is much to be gained from such a comparison.

The many links between East and Southeast Asian societies set the region apart from other regions of the world. Traditional conceptions of the moral basis of the social order—often labeled "Confucian," but also rooted in Chinese popular religion—were first developed in China and were then transmitted to Japan, Korea, and Vietnam. They were also carried to Southeast Asia by the many thousands of Chinese migrants

1

who settled throughout the region (see, for example, DeBernardi in this volume). In several Southeast Asian societies—most notably Singapore and Malaysia, but also including Thailand (see Keyes 1987:208)—these conceptions are still invoked directly or indirectly by some today in their efforts to relate to the modern world.

Japan was the first country in Asia to embark on a project to remake its society as a modern nation-state, and its experience has had a profound impact on nearly every country in East and Southeast Asia. As Anagnost shows in her essay, the genealogy of the antisuperstition campaigns in the People's Republic of China can be traced not to Marxist-Leninist thought but to a Japanese critique of practices deemed unacceptable in a modern society (see also Duara 1988). Both Kendall and Kim (in this volume) note how an adamantly anti-Communist South Korean state similarly attacked "superstition" (see also Choi 1987); the campaign was reminiscent of policies once enacted in Korea by a Japanese colonial adminstration (Ch'oe 1974). The early Vietnamese nationalists explicitly sought to learn from the Japanese experience (Marr 1981:118), and through at least the early years of World War II many nationalists in other Southeast Asian countries looked to Japan for ideas and support for their movements (McCoy 1980).

Today, many East and Southeast Asian politicians and scholars maintain there is a distinctively Asian view of order that contrasts with that of the West. Khien Theeravit, a Thai specialist on China who was the founding head of the Institute of Asian Studies at Chulalongkorn University, Thailand's most prestigious institution of higher learning, has provided a succinct summary of this view. In a recent paper, he wrote: "The attitudes of the Thais and their [East and Southeast Asian] neighbors toward human rights have been traditionally similar: greater emphasis has been given to duty, not right; order and harmony has always been considered more important than pluralism" (Khien Theeravit 1992:12). Such a stance lies at the root of the defense that Korean, Burmese, Vietnamese, and Chinese governments have given for the suppression of democracy movements. It has also been strongly advocated by Lee Kuan Yew, the long-time prime minister of Singapore, and Mahathir Mohammed, the prime minister of Malaysia. While this stance is belied by much of what is reported in this volume, it serves nonetheless to indicate how a common ground in different Asian states has been sought for resisting pressures toward pluralism exerted not only by political but also by ethnic and religious movements.

As the papers on Muslim communities in Indonesia (Hefner), Malaysia (Shamsul), Thailand (Chaiwat Satha-Anand), and China (Gladney) in this volume demonstrate, the adherents of certain religions existing in several different Asian societies see themselves as belonging or linked to the same transnational community. The same is also true of many Asian Christians.[1]

Although we find the case for a comparative study of religious change in contemporary East and Southeast Asia compelling, scholars working on different countries in the region have rarely come together to address this particular issue. The conference from which this book emerged was the first effort in more than a quarter of a century to examine the relationship between religion and modernization within a broad Asian framework. In 1963 a group of scholars held a conference in the Philippines on "Cultural Motivations to Progress in South and Southeast Asia"; their efforts culminated in the book *Religion and Progress in Modern Asia* (Bellah 1965). In our conference and this book we demonstrate that the thesis of the earlier conference—that as Asian states "progress," they will increasingly be secularized—has not been born out in practice. On the contrary, as these states have modernized, religion has become more, not less, significant.[2]

Religion and the Modern Nation-State

The varieties of Asian religious experience considered in this book all relate to a "modern" crisis of authority. This is not to say that Asians lived until recent times within "magical gardens," to use Max Weber's term, in which tradition was never questioned. On the contrary, the hundreds, perhaps thousands, of millenarian movements known to us from Asian history, which are especially well documented for China (Wakeman 1977; Naquin 1976; Overmeyer 1976), indicate that in premodern times people experienced intense crises for which received religio-political authority no longer seemed an adequate or acceptable solution. Even if these millenarian movements proved in the end to be little more than "rituals of rebellion" (Gluckman 1959) that ended with the reassertion of traditional authority, they still indicate that religious challenges to the authority of the past are not distinctively modern phenomena. Traditional authority in Asia was also challenged by missionizing religions—first Buddhism and then Islam—long before modern times, and even early Catholic missionization must be considered premodern. While these "historic" religions were synthesized with local beliefs to generate ahistorical cosmologies, they still contained the seeds of more dynamic views of the world.

What is essentially modern about the religious ferment of today is that fundamental political, economic, and ideological changes that first appeared in Europe and then spread to Asia (and elsewhere) drove, in the words of Benedict Anderson (1991:36)[3] "a harsh wedge between cosmology and history." "Modernity," as R. J. Zwi Werblowsky (1976:14) has written, "renders the past problematic." It is the experience of having a problematic relationship with the past, of being alienated from traditional certainties in which cosmology reflects community and vice versa, of being offered and often pressured to accept an identity with one particular version of one's heritage rather than another that constitutes what we term the modern crisis of authority.

This crisis is a consequence of the efforts by Asian rulers to reshape political orders in the mold of the nation-state. In the premodern Asian states, power was derived from a hierarchy taken as the earthly manifestation of a cosmic order. Over a period from the late nineteenth century to just after World War II, every country in Asia was restructured on a Western model of the nation-state—some as the consequence of direct Western colonial rule and others, most notably Japan and Thailand, as the result of borrowing Western ideas of statecraft by indigenous elites. Although the models varied, all entailed the establishment of political orders under strong central governments administered by trained officials who operated according to function and who followed what were by Western measures rationalized laws and regulations. Further, they included as their subjects all those living within internationally recognized territorial boundaries. The modern state was—and this was probably the most innovative characteristic for those Asian countries that had long known bureaucratic rule—to represent and promote the interests of a "nation," a "people."

No matter what way the process of nation building was begun, everywhere in Asia the nation came to be conceived of as shaped by "modernization". The Western theories of modernization adopted by the rulers of the new nation-states of Asia presupposed the liberation of people from superstition and time-consuming and expensive rituals so that they could participate in a new rationalized order oriented toward the attainment of self-sustaining economic growth. Modernization theory posited that a secular "civil" identity with a nation-state would eventually replace "primordial" identities with traditional local, religious, ethnic, or linguistic communities. The perpetuation of primordial identities was, indeed, seen by political leaders and social scientists alike as a fundamental problem in the development of modern nation-states. Clifford Geertz (1973b:259), expressing what was the dominant view in the social sciences in the early 1960s, observed that the basic problem of so-called new states (i.e., states that had not yet become fully modern) was that such states "are abnormally susceptible to serious disaffection based on primordial attachments."

In pursuit of "progress" free from primordial attachments, the rulers of the modern states of East and Southeast Asia all have instituted policies toward religious institutions. These policies have been predicated on the adoption of official definitions of "religion," definitions that again have tended to be derived from the West. Indeed, in most Asian cultures prior to the modern period, there was no indigenous terminology corresponding to ideas of "religion" held by Christians or Jews.[4] Complex predispositions about the nature of religion—the primacy of texts; creeds pledging exclusive allegiance to a single deity; ethics; and a personal, privatized relation to a deity, all originating in the theologically unadorned varieties of Protestantism—were brought to Asia by missionaries in the nineteenth century. When these predispositions came to inform official discourse on religion, they were often used to devalue other aspects of religious life such as festival, ritual, and communal observances—precisely those aspects that were at the heart of popular religious life in East and Southeast Asia. And as Western notions about religion were incorporated into law and custom, they also came to exercise a great influence on popular religious life in Asia as well.

State policies toward religion in Asia have been shaped not only by modernization goals but also by the needs of states to legitimate their rule and unify their populace. Nation-building requires a very different stance toward the past than does modernization. While commitment to modernization entails rejection of those aspects of a society's past deemed impediments to a rationalized bureaucratic order, nation-building depends on the very opposite move. The nation is always imagined as a community of those who share a common history (Anderson 1991; Chaiwat Satha-Anand 1988b; also see Soedjatmoko 1965:3). The recognition that a nation is an imagined community makes clear that a nation is not a natural precipitate of an inevitable historical process slowed by people's attachment to primordial identities. On the contrary, identity with a nation, if it is to be effective, must be invested with that quality of "givenness" that Geertz associated with primordiality. Ultimately, any particular national identity entails a leap of faith, acceptance of the fundamental givenness of premises about who belongs to the community sharing the same national heritage. It is in this sense that nationalism is in essence religious. As Kapferer (1988:1) notes at the outset of his book on the nationalisms of Sri Lanka and Australia, "Nationalism makes the political religious and places the nation above politics."

The process of creating modern nation-states has, thus, entailed two rather contradictory stances toward religion. While the modernizing stance leads to a deemphasis of ritual practices, the nation-building one leads to the promotion of selected practices and even the invention of new rites (Hobsbawm and Ranger 1983). Modernization emphasizes rational action; nation-building insists on a commitment of faith. The tension between these two stances as well as that between each of them and those religious practices that derive their authority from other than the state have contributed to the crisis of authority with which we are here concerned.

The crisis has become particularly acute in the late twentieth century because, following Chaiwat Satha-Anand's analysis in his chapter in this volume, most if not all Asian societies have entered a new "moment" in the process of legitimation of nation-states. As the particular activities that in any one society constituted nation-building and modernization become social memories rather than on-going experiences, these memories have become the impetus for some Asians to reflect critically on their contemporary situations. Because of the growing significance of transnational linkages there are also citizens of particular states who imagine themselves as belonging to communities other than those confined to the boundaries of the state in which they live. In some cases this heightened self-consciousness of being engaged in a dialogue with both the modern state and local tradition might be characterized as postmodern. We think here, for example, of those participating in shamanistic performances held in connection with student protests against the state in Korea (see Kwang-ok Kim's chapter) or those who find both local and global meanings in the shrine that commemorates those killed by the atomic bomb at Hiroshima (see Foard's chapter).

The Politics of Ritual Displacement and the Persistence of Religion

In pursuit of their modernizing and nation-building projects, all Asian states have engaged in what Anagnost (in this volume) terms the "politics of ritual displacement" to transfer authority from religious communities to the state. Although premodern states sought on occasion to substitute state-approved gods for local deities or to vest some religious practitioners with greater authority than others (one thinks here, for example, of the downgrading of the authority of Buddhist monks in China, Korea, and Vietnam), none had the power and will to undertake, as Anagnost observes, "to reinscribe the local landscape within its own totalizing order." The control of modern "technologies of power" (see Cohn and Dirks 1988; Anderson 1991: chap. 10), including the power to set the calendar by cosmopolitan time; to regulate curricula for a universal educational system; to certify births, marriages, and deaths; to determine land use; to issue building permits; to license the media, and so on has given states a great advantage over religions, which look outside the state for their ultimate authority. Despite this, in no case has any state been successful in preempting the authority of all alternative conceptions of moral community.

The politics of ritual displacement have faltered because no civic order promoted by any state has proven capable of meeting all fundamental existential problems that people encounter. On the contrary, many have confronted new problems as a consequence of the social dislocations and restructuring that modernizing and nation-building policies have generated. The limits of the politics of ritual displacement can be seen in the challenge the dead pose to the authority of the state in a number of cases discussed in this book.

Although rationalization and secularization have undermined many religious beliefs, the belief in the continuing significance of the dead is still a ubiquitous element in conceptions of the world. Those dead who evoke both intimate connections and a larger history are potent symbols. Even the Communist regimes of China, Vietnam, North Korea, and Laos have sought to draw on such beliefs to promote their legitimation by creating shrines and rites to memorialize the dead of their revolutions or of their wars with antagonistic countries. The mausoleums of Mao Zedong and Ho Chi Minh, unlike that of Lenin, are still *the* national shrines of China and Vietnam.

Some dead become ghosts. Belief in ghosts entails a collective memory that symbolizes something of significance to a certain group of people and, often, also evokes strong emotions beause the death that produces a ghost is typically a premature death, one recalled with pain. In the chapters that follow we are introduced to a number of ghosts whose presumed presence in one or another Asian landscape raises fundamental questions about the civil order backed by the state.[5]

Weller discusses a rapidly growing cult in Taiwan that centers on the propitiation of the ghosts of seventeen men and a dog. Ghosts are the most amoral denizens of the Chinese spirit world and can be bribed with appropriate offerings to further the profit-oriented and self-serving interests of their worshipers. The cult of the Eighteen Kings flourishes in the aggressively capitalist milieu of contemporary Taiwanese society, where the Nationalist Chinese state, disaffected from the old ritual idioms of propriety, has been unable by either policy or example to claim moral leadership.

A very different Chinese ghost is the object of ritual attention in Malaysia. The cult of the ghost of A Qeng, a Penang Chinese trishaw driver who was killed by a Japanese bomb, discussed by DeBernardi, provides a commentary not on capitalism but on ethnic relations. Because he died in Malaya and is paired with a Malay spirit, he symbolizes the Chinese community that is rooted in the Malaysian soil. At the same time, his demand, through a spirit medium, for offerings of pork dumplings—a food that would be wholly unacceptable to the Muslim Malays—symbolizes the division between the Chinese and Malays.

In Korea ghosts have been invoked in a direct challenge to the state.

Kwang-ok Kim describes how Korean students and dissidents, under the banner of the Popular Culture Movement, have fashioned from popular religion, including shamanic ritual, a series of performances that blur the lines between ironic drama and intense religious experience. In the most powerful of such performances that improvise on shamanistic rituals for the dead, the souls of two recent victims of police brutality are called back through a danced recitation of their grievances and comforted by the resolve of their comrades. The charged atmosphere of these events, held in a climate of rising dissent, mobilizes for performer and audience alike grief and righteous rage. The performance serves also as an exorcism of the "evil ghosts of dictatorship, corruption, torture, antinationalism, and those who would sell their nation to foreign powers" (also see Seong Nae Kim 1989).

The collective dead who were killed in the atomic bomb blast at Hiroshima (as discussed in Foard's chapter) and those who were victims of the Khmer Rouge in Cambodia (Keyes's chapter) are also shown as having been invoked so that the evil surrounding their deaths can be critiqued. In Cambodia the People's Republic of Kampuchea, a regime put in place by the Vietnamese forces who ousted the Khmer Rouge under Pol Pot, could lay very little claim to political legitimacy. They sought to bolster their position by mobilizing the powerful and painful memory of the Cambodian holocaust by creating monuments and sponsoring Buddhist rites at the places the Khmer Rouge used for their killing fields. The promotion of this cult of the dead is also associated with the restoration of Buddhism. Any future government in Cambodia risks provoking a legitimacy crisis if it chooses to ignore the ghosts that populate the Khmer landscape.

The annual rites at Hiroshima draw representatives from diverse religions, solidarity groups, and nations and are enacted in front of international press crews in the name of world peace. But they draw their legitimacy and moral urgency from a local community made up of surviving bomb victims *(hibakusha),* their kin, and acquaintances. At the core of the Hiroshima commemoration is a Japanese understanding of the obligation of the living to comfort the dead; so long as the world is not at peace, the dead are not at peace. Foard writes, "The particular and universal are therefore allies in their human responsibility to reject chaos, terror, and nothingness."

As a judgment of the past and a vision of the future, the Hiroshima rites vie for pride of place in Japanese national consciousness with the government-sponsored memorial service for the war dead at the Yasukuni Shrine. Hiroshima demands a total break from militarism; the 15 August commemorations at Yasukuni seek maximum continuity with prewar civil religion (see also Hardacre 1989:chap. 7). One set of rites personalizes the tragedy of the past in the civilian dead, in families and school children; the other honors dead warriors. One aspires to be international and generates a genuine communitas; the other is closely managed by the state.

The contention over the memory of the dead reflects the broader struggle over religious authority in Asia. This struggle has its origins in the stances taken toward "religion" by the modernizing states of Asia.

Varieties of Religious Resurgence

The introduction of modernization, albeit at different times for different Asian states, was inevitably accompanied by direct attacks on those religious practices deemed to be superstitious. In many instances such attacks provoked defensive responses that were often millenarian in character. Millennial uprisings occurred in many parts of Asia from the mid-nineteenth through early twentieth centuries; among the more significant were those of the T'ai-p'ings and the Boxers in China, the Tonghak (Eastern Learning) in Korea, the Samist in Java, the "holy men" *(phūmībun)* in northeastern Thailand and southern French Laos, and the Hsaya San in Burma.[6] Because the eschatology of millennial movements leads people to expect an imminent reordering of the world by the direct intervention of a sacred power, such movements have inevitably lost their attraction once they have proved incapable of effectively challenging the power of the states in which they emerged.

In the wake of these movements, a number of "new religions" have emerged in various parts of Asia; these religions continue to interpret worldly events as the manifestation of cosmic forces, but they do not foresee an immediate end to the existing order. The religions are "new" in that they have drawn together an eclectic variety of symbols from foreign and local religions to clothe traditional cosmological ideas. Religions like Kurozumikyō, Reiyūkai, or Mahikari in Japan, Ch'ŏndogyo in Korea, Cao Dai in Vietnam, Iglesia Ni Cristo in the Philippines, or the cult of the Heavenly Valley in Thailand reflect the continuing appeal of religious practice that strives "for continuous integration of self with the body, society, nature, and the universe" (Hardacre 1986:12).[7]

While most new religions, unlike millennial movements, often have a strong nationalist flavor, they can still find themselves at odds with the state. The new religions of Japan, for example, have sometimes worked in tandem with the state, and many maintain ties to Shinto shrines; but their claims of emperorlike charismatic founders and their promulgation of mythologies that conflict with imperial ideology compete with the authority of the emperor system the new religions presume to replicate. Before 1945 certain such sects in Japan were suppressed and their founders charged with the crime of lèse majesté. A similar charge was leveled in the 1980s against the founder of the Thai cult of the Heavenly Valley; and despite strong backing from certain highly placed military leaders, the cult was all but suppressed.

Many students of religion as well as political leaders have been puzzled about why cosmological conceptions central to new religions, millennialism, and even traditional popular religion should continue to appeal to people in a world that has become increasingly rationalized. Why, it is often asked, should faith healing continue to flourish in a society like Japan, which has one of the most technologically advanced medical systems on earth? Why should women embrace the antifeminist ideologies, rites, and practices of fundamentalist movements in democratic societies offering them education, employment, and the franchise? Why would educated men reject the project of a pluralistic civil society in favor of the narrower world view of a religious movement? While part of the answers to these questions must be sought in the specific religious and social conditions in which such activities exist, there is also a more general factor, one attested to by several of the studies in this volume (also see Davis 1980). Ritual and magical symbols continue to hold great appeal even in highly rationalized social orders because they and those who manipulate them offer the immediate eradication of injustice and imperfection through acts aimed at bringing the world into conformity with a cosmic order. Symmetry of earthly and cosmic blueprints promises to bring individual moral conduct into a framework of universal significance on a scale far surpassing the contingent ideals of particular political systems and their inevitably venal bureaucracies. One can expect, thus, that cosmological religions will continue to emerge and to draw adherents throughout Asia as they do also in the West.

A contemporary derivative of older cosmological religion is what Foard has called "endemic religion." Endemic religion in Japan, Foard has written, is "a kind of minimal religious practice that absolutely every Japanese participates in to some degree and which helps bind the Japanese together" (Foard n.d.). Japanese endemic religion is nurtured by mass media and an elaborate commercialization of ritual goods and services as in Juzo Itami's black comedy "The Funeral," wherein the bereaved brush up on condolence etiquette with the aid of a home video. By Foard's description, endemic religion is also a postmodern phenomenon self-consciously acknowledged as "tradition." But this is not the frozen artifactual stuff of museum displays and cultural performances. Endemic religion is saturated with associative meanings that combine remembered personal experience with shared cultural imagery.

Endemic religion derives its authority from its practice, which generates "tradition" as an ongoing process. Because endemic religion is pervasive, representatives of the state may manipulate its rich associations to bolster national identity. At the same time the diffuse authority of endemic religion can be invoked by a variety of different interests and used to generate new meanings, including ones that run counter to those promoted by the state. Because of this potential, endemic religion has on occasion been directly attacked by the state.

The agenda for rural development embraced by the Korean New Village Movement of the 1970s included the destruction of local shrines and generally unsuccessful attempts to ban the performance of shamanic rituals. The many draconian campaigns waged in the Chinese countryside during the forty-year history of the People's Republic are better known. Anagnost asserts that the Chinese state considers the resurgence of popular ritual in the Chinese countryside to be resistance against its own totalizing project, a reclamation of local space against the centralized authority of Beijing. The Chinese government has failed, however, as Anagnost shows, to control endemic religion completely.

Drawing on the idea of endemic religion, Kendall describes Korean weddings as passage rites and vehicles of morality that cut across denominational affiliations. Precisely because of their primary identity as a *Korean* practice, Korean weddings have been a locus of argument for shifting perceptions of "tradition and modernity," "Korean and Western," of what is rational, moral, and good. Recent attempts to revive a "traditional Korean wedding" imply both a self-conscious and a selective reclamation of the past and a tacit recognition of the transformed circumstances in which that past is reclaimed and transacted. Although the state has attempted to impose its own directives for "wholesome family rites," it has only been partially successful, adding its voice to a larger popular clamor. Korean feminists, traditionalists, and dissidents add their glosses to the common structure of the Korean wedding and so underscore their own distinctive messages.

The Chinese who moved to Malaysia carried with them memories of popular religion in China; in the new context, however, the religious practices they instituted did not become part of an endemic religion because, as DeBernardi shows, they now confronted a world in which the civil order was based on quite different premises from those of China. Although they adapted to some extent to the popular religion of the Malays as, for example, by adopting local animistic spirits as minor tutelaries in a Chinese pantheon within whose temporal jurisdiction they had come to dwell, few Chinese converted to Islam. The tension between the meaning embedded in Chinese temple festivals and the experience of living in an increasingly Islamic society was intensified after Malaysian independence in 1957 and especially after the institution in the early 1970s of government policies that recognized the Malays as having a preferred place within the society. Today, as part of an unfavored minority group within the Malaysian state, Penang Chinese give local rituals a new gloss as assertions of ethnic sovereignty and pride. DeBernardi describes the religious space of the Penang Chinese community as an arena wherein Chinese identity may be asserted and commented upon through a longstanding Chinese discourse of obliquely political religious symbols.

Many other Asians have also become self-conscious about their religious identity because of policies instituted by the states in which they live. This self-consciousness is most marked among adherents of organized religions or religious movements. Members of the Islamic missionary *(dakwah)* movement in Malaysia described in Shamsul's chapter and the Santi Asoke Buddhist movement in Thailand (Keyes 1989, 1992) each claim that their beliefs represent the "true" version of the dominant religion of their society. Hefner describes the historical shifts and political maneuvers that won for advocates of orthodox Islam a favored position both in the formulation of Indonesian national religious policy and in its local implementation. By law, all Indonesian citizens must claim membership in one of a limited list of "true religions" as defined by essentially Islamic criteria: monotheism, scriptural revelation, origins in prophecy, and routinized ritual. In these varied contexts the political claims of "fundamentalism" or orthodoxy may be understood not as atavistic reassertions of tradition, but as the product of a confrontation with a pluralistic world.

It is possible to recognize some broad comparative themes among Muslims and Buddhists as well as Christians that, for want of a better term, may be called "fundamentalist" (see Marty 1988). Fundamentalists point to an authority found in scriptures in order to undermine religious pluralism; they reject the legitimacy of different forms of their religion existing in various societies. They also challenge particularistic forms of their religion restricted to a particular nation. Ironically, as Hefner, Shamsul, and Gladney show, they may do this at the same time they make use of the state to promote their cause. Finally, they reject the claims of any other religion to universalism, and they oppose themselves to missionizing religions.

Hefner provides a detailed description of the struggle between orthodox Muslims and Javanists to determine the content of religious education in East Java, a conflict cast in terms of scriptural authority versus local practice. At issue was the requirement that all Muslim children receive instruction in orthodox Islam through a course of study emphasizing the fundamentals of Indonesian "civil religion" while making few concessions to regional custom or belief. An ethnically constituted Javanist religious identity, combining Muslim practice with indigenous ritual traditions and respect for local spirits, could not compete with the orthodox Muslims' well-organized, longstanding effort to standardize, disseminate, and "rationalize" popular religion.

Shamsul examines the phenomenon of Islamic resurgence in the context of Malaysia's ethnic politics. When the Malaysian government restricted student activities in the early 1970s, the *dakwah* movement became "the only safe avenue through which students could air their grievances, fulfill a need to serve society, and find relief from the pressures of university life and urban living." Drawing support from a larger Islamic world that regarded Islam not only as a possible alternative to Western civilization, but also as an ideological framework for practical action, the movement was phenomenally successful in re-Islamicizing much of Malay life and at gaining powerful protectors in the high reaches of government. At the same time it polarized the Malay community between secular and religious adherents and contributed to the uneasiness felt by non-Malay groups within the Malaysian state (see DeBernardi in this volume). The government, wary of what it saw as radical tendencies within the *dakwah* movement, attempted to co-opt it with its own Islamicization program or to control it through harsher security measures. Both of these strategies were viewed with alarm by Malaysia's non-Malay population.

In China the Hui, a Muslim minority, found it possible, as Gladney describes, to win concessions from the Chinese government through a successful public demonstration even as the same government prepared for its bloody suppression of the 1989 Democracy Movement. The Hui gained leverage through the state's definition of their minority status as a people who practice Islam—and as such, whose freedom of religious practice is guaranteed by the state. Thus defined, the Hui benefited by the importance of China's trade relationships with Middle Eastern Muslim nations and consequent vulnerability on issues of Islamic religious freedom. Gladney notes that the demonstrators self-consciously aimed their protest at a transnational audience. They linked their complaints regarding an offensive Chinese publication to international protest over Salman Rushdie's *The Satanic Verses*. Seizing a moment when Beijing was filled with foreign press crews, they marched with placards in English and Arabic as well as Chinese. They made opportunistic use of full veils, not commonly worn by Muslim women in China but readily identified by the media as an icon of resurgent Islam.

Identification with a transnational community of coreligionists can enhance the moral force and political consequences of protest, as in the case of the Malaysian *dakwah* movement or in the Chinese Hui demonstration. Deploying transnational religious identities is, however, a double-edged sword; such identities are a liability to the Thai Muslims described in Chaiwat Satha-Anand's chapter. In Thailand the Muslim students and civil servants who claim the right to wear *hijab* (prescribed Muslim dress for women) underscore their dual identity as Muslims and citizens of the Thai nation. Their vision of a national community that admits plurality confounds other definitions of the Thai as a Buddhist people whose history is that of a Buddhist state. Their protest ignited a national debate on the nature of Thai identity. As Chaiwat notes, Thai Muslim claims are undermined when observers ascribe the *hijab* to "Iranian influence" or see the students' protest as linked to the activities of *dakwah* groups just across the Malaysian border, associations that marginalize the Muslim minority, rendering them less Thai.

Kwang-ok Kim's discussion of the dilemma of liberal Christian protest in the Republic of Korea also presents a tension between appeals to an international moral community and dissident assertions of national identity. Since the colonial period, Christianity in Korea has provided a space for political discontent and, under the eye of pervasive censorship, has been a conduit of information to concerned communities outside Korea (Clark 1986). In a rising tide of national pride and xenophobia, the government has effectively stigmatized activist missionaries as foreign meddlers and Korean Christian activists as the puppets of foreign powers. Kim suggests that this stigma and the close cooperation between the government and numerous conservative Christians who have opportunistically worked with the government to propagate an anti-Communist message have blunted the efficacy of Korean Christianity as an idiom of protest. Instead, dissident Korean intellectuals have reclaimed popular religion (with some barely acknowledged inspiration from liberation theology) as a wellspring of distinctively Korean, emotionally charged idioms of protest.

Because Buddhism is not organized transnationally in ways comparable to Christianity or Islam, the Buddhist religion in those societies where it is dominant—in Burma, Thailand, Laos, and Cambodia—has been vulnerable to control and manipulation by the state. But because Buddhist practices are part of the endemic religion for a large majority of peoples in these societies and because the Buddhist *sangha* must serve the religious needs of their congregations before carrying out the policies of the state, authoritative voices speaking in the name of Buddhism can and do question the state's hegemony. In Thailand the theologian Buddhadasa, whose teachings have inspired many liberal social activist nongovernmental organizations, has developed a role quite independent of the religious hierarchy headed by a supreme patriarch called on to lend sanctity to state affairs. In Burma monks have been at the forefront of the movement questioning the government's legitimacy. And in Cambodia, as Keyes shows in his chapter, the effort of the Khmer Rouge to destroy

Buddhism led the successor regime, although still led by a Communist party, to embrace Buddhism in order to vest itself with legitimacy. The designation of Buddhism as Cambodia's official religion was as much a consequence of the state's recognition that the populace still find in Buddhism a source of authority that transcends that of the state as it was an effort by the state to assert its control over the religion.

Conclusion

In her epilogue Comaroff reflects that the essays in this volume demonstrate "that religion and ritual are crucial in the life of 'modern' nations and communities, in Asia as elsewhere." These essays serve to challenge, she observes, long-held views by social scientists as well as by political leaders that the civil orders produced by modernization and nation-building would ultimately relegate "primordial" attachments to religion to the personal rather than the public sphere. Those who adopted this position misunderstood the nature of religion.

By asserting the right to define communities whose members share the values derived from a common national heritage, nationalist leaders have stimulated rather than preempted religious debates about the constitution of moral communities. By insisting on the superiority of rational action over traditional practice, the modernizers have made the limits of rationality much more clear; the gap between the conclusions reached about the world through recourse to rational decision making and the practical reality of the world generates uncertainty and ambiguity that many seek to resolve through turning to religion. By seeking to regulate, control, or even suppress religious practices, states have stimulated people to look to religion for authority in criticizing, resisting, and challenging those who control state power.

The variety and intensity of religious activities in Asia today should, thus, not be taken as indicative (as a previous generation of theorists would have assumed) of the incompleteness of modernizing and nation-building projects undertaken in these societies. On the contrary, these activities point to a crisis of authority that has been created by the very success of these projects.

NOTES

1. We are acutely aware that there is little attention to Christianity in this volume. We hope, however, that our work will stimulate comparable work on Christianity.

2. The "Asia" of that earlier project included the Philippines, Indonesia,

Japan, India, Sri Lanka, and "the Arab World." It did not, however, include any of the Communist countries of Asia. Our project has focused specifically on the countries of East and Southeast Asia and, as the chapters on China and Cambodia indicate, has sought to bring Communist states into a comparative analysis.

3. The first edition of Anderson's book (1983a) was a key work for most who attended the conference and contributed to this book. Since the revised edition did not come out until after most of the contributions to this volume were written, we have left references to the first edition in them. In our introduction, however, we refer to the revised edition.

4. Even the Buddhist term *sāsanā*, which today is used as the equivalent of "religion," only came into general usage in the late nineteenth/early twentieth century.

5. Christine Pelzer White has written evocatively of the significance of the "wandering ghosts" of the Americans who disappeared during the Vietnam War and who are still labeled as POWs or MIAs by the United States and Vietnam (White 1992).

6. See Wakeman (1977:208–209; 219–220) for a review of the work on the T'ai-p'ing and the Boxer rebellions. On Tonghak, see Weems (1964) and Shin (1978–1979); on the Samist, Benda and Castles (1969) and Anderson (1977); the *phūmībun*, Ishii (1975), Murdoch (1974), and Keyes (1977); and the Hsaya San, Sarkisyanz (1965), Solomon (1969), Scott (1976), Adas (1979), and Herbert (1982).

7. When we originally conceived of this project we thought of focusing specifically on the "new religions" of Asia. We soon became persuaded that such a focus would lead to an emphasis on only one type of religious practice—and by no means the most important type—that has emerged in the context of the radically changed world of contemporary Asian societies. For a general discussion of the phenomenon of "new religions" see Beckford (1987). On the new religions of Japan, see Ellwood (1987), McFarland (1967), and, for the particular religions of Kurozumikyō, Reiyūkai, and Mahikari, see Hardacre (1984, 1986) and Davis (1980). On Ch'öndogyo see Yong-choon Kim (1978) and for other Korean "new religions" see Palmer (1967); on Cao Dai see Nguyen Tran Huan (1971), Oliver (1976, 1978), and Werner (1981); on Iglesia Ni Cristo see Ando (1969) and Tuggy (1978); and for the cult of the Heavenly Valley in Thailand, see Jackson (1988) and Yagi (1988).

PART I   STATE AUTHORITY AND RELIGION

1 The Universal and the Particular in the Rites of Hiroshima

JAMES H. FOARD

In August 1985 the American mass media covered, on an unprecedented scale, the commemorations in Hiroshima of the atomic bombing of that city. *Time* and *Newsweek* devoted whole issues to the fortieth anniversary of the catastrophe, and all three major television networks reported prominently the events of 6 August then and now. For most Americans the Hiroshima commemorations were one of a series of ceremonies, widely publicized that year, marking the fortieth anniversary of the conclusion of World War II, although the Hiroshima bombing was presented as a beginning as well as an end. In Hiroshima Americans perhaps caught a glimpse of something even more: an annual rite, or actually a collection of rites, of remarkable complexity involving distinctly Japanese elements, such as incense and gaily colored lanterns. What they saw was in fact an array of symbolic actions that has evolved over a generation, is rooted in some of the fundamental religious orientations of Japanese culture, and provides a powerful moral force in contemporary Japanese imaginations of themselves as Japanese.

The rites of 6 August in Hiroshima, which have been held in some fashion since 1946, are among the largest public gatherings in modern Japan, and yet, while covered heavily by Japanese journalists, they have received virtually no scholarly attention.[1] The purpose of this chapter is first to interpret the rites as a distinctly Japanese religious response to the bombing, a response grounded in the traditional handling of the dead, but also to show how this response developed rituals addressing a national and even international community. As what was familial and local became public and universal, private expressions served simultaneously as national and global metaphors of considerable political force. At the same time this appropriation of traditional rites has engendered tension over the ritual space of Hiroshima. This tension, I will suggest, is rendered acceptable only by what I wish to call the postmodern character of the rites themselves, by which the particularism of the traditional handling of the dead is reconciled with the universalism of national and global meanings.

A complete description of the Hiroshima rites is impossible here, for there are an awesome variety and number of them (in itself a significant fact). My basic sources have been newspapers from the past forty-five years—particularly the Tokyo edition of the *Asahi Shinbun* and Hiroshima's leading regional paper, the *Chūgoku Shinbun*—as well as my own observations and interviews conducted in the summers of 1985 and 1989.[2] There are many other ways in which the atomic bombing has been symbolized in Japan—in fiction, poetry, drama, even comics, as well as the event's role in political ideology and the continuing medical and social tragedies of the *hibakusha* (surviving victims of the atomic bombing). Although these are connected, I will concentrate on the rites themselves.

A short newspaper item, a small civil religious datum if you will, appeared in the 3 August 1970 *Asahi Shinbun,* morning edition, middle of page three. It is not startling, but just the opposite: so typical that it is rather incidental as news.

Six Hundred Seventeen Pictures of the Dead are Gathered

In Hiroshima, a United Memorial Service (gōdō hōyō) for the Victims of the Atomic Bombs

(Hiroshima) The faces of 617 people. A smiling baby. A young girl dressed as a bride. A dignified middle school student. And a uniform. . . . The pictures of those who died in the Nakajima district of Hiroshima, which on that day was directly under the atomic bomb, were arranged together; and from 10:00 A.M. on the second, a united memorial service was held before the Atomic Bomb Ossuary *(genbaku kuyōtō)* in the Peace Memorial Park. That district was composed of four sections *(chō)*—Nakajima Honmachi, Zaimokuchō, Tenjinchō, and Motoyanagichō—in the vicinity of the present Peace Memorial Park and within close range of the blast so that people and buildings alike were entirely obliterated. Last year, the families of the victims organized the Committee for the Reconstruction of the Center of the Explosion in the Peace Park (Heiwa Kōen Bakushin Fukugen Iinkai) with Narumiya Sōgorō as chairman and began the movement to gather the pictures of the dead.

On this day, 300 people from the victims' families attended. "Now, at last she has attained Buddhahood" *(korede yatto jōbutsu dekita jarō),* said an old woman pointing to the picture of her daughter as a bride. One could also see mothers telling their children, "That person is your grandfather." [ellipsis in original]

In this short article are many elements consistent with traditional Japanese symbolic handling of the dead and some that are novel. Determining what is consistent and what is novel is, I think, the key to understanding not only this single ritual moment, but the whole Hiroshima ritual complex.

Death in Japan

Let us turn first to how the events described in the newspaper article are consistent with traditional Japanese handling of death. Recent anthropological work on funerals and other mortuary rites (Huntington and Metcalf 1979) has drawn heavily on very old theories indeed, with extensive use of Arnold van Gennep's classic 1909 study of "rites of passage," wherein "death" is described as an elaborate transition between the two states of being alive and being dead. Hence, between the two states there is a period during which the deceased is no longer alive and yet not fully dead, what van Gennep termed a "liminal" period. Three stages, then, reflect the general pattern of rites of passage: separation, transition, and incorporation—in this case, separation from the living and incorporation into the world of the dead. Both van Gennep and, in a different fashion, Robert Hertz before him, pointed to two elements in this pattern that are distinct to death ritual and apply to Japan: both the deceased individual and his or her society or community pass through these stages; and both processes (that of the individual and that of the community) are bound together through the symbolism of the corpse, whose changes refer to changes both in the deceased and in the community. The deceased and the community are bound together in parallel fates within a single symbolic process. The success or failure of this process, then, is the success or failure of both. (Failure is often symbolized by a ghost, a liminal being who would terrify the community.)

More recently, Victor Turner (1969) has extended van Gennep's scheme by stressing the distinction between liminal, "anti-structural" moments and ordinary life within social structure as two "social modalities" found throughout many cultural processes. Hence, liminal periods in ritual, even those of funerals, have affinity with other moments of liminality, those periods of what Turner calls *communitas*, which are characterized by antihierarchical social relationships, the breaking down of cultural structures and barriers, and the emergence of generic human bonds, as in pilgrimages and festivals.

This very general theoretical perspective can help us outline the basic features of Japanese patterns of death, patterns that have been rather stable, but with less and less regional variation, since the Tokugawa period. Throughout history, relationships with the dead have had tremendous importance for Japanese religion and have even been pivotal in religious change.

Discussion of these relationships usually focuses on something called "ancestor worship," but this term is only sometimes accurate. The term "ancestor" is, of course, literally untrue in such cases as the mother in the article performing a rite for her daughter, but the more basic problem, I think, is the word "worship." Robert Smith (1974:115–151) has shown that attitudes toward the ancestors are extremely diverse and complicated. Nevertheless, the entire structure of Japanese deathways consists of conducting a deceased individual from the end of his or her life to the final state of collective ancestorhood. While there are reasonably short periods of mourning, the full range of rites for an individual can extend for thirty-three or fifty years, in the course of which the rituals for any given individual will cease to be held on the anniversary of his or her death and merge with the annual observances for all ancestors. This period will always be liminal to a degree.

Furthermore, Smith (1974:128) distinguishes "praying for" *(kuyō)* and "praying to" *(sūhai)* the ancestors, a distinction that often reflects the status of the family member while alive. In general the comforting of the dead and the seeking of their tutelary protection represent a continuation of the intimacy and dependency of family life. Indeed, the liminality of Japanese death ritual reflects the mode by which human experience is ordered within life, the intimacy and harmony of the family. What are being manipulated and restored in Japanese death ritual, then, are not principally cosmological or social structures but interpersonal sentiments objectified and valorized by ritual. (In this respect, Japanese death ritual is consistent with Japanese ritual generally.) This point has been largely obscured by research into "ancestor worship," because the functional approach of this research, in which these rites are seen as mirrors or ideals of social structure, obscures what performers of the rituals feel is going on. Smith (1974:184–210) found that many people do not perform these rites for any of the sociological rules he had been searching for, but simply out of sentimental bonds with the deceased.

Hence not just social structures but, more basically and normatively, social sentiments are reflected in Japanese death ritual. The "steady states" of life and death, as well as the liminality of the transition from one to the other, are primarily affective rather than cognitive categories. The parallel processes of the deceased and the living community, generally a family, reflect this: the peace and happiness of the deceased are that of the living, and their disruption are the opposite (for both living and deceased). This attitude is reflected in the words that describe what the Japanese believe they are doing ritually—*nagusameru* (comforting), *irei* (comforting spirits), *ian* (consoling)—and in the ongoing sentimentality directed toward the dead until a new place can be found for them in the intimate hierarchy of the family. A sense of the importance of sentimentality, I think, explains the tone of the newspaper article above, as well as the simultaneous relief of the mother and release of her daughter.

It is also important to note that belief in the literal efficacy of rites for the dead is subordinate to this ritual expression of sentiment. Indeed, the ritual articulation of who and where the ancestors are is full of contradictions. As Plath has put it:

The world beyond cannot be described in any but equivocal phrases. Spatially it is both here and there, temporally both then and now. The departed and ancestors always are close by; they can be contacted immediately at the household shelf, the graveyard, or elsewhere. Yet when they return "there" after the midsummer reunion they are seen off as for a great journey. They are perpetually present. Yet they come to and go from periodic household foregatherings. (1964:308)

The mother's statement—"Now, at last, she has attained Buddhahood" —is an expression of sentiment, not a confession of faith, and certainly not the last word on how she understands her daughter's postmortem existence. In the Japanese context, however, it is no less religious because of that.

The motifs of rites for the dead are predominantly Buddhist—indeed, the chanting of sutras is the principal means of comforting the dead at funerals and death anniversaries—but the main actors are generally the household members themselves, even to the point of handling the bodies and bones of the immediate deceased. They offer incense at formal and informal occasions and offer highly idiosyncratic foods, drink, and mementos of family achievements daily or whenever they feel like it. Most telling of all is the common practice of announcing something to the ancestors. (Smith [1974:143] tells of a woman who shouted into the family altar because her father had been hard of hearing.) In this fashion the care of the deceased remains in the hands of the family.

The dead are present in either their ashes (eventually placed in a grave) or their mortuary tablets. In funeral rites the ritual substitution of the latter for the former is made quite clear. Although always present in the tablets, the ancestors nevertheless return to them periodically, in modern Japan most notably at *obon,* the midsummer festival. It is not unusual— indeed, it is expected—for these mortuary tablets to be saved from burning buildings or for remains to be desperately sought so that the dead can be comforted. The performance of the living requires some concrete presence of the dead.

The dead are also the basis for the most fundamental Japanese theodicy and ethical motivation for self-sacrifice among the living. Perhaps the role of the ancestors as a collective conscience has been overemphasized (Plath 1964:309), but if so, only because there is truth to it. Here we find the family not only writ large but rendered ultimate in its authority by virtue of its ancestors.

Such, then, are some of the Japanese approaches to the dead. The entire process can be said to maintain family dependence, intimacy, and hierarchy throughout the liminal transformation from living family member to ancestor. However, things can go wrong so that the process is not completed, with serious implications for both the dead and the living. Any failure in this process is defined as the opposite of what is sought: the suffering of the dead rather than their comfort. Two things can bring about such suffering: some kind of bitterness on the part of the dead, often tied to death by unusual circumstances, and ritual or ethical failings on the part of the living. In either case the burden of rectifying the situation is on the living. The final peace of the dead can be left neither to a deity nor to the dead themselves, but is a fundamental—some might say ultimate—responsibility of the living.

Traditionally, the inability to find peace as an ancestor has resulted in a ghost. Far more common is the sense of people suffering in an unresolved limbo, simply unable to find rest regardless of how much time passes. Most pitiful of all are the *muen-botoke,* the "unconnected dead" who have no one to care for them and for whom many Japanese perform special services *(segaki-e).* This sense of the dead not yet at rest is strong in Hiroshima, a kind of indefinite liminality that disturbs the living, as symbolized by the "eternal" flame that will burn, not necessarily eternally, but until all nuclear weapons are abolished. I have also observed in the rebuilt temples of Hiroshima what appear to be extraordinary numbers of "unconnected" graves, those with no one to look after them, piled like rubble in the back of graveyards.

Let us return once again to our newspaper article. Here we find many of the elements of traditional Japanese handling of the dead, including overt sentimentality (not just of the participants but also, I think, of the newspaper reporter) and the basic motif of the service (best provided by the mother's statement that her daughter has at last found rest). Pictures, always present in funerals, substitute for the individual remains of the deceased and hence are the objects before which the Buddhist priest chants (which I take to be the meaning of *hōyō* [memorial service]). Finally, the mother pointing out a child's grandfather underscores that this is an assembly of families.

The Distinctive Rites of Hiroshima

There are, however, facts in this case that are *not* typical of the Japanese handling of death. This rite was not done in a temple or home, but in a public park; it was done not before any distinguishable ashes, but before a huge collection of remains (the community of the dead, many anonymous, in the ossuary [the *kuyōtō,* literally, a votive pillar for the dead]); and, above all, it was done not by a family alone, but by a collection of them directed by an *ad hoc* committee of representatives from families unrelated to each other. All of these indicate that this rite moved beyond traditional family religious practices into a larger civic world.

These differences from traditional religious action were not brought about because people desired to do things differently for the bombing deaths, but because they had to. In other words, the character of the bombing deaths forced ritual changes initially for logistic rather than conceptual reasons. These rites therefore differ from Japanese civic efforts to exploit images of family solidarity for other purposes. Here, the reverse is true: the civic is exploited for family purposes. These rites also differ from others resulting from bus accidents, plane crashes, and similar disasters, because in those cases families generally have to rely less on the civic for memorialization. In Hiroshima the civic space is often all they have. Hence, during the equinoxes, which are traditional times for visiting graves, large numbers of people treat monuments in Hiroshima's Peace Park as they would family graves.

The first commemorations in Hiroshima were Buddhist, in as traditional a fashion as possible. For most of those in Hiroshima, this meant relying on the Akimonto of Shinshū, to which perhaps 80 percent of the city had belonged. Immediately after the bombing, corpses were burned by the thousands in several places throughout the city, including the eventual site of the *kuyōtō*. Many remains were recovered by kin, but thousands were not. The city government gathered remains from various sites, including some temporarily interred at temples.[3] Other bones were uncovered during reconstruction. At such times construction would be halted and a priest would be called for a *hōyō*. I interviewed one elderly priest who spoke of how busy priests were throughout the early years of the Occupation. Eventually, the remains of the unidentified, as well as the identified but unclaimed, were gathered together at the *kuyōtō*. This was originally a pillar with a small chapel next to it containing a Buddhist altar. Photographs from the immediate postwar period show Buddhist services held there.

Immediately after the dropping of the bomb, though, there were ritual problems that could not be resolved by even these courses of action. The sheer scope of mass death meant that traditional services could not be held. Remains could not be found or distinguished from one another, and whole families had been killed, leaving no one to initiate the rituals. Hayashi Kyōko (1984) writes of a schoolgirl who picked the bones of her parents out of the ruins of her house and carried them everywhere she went in an empty can covered with newspaper. Furthermore (although this is nowhere stated), I suspect the unnatural character of atomic death meant that pacification of the dead was all the more urgent at the very time that it had been rendered impossible.

Here, too, the city stepped in to resolve ritual problems or at least provide the means for its citizens to do so. According to a law passed by the Diet in 1949, Hiroshima was to be reconstructed as the "Peace Memorial City." Then, as the reconstruction took place, the memorial sites and ceremonies of the city assumed roles in comforting the dead as well. In the beginning, though, there was a physical and ritual separation between comforting the dead and extolling peace. In 1950, for example, when Occupation authorities prohibited the "Peace Festival," rites for the dead at the *kuyōtō* were permitted. The ritual connection between comforting the dead and praying for peace began only in 1952, when the *ireihi* (cenotaph), designed by Tange Kenzō, was dedicated. Included in it was a list of names of the deceased *(kakochō),* which has grown annually, numbering 167,243 in 1990. Through the city's exhaustive research and recording of names over the years, virtually anyone connected with a bombing victim now has a ritual site. For example, the *Asahi* for 7 August 1959 records a woman calling the cenotaph the grave of her child.

Today, there are two ritual centers, the ossuary and the cenotaph.[4] The ossuary replaced the old votive pillar and its Buddhist-style reliquary chapel. Out of habit this ossuary is still called the Genbaku Kuyōtō (Atomic Bomb Votive Pillar), even though it is actually a grass-covered mound covering the half-underground room that holds the ashes of approximately seventy thousand victims. (Hence, the standard English name is "Atomic Bomb Mound.") Behind the ossuary, however, the old pillar still remains, badly rotted with its top broken off, and there is an image of the bodhisattva Kannon in the ossuary itself. Many older, local people prefer this ossuary to the later sites constructed by the city. It is the only structure in the current Peace Park that houses remains of the dead.

Though the ritual problem had been solved by the construction of the Peace Park, a constitutional problem was introduced: the handling of religious plurality and the separation of religion from state support. It was decreed that no expressly religious objects should be included in the park, although this decree has been circumvented more than once. The result was the development of rites and icons many of which seem more generically Buddhist than "nonreligious" to the outsider. The ossuary and its altar, the peace bell built like a Buddhist temple bell and surrounded by a lotus pond, and the *kakochō* indicate a general, civic sense of what is appropriate for the dead. The cenotaph, however, was designed expressly following the model of *haniwa,* the clay sculptures surrounding ancient (and pre-Buddhist) Japanese tombs.

In general, though, the present Peace Park, like much of the city itself, is filled with memorial stones established by ad hoc, private groups. Nearly all of these can be classified into three categories according to the victims they commemorate: those devoted to students of particular schools; those devoted to residents of particular areas; and—the largest group—those devoted to members of particular occupations, labor unions, or workplaces (Kurokawa 1982). There are others, including some of the most famous: the monument to students mobilized for war work, for example, or the monument to the Koreans, mostly forced laborers, who died in the blast. (The latter was kept out of the park itself in what is widely perceived as an act of racial bigotry.[5]) Only two individuals are honored: the poet Tōge Sankichi, and Marcel Junod, a Swiss Red Cross worker who strove to help the stricken city. Nearly all of these serve as sites for special rites by the groups that established them. These rites can be expressly Buddhist, involving a priest, but most are not.

The Memorial to the Atomic Bomb Children plays a role much larger than that played by any of the other specialized memorials. The story behind this statue is world famous. In 1955 Sasaki Sadako, a girl in the seventh grade who had been two years old when the bomb was dropped, suddenly developed leukemia. Believing she would recover if she folded a thousand paper cranes, she did so with her classmates. (The crane is a symbol of longevity and good fortune, and a bouquet of a thousand paper cranes is a common shrine offering when making a request.) When the first thousand were finished, she began another thousand but died before completing them. After her death a movement to establish a memorial to all the bombed children swept Japanese schools and even touched many in other countries. Since the memorial was dedicated in 1958 there have been, at any given time, hundreds of such bouquets of paper cranes lying beneath it. On 6 August in particular, children representing schools from around the country can be seen offering paper cranes in Sadako's memory. From this beginning, paper cranes became the ubiquitous offering in Hiroshima and Nagasaki, the most common expression of consolation of the dead victims and a desire for peace. The various memorial stones, regardless of type, are draped with them, as are visiting dignitaries. At the Urakami Cathedral in Nagasaki, a bust of John Paul II is draped with cranes on the anniversary of that bombing.

During most of the year, activities peculiar to the Peace Park mix with those that could be found in any other large urban park in Japan. Visits by tourists and schoolchildren on field trips and devotional acts before the *ireihi* and ossuary combine with gatherings of the local *shōgi* (chess) society and young lovers on the benches. Most of the time this mixture is harmonious, but there are limits. In April 1989 a controversy erupted in the *Chūgoku Shinbun* over the practice of cherry blossom viewing *(hanami)* in the park. As everywhere in Japan, this custom had long been accompanied by mass drinking and revelry. The immediate cause of the controversy was the introduction of portable electronic equipment for singing to musical accompaniment *(karaoke)*. "How," one elderly *hibakusha* was quoted, "can the dead sleep with all that noise?" Several opinions were offered, ranging from those advocating prohibition of blossom viewing altogether to the assertion that such behavior was what peace was all about. By 1990 the controversy had died away; the revelers were still there, but so were signs prohibiting amplification equipment.

This compromise is reminiscent of others involving sacred space in Japan, such as the use of shrine grounds for children's baseball games. Even in those places, though, there are limits, and there are certainly sacred times. In preparation for 6 August, the activities in Peace Park designate it as a sacred space. It is meticulously cleaned by all sorts of volunteers, and more "parklike" uses give way entirely to those devoted to the dead and to peace. One would not think of having a drinking party. In the course of its history, this ritual time has on occasion been tainted by frivolity and the domination of political movements. In 1947, for example, the city blundered with its attempt to hold a "carnival" complete with samba dancers; and in 1963 radical students battled police over the cenotaph. In each instance the people of Hiroshima have restored what they felt to be the proper tone.

The congregation of various people is reminiscent of the great pilgrimage sites of Japan's recent past (Foard 1982). On 6 August one can find in the park virtually every imaginable type of group: political organizations, the ad hoc groups for the various memorials, schoolchildren, religious organizations, families, artistic societies, foreign delegations, athletic clubs—even a few people who are obviously mentally ill. The list, if not endless, is open. The mood, while not jovial, is everywhere civil and cordial, with an openness to strangers, including foreigners, that is unusual in Japan. Most telling of all are the religious and women's groups who offer free gifts of tea or cold, wet towels to all. I was reminded of the meritorious gifts offered Buddhist pilgrims in medieval and early modern Japan (see Foard 1982). The diversity and size of the crowd make a point: for one day a kind of generic human bond, a national and even international communitas, if not opposed to the state at least apart from it, emerges from imagination into reality.

The performance of ritual acts, down to individuals offering incense and small offerings, is carried on with striking piety. I witnessed several people kneeling on the ground as they approached the cenotaph (which is not common in Japan), and even children were restrained (which is almost unheard of).

The day begins early, about 3:00 A.M., when many of the *hibakusha* and relatives of the dead make their offerings. Buddhist groups may also chant sutras. In these early hours the ossuary attracts more activity than the cenotaph, although a large number of people burn incense and make other offerings at both. About 6:30 A.M. joint religious services are held at the ossuary by Buddhist, Christian (both Catholic and Protestant), and Shinto clergy. Under the auspices of the city, the three groups take turns in an order that changes each year. (In interviews with members of each clergy, I did not find a single member who was fully comfortable with the participation of the others.) About 7:30 A.M. the area around the cenotaph is cleared and cleaned in preparation for the city's ceremony, which lasts about an hour. Anyone may attend this, and it is broadcast on closed-circuit television to several areas of the park. The climax of the ceremony is at 8:15 A.M., the time of the bombing, when there is a moment of silence both in the park and throughout the city. Afterward, an enormous but orderly crowd makes its way past the cenotaph to offer incense and other items. Throughout the rest of the day, various special memorial services are held before the memorial stones and statues. In front of the large memorial to the mobilized students, for example, a statue of the *bodhisattva* Jizō, the savior of children, is set upon a temporary altar. Representatives of various groups, relatives, and political authorities offer flowers in turn. Many then go to a Buddhist temple across the street. In the afternoon several of the "new religions" of Japan perform their own special rituals; I witnessed Sūkyō Mahikari, one of those new religions, exorcising the rivers of Hiroshima (see Davis 1980).

In the early evening, for a nominal fee anyone may have a name written on a colored lantern. These are constructed by the local merchants' association and floated that night on the river next to the park, while a priest on a barge intones sutras through a loudspeaker. The floating of the lanterns is derived from the traditions of *obon,* the return of the dead in summer. As in *obon,* the dead are being guided back for another year in a moving reminder of Buddhist impermanence. The lanterns' gay colors are reminiscent of Hiroshima's distinctively festive *obon,* during which colored lanterns are set up in graveyards. Indeed, for many in Hiroshima the end of the rites of 6 August marks the beginning of *obon.* On the side streets around the park, the food and toy vendors have set up their booths as they would at any Japanese festival.

This minimal sketch of the Hiroshima rites shows how the rituals devoted to the bombing victims are not traditional kin-group activities carried out under sectarian Buddhist auspices. Nevertheless, they are derived from such traditional practices and transformed only to the degree made necessary by the size and nature of this catastrophic death and by the consequent assumption of responsibility by civic authorities. Although by these arrangements the city provides for family rites, it and other civic groups have come to claim a role in the ritual handling of the dead in Hiroshima.

The traditional motif of death rites, however, remains unchanged. The formal name of the city's major ceremony on 6 August is Hiroshima-shi Genbaku Shibotsusha Irei Shiki Narabini Heiwa Kinen Shiki. The term *irei* is generally rendered into English as "memorial," but actually means "comforting." The *ki* of *kinen* means "prayer." The title should therefore be translated as "The Hiroshima City Ceremony for the Comfort of the Atomic Bomb Dead Together with the Ceremony to Pray for Peace." The ceremony, then, unites the suffering of these particular victims with a universalistic, and rather vaguely directed, prayer for peace. By the very fact that these rites continue, we know that the process, too, goes on—the liminal dead have not been finally pacified and the world of the living is not at peace. In these rites we have a transitional, liminal period that proceeds in spurts every year. The continuing growth of these rites, in complexity and number of participants, indicates that the walls that traditional Japanese theodicy erected against the meaninglessness of suffering and death were shattered by the bomb, resulting in a tremendous effort to repair them.

These sentiments are expressed in the following passage from Kamezawa Miyuki's autobiographical short story, "Hiroshima Pilgrimage." The main character, herself suffering the effects of radiation sickness, despises Hiroshima and wants never to return, until she sees photographs of the memorial stones and sculptures:

> Then, a homesickness I had never felt before began to stir in my breast. Should I go once, to Hiroshima? I had stubbornly hated Hiroshima, where the bones of my parents and relatives are buried, and never had I pressed my hands together before their souls. K's collection of photographs awakened my spirit. At least I wanted to offer flowers before the memorial stone of my younger sister's alma mater. These sweet girls enclosed in one thin grave-marker, these gay maidens unable to say what they wish, what had I, in their stead, been doing? I had neglected even to offer one flower. I would go on a pilgrimage *(junrei)*. The Hiroshima that I had lived in was above all a place for caring for the dead. Therefore, I remember *obon* as especially bustling. The graveyards blossomed brightly with the lanterns peculiar to Hiroshima. (Kamezawa 1983 [1982]:419)

The Universal and the Particular

The short article on the Nakajima district ceremony appeared in the pages of a national newspaper, so the rites held in the Peace Park that day were considered (at least by an editor) of some importance to people other than just the participants. Since countless memorial rites take place every day in Japan and go unreported, the reporting of these to the "imagined community" (Anderson 1983a) of the Japanese must hold some significance. Indeed, any perusal of Japanese newspapers in August would reveal a great many stories concerning commemorations of the atomic bombings and the end of the war, as well as the attendant controversies, but their regularity should not blind us to the passion and attention they command.

With the development of civic rites, as symbolized by the ascent of the cenotaph over the ossuary, the rites of Hiroshima were increasingly disengaged from the traditional communities defined by kinship, temple affiliation, and locale, which have both supported and been authorized by death rites in Japan. It was the national government, after all, that designated Hiroshima the "Peace Memorial City" for the whole country, and an international role was assumed from the beginning as well. Ironically, and sometimes painfully, the mode of religion most exemplary of the bonds of kinship and intimate association, namely "ancestor worship," was pressed into increasingly universalistic service. To represent this change, a distinction is often made between Hiroshima as written in characters and Hiroshima as written in *katakana*, the syllabary used when translating foreign words (Kuroko 1983:11–12). Today the characters represent the actual city, both prior to and after the bomb, while the *katakana* indicates the city as a universal symbol—of peace, the nuclear age, or whatever. Undoubtedly, this latter orthography became prevalent with the early popularity of the phrase "no more Hiroshimas," originally in English and then in *katakana (nō mōa Hiroshima)*, which was ubiquitous in the early ceremonies.

One result of the increased disengagement of rites from traditional communities has been the multitude of ritual actions described above. Another has been real tension concerning acceptable ritual and legitimate community. In the past few years tens of thousands of people have participated each year in the annual rites alone. The sociologist Ejima Shūsaku (1977) has classified the participants according to a rather complex scheme involving their relative orientation toward the particular (the Hiroshima dead) or the universal (humanity), the past (the bombing) or the future (the peace movement). He then analyzes the various events from 1 August to 8 August according to the participation of people so classified. While his analysis is rich in detail, the basic scheme is that in passing from the earlier to the later days, the participants change from domination by those oriented toward the universal and the future to those oriented toward the particular and the past. They intersect—with some tension—on 6 August, which has the most intensely sacred character.

Although my own observations confirm many of Ejima's, I would like to work from a classification of participant communities exclusively according to their relative particularity and universality. I believe this is the more fundamental distinction among participant groups, for it is the discourse among groups of differing degrees of particularity and universality that has articulated the issues of legitimacy in the ritual space of Hiroshima, including those concerning the relationship of past death to future world peace. The most careful discussion of "universal" and "particular" is still that of Talcott Parsons, for whom this distinction was one

of the "pattern variables" derived from breaking down Ferdinand Ton-
nies's *Gemeinschaft-Gesellschaft* distinction into its more elementary
components (Parsons 1949:359–360). For Parsons, the question of "universal" concerned the type of value standard relevant to role expectation:
"The question is whether or not a discrimination is made between those
objects with which ego stands in a particularistic relationship and other
objects possessing the same attributes" (1949:63). Hence, the question
has nothing to do with the prevalence of a value standard. "Honor thy
father and mother" may be widely accepted, even in many cultures and
nations, but it is still particularistic. A universalistic standard would
require, say, an obligation to honor all parents, one's own and others'
equally. In Parson's usage, then, the universal-particular distinction was
one of the *content* of particular values and norms as measured by the
social roles they expected. Hypothetically, we can imagine one person or
a billion, a village or a region of nations, holding to either a universalistic
or particularistic value.

A similar distinction has recently been addressed, most clearly in
scholarship on Islam. In some of this work, however, we find a usage
very different from that of Parsons, one that I would call "empirical"
(Eickelman 1982; Woodward 1988). By empirical I mean that no attention is given to either the content or what Parsons would call "role expectation" of values or norms. Instead, they are either universal (essentialist)
or local solely on the basis of their presence or absence cross-culturally.

Turning to certain classics in the sociology of religion, we find a sense
of "universal" that implies both a certain kind of content and an empirical presence cross-culturally. Generally, this is ascribed to the great "historic" religions, whose growth accompanied that of empires (Weber
1963:23). This universalism can be found in the deity, in ethics, or (as in
the case of Robert Bellah) the anthropology of the tradition.

> Relative to earlier forms, the historic religions are all universalistic. From
> the point of view of these religions a man is no longer defined chiefly in
> terms of what tribe or clan he comes from or what particular god he serves,
> but rather as a being capable of salvation. That is to say that it is for the first
> time possible to conceive of man as such. (Bellah 1970:33)

Bellah connects this universalism to transcendentalism, dualism, and salvation. Joachim Wach (1944:310) attributed it to the "intensity" of religious experience, in which a universal moral obligation results from "the
widening and deepening of religious experience" (ibid., 377). For Wach,
the institution of universal religions represented the "final stage" (!) in
religion-state relations (ibid., 310).

In the following classification I will measure particularity and universality by both content and empirical evidence. Following Parsons, I measure the content by whether the relationship formed with the objects of ritual is particularistic or not—in this case, between kin and the Hiroshima dead at one extreme and between virtually any participant and an imagined global community on the other. I measure the empirical universality by the relative exclusiveness and openness of each group's actual membership. In fact, in the case of Hiroshima, there is such a close correlation between the two measures that they can function together as a single standard.

I see four categories of communities participating in the Hiroshima rites, on a scale from particularistic to universalistic: those personally connected with the dead; the city; the nation; and the world.

Those personally connected with the dead. This category naturally includes those with traditional ties of kinship, who use the Peace Park as a kind of family grave. In addition, I include all those with occupational or school ties with the dead, since they have a "particularistic" responsibility that mimics kinship ties. They are therefore responsible for the rites at many of the memorial stones in the park. Nearly all *hibakusha* fall into this group, and they are singled out for special recognition.

The city. By this I mean first of all the city government, which is responsible for the park and the major ceremony on the morning of 6 August, including the mayor's appeal *(sengen)*. It also organizes and coordinates many other events, including the use of the ossuary by religious groups, concerts, conferences, exhibits, and the like. In addition, I mean the city as an imagined community sustained by the bonds ordinary people have to these rites and this civic identity (*Hiroshima no kokoro,* etc.) even though, as with most residents of the city today, they may have no personal relationship to the bombing or the dead (e.g., the cleaning of the park on the days before 6 August and the moment of silence observed at 8:15 A.M. on that day throughout the city).

The nation. Here, too, I mean both the government and the imagined community, more the latter than the former.[6] Eight prime ministers have attended the ceremonies, and a representative from the cabinet is always present, but the national government has no hand in the proceedings. The late emperor and current emperor as crown prince have both visited the Peace Park, although not on 6 August. More significant is the widespread media coverage of the rites and related events, which since the mid-1950s has profoundly affected Japanese national identity. Newspaper editorials and Japanese diplomats alike routinely refer to Japan as having a special role in the world because it is the only nation to have suffered nuclear attack, and the "three principles" against nuclear weapons (no manufacture, possession, or introduction) rest on this identity. Since 1947 both the city and citizen groups have urged that 6 August be declared a national holiday, to be called "Peace Day," and currently between one hundred and two hundred local governments recognize it every year. On 6 August numerous nationally based groups, such as labor unions, teachers, and the new religions are represented, and throughout the year Hiroshima is visited by school tours. Increasingly, Hiroshima has become something of a national pilgrimage site.

So far there have been few explicit connections between Hiroshima and the *Nihonjinron,* the ideological discourse on Japanese uniqueness (Mouer and Sugimoto 1986). One recent work (Akiba 1986), published by the Asahi Shinbun Press and written by a long-time Japanese resident of America, a peace activist who after moving to Hiroshima was elected in 1989 to the lower house of the Japanese legislature, connects Americans' lack of understanding of Hiroshima with certain pathologies of American national character. These are in turn contrasted with an implicit (and occasionally explicit) discussion of Japanese national character, but the book displays little of the closed polemic and sloganeering of *Nihonjinron.* Aspirations for international meaning will, I believe, always retard efforts to embed Hiroshima in Japanese uniqueness.

The world. From the beginning, the city and citizens' groups have appealed for world participation in the rites of Hiroshima. Currently, one official logo for the city has a dove surrounded by the motto, in English, "Hiroshima Belongs to the World." Peace groups around the world, although mainly in Western Europe, have commemorated 6 August, and such groups often send delegations to the ceremonies in the Peace Park. In addition, a great number of cultural and political luminaries have been visitors: Helen Keller, Jawaharlal Nehru, Pope John Paul II, Eleanor Roosevelt, Che Guevera, to name but a few. Their own purposes vary, but the great attention they receive confirms Hiroshima's international status. Most significant for long-term connections with the rites have been international religious institutions, notably the Roman Catholic Church and the Society of Friends, as well as occasional visits by international Buddhist groups. Among the traditional Japanese Buddhist sects Shinshū is by far the most prominent because of its dominance among residents of the city; Shinshū draws upon both its national organization and its international ties in its connections with the rites.[7]

The Conjunction of the Particular and the Universal

The relationships among these categories of communities revolve around questions of legitimacy and hence the authority to define meaning. In general, the more universal concede greater legitimacy to the more particular, except that the third and fourth categories each accept separately the legitimacy of the first two while having little to do with one another. Because the smaller categories of communities have the greatest claims to legitimacy, acceptance of both their ritual claims and their assertion of the absolute and unique evil of the bombing is necessary for the participation of the larger communities. Thus, the more all-encompassing groups depend on the more local: the city on the personally connected, and the national and international groups on both categories of local communities. Objections from the center (category 1) can have virtual veto power over ritual performances or statements of meaning from the other sorts of communities. A dramatic illustration of this came in 1975, when the Imperial Household Agency was forced, after objections from *hibakusha* groups and the city, to make an extraordinary "clarification" of remarks by the emperor that seemed to justify the bombing as an act of war and ignore what is regarded in Hiroshima as its unique significance.

Perhaps the priority assigned to the more particular communities by those who do participate can be most clearly seen in contrast to the denial of that priority by those who do not participate. This denial takes place at the city, national, and global levels. In other words, for each of the three larger categories of participant communities listed above, there is a corresponding category of nonparticipants who reject or are indifferent to the claims of the more particularistic groups. This rejection comes from those in the city who think there is too much attention given the atomic bomb, from those in the nation who are attracted to competing ritual formulations of the Pacific War, and globally from those who believe that Hiroshima is being used to deflect memories of Japanese aggression.

In the city itself many citizens of Hiroshima feel that the identity of the city has been too tied to the past and that other civic images should be promoted. Their voice was made clear in the failed effort to tear down the ruins of the Hiroshima Prefectural Industrial Promotion Hall, now known as the A-Bomb Dome and the most widely recognized symbol of the city.

Rejection of the claims of the smaller groups is even stronger on the national level, because the rites of Hiroshima encounter serious competition in the ritual handling of the war dead at Yasukuni Shrine, in which Japan's military dead are enshrined, and in the government-sponsored memorial service for the war dead (Zenkoku Senbotsusha Tsuitōshiki) held on 15 August. For many years Japan's conservatives have wanted to remove by law the Yasukuni Shrine's identity with a specific religion within a plurality of religions and make it something honored by all Japanese as Japanese—in short, make it part of a new civil religion. Begun shortly after the Occupation by a quasi-governmental entity, the ceremony of 15 August—the anniversary of the emperor's surrender broadcast—is now held under the strictest security at the Budōkan in Tokyo. In attendance are the emperor, the cabinet, and other conservative politicians; the audience is made up of carefully selected veterans' groups and organizations of the kin of military dead from within the politicians' constituencies. Obeisance to an enormous pillar inscribed "The Souls of the War Dead of the Entire Country" is, arguably, the only public religious act the emperor now performs (and was the last public appearance of the late emperor).

The distinctions between Hiroshima on the one hand and Yasukuni and 15 August on the other are significant. Yasukuni honors the military dead; Hiroshima all the dead.[8] Yasukuni is innately Shinto, and even within Shinto is particularly tied to the emperor; Hiroshima aspires to be international. Hiroshima's rites present a genuine communitas; those at the Budōkan are closely managed by the state and its police. Yasukuni and 15 August seek maximum continuity with prewar civil religion; Hiroshima demands a total break from militarism. Whereas the Japanese left would like to see Hiroshima Day be the national holiday, the right wants it to be 15 August. In 1985 a new complication emerged on 15 August, when immediately after the ceremonies at the Budōkan, Prime Minister Nakasone Yasushiro made the first official visit of a government official to the Yasukuni Shrine. The ensuing controversy was severe, and there were protests in other Asian nations.

Internationally, there is open rejection on the part of many who encounter the Hiroshima rites through the international media, particularly among Japan's former enemies in Western Europe, Asia, and America. As with the other types of communities, those who could potentially participate in this category are rejecting the meanings defined by the more local groups. Specifically, they reject the separation of the meaning of Hiroshima from the context of World War II, a separation that is insisted upon by the city of Hiroshima (Committee for the Compilation 1981:335, 340). For example, the Akiba Project, begun in 1979, is an effort to bring reporters from regional American newspapers to Hiroshima about the time of the rites. Akiba (1986) gives many examples of the angry, often venomous reactions of Americans to the stories produced by these reporters. While the details differ, in each case cited, Americans regard acceptance of the claims of the local participants concerning the dead and universal peace as requiring a denial of Pearl Harbor and Japanese atrocities. In other words, many Americans refuse to accept the particularity of the Hiroshima dead.

Even though their legitimacy is paramount, there is clearly an assumption on the part of the local communities of a national and an international role. The mayor, for example, regularly cables appeals for peace and objections to nuclear testing around the world, and the tying of the comfort of the dead to world peace or, as the case may be, a peaceful Japan, virtually requires an aggressive pursuit of national and international recognition of the "meaning" of the city, if only out of obligation to the dead. Therefore, citizens' groups and the city itself are, in turn, legitimated by national and international attention. Nevertheless, priority in these matters is clearly given to the particular legitimacy, indeed the particular dead, of Hiroshima. According to newspaper accounts, for example, it is common for prayers to be offered before the cenotaph after major nuclear tests around the world; and Hiroshima activists firmly believe that peace will come only when the world appreciates the meaning and spirit of Hiroshima.

Tensions between specific communities from different categories are generally at the heart of controversies surrounding the ritual space of Hiroshima. There were considerable tensions in the 1950s between *hibakusha* groups and the city government over their respective roles in the development of the city and its monuments. For example, there was widespread criticism of the construction of the hundred-meter-wide Peace Avenue as a monumental waste of money and land while *hibakusha* suffered. Even today, there are those who feel cut off from all rites in the Peace Park because they feel them contrived,[9] while some object to particular things in the park, such as the national flag. While many of these issues have been resolved, each year seems to bring some negotiation over details or some objection to the mayor's appeal. Between these local groups and the nationally based communities there is often a suspicion, sometimes well founded, of exploitation by political or religious interests. These suspicions reached their peak in the dramatic events of 1963, during which the *hibakusha* voices were lost in political clamor and demonstration (Ōe 1965). Cultural misunderstandings and clashes inevitably arise between the local groups and international communities. Akiba (1986), for example, discusses the difficulty *hibakusha* had with one American's well-meaning intentions to make Hiroshima Day into a "celebration of life."

Despite such controversies, there is in the performance of the rites themselves remarkable coordination and harmony, accomplished through the now widely agreed upon patterns of time and space described above. There are also spontaneous events, such as Leonard Bernstein and Seiji Ozawa leading a superb impromptu choral concert near the ossuary in 1985. The different types of communities do different things at different places and different times, but everyone participates in the moment of silence at 8:15 A.M. Like the American parade in Warner's 1959 "Yankee

City," this is the sole event in which all categories of communities are brought together. Taxis, streetcars, those gathered in the park, people at work—the whole city just stops.

Conclusion: The Postmodernity of Hiroshima

In the rites of Hiroshima we find traditional kinship, local, national, and universal communities all operating at once. There is rejection of the authority of the local groups by those that do not participate, and among those that do there can be tension with them. Nevertheless, there is a remarkable conjunction of the particular and the universal in the relationships described above.

Conjunctions of universal and local traditions can be seen throughout the world, but Hiroshima seems to invert the usual relationship found in, say, a Romanian Easter or Javanese Ramadan, in which greater authority lies in the universal. What is challenging about Hiroshima is that the rites seek to be for the world universally and yet give clear priority to ancestor veneration and its derivatives, what to many sociologists would be the classic case of particularism. In other words, the rites have both universal and particularistic expressions and communities, but seem to insist on an impossible relationship between the two. This is more than a theoretical problem: it is a ritual and cognitive problem among the participants themselves. What precisely is the connection between the comforting of the dead by those connected with them and the peace of the entire world? And how can the world participate in the former to attain the latter? This problem is not finally answered in Hiroshima. However, since the rites of Hiroshima have for forty-five years maintained both the priority of the particular and aspirations to the universal, we should expect that some character of the rites has made this possible.

I would describe this character as "postmodern." For the purposes of this discussion, let me define as postmodern any cultural expression that treats modernity as modernity has treated tradition (Werblowsky 1976:18). Growing out of modernity itself, such expressions treat whatever they see as the most salient features of modernity with the same relativizing historicism that modernity used to undercut the authority of tradition. Often, in its opposition to secular rationalism, postmodern religion appears to be a "reenchantment" of the world; but it is not simply a return to tradition, for it recognizes its own relativizing history, its own rhetorical character. Hence, its opposition is not so much to the rationality of modern discourse as to its hegemonic claims of representation.[10]

In the case of Hiroshima this opposition to hegemony is rooted in the initial, local solutions to the ritual problems engendered by mass death. The ad hoc creation of the particularistic rites and their seeming incommensurability with annihilation, both in the local past and in the global future, was never hidden. On the contrary, the process and pain of their human creation have been told and retold in narratives and monuments. The particularistic rituals that have developed from ancestor veneration are therefore performed with great religious sentiment in a patently sacred place, but the human origin of ritual is not disguised—there are no "objectivation" and "alienation" in Berger's sense (1967)—because their historic origins are part of what they communicate to their participants, namely, that these are historic human responses to historic human acts.

This historical relativizing, first developed and expressed in the local rites, permits, even seeks, Buddhist and Christian participation, since it sees all such traditions as historical human expressions. These "historic" religions and all other universal discourses are accepted, however, as rhetorical rather than referential and hence can never attain a closure of meaning within the ritual space of Hiroshima, whatever they may do outside of it. In Hiroshima the particularistic rites have already set limits on what ritual can claim for itself: since the particular has relativized itself, it will permit no less from the universal.

The universal, furthermore, is accepted by the particular as an ally in the common human responsibility to reject chaos, terror, and nothingness. Rather than "formulating a general order of existence" (Geertz 1973c:90), therefore, the alliance is meaningful only in what it opposes and seeks to overcome. Other than "peace" there is little agreement about what the rites are to accomplish (a fact that has consistently frustrated the political left). This discovery of meaning in opposition also has its roots in local developments. As with many other sources of postmodernity (Trachtenberg 1985:3–4), the ritual representations of the *hibakusha* came from the cultural and social margins in opposition to the master narrative of the bomb that brought peace (Ubuki 1976). Like a guerrilla resistance, they have found unity with others in a common enemy—"the Bomb"—that has invaded Hiroshima particularly and the consciousness of humanity universally.

The particularistic rites of Hiroshima, then, accommodate the universal through a postmodern rejection of hegemonic meaning. This rejection grew from two characteristics developed initially in the local rites: their historical consciousness and their discovery of meaning in opposition. These characteristics not only opened the ritual space of Hiroshima to other articulations but also denied the closure of ideological and religious certainty. Both the universal and the particular, therefore, have been able to join the cultural *bricolage* every 6 August. Writing as early as 1952

(Hiroshima Jōkōshi 1985:189), a *hibakusha* attending the rites for a group of school children was able to wonder, "Are there really this many kinds of religions?"

NOTES

1. The notable exception is the sociological analysis by Ejima, Kasuga, and Aoki (1977). Best known in America is Robert Lifton's *Death in Life: Survivors of Hiroshima* (1967). Lifton is a psychologist concerned with the *hibakusha,* or surviving victims of the bombing, who reduces all Japanese cultural traits to examples of psychological universals. I, on the other hand, am interested more in the public symbolic actions of various groups, including *hibakusha* but also many others, and I find many of these actions incomprehensible except as culturally specific to Japan.

2. Research for this essay was initially supported in part by a summer travel grant from the Northeast Asia Council of the Association for Asian Studies and was continued while the author participated in an exchange program between Arizona State University and Hiroshima Shūdō University. I want to thank particularly Mr. Ōmuta Minoru of the *Chūgoku Shinbun* and Professors Akiba Tadatoshi and Aoki Hideo of Hiroshima Shūdo University. The 1985 interviews were principally with leaders of religious groups: the Shin sect of Buddhism, Catholic and Protestant Christianity, and the local association of Shinto shrines. The 1989 interviews were with *hibakusha* themselves.

3. The complexity of the disposal of the dead is only indicated here. The details can be found throughout volume two of Hiroshima Shiyakusho (1971).

4. Originally, the city wanted to move the remains from the *kuyōtō* to a new ossuary underneath the planned cenotaph *(ireihi)* at the center of the park, but this was vetoed by the Tokyo government, which deemed such a thing inappropriate in the center of a public park and which was providing two-thirds of the funding (Hiroshima City 1984:100–103). Hence, there are now two ritual sites.

5. The reason given for the exclusion was that the deadline for private groups establishing such stones in the park had passed. Under the auspices of the city itself, it could be placed there, as indeed other monuments have been, including an inscription of a rather ridiculous poem by former Prime Minister Nakasone. The demand that the Korean memorial be moved into the park was revived in 1990 by a delegation of Korean *hibakusha* who visited Hiroshima and later met with the foreign minister. The city responded to this pressure by promising to move the stone to the park in time for the 6 August 1990 ceremonies. However, it failed to do so because of disputes between Korean residents loyal to each of the two Korean regimes and between both groups and the city over the inscription on the stone.

6. Some may object to designating the national communities as more "universalistic," but those national communities that participate in Hiroshima must be considered relatively universalistic, since they seek peace for all humanity. Among the competing claims for the meaning of "Japaneseness," including those

that articulate difference and supremacy, theirs seeks to tie Japan's experience to universal, internationalist goals.

7. My placing the new religions with nationally based groups and these religions with the international is somewhat arbitrary. Groups such as Risshō Kōsei Kai, for example, seek strong international and interreligious ties and hold rites in Hiroshima. My distinction here is based first on how much Japan looms in the doctrines of a group and also on how international its institutions really are.

8. In Hiroshima there are no monuments to the numerous military dead from the bombing, at least in part because the identity and remains of the dead were handled efficiently by the military rather than the city. The names of military dead, however, are recorded in the *kakochō*.

9. The most well known of these nonparticipants are surely the painters Iri and Toshi Maruki, who nevertheless hold their own rites, including a *toronagashi* (lantern floating), at their museum on the outskirts of Tokyo.

10. Several of these characteristics are outlined in Trachtenberg (1985). For a helpful discussion of Japan and postmodernism, see Harootunian and Miyoshi (1988).

2 Communist Revolution and the Buddhist Past in Cambodia

CHARLES F. KEYES

In 1975 a Communist-led government took power in Cambodia;[1] the leaders of the country they renamed Democratic Kampuchea viewed religion as an impediment to the development of their country. Under Pol Pot the government of Democratic Kampuchea from 1975 to 1979 interpreted Marxist ideology as a mandate for the elimination of religion from Khmer life. In 1979 the Pol Pot government was replaced by another Communist-led government, backed by the Vietnamese and led by Heng Samrin. Although the new government of the Peoples' Republic of Kampuchea (PRK) supported the restoration of Buddhism in Cambodia, it sought to severely circumscribe the role that religion could play in Khmer life. In the late 1980s, however, the PRK government made Buddhism the state religion; its leaders became conspicuous in their public support of the religion, and the stance it currently takes toward Buddhism is no longer impelled by Marxist ideology. On the contrary, the government's present position although impelled by immediate political concerns still demonstrates a recognition of the deep significance of Buddhism for Khmer national identity.[2]

Cosmological Buddhism and the Traditional Social Order in Cambodia

Khmer look to the Indianized civilization, centered on Angkor near the Great Lake (Tonlé Sap) in northwestern Cambodia, which flourished from the ninth to the fourteenth centuries, as the source of their national culture. Angkorean civilization is remembered by all contemporary contenders for power in Cambodia through the images of Angkor Wat they depict on their flags, the political rhetoric they use, and the support they give for dance, the movements of which are depicted in the bas reliefs at that ancient city. Despite the emphasis on Angkor as the source of Khmer nationalism (a product, in fact, of the colonial period),[3] the significance of Buddhism in Khmer life derives primarily from the post-Angkorean period.

From the eleventh through the fifteenth centuries, Buddhist monks gained the patronage of most rulers of principalities and kingdoms in what are today Burma (Myanmar), Thailand, and Laos as well as Cambodia. These monks derived their understanding of Buddhism from interpretations of Pāli texts that had become authoritative in the fourth century A.D. in Sri Lanka. These interpretations constituted what became known as Theravāda Buddhism, or the "way of the elders." The *sangha*,[4] or Buddhist order of monks, is seen as the exemplar, teacher, and embodiment of the *dhamma*, the message of the Buddha.[5]

The missionary monks of the period carried the *dhamma* not only to the capitals of the kingdoms, but into the villages as well. By the end of the fifteenth century if not earlier, temple-monasteries *(wat)* with local chapters of monks had been established in most villages throughout what is now Cambodia as they had also been in what are today Thailand, Laos, and Burma. The *wat* became, as Ebihara (1990:21) has observed, the "moral, social and educational center" of Khmer villages (also see Ebihara 1966).

From monks' teachings and even more through participation in rituals led by monks, followers of Buddhism came to conceive of the social orders in which they lived as manifestations of a cosmological system based on the principle of *kamma* (*karma* in Sanskrit). The root meaning of *kamma* is "action," and in either Buddhist or Hindu thought the concept refers to the moral consequences of human acts. The doctrine of *kamma* explains how certain aspects of one's present experience are consequences of previous acts, including acts in former existences, while also providing an incentive to perform certain acts that will ensure greater freedom from suffering in this life or future ones (cf. Keyes 1983:13).

Khmer, like other Southeast Asian peoples, conceived of the effects of previous *kamma* in terms of a Hindu-Buddhist cosmology. This cosmology, as Craig Reynolds (1976:203) has written, stood as "an all-embracing statement of the world." Within "cosmological Buddhism," as I term the traditional Buddhist system in Southeast Asia, the status at birth of all beings—both human and nonhuman—was deemed to reflect the relative amounts of merit (Pāli *puñña*; Khmer *bon*), or positive *kamma*, and demerit *(pāpa, bap)*, or negative *kamma*, inherited from previous existences.

In the Khmer version of this cosmology,[6] certain powerful beings—such as demons *(yeak)*, spirits (including the *neak ta* or guardian spirits, *praet* or ghosts, and others), and some animals (e.g., elephants and tigers)—were considered to belong to a lower or outer realm because their power was not constrained by the moral injunctions of the Buddha. These beings were associated with the "wild" or "forest" *(prei)* as opposed to the "civilized" of the realm under a king *(srok)*. While these beings might from time to time disrupt the *srok*, their lack of merit ensured their power would eventually be controlled by morally superior beings, those who possessed merit. The Khmer cosmos also included gods *(tevoda,* Pāli *devatā)* who were the inheritors of much positive *kamma* but who had little power to influence events in the world.

Buddhist cosmological ideas were seen as relevant for understanding not only the relations between humans and other beings but also among humans themselves. Whereas other beings were deemed to be fixed by their *kammic* legacy in a particular status, this was not thought true of humans. Rather it was believed to be in the nature of being human that one could choose between acting on one's natural desires (Pāli *tanhā),* even though in doing so one would acquire demerit, or following Buddhist precepts to control one's desires and devote oneself to acts that produced merit. Single-minded pursuit of one's desires might result in the accumulation of worldly power or wealth, but the law of *kamma* ensured that such actions would ultimately result in intense suffering for oneself and others in this life or in future ones. A good Buddhist therefore, aware of the consequences of desires, tempered them and sought to perform only those acts that yield merit.

This Buddhist perspective on human action was deeply embedded, as Ebihara (1966:177) found, in traditional Khmer culture:

> By living according to the "law" *(chbap)* [i.e., the law of *kamma*], abstaining from evil *(bap),* and earning merit in numerous ways, an individual moves forward on the righteous path. The concept of achieving merit and avoiding evil is the basic principle underlying the influence of religion on behavior, for living by the "law" involves numerous aspects of daily life. (also see Chandler 1982:54–55).

The *sangha* served as the religious gyroscope for traditional Cambodian society as it did for other Theravāda Buddhist countries. By following the discipline *(vinaya),* monks emulated the ideal of the *arahant,* the saint who has achieved the liberation that lies at the end of the path established by the Buddha. Through sermons and ritual acts, monks make the path known to others. And by receiving the alms *(dāna)* offered by the laity, monks served as "fields of merit" and made it possible for laypeople to gain the merit that in turn advanced them along the path to ultimate salvation.

Unlike religious elites in certain other societies, membership in the *sangha* was open to all males from any segment of society. In Cambodia, as in other Buddhist societies in Southeast Asia—although not in Sri Lanka—it was the custom for a male to spend time (ideally, at least one Buddhist lent of three months) as a member of the order (Leclère

1899:401). This custom was still observed in many villages in Cambodia even into the 1960s. A village about thirty kilometers west of Phnom Penh where Ebihara carried out research in 1959–1960 was typical; three-quarters of men over seventeen had been in the _sangha_ as novices or monks for an average of two to three years.

Although each congregation of monks was relatively autonomous in premodern Cambodia, there were links between congregations that ultimately tied each to a _sangha_ whose supreme patron was the king. A king demonstrated that he was the possessor of extraordinary virtue (Pāli _bāramī_)—that is, merit that greatly transcended the _kammic_ heritages of others in the realm—by his conspicuous support for the _sangha_ as well as by acting in accord with the moral instruction he received from palace chaplains. If the king were truly virtuous, the realm would prosper. In premodern Cambodia, even more than in traditional Siam and perhaps even Burma, virtuous kings were rare and the world was often, as Chandler (1982:72) has written, "a desperate, cacophonous place." Nonetheless, so long as monks remained to perform the cyclical rituals in local _wats,_ the world still remained an intelligible one. Although demons, spirits, and beasts could invade the _srok_ from the forests, cruel kings could sit on the throne, and outside powers such as the Vietnamese or Thai could gain control over the realm, those who devoted themselves to constraining their passions and to making merit would in the next life, if not in this, reap the fruits of their acts.[7]

The Development of Buddhist-based Nationalism in Cambodia

The world of premodern Cambodia was particularly unsettled in the early nineteenth century. Powerful new Siamese and Vietnamese courts in their efforts to expand their realms threatened the very existence of an independent Khmer kingdom. Although the Khmer resisted domination by either power, they found Vietnamese rule far more threatening than that of Siamese because the Vietnamese sought to impose a very alien cultural tradition on them. The Khmer shared, in contrast, much of the same cultural tradition as the Siamese.[8] But despite their cultural connections, Khmer still felt threatened by the Siamese interest in extending political control over their country.

This threat was ended, temporarily at least, in 1863, when King Norodom (r. 1860–1904), a man who came under Siamese patronage, agreed to the establishment of French protection over Cambodia. It was during the colonial period (1863–1953) that the basis was laid for the Khmer revolution.

One source of this revolution was Buddhist. In 1864 a Khmer monk, Preah Saukonn (Pan), introduced in Cambodia a new Buddhist order that promoted a radical Buddhist world view (Leclère 1899:403). This order had its origins in Siam, where the monk had spent a long time. The Siamese reforms, begun by a princely monk who in 1851 became King Mongkut, entailed an emphasis on rational theology over traditional mythology and on asceticism for monks and ethical action for laity instead of traditional ritual practices.[9] While a member of the *sangha* Mongkut had gathered around him a group of monks who shared his interest in eliminating those aspects of traditional Buddhist practice that they considered obscured the fundamental truths of the religion. These monks founded a new order (Pāli *nikāya*) with a separate ordination tradition and a distinctive interpretation of *sangha* discipline. Mongkut named the new order Dhammayutika, "adhering to the *dhamma*" (Thai, Thammayut) (Reynolds 1973:95).

Preah Saukonn, the Khmer adherent to the Thammayut order, went to Phnom Penh, probably by royal invitation, in 1864. Norodom was close to the Siamese court, and his own ordination as a temporary member of the *sangha* had been sponsored by King Mongkut himself (Wilson 1970:544). Although after leaving the *sangha* and returning to Cambodia King Norodom had not, as Yang Sam (1990:116) notes, been conspicuous in his devotion to the religion, he still followed Mongkut's lead in providing royal patronage for the new order (called Thommayut in Khmer) in Cambodia (Kiernan 1985:3). Unlike Mongkut, Norodom did not, however, give the Thommayut unquestioned preeminence over the Mohanikay (Pāli, *Mahā-nikāya,* the great order), the order that included most monks in the country. When King Norodom emulated Siam in creating a national *sangha* under a court-appointed patriarch,[10] he appointed a Mohanikay monk to this post. Preah Saukonn, as head of the Thommayut order was, however, given almost equal authority to the patriarch; he also received the patronage of the royal family.[11]

With Preah Saukonn's death in 1893, the reformist approach to Buddhism lost its major advocate in Cambodia. A rationalized approach to understanding Buddhist doctrines was, however, again taken up by several young Mohanikay monks—most notably, Chuon Nath (1883–1969) and Huot Tath (1891–1975?)—in the early part of the twentieth century. These monks first gained recognition for their sermons on the discipline of the *sangha* based on their own reading of the Pāli scriptures. Their criticisms of the traditional practices of the Khmer *sangha* soon aroused the animosity of the ranking monks of the time, and in 1918 the latter persuaded the king, with the blessing of the French, to issue an ordinance prohibiting monks "from teaching reforms or . . . from spreading among the faithful modern ideas which conflict with traditional religion."[12]

The French found traditional cosmological Buddhism more conducive for their purposes than modernist Buddhism (see Chandler 1983a:157). The maintenance of a traditional social order, at least in form, with a monarch at its apex, made it easier for the French to administer the country and extract indirect taxes from it. The French also moved very slowly in introducing modern secular education in Cambodia. Whatever education villagers received throughout the colonial period was provided by traditional monks in local monastic schools (Chandler 1983a:160, 161–162).

Despite the restrictions placed on the introduction of ideas that might lead to a questioning of the premises of cosmological Buddhism, some Khmer peasants still resisted the new forms of domination introduced by the French. As early as 1916, tax revolts involving thousands of peasants took place; in 1925 a French *résident,* Bardez, was beaten to death by villagers from whom he was trying to collect increased taxes. During the Great Depression demands for reductions in taxes continued to increase (Chandler 1983a:153f). Some peasants during this period, disturbed by the changes that colonialism had introduced into their world, embraced Buddhist millenarian ideas; others turned to the Cao Dai cult, a new religion introduced from Vietnam (Bernardini 1976; Chandler 1983a:162; Kiernan 1985:4–7; Yang Sam 1987:40–41).

Reformed Buddhist ideas were also beginning to gain some ground, albeit mainly among people living in Phnom Penh rather than in the villages. The Venerable Chuon Nath and Huot Tath continued, despite the ordinance of 1918 proscribing teaching of modern interpretations of Buddhism, to promote reformist ideas within a faction of the *sangha* known as Thommakay (Kiernan 1985:3–4). In the early 1920s both were selected to study in Hanoi with Louis Finot, the great French philologist who was then the director of the École Française d'Extrême-Orient. On return to Phnom Penh, they began to work on a monumental project, the translation of the *Tripitaka,* the Buddhist scriptures, into Khmer and the printing of the work in both Khmer and Pāli.

This project was spurred not only by the commitment of the monks involved in an approach to Buddhism that posited that religious truth could better be gained through direct access to the Buddhist scriptures than through acceptance of traditional authority but also by the development in the early part of the twentieth century of ways to print the Khmer language. By publishing and circulating their translations and their sermons, the reformist monks began stimulating the imagining, to use Anderson's (1983a) term, of a Khmer community whose members shared a common culture expressed in a printed language.

The imagining of a Khmer nation was further spurred by the founding of the Buddhist Institute in 1930. The French founded the institute "to lessen the influence of Thai Buddhism (and Thai politics) on the Cambodian sangha and to substitute more Indo-Chinese loyalties between the Lao sangha and their Cambodian counterparts" (Chandler 1991:18). Suzanne Karpelès, who was placed in charge of the institute, recruited as her chief associates several men who were to have a lasting impact on the development of Khmer nationalism.

In 1935 Son Ngoc Thanh, an ethnic Khmer from southern Vietnam who had studied in France for many years, was recruited as the secretary of the institute. Thanh would within a few years help create and then lead Cambodia's nascent nationalist movement. Although he was over-shadowed in the 1950s by Prince Norodom Sihanouk, he is still recog-nized as one of the key architects of Khmer nationalism. Karpelès also recruited two *achar,* former monks with a reputation for their knowledge of traditional Buddhist culture, who were to play arguably even more important roles than Thanh. Like him, both Mean (who later took the nom de guerre of Son Ngoc Minh) and Sok (better known as Tou Samouth) were ethnic Khmer from southern Vietnam. Mean/Son Ngoc Minh, who died in Vietnam in 1972, is today looked to by the Kampu-chean People's party, the Communist party that came to power following the Vietnamese invasion of Cambodia in 1979, as the founder of the Party.[13] Sok/Tou Samouth was the secretary of the Party in 1962 when he was assassinated, probably by Sihanouk's police.

In 1936 Son Ngoc Thanh and two other men associated with the insti-tute founded the first Khmer-language newspaper, *Nagara Vatta* (Ang-kor Wat). The newspaper was read primarily by monks and others who had received their education in Khmer from monastic schools rather than by the small French-educated elite (see Bunchan Mul 1982:116). *Nagara Vatta* served as the first forum for making a form of Buddhism that was not simply a reflex of traditional cosmological ideas central to Khmer nationalism.

The Buddhist-based nationalism inspired by those associated with the Buddhist Institute and formulated in the pages of *Nagara Vatta* acquired a significant following in the context of the challenge posed to French rule during World War II. The authority of the French colonial adminis-tration was undermined by the Nazi defeat of France and the establish-ment of the Vichy regime in July 1940. The Vichy administration of Cambodia entailed little change of personnel, but the isolation of the colonial officials from France rendered them far more dependent on local resources than had been the case before. The weakness of the colonial administration became obvious when in early 1941 Thai forces launched a successful attack on French colonial forces to "recover" territories in Cambodia and Laos. Following a brief war, France—under Japanese urging—ceded a large part of northwestern Cambodia as well as parts of Laos to the Thai. This cession was a severe blow to Khmer pride, not only in view of the loss of territory, but also because the Khmer court had no role in the negotiations. French authority was further eroded in August 1941 when eight thousand Japanese troops were sent to Cambodia as part of the movement of Japanese forces throughout Indochina.

The Vichy colonial regime sought to shore up its authority through a number of repressive acts. *Nagara Vatta* was closed in 1942 after its editors took part in anti-French demonstrations. Before suppressing the paper, the French arrested the Venerable Hem Chieu, a ranking Thommayut monk, and another monk, for antigovernment activities. "Hem Chieu was an important member of the *sangha,* and the manner of his arrest—by civil authorities who failed to allow him the ritual of leaving the monastic order—affronted his religious colleagues while giving nationalists of the *Nagara Vatta* clique a cause célèbre" (Chandler 1983a:169). On 20 July 1942—a day still looked back to by many Khmer as an important one in the history of Cambodian nationalism— several hundred monks led a large demonstration of more than a thousand people to demand the release of Hem Chieu and his colleague (Bunchan Mul 1982:120–123; Chandler 1986:83). The nationalists mistakenly assumed that the Japanese would support the demonstration; instead, Vichy officials arrested its leaders. A number of the latter, including the former editor of *Nagara Vatta,* were quickly tried and sentenced to death, although their sentences were subsequently commuted to life imprisonment. The Venerable Hem Chieu himself died in 1943 in the infamous French penal colony of Poulo Condore, an island off southern Vietnam (Bunchan Mul 1982:124; Chandler 1983a:170).

The Vichy colonial government further sought to render Buddhist-based nationalism impotent by moving in 1943 to replace the traditional Khmer writing system with a romanized system devised by French officials. "Many Cambodians . . . , and especially the *sangha,* saw the reform as an attack on traditional education and on the high status enjoyed by traditional educators in Cambodian society" (Chandler 1983a:170; also see Chandler 1986:81). The French effort was, however, shortlived. In March 1945 Japanese forces staged a coup d'état against the French throughout Indochina. In Cambodia the Japanese recognized the young Norodom Sihanouk, who had been placed on the throne by the French in 1941, as the head of an independent government. Not only was the romanization effort aborted, but the new government made the Buddhist rather than the Gregorian the official calendar (Chandler 1986:81–82).

Although the Japanese-sponsored independent government of Cambodia lasted only a short time, French rule being reestablished in October 1945, it left a significant legacy. The monarchy, which previously had been a compliant tool of the French, was to become under Sihanouk the leading institution in the promotion of Khmer nationalism. Before it could fulfill this role, however, Sihanouk first had to win the support of the peasantry who made up the vast majority of the populace, as well as gain that of the small elite in Phnom Penh who had the skills to administer the country.

Political Crisis in Postcolonial Cambodia

The return of the French in October 1945 placed Sihanouk in a difficult position. He had been seen briefly by the people as the leader of an independent Cambodia; now he was once again the puppet of a colonial regime. In the immediate post–World War II period the initiative for shaping Khmer nationalism shifted from Sihanouk to the successors of the reformist Buddhist *(Nagara Vatta)* group who established the Democratic party after 1946 when the French permitted the formation of political parties. This party appears to have taken inspiration in part from the "promoters" of the revolution of 1932 in Siam. Like the promoters the Democrats sought to create a constitutional monarchy in which effective power would rest with an elected parliament. They appeared to gain the mandate of the populace when they won more than two-thirds of the seats in a Consultative Assembly in elections held in September 1946 (Chandler 1983a:177; Chandler 1991:31). This election led, however, to no real devolution of power by the colonial government.

The inability of the Democrats to win any concessions from the French paved the way for Sihanouk to reassert his claim to be the embodiment of Khmer nationalism. In a dramatic act in 1947 he left the throne and entered into the monkhood for three months. As Yang Sam (1987:8) has written, "His participation in the monastic life certainly raised the spirit of Buddhist worshippers and made them very proud of this pious act." By becoming a monk, Sihanouk followed a traditional ideal of Buddhist monarchs (see Reynolds 1972). When he left the monkhood, he also became a conspicuous public supporter of the *sangha,* again following the traditional model of the Buddhist monarch.

Having established in ritual act his claim to the merit and virtue required of a great king in traditional times, Sihanouk then turned to demonstrate his Buddhist charisma in the political arena. Over the opposition of the Democrats, he accepted a treaty for partial independence offered by the French in 1949, a treaty that they agreed to in part because of their involvement in the growing conflict with the Communist-led Viet Minh in Vietnam.

With Sihanouk commanding the stage in Phnom Penh, some who had been at the forefront of a Buddhist-based nationalism turned to the Viet Minh for support. Son Ngoc Minh became the leader of a Cambodian section of the Indochina Communist party, but he still retained his links to a Khmer Buddhist nationalism. In April 1950, under the aegis of the Viet Minh, the *Samakhum Khmer Issarak*—literally, the Khmer Independence Association, but known in English as the Unified Issarak Front (UIF)—was created. At the first meeting, 105 of the 200 in attendance were said to have been Buddhist monks (Kiernan 1985:79). The main leaders of the new Communist-led movement, like Minh and Tou Samouth, had been monks, and the main local organizers appear to have been monks (Kiernan 1985:93–94). In early 1951 the UIF sponsored a Khmer Buddhist Conference at which a play was presented about Hem Chieu, the monk who died in a French prison after having led the 1942 demonstrations. Later in the same year Son Ngoc Minh, speaking to Khmer in southern Vietnam, linked national liberation with saving the religion (Kiernan 1985:93). It was only later, when the leadership was replaced by men and women who had studied in France and there came strongly under the influence of other ideologies, that Buddhism was to be viewed as an impediment to rather than an essential component of the revolution.

In 1952 Prince Sihanouk took over the control of the government himself, ignoring the electoral mandate that the Democrats had again won in the National Assembly. He became his own prime minister, and in this role as well as that of king, he played for support on both the local and an international stage. His Royal Crusade for Independence, begun in 1953, quickly succeeded in making him the dominant nationalist figure. The Democrats had been shown to be impotent by Sihanouk's total disregard of them. Although the UIF by the start of the crusade controlled perhaps as much as one-third of the territory and 15 percent of the population of the country (Kiernan 1985:128), it, like other groups, "underestimated the King's ability to establish himself as an effective national leader" (Kiernan 1985:131). When at the Geneva Conference in 1954 China withdrew support for some recognition of the UIF and the Viet Minh followed suit, Sihanouk was able to claim that he led the sole legitimate Khmer nationalist movement (see Kiernan and Boua 1982:131–132). When Cambodia became independent as a consequence of the conference, the opposition to Sihanouk had been left with no internationally recognized base of support.

In 1955 Sihanouk abdicated the throne in favor of his father and then took the position of head of government. Even after his father's death in 1960 he did not reassume the throne but rather became head of state so that he could continue to guide the political fortunes of his country rather than play only ceremonial roles. The fact that he was still de facto king, however, gave him a status in the eyes of the populace that could be matched by no other political leader.

Sihanouk could trace his heritage to precolonial kings and could, thus, claim the mantle of the past, including the past of the great Khmer empire of Angkor. The monarchy was, however, only one wheel of the chariot of Khmer nationalism. The other wheel was the Buddhist religion. "These two wheels must turn at the same speed in order for the cart, i.e., Cambodia, to advance smoothly on the path of peace and progress" (Chau Seng 1962:11; quoted in English translation by Zago 1976:111). Prince Sihanouk himself often employed this metaphor of the two wheels of the chariot, thereby linking himself with a notion of the Buddhist state based on the "two wheels of the Dhamma" that had its origins in the third century B.C. under the first great Buddhist king, Aśoka (in this connection, see, especially, Reynolds 1972).

Sihanouk sought to do more than to restore the past, however. He sought recognition of Cambodia as a modern state and linked his nationalist goals to socialism, albeit a socialism that he claimed was to be rooted in the teachings of the Buddha. "We are socialists," Sihanouk said, "but our socialism is inspired far more by Buddhist morality and the religious traditions of our national existence than by doctrines imported from abroad" (quoted in Zago 1976:112).[14] In keeping with his vision of a society based on its own traditions rather than on foreign ideologies, Sihanouk sought to maintain a neutral foreign policy.[15] Events in neighboring Vietnam were soon, however, to make this effort untenable.

In March 1970 Prince Sihanouk was deposed in a coup d'état, and General Lon Nol became the new prime minister. This change was not simply the replacement of one political leader by another; with Prince Sihanouk gone, gone too was the legitimacy of power that he as successor to the Khmer kings had brought with him. Although Lon Nol attempted to rally his countrymen around him in a religious crusade against communism (Whitaker, et al. 1973:145, 191–197), he gained little support beyond the city of Phnom Penh. The country was soon plunged into chaos. Many members of the Buddhist *sangha* living outside Phnom Penh had to make their own decisions about appropriate relations with the warring parties as communication with higher levels of the order became difficult or impossible. The legitimacy of the Lon Nol government was also seriously challenged when Prince Sihanouk, who had been traveling abroad when the coup occurred, arrived in Beijing and shortly afterward declared himself the head of the Royal Government of National Union of Kampuchea and nominal chairman of the Communist-led National United Front of Kampuchea.

The Lon Nol government broke not only with Sihanouk's domestic policies, but also with his foreign policy. No longer did Cambodia remain neutral; rather the short-lived Khmer Republic under Lon Nol became an unequivocal American pawn in the war in Vietnam (in this connection, see, especially, Shawcross 1979). In April 1970, only a little more than a month after the Lon Nol coup, American and South Vietnamese forces entered eastern Cambodia with the agreement of the Lon Nol government. While this invasion failed in its goal to destroy the headquarters of the Vietnamese Communist military command for South Vietnam, it succeeded all too well in exacerbating the civil war in Cambodia. From this time on the United States steadily increased bombing missions over Cambodia until they were finally halted, through an Act of Congress, in 1973.

The civil war in Cambodia was waged between the forces of the Khmer Republic and those who collectively came to be known as the Khmer Rouge. The leadership of the Khmer Rouge was provided by the Communist party of Kampuchea under Saloth Sar or, as he is better known, Pol Pot.[16] Although the Party claimed to be aligned in a National Front under Sihanouk with non-Communist elements, these elements had no influence over the Party.

The war, together with the bombing, took a brutal toll on the population of Cambodia. It is estimated that at least six hundred thousand people were killed in the war between 1970 and 1975. The victims were often civilians and included Vietnamese who resided in Cambodia, who became the object of racially motivated attacks encouraged by the Lon Nol government. In 1970 Vietnamese living inside Cambodia were massacred in large numbers (see Poole 1975).[17] It is also estimated that more than a third of the population of the country, which in 1974 was said to contain 7.89 (Kiernan 1990:38) million people, became refugees from the war. The vast majority of these refugees sought sanctuary in the towns and particularly in the capital city of Phnom Penh. The city grew from about six hundred thousand in 1970 to nearly two million when the country collapsed in April 1975.[18]

The refugee population could not be supported on food produced within the country since so much land had been abandoned or had fallen under Khmer Rouge control, while transportation had come to a near standstill. Despite a massive airlift by the United States of food into the country, starvation became a fact of life—or rather a fact of death—to perhaps tens of thousands of Khmer in 1974 and 1975.[19] Starvation accelerated after the fall of the country to the Khmer Rouge and the concomitant ending of the airlift of food supplies by the Americans. The new government was incapable of feeding its large refugee population even if it had been willing to do so. While it is impossible to calculate the number of deaths from starvation between 1973 and the end of 1975, they could not have been fewer than a hundred thousand.

By April 1975 Cambodia had been reduced to a Hobbesian state in which all moral standards had been destroyed or abandoned. It was in this moral vacuum that the Khmer Rouge set out to create a wholly new social order.

The Destruction of Buddhism in Cambodia under the Khmer Rouge

From April 1975 until the Vietnamese invasion of Cambodia at the very end of 1978, the government of what was known as Democratic Kampuchea under Pol Pot attempted in a ruthless manner to institute one of the most radical revolutions in modern history.[20] The new society was to be racially pure—one that above all was purged of Vietnamese (Thion 1983a:28; Frieson 1988:413–414; Chandler 1991:238). Furthermore, it was also to have no antecedents; all institutions of the past were to be destroyed. Not only were institutions associated with the pro-American government of Lon Nol, the neutralist government of Prince Sihanouk, and the colonial regime under the French to be rejected, but even bona fide Khmer institutions that could be traced to the precolonial past were to be rooted out and destroyed. Foremost among these was the *sangha,* or the Buddhist order of monks.

In 1969/1970, the last time a count was made, there were some 65,000 monks and novices in Cambodia's 3,369 *wats.* Of these, 2,385 monks and 139 *wats* were affiliated with the Thommayut order.[21] During the war between 1970 and 1975 more than one-third of the *wats* were destroyed; many monks and novices were killed, left the order, or became refugees (Yang Sam 1987:58–59). Despite this, Buddhism remained a vital basis for Khmer life until the end of the war in 1975. Cambodian Buddhism was, however, not to benefit by the end of the war in April 1975. The new Khmer Rouge government under Pol Pot sought in a systematic manner to obliterate Buddhism from Cambodian society.

Although the Communist movement in Cambodia had its origins in the Buddhist nationalism of the 1940s and although former monks and monks had been prominent in the movement in the 1950s, since its reorganization in 1960 the Party had begun to shed its Buddhist mantle. Between 1970 and 1975 a few monks still appeared among the membership of the National Front, but there is evidence that by this period the Party had already begun to place very severe constraints on the practice of religion in areas under its control (see Kiernan 1985:346, 376–377).

In the immediate aftermath of its takeover in 1975, the Khmer Rouge did not immediately move to ban Buddhism (Yang Sam 1987:70–72), but by the end of the year it had been declared to be a "reactionary religion." Monks and novices, even those in the base areas that Khmer Rouge had controlled before April 1975, were compelled to disrobe. One eyewitness describes how after he and his family had been forced to leave Phnom Penh, they made their way to a village where they had relatives.

> When Bun arrived in the village there were still three monks in Phum Andong pagoda. Soon after they were ordered to leave the *Sangha* and get married, which they did, even one old monk who had lived in the pagoda all his life and had been a friend of Bun's father. Not to have done so would have been to risk re-education. (Stuart-Fox and Bunhaeng Ung 1986:53)

Being sent for reeducation often meant being sent to be killed. In 1980 it was estimated that five out of every eight monks were executed during the Pol Pot regime (DeVoss 1980:90). Major temple-monasteries were destroyed and lesser ones were converted into storage centers, prisons, or extermination camps. The former cremation grounds at Choeung Ek *wat* on the edge of Phnom Penh became one of the major sites for mass executions (Yang Sam 1987:74).[22] Images of the Buddha were often decapitated or desecrated in other ways; copies of the Buddhist scriptures were burned or thrown into rivers (Sophath Pak and Colm 1990).

The story of the Venerable Chea Tong, a monk who survived the 1975–1979 period, is typical. In 1975 this monk was forced with about a hundred of his fellow monks and novices to leave their *wat* in Phnom Penh. They walked to a community about 50 kilometers north. Here they were forced to disrobe and were told that "religion was feudal and oppressive and monks were useless parasites . . . , leeches living on the blood of the people." During the Pol Pot period, Chea Tong's monastic companions disappeared; some, he heard, had been executed. The temple-monastery in the community in which he continued to live and labor was "turned into a food storehouse and pigs were kept in front of the temple." Khmer Rouge soldiers, in an act that was a violent reversal of the rite of dedication of a new image, "shot the giant cement statue of the Buddha inside the temple between the eyes."[23]

The hostility of the Khmer Rouge toward Buddhism cannot be explained solely in terms of Marxist ideas about religion being the opiate of the people. As the Khmer Rouge have become better understood, it has become clear that the potency of their ideology derived in part from its relationship to Khmer Buddhist culture.

Pol Pot's own roots were in this culture. He told Yugoslav journalists in 1978 that "according to custom, I lived in a [*wat*] to learn how to read and write. I spent six years in a [*wat*] and I was a monk for two years" (quoted in Kiernan 1985:26–27). Although this was an overstatement—

his actual time in the *sangha* was between three months and one year[24]—
it is indicative of Pol Pot's recognition of the high cultural value attached
to service in the *sangha* in period when he was growing up. Later, when
Pol Pot joined the Communist movement, he worked under Tou Samouth,
secretary-general of the Party, who had been a monk and made use of his
network of connections in the *sangha* to gain support for antigovernment
activities (see Chandler 1992:64–65). By the time he assumed control of
the Party, however, Pol Pot had turned away from the *sangha* and had
adopted a very hostile stance toward organized Buddhism.[25]

After Pol Pot gained control of the Party, he remade it into a disciplined organization (known in Khmer as Angkar, the organization, or
Angkar Loeu, the high organization) that was to be substituted for the
sangha as the ultimate source of moral authority in Khmer society. Yang
Sam records that in the village in Battambang province where he had
been moved, a cadre made this substitution (the Khmer version of the
"politics of ritual displacement"—see Anagnost's chapter in this volume)
explicit:

> To his view the conduct of the Communist Party's members was far more
> perfect than the practices of monks. As a comparison, each Khmer Rouge
> cadre observed more than ten Sila [ethical precepts incumbent on monks] in
> the Buddhist teachings. He/she persevered in improving his/her personality
> by loving and respecting people, being honest, protecting people's interests,
> confessing his/her misdeeds, using modest and polite words, and avoiding
> adultery and polygamy, avoiding drinking, avoiding gambling, avoiding
> thievery. (Yang Sam 1987:70)

Although many rural people appear to have been impressed by the similarity between the disciplined morality of the Khmer Rouge cadre and
that of members of the *sangha,* the Khmer Rouge sought to create a
world that was the moral inversion of that of Buddhism.

Smith (1989:25–30) has recorded observations of Khmer refugees
who viewed the Khmer Rouge in Buddhist cosmological terms as belonging to a subhuman realm—as animals, *yeak,* or spirits. These beings,
belonging to the forest (see Ponchaud 1989:161), that is, outside of society, were credited as having black powers.

> One of the most important concepts in Khmer world view is that good and
> evil in the cosmic order are held in perpetual balance. Each must exist, so
> neither ever completely and conclusively triumphs over the other. Existence
> is above all *ordered* . . . . In the Khmer Rouge years, evil did seem to tri-
> umph. (Smith 1989:30)

The Khmer Rouge conceived of a new order in which evil and good were fused in the Angkar and cadres were both subhuman beings with immense magical powers and morally superior beings equivalent to Buddhist monks. Organized Buddhism had to be eliminated for this new order to be established.

In 1978 Yun Yat, minister of culture in the Khmer Rouge regime, told Yugoslav journalists that "Buddhism is dead, and the ground had been cleared for the foundations of a new revolutionary culture."[26] By this time all the monks in the country, including even those who had supported the Khmer Rouge before 1975, had been compelled to disrobe (see Boua 1991). Without the *sangha,* the Buddhist ritual life of the populace had been totally eradicated; in its stead, the people were supposed to dedicate themselves to work. In no other Communist state, including even Tibet, was a materialist ideology so radically imposed at the expense of a spiritual tradition.[27]

The attack on Cambodian Buddhism went well beyond the Marxist notion that religion serves to disguise class relations. The Khmer Rouge sought, by eliminating the institution that had for so long served as a basic source of Khmer identity, to create a new order with few roots in the past. The history of the new Democratic Kampuchean utopia was to be written by the revolution alone (see, in this connection, Thion 1983a and Chandler 1983b and 1983c).

In the end, the effort to create an agrarian utopia purged of all "undesirable" elements failed. Although the Khmer Rouge had come to power in no small part because of their alliance with the military forces of the Vietnamese Communists, by early 1977 relations between Democratic Kampuchea and the Socialist Republic of Vietnam had become extremely hostile. In late December 1978, after two years of border clashes, the Vietnamese sent a military force into Cambodia, driving the Democratic Kampuchean government out of Phnom Penh. While the Vietnamese forces quickly captured Phnom Penh and installed a new government under the People's Revolutionary Council headed by Heng Samrin, it encountered some resistance in the countryside. Eventually, the Khmer Rouge were forced to retreat to the hilly areas along the Thai frontier, taking with them between twenty-five thousand and forty thousand people.[28]

The invasion released the hold that Angkar had over the populace, and at least a million people moved during 1979. About 600,000 made their way toward the Thai border (Vickery 1984:34; also see Ea 1990:8–10), most impelled by starvation as there had been a total collapse in rice production and distribution in 1979. Although from 1979 until 1992 more than 200,000 Khmer refugees were resettled in third countries—especially the United States, France, Canada, and Australia—for many years refugee camps in Thailand defined the only Cambodian world for another 350,000 or more.[29]

The Reestablishment of Buddhism in Cambodia after 1979

Following their invasion of Cambodia, the Vietnamese installed a new government under Heng Samrin in Phnom Penh. The country was called the People's Republic of Kampuchea, a name that was to be replaced in 1989 by the State of Cambodia.[30] Despite the fact that the Khmer Rouge had sought to maintain power through a reign of terror that had left up to one-fifth of the population of Cambodia dead,[31] the United States, Western European Countries, Japan, the People's Republic of China, the countries associated with the Association of Southeast Asian Nations (ASEAN)[32]—indeed, an overwhelming majority of the members of the United Nations—did not recognize the PRK. Rather, the PRK was ostracized for having been set up by the Vietnamese. Only members of the former Soviet bloc and India extended recognition to the PRK.

Because of their powerful support, the Khmer Rouge who fled to the Thai border were able to gain sufficient support (mainly from China and Thailand) to regroup and launch a guerrilla war against the PRK. In addition, two new political movements that proclaimed as their goal the liberation of Cambodia from Vietnamese domination were created among refugees in the camps in Thailand. One of these movements, the Khmer People's National Liberation Front (KPNLF) under Son Sann, a former prime minister, was the descendant of the Khmer Republic. The other, known by its French acronym, FUNCINPEC,[33] was headed by Prince Sihanouk. In 1982, under prodding from the United States, the People's Republic of China, and the ASEAN countries, the two refugee-based movements agreed to join the Khmer Rouge in a Coalition Government of Democratic Kampuchea under the nominal leadership of Sihanouk. The real power within the coalition lay, however, with the Khmer Rouge.

Despite the continuing threat of the Khmer Rouge and the international isolation imposed by a de facto anti-Vietnamese alliance, the PRK had still begun by 1980 to establish some semblance of a new order within most of Cambodia. The PRK based its moral authority primarily on its having restored order to the country following the destruction that the "murderous Pol Pot clique" had inflicted upon the Khmer people. The PRK sought to distance itself from the Khmer Rouge regime by making national monuments out of the mass graves and, especially, the former Khmer Rouge prison at Tuol Sleng, where thousands were tortured and executed. The government also instituted a national holiday on 7 January to mark the "liberation" of the country from the Pol Pot regime. Not being the Khmer Rouge, however, provided the PRK government with only a negative legitimacy. Although the PRK eschewed the perverted ultranationalism of Pol Pot, it still had to demonstrate that it had the authority to represent the Khmer nation.

Before the signing of peace accords in late 1991, the PRK was unable and probably unwilling to reclaim the monarchical tradition as part of its own legacy. While the grand palace was accorded a prominent place among the tourist attractions of Phnom Penh, the fact that its last inhabitant, Prince Sihanouk, had associated himself with the opposition Coalition Government of Democratic Kampuchea prevented the PRK, at least so long as Sihanouk remained outside the country, from reinterpreting the monarchy for its own purpose. Because the monarchy still held positive significance for many Khmer, however, it was not surprising that the government in Phnom Penh became in 1991 party to an agreement that recognized Prince Sihanouk as head of state. When Sihanouk returned to Phnom Penh in late 1991, the leaders of the PRK, Hun Sen and Chea Sim, were conspicuous in their public association with the prince in the welcoming ceremonies.[34]

For twelve years the PRK had, therefore, to find institutions other than the monarchy through which to bolster its legitimacy. Despite the dominance of a Communist party, the PRK recognized that the Buddhist heritage of Cambodia should be accepted as part of the culture of the Khmer nation. One of the first acts of the Heng Samrin government after it came to power was to permit the partial restoration of Buddhism.

The restoration was described to me in 1990 by the Venerable Tep Vong, the highest-ranking monk in the PRK, and the Venerable Oum Sum, another high-ranking monk and the monk with the most clerical education in post–Pol Pot Cambodia.[35] Early in 1979 a delegation of Theravādin monks was brought from Vietnam to Cambodia to carry out the reordination of some of the monks who had been forced to leave the order during the Khmer Rouge period. According to the Venerable Tep Vong, the monk who served as the preceptor (Pāli *upajjhāya;* Khmer *oppachchea*) for this ordination was a Khmer who had been in the monkhood for fourteen years, served as a preceptor in Cambodia before 1975, and escaped to Vietnam after the arrival of the Khmer Rouge.[36] The qualifications of the preceptor are critical since the major schisms in Theravāda Buddhism are traceable to the nonrecognition by some monks of the ordination genealogy of other monks.

The Venerable Tep Vong said that seven carefully chosen former monks were reordained at Wat Unnalom in Phnom Penh in September 1979. By "carefully chosen" he meant that they were men who had good reputations as monks before 1975. According to Yang Sam (1987:80), the seven had all been in the *sangha* for twenty to sixty years.[37] These monks were then able to constitute the chapter required by the rules of the *sangha* for an ordination. The Venerable Oum Sum was in the second group of monks ordained by the first group. It would appear that seniority in the Khmer monkhood now is traceable to the order in which monks were reordained rather than to the order in which they were originally ordained. The Venerable Tep Vong is the ranking monk because he was the first to be reordained.

The Venerable Tep Vong said that from late 1979 to late 1981 the monks who had first been reordained reestablished the Khmer *sangha* by ordaining other former monks, first in Phnom Penh and then for each province. The goal, he said, was the creation of chapters of seven monks each, which could reestablish the ordination genealogy in each province.[38] He also noted that those chosen for reordination had all previously been preceptors or abbots, that is, senior monks.

Many *wat*s were reopened during this period not only to accommodate the members of the *sangha* but also to make possible the resumption of traditional ritual life. Ben Kiernan (1982), who visited Cambodia in mid-1980, reports seeing festivals at Buddhist temples at that time, and the government allowed a factory manufacturing Buddha images to open (Hawk 1982). The new government was allowing the people to reclaim some of the ritual landscape.

In the first years of the PRK, the government, or, more precisely, the Party, allowed the *sangha* to reemerge only very slowly. By 1981, according to a report by Michael Richardson, 500 monks had returned to the *sangha* and about 1,500 novices had been ordained, and about three thousand *wat*s had been restored "with official encouragement" (Richardson 1981:104). An official report in 1982 put the figures at 2,311 monks, of whom 800 were former monks (Yang Sam 1987:81).

In 1980 in its early stages of consolidating power, the new PRK government convened a national conference of monks in Siem Reap to consider the role of Buddhism in the development of the country.[39] The National United Front for the Salvation of Cambodia, set up by the Party to represent interests of groups other than the Party, included members of the *sangha*. Three monks were members of its thirty-member Central Committee (Kiernan 1982:368), and the Venerable Tep Vong was made vice-president of the Central Committee (Yang Sam 1987:80).

In 1980 it seemed as though the Heng Samrin government, while led by members of a Communist party, might be moving toward drawing upon the Buddhist tradition to shore up or establish its legitimacy in the eyes of the Khmer people. However, by 1981 the PRK government began to make it difficult for Buddhism to be restored in the form in which it had existed before 1970. It started restricting ordinations, permitting only those over fifty years of age to enter the *sangha*.[40] Although a few younger men were allowed to be ordained, especially if they were following the traditional custom of doing so to make merit for a parent at the time of the parent's funeral (Laurie 1985), the number of monks was kept quite small. Various estimates place the total of monks in the 1985–1989 period at between 6,500 and 8,000.[41] In other words, the total number following the discipline of the *sangha* under the PRK was then less than 10 percent of the number in pre-Khmer Rouge times.

Kiernan reports that in 1980 the government justified restriction on ordinations because "it would . . . seem that the country is not yet productive enough to support large numbers of monks living from alms donated by the population" (Kiernan 1982:368). It is also likely that the restrictive policy toward Buddhism reflected an effort to ensure that the *sangha* did not emerge as an institution independent of or resistant to the state. Buddhism was still viewed in Marxist terms as having a potential for offering people "unhealthy beliefs." At a second congress of monks held in July 1984, a resolution imposed by the Party leadership included the admonition to "completely discard unhealthy beliefs."[42]

Although the government imposed strict restrictions on the numbers of monks being ordained, it permitted the restoration of *wat*s. By 1989, according to official figures, there were twenty-four hundred temple-monasteries in the country, or about two-thirds of the number that had existed before 1970.[43] I saw many restored *wat*s in and around Phnom Penh when I visited the city in early 1988 and again in 1989. I also saw many new images of the Buddha. It should be noted, however, that while the government permitted reconstruction of religious structures and the casting of new images, it did not, at least until very recently, allocate any government monies for such projects.

In mid-1988 there was an abrupt change in the policy of the PRK toward Buddhism. Just before this shift the PRK and Vietnamese governments announced an agreement for the withdrawal of Vietnamese forces from Cambodia. Hun Sen, the prime minister of the PRK, had met twice with Prince Sihanouk in late 1987 and again in early 1988 and had agreed in principle to the creation of a government that would include not only representatives of the PRK and Sihanouk himself, but also representatives of the Khmer Peoples National Liberation Front. As the leaders of the PRK began to foresee a time when they would have to compete with those from other factions in elections in Cambodia, they must have felt the need to develop a broader popular appeal. They sought to build this popular support by becoming, as had kings in the past, conspicuous patrons of Buddhism.

In January 1989 Hun Sen apologized to audiences around the country for the "government's 'mistakes' towards religion" (Hiebert 1989:36).

Restrictions on ordinations of men under the age of fifty were removed. The consequences of the change were evident when I was in Cambodia in May 1989. Whereas the previous year I had seen very few monks, and only one under fifty, this time I saw more monks, especially in the countryside, and many of those were young.[44] The number of members of the *sangha* grew significantly after 1988; the Venerable Tep Vong told me that in 1990 the total membership of the *sangha* was 16,400, of whom about 40 percent were novices.[45] The government also removed a detested tax on temple-monasteries and has even contributed monies for the construction of some shrines.

Hun Sen and other leaders became conspicuous for their public piety. In a speech in Kampot, Hun Sen made a point of telling people that Heng Samrin, the general secretary of the Party, and Chea Sim, the chairman of the National Assembly, had been members of the *sangha*. Hun Sen told the reporter Susan Downie that he himself has "good memories" of his period living in a *wat* as a boy in Phnom Penh (Downie 1989).[46] Although a cynical interpretation could be given to these statements, they also could be seen as an acknowledgment that Buddhism had been a formative influence in shaping the nationalism of the non–Khmer Rouge segment of the Communist party. Hun Sen, Heng Samrin, and Chea Sim look to two former monks, Son Ngoc Minh and Tou Samouth, as the founders of the Party they now head.

In April 1989 Radio Phnom Penh reported that Hun Sen, Heng Samrin, and other officials were present at a ceremony at which a relic of the Buddha was enshrined at a temple in front of the Phnom Penh railway station.[47] The most important public religious acts involving government officials were those held at the recently constructed shrines to those killed by the Khmer Rouge. These shrines—such as the ones at the Tuol Sleng extermination camp in Phnom Penh and at Choeung Ek on the edge of the city—are in the form of a traditional Buddhist funerary structure, symbolizing both Mount Meru and the impermanence of life. The rites held at these shrines involve monks who are invited by the government to chant appropriate texts.

In April 1989 the National Assembly of the PRK voted to amend the constitution to make Buddhism once again the national religion of Cambodia. The director for the Center of Reproduction of Cultural Art Objects of the Ministry of Information and Culture—a man who is also a sculptor involved, with government backing, in restoring Buddha images—provided a clue regarding the government's reason for having changed its position toward Buddhism: "We know we have a great difficulty. . . . On the one side the country is a battlefield. But on the other hand, we have to reconstruct the nation" (quoted in Sophath Pak and Colm 1990). A government run by men who remain members of a Communist party

has discovered that communism has little to say about national reconstruction (or construction, for that matter). The pursuit of that goal in
Cambodia, the leaders have come to accept, requires looking to the Buddhist religion.

Given the near total destruction of Buddhism in Cambodia under Pol
Pot, the question of what might be the nationalist character of Khmer
Buddhism does not have a clear answer. The Venerable Tep Vong and the
Venerable Oum Sum both point to the parlous state of religious education in Cambodia today. A first task after the ouster of the Khmer Rouge
was to collect what remaining Buddhist texts could be found; the two
monks told me that some were discovered in provincial *wat*s and other
copies were obtained from Thailand, where scriptures in Khmer have
long existed. The Buddhist Institute has been reestablished at Wat Unnalom; in 1990 an effort was begun to reopen a press at this *wat*.[48] Among
the books that have already been published for wide public dissemination
is a work by the Venerable Huot Tath, a leader of the modernist
approach since the late 1920s (Sophath Pak and Colm 1990). It appears
that the modernist approach to Buddhism first championed by the
Thommakay faction of the Mohanikay order may be the most favored in
the PRK. Religious texts still are rare in the bookstores and stalls of Cambodia, and religious texts are not yet used in the schools. According to
the Venerable Tep Vong, even though schoolchildren have, since 1988,
been taught in the schools to "respect the religion," the exposure that students receive to religion is still far from that which most received before
1975. Even schools for novices and monks are few, and in 1990 a curriculum existed only for the primary level of monastic education.[49]

The restoration of Buddhism in Cambodia took a new direction in late
1991 after representatives of the PRK (now known as the State of Cambodia), the Khmer Rouge, the KPNLF, and FUNCINDEL agreed to
accept a UN-supervised settlement of the Cambodian conflict. The most
important immediate consequence of the agreement was the return on 14
November 1991 of Prince Sihanouk to Phnom Penh where he became, as
the chair of the transitional Supreme National Council on which all four
factions are represented, the head of state. Monks played critical ritual
roles in many of the festivities staged for the prince, and he himself
resumed his royal role as supreme patron of the *sangha*. This role, which
has been welcomed by Hun Sen and Chea Sim, must have distressed
those in the KPNLF who would make Buddhism serve republican objectives (see, in this regard, Son Soubert et al. 1986).[50]

The 1991 peace accords made possible the return of the Cambodian
refugees living in camps in Thailand. Among these refugees were hundreds of monks and novices who had been ordained outside of Cambodia. It is possible that the monks ordained in Thailand will raise serious

questions about the legitimacy of the ordination tradition of those monks who were reordained in the PRK in 1979. It is possible to interpret the rules of the *sangha* as requiring that monks who have left the monkhood, even against their will, be in the monkhood for an additional ten years following reordination before they can ordain other monks. If this interpretation is adopted, then the ordination of almost all monks in Cambodia would be in doubt. A question could also be raised whether a rupture in service makes reordained monks less senior than those few Khmer monks who were outside Cambodia in 1975. Whatever form debates about Buddhism in postsettlement Cambodia may take, it seems certain that Buddhism will once again become central to the nation-building project of most Khmer leaders.

Conclusion

The revolutionary parties that have led the governments of Cambodia since 1975 have sought to exercise state power in light of theories drawn from Marxist, Leninist, and Maoist thought. The resurgence of Buddhism in Cambodia, as the turn to religion by many in China (see Gladney's chapter in this volume), demonstrates that Communist theories of state fail to account for the compelling attraction to religious visions of community repudiated by the Communist holders of state power.

A full understanding of this failure for Cambodia would require the tracing of a genealogy, in the Foucaultian sense (Foucault 1977), of Khmer Communist thought. Such a genealogy—which is only beginning to be written—must attend to the relationship of Khmer Communist thought to the modernizing project of the West as refracted through French liberalism, Vietnamese interpretations of Leninism, and Maoist interpretations of Marxism, Leninism, and Stalinism.[51] It must also attend to the connections and disjunctures with both cosmological and reformist Buddhism.

As Ben Anderson (1983a:40) has shown, the genesis of nationalism entails a rupture with an unself-conscious acceptance of the suzerainty of those who rule "by some form of cosmological (divine) dispensation" and of "a conception of temporality in which cosmology and history [are] indistinguishable." This rupture does not, however, presuppose, as Marxist thought has assumed, a rejection of religion as the source for visions of a national community. Rather, what it does entail is a break with unreflected acceptance of the intrinsic relationship between the world as it is experienced and the cosmology as it is imagined. What this rupture opens up is not a new imagining of social order untrammeled by the past, but a dialogue with the past (in this connection, see Anagnost's chapter in this volume).

When the Khmer Rouge took power in 1975 they were confronted everywhere by the physical presence of the past in the *wat*s and shrines found in every village as well as in Phnom Penh and other towns. They did not ignore these icons of a Buddhist world, but set out literally to remove them from the Cambodian landscape or to convert them to non-religious purposes. But in the very act of doing so, they made the world they pointed to more significant for many people. In becoming self-conscious about the rupture with the old *wat*-centered world they had known, they found the vision of the Khmer Rouge one not of order but of chaos.

At least some in the Khmer Rouge were conscious that they must engage the Buddhist past in more active terms if they were to succeed in the revolution. This is evident in the view offered by the cadre quoted above that Angkar was a moral substitute for the *sangha*. For all their discipline, the record of the Angkar belies this claim. The Khmer Rouge were—and are—powerful, but their power derives not from moral superiority but from disciplined immorality, the immorality of anger and hatred—cardinal vices in the Buddhist perspective.

The remembrance of the Buddhist past made Cambodia in 1979 a haunted landscape, one filled with the ghosts of the hundreds of thousands who were killed or died during the Pol Pot period. The PRK government had to attend not only to the needs of the living, but also to those of the dead. It is noteworthy that the most significant monuments built by the PRK were those honoring the dead at the sites of mass execution. It is even more noteworthy that the forms of these monuments were unequivocally Buddhist. The restored *wat*s of Cambodia have also been used to effect a relinking between the living and the dead through communal sponsorship of rituals to make merit for the dead.[52]

The ghosts of Cambodia, like those of the Nazi extermination camps, haunt not only their relatives and fellow countrymen; they also haunt the world. In May 1989 on a trip to Angkor, I encountered a Japanese who had been ordained in the Theravādin tradition. I discovered that although he spoke no English, we still could communicate in Thai—a language he learned because he had become a monk in Thailand. I asked him why he was in Cambodia, a not unreasonable question even if he had not been a monk since so few between 1970 and 1990 were fortunate enough to visit the famous monuments. He replied he had felt compelled to make a pilgrimage to Cambodia because of the massive deaths that had occurred there. He had come as a Japanese, dressed in Thai Buddhist robes, to make merit for the dead of the Khmer revolution. His presence was a powerful icon of the transnational support for a vision of a Cambodian nation that has reaffirmed its link with its Buddhist past. Given this support, how could even the most committed Cambodian Marxist continue to deny the Buddhist basis of Khmer identity?

NOTES

I am indebted to David Chandler, May Ebihara, and Ben Kiernan for comments on earlier drafts of this paper. None of them is responsible, however, for whatever faults remain. I am also indebted to Mr. Ou Long, a leader of the Khmer community in the Seattle area, and Mr. John Marston, a scholar specializing in Khmer language and culture, for arranging my interviews with the Venerable Tep Vong and the Venerable Oum Sum, and to Mr. Tarun Khemardhipat, a Khmer-American from the Washington, D.C., area and an employee of Voice of America, for serving as interpreter at my interviews. My trips to Cambodia in 1988 and 1989 were made under the auspices of the Social Science Research Council which, at the time, had undertaken to promote scholarly cooperation with institutions in Cambodia.

1. The country today known once again as Cambodia has been officially called Kampuchea and the Khmer Republic by previous regimes. "Cambodia" is an Anglicized rendition of the French "Cambodge" which, in turn, derives from an indigenous word best transliterated as "Kampuchea." Cambodia became the official English name of the country during the colonial period, was used during the period from 1954 to 1970, and has been used again since 1989. The country was known as the Kingdom of Kampuchea in 1945, Democratic Kampuchea from 1975 to 1979, and the People's Republic of Kampuchea from 1979 to 1989.

2. The volte face of a Communist-led government toward Buddhism in Cambodia must be seen as part of a wider process in which people in Burma, Laos, and Thailand have turned to Buddhism in rethinking assumptions about political authority (see, in this connection, Keyes 1989 and 1992). The socialist revolution initiated in Burma after General Ne Win took power in 1962 in some ways foreshadowed the Communist revolutions in Cambodia and Laos. There do not, however, appear to have been any direct links between Buddhist politics in Burma and in Cambodia or Laos. There are links, however, between Cambodia and Laos since both countries, together with Vietnam, have since 1979 been "fraternal" countries in an Indochinese alliance. The initial policies toward religion of the post-1979 government in Cambodia were quite similar to those shown by the Communist-led government of Laos. From 1975 until the mid-1980s the Lao government sought to purge Buddhism of "superstitious" practices and to bring Buddhist monks under the strict control of the state. The Lao government's more recent public support of Buddhism as central to Lao national identity is also similar to the stance currently taken by the government in Cambodia.

3. The heritage of Angkor is based, in part, on the world recognition accorded Angkorean civilization following the work of French archaeologists, historians, and writers and, in part, on the difficulty that Khmer have had in finding in the history of the fifteenth to nineteenth centuries events that could be worked into compelling narratives of national identity (see Keyes 1990a).

4. Unless otherwise indicated, I give Pāli rather than vernacular or Sanskritic forms of Buddhist terms.

5. For a general overview of Theravāda Buddhism, see Reynolds and Clifford (1987).

6. The most extensive discussion in a Western language of the traditional Khmer cosmology is to be found in Leclère (1899:35–172). The monumental

study of the agrarian rituals of the Khmer by Porée-Maspero (1962–1969) also contains much information inter alia on the cosmology. Forest (1980:35–57) provides a summary; also see Chandler (1982) and Ebihara (1966). Although Khmer treatises, usually known under the name of *Trey phum,* the "Three Worlds," provided—as did their counterparts in the Thai and Lao traditions (see Reynolds and Reynolds 1982)—systematic discussions of the cosmology, most Khmer gained an understanding of the cosmology through participation in an annual cycle of rituals that constituted, as Tambiah (1970:35) has observed for the Lao of northeastern Thailand, a "cosmology in action." For an overview of traditional Khmer Buddhism, see Ebihara (1987). Aymonier (1883 and 1900–1904) and Leclère (1899 and 1917) provide detailed descriptions of traditional practices as they observed them in the late nineteenth century, while Ebihara (1966, 1968) and Kalab (1976) document the persistence of such practices in the 1960s and early 1970s. Bitard (1966), Porée-Maspero (1962–1969), and especially Bizot (1976, 1980, 1981) have studied the distinctive features of traditional Khmer Buddhism.

7. The instability of the Khmer monarchy and concomitant disorder for much of the period between the fifteenth and nineteenth centuries provided a context in which certain local monks could promote some distinctive practices, ones typically involving the magical manipulation of Buddhist sacra for this-worldly ends.

8. This was evident in the fact that the Siamese had used Khmer orthography for the writing of Pāli religious texts from the fifteenth century on. Vernacular religious texts were also adapted from Khmer into Thai or vice versa. Many other customs were common to both peoples. Even the languages, although belonging to different language families (Tai in the case of Siamese and Austroasiatic in the case of Khmer), shared much of the same vocabulary for government, religion, and the arts. Although this vocabulary was derived ultimately from Sanskrit, it had entered into Siamese from the Khmer. In calling attention to the deep connections between Khmer and Siamese cultures, I do not wish to imply that Siamese domination was acceptable to the Khmer while Vietnamese domination was not.

9. See, especially, Reynolds (1973) and Kirsch (1973). In my paper on Buddhist politics (Keyes 1989:123–126) I also analyze the consequence of these reforms and provide references to other relevant literature.

10. *Sangha-rāja* in Pāli; *sanghareach (sangharāc)* in Khmer.

11. The patriarch and the head of the Thommayut order, following a traditional model, divided responsibilities for the *wats* of the "right" and of the "left." That is, they each assumed supervision of half the *sangha* in the country (Leclère 1898:391).

12. Quoted in Chandler (1983a:157); Chandler does not give a source for the edict. Also see Yang Sam (1990:137) and Kiernan (1985:3–4).

13. His face appears on the 100-riel notes of the PRK.

14. Neither Sihanouk nor his associates ever appear to have worked out a coherent ideology of Buddhist socialism comparable to that attempted in Burma or in Laos after 1975.

15. Chandler (1991:87–88) observes that Sihanouk's rejection of foreign mod-

els and his emphasis on the indigenous basis of his nationalist ideology "foreshadowed policies espoused by the Khmer Rouge."

16. Although the Khmer People's Revolutionary party (KPRP), under Heng Samrin, Chea Sim, and Hun Sen, which has ruled the country since 1979, is also a Communist party, the term "Khmer Rouge" has been used to refer only to the Pol Pot party. In Cambodia under the KPRP, the Khmer Rouge were referred to as Pol Potists.

17. It is cruel irony that the Lon Nol and Pol Pot sides both agreed that all Vietnamese should be eliminated from Cambodian society.

18. Hildebrand and Porter (1976:20) estimated the population of Phnom Penh in 1975 to be nearly 3 million, but Ben Kiernan (personal communication) thinks this is wrong. Basing his own estimate on a rough census made by a New Zealander who was working for an international agency in the city at the time, Kiernan places the total at about 1.8 million. All statistics relating to the population movements and especially deaths occurring in Cambodia from 1970 through 1978 are only rough estimates. While such statistics and their interpretation have been subject to considerable debate, I do believe that those I have cited give a rough idea of what actually occurred.

19. It is estimated that at least fifteen thousand people died during the last five months alone before the collapse of Phnom Penh (Hildebrand and Porter 1976:29).

20. This, and the following section, expand on a previous paper on Buddhism and revolution in Cambodia (Keyes 1990b).

21. These statistics are from Zago (1976:110; 117n), who gives his source as the Khmer Ministry of Cults. The same statistics are given by Yang Sam (1987:17, 23), who gives as his source a work in Khmer by the Venerable Huot Tath, the head of the Mohanikay order. The estimates by Whitaker et al. (1973:139–140) of a hundred thousand monks in twenty-eight hundred temple-monasteries are obviously inaccurate.

22. The mass executions at Choeung Ek had taken place mainly on the grounds associated with the *wat* that had formerly been used for cremations and burials. I observed on first visiting the place in 1988 that there were many Chinese grave sites and that these had been desecrated. When I visited the site again in 1989, I noted that with the organization of the place into a shrine these graves are no longer so obvious.

23. This account is taken from Richardson (1981:104). The dedication of a new image culminates in a ritual act of "opening the eyes" of the image.

24. David Chandler in his research for a biography of Pol Pot says he was told by a brother that Pol Pot actually was in the *sangha* for a total of only three months (Chandler, personal communication; Chandler 1992:9). Kiernan (1985:27) was told in an earlier interview with the same brother that Pol Pot entered the novitiate at age six and spent a year as a novice at Wat Botumvodey in Phnom Penh, "the religious centre of the small, royalist Thommayut order."

25. The reasons why Pol Pot turned so violently against Buddhism are not yet clear. David Chandler (personal communication) says he suspects "his hostility came from his wife, from fellow intellectuals, and from people like Nuon Chea" (long a close associate of Pol Pot in the Party).

26. Radio Belgrade, Tanjug Domestic Service in Serbo-Croatian, 21 April 1978, in Foreign Broadcast Information Service (FBIS), *Daily Report—IV,* 24 April 1978, cited in van der Kroef (1979:737); also see Jackson (1989b:33–34n).

27. There may have been a direct link between the Chinese effort during the Cultural Revolution to destroy Buddhism in Tibet and among the Dai people of southern Yunnan and the similar effort by the Khmer Rouge. Descriptions of the desecration of temples and the forcing of monks and novices to leave the *sangha* are strikingly similar for Yunnan and Cambodia (see Hsieh 1989:224–235). The Khmer Rouge clearly drew inspiration for some of their policies from the Cultural Revolution (Quinn 1989:219–231).

28. The estimate of twenty-five thousand is from Kiernan, who also estimates that the Khmer Rouge were later able to increase their following to forty thousand (1982:377).

29. Most Khmer living in camps on the border between Thailand and Cambodia were never accorded official refugee status. In 1986, for example, there were nearly 250,000 living in border camps created for those who had not been accorded legal refugee status; only some 27,000, who lived in other camps, had been accorded this status and were, thus, eligible for resettlement (see Lawyers Committee for Human Rights 1987). See Amara and Noppawan (1988) for statistics on resettlement. In 1992 and 1993, the refugees in camps in Thailand were all repatriated to Cambodia.

30. For convenience, I will refer to the post-1979 government of Cambodia as the People's Republic of Kampuchea (PRK) for the entire period.

31. The number of deaths under the Khmer Rouge has been the subject of much debate (see, for example, Vickery 1988; Ea 1990; Kiernan 1990). Although refugees often cite a figure of 3 million, those who have closely examined the available demographic data place the figure at a still horrifying 1–1.7 million. Chandler (1991:236), following Vickery (1988), who, in turn, based his estimates on data from the U.S. Central Intelligence Agency, estimates that 1 million out of a total of 7 million in 1975 died. A similar estimate is accepted by Ea (1990:4). I am persuaded, however, by the analysis made by Kiernan (1990), which leads to an estimate of a total of 1.7 million dead out of a 1975 population of 7.9 million.

32. Indonesia, Malaysia, the Philippines, Singapore, and Thailand.

33. Its full name in French is Front Uni National pour un Cambodge Indépendent, Neutre, Pacifique et Cooperatif; in English, the National United Front for a Cooperative, Independent, Neutral, and Peaceful Cambodia.

34. The videotape of Prince Sihanouk's return produced for television in Cambodia shows Hun Sen and, less often, Chea Sim demonstrating their respect for the prince while at the same time acting as the stage managers for the whole event. I am indebted to Dr. Sam-ang Sam for making this tape available to me.

35. I conducted interviews with these two monks in Seattle, Washington, on 17 June 1990 while they were on a visit to the Khmer communities in Seattle and Tacoma. The monks had come to the United States primarily to attend a conference on "Cambodia in the 1990s: The Role of Buddhism in Khmer Society," held 2–3 June in Berkeley, California. They had taken the opportunity while in the United States of visiting Khmer communities on the West Coast.

At the time the Venerable Tep Vong was the *sangha nayaka* (president of the *sangha;* Khmer *sangha nayok*) in the PRK. He explained that the rank of patri- arch *(sanghareach)* had been abolished by Pol Pot. In early 1992 Prince Siha- nouk, after returning to Cambodia, conferred on Tep Vong the title of Prah Sumedhatipoti, which was said to have been equivalent to patriarch (Gray 1992). The Venerable Tep Vong was born in 1932 and was abbot of Wat Po in Siemreap province before 1975 (also see Sam 1987:68, 80). During the Pol Pot period he had been forced "by ten armed men" to disrobe. He was ordered to marry, and when he resisted he was imprisoned. Since being re-ordained in 1979, he has been the main spokesman for Buddhism under the PRK government.

As of 1990 the Venerable Oum Sum was head *(me khum)* of the *sangha* in Phnom Penh. He was born in 1918 or 1919, was ordained in his home province of Kampong Cham as a novice in 1934 and as a monk in 1938. In 1943 he moved to Wat Saravane in Phnom Penh, where he remained until 1975. He was a scholar monk who taught Pāli at the Buddhist Institute and later the Buddhist University and worked on the Khmer version of the Tripitaka. In 1975 he was forced along with the other inhabitants of Phnom Penh to leave the city. He was also forced to disrobe, and said that if he had resisted he would have been "sent to a higher level"—a euphemism for being sent to be executed. He said, in answer to my question, that he never considered in his heart to have left the monkhood. He was not forced to marry.

36. According to Yang Sam (1987:80), who gives as his source Phnom Penh radio broadcasts in September 1979 as translated by FBIS, the head of the delega- tion was an ethnic Vietnamese Theravādin monk, Thich Bou Chon, who was adviser to the Central Commission of Vietnamese Theravāda Buddhism. The other monks in the delegation, the Venerables Thita Silo, Koralo, and Kosala Chetta, appear to have Khmer names. Some could, however, have been Khmer Krom, that is, Khmer from Vietnam. Some may have been Khmer monks who fled to Vietnam. (The Venerables Tep Vong and Oum Sum were uncertain as to how many monks had escaped to Vietnam—or to Thailand—during the Pol Pot period, but there were probably not many.)

There must have been at least five monks in the delegation since five are required by the *vinaya* to hold an ordination. I had first learned of the delegation of monks from Vietnam to Cambodia when I saw a slide photograph of Theravā- din monks disembarking from a plane coming from Vietnam in early 1979, and I recall that there were more than five monks in the picture. The photograph had been taken by an American Friends Service Committee representative who accompanied a shipment of goods for humanitarian aid to Phnom Penh.

Both the Venerable Tep Vong and the Venerable Oum Sum were reluctant to talk about the membership of this delegation because of their sensitivity to being branded "Vietnamese monks in Khmer robes" (which, I learned from a Khmer- American, some Cambodians in Los Angeles accused the two monks of being).

37. Yang Sam (1987:80) gives the names of the five most senior monks. The Venerable Tep Vong said that only five of the seven remain as monks today, but I did not ascertain which monks they were. Since the eldest monk ordained in 1979 was eighty-two, it is not unlikely that at least this monk has since died.

38. The Venerable Tep Vong said that although in Khmer custom there should

be seven monks to constitute a chapter to ordain new monks, this was not possible in small provinces given the few former monks who were qualified. Thus, in these provinces, the more ancient pattern of having a chapter of five monks was followed.

39. The Venerable Tep Vong said that there were thirty monks at this meeting. Ros Chhnum, general secretary of the Council of the United Front for the Construction and Defense of the Kampuchean Fatherland, a front organization composed of representatives of nonparty sectors of Khmer society, reported in 1989 that "two Buddhist conferences and one enlarged meeting on Buddhist affairs have been held" (in *Daily Report—East Asia,* FBIS-EAS-89-020, 1 February 1989:43). The first of these was probably the one held in Siemreap. Also see Sam (1987:81).

40. Ben Kiernan (private communication) reports that despite the official restriction there were always monks under fifty in the countryside.

41. In 1985, correspondent Jim Laurie was told that there were about 8,000 monks in the country (Laurie 1985). In 1989 Ros Chhnum reported to the Council of the United Front for the Construction and Defense of the Kampuchean Fatherland that there were 6,500 monks (from a radio broadcast translated in FBIS-EAS-89-020, 1 February 1989:44). The Venerable Tep Vong (Hiebert 1989:37), however, put the total at 8,000 in 1989.

42. Reported on Radio Phnom Penh, 2 July 1984; translated in FBIS-Daily Report on Asia, FBIS YB, 9 July, and summarized in *Indochina Chronology* 3 (3): 8 (July–September 1984). What beliefs were "unhealthy" was not specified.

43. This figure was given by Tep Vong in an interview in mid-1989 (Hiebert 1989:37). The same figure was given to me in an interview in 1989 by Dr. My Samedi, who was at the time, along with being head of the Cambodian Medical School, the deputy head of the National Front.

44. Sophath Pak and Colm (1990) interviewed a young twenty-two-year-old monk at Wat Unnalom who had been ordained early in 1990 but then noted that "some observers question how easy it really is for young men to get approval to join the monkhood—rather than the army—when the country is at war and a conscription was recently instituted."

45. In 1989 the Venerable Tep Vong told Murray Hiebert that there were eight thousand monks in the country (Hiebert 1989:37). In 1990 he told Sophath Pak and Sara Colm (1990) that there were ten thousand, a figure about the same as the one that can be calculated from the information he gave me. It would appear, thus, that there had been an increase of nearly a thousand monks in about a year's time. By 1991 the total membership of the *sangha* had grown to about twenty thousand (Pongpet Mekloy 1991; Gray 1992).

46. Chandler (1991:162) says that Hun Sen had been a monk in his youth.

47. Translated in FBIS-Daily Report/East Asia, FBIS-EAS-89-75 and excerpted in *Indochina Chronology,* 8 (2): 11 (April–June 1989). This act was repeated again in the following years. In 1991, for example, Heng Samrin and Chea Sim led the rite, and Heng Samrin "made an address on Buddhism in Cambodia and called for peace" (*The Nation* [Bangkok], 29 April 1991).

48. The intention is to purchase computers and printers for desktop publishing. The two monks from Phnom Penh obtained promises of significant support

for this endeavor from Cambodian communities living on the West Coast of the United States. The potential for desktop publishing of works in Khmer is an ironical consequence of the resettlement of Khmer refugees in the United States, France, and elsewhere. There now exists sophisticated software for production of works in Khmer because of the demands for Khmer works by these refugee communities.

49. This again from information provided by the Venerable Tep Vong.

50. In May 1992 Son Sann, the head of the KPNLF, was reported as launching a new "Buddhist Liberal Democratic Party." The goals of the party, Son Sann said, are to combat three enemies: the Vietnamese, the Khmer Rouge, and corruption. The appeal to Buddhism for a militant and racist nationalism prompted a representative of the United Nations in Cambodia to warn against "the use of the right (of free expression) to incite divisiveness or discrimination" (*Indochina Digest,* 22 May 1992).

51. See, especially, the work of Chandler (1979, 1983b, 1983c, 1991), Frieson (1988), Kiernan (1980, 1982, 1985), Kiernan and Chanthou Boua (1982), Thion (1983a, 1983b), and Vickery (1984, 1986). Also see the essays in the volumes edited by Chandler and Kiernan (1983) and Jackson (1989a) and the works of Chanda (1986), Heder (1979), and Willmott (1981). Some writings of the leaders of the Khmer Rouge, including work written when they were in France, have been translated (see Carney 1977; Khieu Samphan 1979). Chandler has pursued this "genealogical" effort in the basic sense of the word in his forthcoming biography of Pol Pot (Chandler 1992).

52. Hun Sen carried this commemoration of the dead of the Pol Pot period to the United States, which he visited for the first time in March 1992. On this occasion he placed a plaque at the Tomb of the Unknown Soldier "in honor of the American MIAs 'from the millions of Cambodian families who also lost a relative in some Cambodian place they know not where' " (*Indochina Digest,* 27 March 1992).

Reimagined Community

A Social History of Muslim Education in Pasuruan, East Java

ROBERT W. HEFNER

Prologue: "High Ethnicity" and Asian Religion

A casual comparison of the premodern traditions of East and Southeast Asia reveals a startling contrast. Countries with the strongest and most enduring states—Japan and China, most strikingly—have engendered the most versatile and encompassing forms of ethnicity. By comparison with the polyglot ethnicity of premodern Southeast Asia, Han and Japanese ethnicities took shape early in their countries' histories and proved to be effective tools for the standardization of political culture and for the conquest and assimilation of neighboring minorities.

The success of this ethnocultural politics is most clearly illustrated in premodern China. There, over the course of many centuries, the dynastic state integrated a large and diverse population into a common ethnic mold. The fact that people could be Han and speak mutually unintelligible "dialects," relish different cuisines, esteem different aesthetic traditions, and even worship different deities in no way diminishes this social achievement. The example does indicate, however, that with Han ethnicity we are dealing with a cultural entity significantly more expansive than the minimal recognition of common descent that Keyes (1976) has rightly stressed as the universal core of ethnicity. In East Asia ethnicity became not just a matter of common descent but a marker of civilized identity within a state-based society. It became, in other words, "high ethnicity"—a constellation of practices and ideas that uses literacy, ritual, and the machinery of state to standardize popular identity along ethnic lines across vast social terrains.

Sociologically, in fact, Han ethnicity varied enormously throughout the land expanse of China, creating cultural differences as significant by some measures as those distinguishing ethnic groups in the countries of Southeast Asia. In China, however, agrarian variants of Han culture were sufficiently connected to high-cultural traditions to prevent the fragmentation of populations into disparate ethnic groups. With only minor qualifications, the Han example also applies to Japan. There, too, ethnicity was codified and standardized through its ties to a high culture sustained by literacy and the state.

In East Asia, then, ethnic "primordialism" (Geertz 1973b) bore the distinctly nonprimordial imprint of high culture and dynastic history. Ethnicity was not an unreflexive "given" rooted in the "nonrational foundations of personality" (Geertz 1973b:277). It was a complex of discourse and action for defining social identity, shaped by the interaction of courts, intellectuals, and high-cultural media with popular society.

The religious consequences of East Asian ethnicity were equally distinctive. Not only did these premodern states engender Asia's strongest and most expansive ethnic communities, they also proved the most successful at resisting the challenge of world religions. It is only a slight exaggeration to say that Buddhism, Islam, and Christianity were all effectively domesticated or marginalized within these premodern societies. By contrast, the empires of the Middle East and Europe created an unusually fertile environment for the development and spread of world religions. Insular Southeast Asia has proven a similarly fertile ground.

The reasons the world religions made less headway in premodern East Asia are too complex to detail here, but clearly one obstacle to their diffusion was the influence of high ethnicity on popular identity. To borrow a phrase from Benedict Anderson (1983a), high ethnicity was a form of "imagined community," a way of talking about and organizing social and political life beyond the boundaries of a face-to-face community. In East Asia the cultural influence of high ethnicity was so strong that it made conversion to a foreign religion tantamount to the repudiation of one's ethnicity and, thus, of the sociopolitical privileges that ethnicity allowed. Until the abolishment of East Asia's dynastic states in the modern era, then, the world religions thrived in East Asia only to the extent that they resigned themselves to working within, not against, the terms of high-ethnic culture.

The situation in insular Southeast Asia was, at first, not unlike that of East Asia. In pre-Islamic times indigenous states were also headed by rulers claiming god-king status. Similarly, many of the premodern states in this region were built around an ethnic core in which, as in East Asia, filial devotion and kinship were linked to a cult of imperial ancestors. Thus, here too local identities were transformed into high ethnicity through their ties to the ritual, arts, and politics of state-based society.

In the long run, however, the states of insular Southeast Asia lacked the staying power of those in East Asia, and the long-term influence of high ethnicity proved much weaker. The reasons for this are also complex, but in general the lack of an effective bureaucracy like that in China caused great political instability. In insular Southeast Asia the periodic collapse of the state was not cushioned by the survival of culture-bearing mandarins. Instead, state collapse often resulted in the destruction of the sociopolitical bonds linking popular society to high culture, fragmenting political community and undermining the moral and political influence of high ethnicity. In the absence of such a stable ethnopolitical complex, Islam—a religion with different ideas on the proper mix of religion, ethnicity, and politics—was able to penetrate the region.

Pre-Islamic Java, of all societies in insular Southeast Asia, had institutionalized the most enduring high-ethnic culture. Building on Indian-derived prototypes, Java developed the liturgy, language, literature, and legal instruments of high civilization. Had it shown greater success at establishing a durable state, Java's religious evolution probably would have more closely resembled that of the great East Asian civilizations. Religions like Islam that refused to resign themselves to working within a high-ethnic religious complex would have been effectively marginalized through their identification as "foreign" and antithetical to civilized identity.

In the end, however, the imperial states of pre-Islamic Java did not succeed in marginalizing Islam in this way. Political instability provided an opportunity for the bearers of an alternative high culture eventually to push aside Java's pre-Islamic rulers. Having seized state power in the early sixteenth century, Java's first Muslim states destroyed much of the pre-Islamic high culture and set the island on a course of religious evolution markedly distinct from that of East Asia. Curiously, however, enough of Java's pre-Islamic high culture survived—or was deliberately revived—to challenge Islamic hegemony. This history is critical to understanding the development of Javanese religion to the present day. In the first decades of the sixteenth century, Muslim courts destroyed the hundreds of Hindu-Buddhist ecclesiastical communities that had existed on the island just a century earlier (Hefner 1985:6). After this point, with their standardbearers annihilated, ecclesiastical Hinduism and Buddhism played no significant role in the reformulation of high-Javanese civilization. Resistance to orthodox Islam emerged nonetheless. It was grounded not on the formal doctrines of Hindu-Buddhism, but on a more diffuse sense of "Javaneseness." This sense of Javaneseness—high ethnicity par excellence—was primarily expressed in ritual, aesthetics, language, and etiquette. The political tension that lay behind this elaboration of high-ethnic culture was given sociological expression in the opposition between the bearers of Java's two most important religious traditions. On the one hand, there were those Javanese, known as *santri,* who insisted on strict conformity to Islamic ritual and legal prescriptions *(shariah).* On the other, there were those, usually known as *kejawen* or "Javanists," who believed that even while embracing Islam one should qualify or neglect many of its formal strictures in favor of high-Javanese traditions. For Javanists, Islam should wear a Javanese face.

This sociocultural contrast was also expressed in political contests.

Less than a century after the founding of Java's first Muslim states, the Javanist-Muslim court of Mataram (in inland Central Java) slaughtered thousands of Muslim religious teachers *(ulama)* and took steps to restrict the application of Islamic law to Javanese social life (Ricklefs 1981:43). Publicly the court insisted that Javanese were Muslims, and it did not hesitate to use Islam as a rallying cry against European rivals. But the court promoted a style of religiosity in which high-ethnic customs influenced or even overrode formal Muslim doctrine. Islam was thereby embedded within a high-ethnic complex. The entire arrangement was poignantly expressed in the popular Javanese distinction between "Javanese" Islam (Islam Jawa) and "Arab" Islam. The identification of orthodox Islam with Arab ethnicity relativized Islam's universalist claims, allowing Javanist Muslims to claim Islamic identity even while rejecting normative orthodoxy.

As these examples indicate, religion, politics, and ethnicity have had a divergent impact on religious developments in East and Southeast Asia. In East Asia high ethnicity provided a ritual-political-moral framework of such enduring influence that it effectively neutralized the demand by Islam or Christianity for exclusive adherence to a single faith. In insular Southeast Asia a similar high-ethnic complex once existed, but the weakness of indigenous states compromised its social force. In both regions state policies and media shaped the form, meaning, and influence of ethnicity. In turn, politics and high ethnicity affected the receptivity of local populations to new notions of community promulgated by the bearers of world religions.

As the essays in the present volume indicate, these same influences are reshaping religious communities in East and Southeast Asia today. In the modern era, however, East Asian trends still differ in important ways from those in insular Southeast Asia. Despite the collapse of imperial dynasties outside of Japan, East Asian religions show the lingering influence of high-ethnic legacies. What James Foard (n.d.) calls "endemic religion" builds not so much on unreflective traditionalism, as some modernization theorists might speculate, but on a deep and regularly renewed sense of high ethnicity. The fact that elements of this tradition are distributed over vast territories with enormous populations should make one suspicious of the idea that endemic religion is merely the spontaneous product of such local realities as family, kinship, and village. Quite the contrary, religion and ethnicity alike show the powerful influence of statewide media, ritual, and customs.

Widespread Korean conversion to Christianity provides partial exception to this East Asian pattern, although some would argue that Korean Christianity has been effectively domesticated (Clark 1986:36–37; Kim in this volume). Elsewhere in East Asia, whether with Korean shamanism, state-sponsored Shinto, Japan's new religions, or Taiwanese ghost cults, religious developments demonstrate that high ethnicity remains a fertile source of ideas for new forms of religious community.

This is much less the case in insular Southeast Asia, as on the island of Java. On the whole, the influence of high ethnicity on popular religion has waned. Conversely, the appeal of universalist religions, which deny the importance of ethnicity as the basis of religious community, has grown. In what follows I seek to analyze this crisis of endemic religion through *santri* and Javanist efforts to develop formal institutions for religious education. The sphere of education reveals with dramatic clarity the reasons for the declining influence of high-ethnic ideals.

My discussion examines this crisis from the perspective of one area of Java, the regency of Pasuruan in the province of East Java. The analysis has two larger goals: to evaluate the impact of modern religious instruction on popular religion and to examine the way in which political struggles stimulated the drive for religious education. Here, as in most of Java, *santri* took the lead in systematizing their faith and in developing institutions to promote its dissemination. In so doing they were better prepared than Javanists to benefit from the processes of nation-state development that transformed all of Indonesia in the twentieth century.

The example points to a general truth. Contrary to the pattern Benedict Anderson (1983a:19) has described for Western Europe, in Java and much of the rest of Asia the growth of the nation-state did not erode religiously imagined communities. Instead, the rise of the nation-state, along with national media and markets, has pushed religion into the center of the contest to define what the nation should become. These developments have provoked far-reaching changes in popular religion.

Politics and Religious Education in Pasuruan

In the 1970s a quiet change occurred in primary schools throughout Java. Graduates of Indonesia's newly expanded Islamic teacher-training colleges arrived to begin providing mandatory classroom instruction in orthodox Islam. Among the 10 to 12 percent of the Javanese population that is non-Islamic, a similar process unfolded, as Christian, Hindu, or Buddhist teachers arrived to work in village schools. Despite the fact that religion classes had, in principle, been mandatory since the 1950s (Boland 1982:196; Noer 1978:31), in many communities this was the first time that formal instruction had actually been provided. Elsewhere—especially in staunchly Javanist communities resistant to orthodox Islam—the teachers replaced older instructors who had no background in Muslim orthodoxy and were often less interested in scriptural Islam than in customary Javanese ways *(adat Jawa; ngaluri Jawa).*

The new teachers had no such inclination toward heterodoxy. They prepared their lessons from textbooks created by Indonesia's Department of Religion, and these made few concessions to regional custom or belief. Textbooks written for all citizens, no matter which faith they adhered to, stressed five general principles: the singular essence of God, the basis of true religion in prophecy and scripture *(kitab)*, the difference between divinely inspired religion *(agama)* and humanly elaborated belief *(keper-cayaan)*, the importance of daily prayer, and the centrality of religion in national development. In short, all emphasized what might be called the fundamentals of Indonesian "civil religion" (Bellah 1970; Atkinson 1983). This is a body of interdenominational doctrine developed by the Department of Religion and promoted by religious modernists over the years since Indonesian independence. From the start Indonesian civil religion was designed to unite the country's diverse religious communities and domesticate its sometimes turbulent religious passions. Contrary to characterizations of civil religion in some parts of the world, however, this national creed bore the imprint not so much of "common elements of religious orientation" shared by the "great majority" (Bellah 1970:171) of people, but of the struggle between Muslim and nationalist Indonesians to define the role of religion in the modern nation-state. Education, as we shall see, has been central to this struggle.

The history and background to these modern developments are clearly evident in the regency of Pasuruan, on the northeastern coast of the province of East Java. From a religious perspective Pasuruan is one of the most diverse regencies in all Java. Its lowlands are dominated by Muslims associated with the party of traditionalist Muslim clerics, Nahdatul Ulama (Jones 1984; Wahid 1986). Its southern uplands, by contrast, are home to Javanist Muslims, resistant to Islamic orthodoxy and traditionally committed to ancestral and guardian spirit cults (Hefner 1987). In the period before the 1965 coup this latter population sided with the Indonesian Nationalist party or, to a lesser degree, the Communist party, against Nahdatul Ulama. In the highest reaches of these southern mountains, finally, lives a third population of Javanese Hindus (Hefner 1985; Jasper 1926; Rouffaer 1921). Though ethnically Javanese, this mountain people has resisted Islam since the fall of the last major Hindu-Buddhist court some five centuries ago (Robson 1981). In modern times they have nurtured strong ties with the Javanist Muslims living just below them in the southern highlands.

The dominance of traditionalist Islam in Pasuruan's lowlands was largely due to the earlier impact of colonialism on native society. At the end of the eighteenth century, Pasuruan was a "cauldron of warfare" (Elson 1984:1), as an alliance of eastern Javanese forces under the rebel leader Surapati rose up against the allied armies of Central Java's

Mataram kingdom and the Dutch (Kumar 1976). After a bloody campaign the rebels were defeated in 1706–1707; in 1743, the Dutch assumed control over the entire eastern territory of which Pasuruan was part. In the regency's southern mountains rebels continued to put up resistance to the Dutch and their native allies well into the 1760s (Jasper 1926).

With the indigenous population depleted by warfare, the colonial government was forced to encourage a migratory influx of ethnic Madurese —people from the island of Madura off the north coast of eastern Java— and Javanese, most of whom came from Muslim coastal regions *(pasisir)* to the west. Fleeing the exactions of their own native aristocrats and coming from areas where orthodox Islam had greater influence than in inland Central Java (De Vries 1931:31; Elson 1984:15), the immigrants created a "freewheeling and open" (Elson 1984:16) society, more Islamic in its faith and markedly resistant to the hierarchical ways of inland Central Java. Eventually the lowland frontier closed, as population grew and the Dutch implemented their program for the forced cultivation of export crops (Geertz 1963b:52; De Vries 1931). Colonial activities increased landlessness and enhanced rural inequality by creating a native elite, which the government needed to coordinate its exactions (Elson 1984:90–94; Alexander and Alexander 1979:31). The authority of this elite was solidly grounded in European might, however, and it appears to have enjoyed considerably less legitimacy than its counterpart in areas of Central Java where native rulers were still somewhat independent from the Dutch. Sartono Kartodirjo's (1972:89) observation that the co-option of the Javanese gentry *(priyayi)* by the colonial regime estranged them from the peasantry thus rings all the truer in Pasuruan. There was a crisis of traditional authority throughout this eastern territory that was conducive to the emergence of an alternative native leadership.

In lowland Pasuruan the primary beneficiaries of this political crisis were Muslim religious teachers, known as *kyai*. Independent of the gentry and untainted by association with the Dutch, the *kyai* were the most prominent extravillage leaders to whom the peasantry could look. *Kyai* influence was abetted, moreover, by the expansion of Muslim boarding schools *(pesantren)* across lowland Pasuruan in the last half of the nineteenth century.

The *pesantren* provided an institution for cultural socialization that cut across the ethnic divide separating Madurese from Javanese. The most prominent *kyai* were linked by ties of descent, marriage, and educational pedigree, creating an Islamic network that extended across vast areas of the Javanese countryside and into Madura. As throughout Java (Jones 1991; Woodward 1989:145), *kyai* authority was reinforced by marital and educational ties to prominent landowning families. The latter regarded *pesantren* education as a vital element in their sons' formation.

Through these and other arrangements, popular society in lowland Pasuruan slowly developed a flavor distinct from that of the Javanist countryside. The mosque replaced the guardian spirit shrine *(dhanyang)* as the ritual center of the lowland village. The pilgrimage to Mecca and donations of land and money to Muslim schools became the preferred form of conspicuous consumption, replacing the *slametan* religious festival prized among Javanists. To borrow a phrase from Mitsuo Nakamura (1983), the "ascent of the Muslim crescent over the Javanist banyan tree" was part of a larger crisis of identity and authority in popular society. Stimulated by the advance of European colonialism, the spread of boarding schools played a key role in the construction of a new, multiethnic, Muslim culture.

The impact of this detraditionalization was in some ways similar to the cultural deracination Benedict Anderson (1983a) has described among native intellectuals recruited to colonial service at the beginning of this century. That process, Anderson explains, uprooted youths from around the Indonesian archipelago, concentrated them in a few urban centers, and resocialized them in the language of Western liberalism. In doing so, colonial education broke down traditional ethnic barriers and unwittingly provided the leadership and idioms for a new form of imagined community, Indonesian nationalism.

Traditional society in colonial Pasuruan was also shattered by the forced "pilgrimage" of colonial migration. But the Muslim schools that responded to this crisis were native-run institutions, to which the language of Western liberalism was still foreign. Muslim leaders spoke of the need for moral revitalization through the creation of a new social order. But their vision was strikingly different from that of the "lonely bilingual intelligentsias" whom Anderson rightly regards as the first spokesmen for modern nationalism. Muslims emphasized not the ideas of political independence and a multiethnic Indonesia, but religious revitalization through education and repudiation of European culture.

This, then, was the context in which Pasuruan's lowlands became a stronghold of Muslim traditionalism. Events of the early twentieth century reinforced the Muslim drive and eventually provided it with a more sophisticated political organization. Indonesia's first mass-based political organization, Sarekat Islam (Islamic Union), swept through Pasuruan in the 1910s, attracting a following among a peasantry hard pressed by declining circumstances (Benda 1983:42; Elson 1984:196). In some parts of Java, Sarekat Islam's membership was divided between orthodox and Javanist Muslims; as a result, specifically "Muslim" issues were often relegated to the background in favor of economic ones. In lowland Pasuruan (as on nearby Madura; see Kuntowijoyo 1986), however, Sarekat Islam was strongly identified with traditionalist Islam. Demands for "a purified and more devout practice of Islam" (Elson 1984:199) were central to its campaign appeals.

Sarekat Islam declined during the 1920s, as a result of government repression and, at a national level, infighting between Muslims and left-wing nationalists, most of whom were, in religious terms, Javanists (Benda 1983:44; Ricklefs 1981:164–167). Sarekat Islam had served, however, to accelerate the process of Islamic resurgence and had also politicized Muslim education. Schools that a few years earlier had been providing an interethnic forum became more directly involved in the struggle against colonialism.

By the late 1920s, Dutch and *priyayi* repression had taken their toll on native political parties, including Sarekat Islam. In the Pasuruan regency the repression was so effective that even during the difficult years of the Great Depression there were few large demonstrations of anticolonial sentiment (Elson 1984:247). The quiet was belied, however, by the spectacular advance of a new Muslim organization: Nahdatul Ulama, the association of Muslim (Javanese) clerics. Founded in 1926 in Jombang, East Java, this party adopted what Harry Benda (1983:55) has called a "consciously non-political course," avoiding large demonstrations and devoting its attention to Islamic revitalization. However, Nahdatul Ulama was "nonpolitical" only in a conventional understanding of politics. From its own perspective, the party's actions showed clear political priorities and an astute awareness of how best to achieve them. While eschewing confrontation with the government, it quietly promoted Islamic regeneration. In its eyes, after all, Java's ills were a product not simply of infidel colonialism but of irreligious Javanism as well.

Not surprisingly, then, religious education lay at the heart of Nahdatul Ulama's political efforts. Building on the network of Muslim teachers established in the late nineteenth century, Nahdatul Ulama sent *santri* students into remote villages to establish party chapters, organize classes in Qur'anic study *(pengajian),* and confront and abolish Javanist ritual cults (Hefner 1987). The results of this simple program were quickly evident in Pasuruan. In just a few years the party extended its organization beyond the Muslim lowlands into the foothills of Pasuruan's southern highlands. Decades earlier this southern region had been a bastion of Javanism. Roadbuilding and commercial expansion at the end of the nineteenth century, however, had brought an influx of Muslim traders with ties to lowland *santri* (Hefner 1990). As a result, in lower-lying areas of the southern highlands the contest between Islam and Javanism intensified. The arrival of Nahdatul Ulama organizers was sometimes sufficient to shift the balance of power to Muslim villagers. Indeed, during the 1930s, many lower-lying hill villages repudiated traditions once shared with their Javanist and Hindu neighbors higher up the mountainside. Though incapable of challenging Dutch colonialism, Nahdatul Ulama was making headway toward its goal of abolishing Javanism and promoting Islamic education.

By the end of the Japanese occupation the last bastions of Javanism had disappeared from lowland Pasuruan, and Nahdatul Ulama thoroughly dominated the political scene. Only the middle and higher reaches of the southern highlands had escaped the Muslim advance. People in these latter regions, however, had not yet taken the first steps toward building political and educational institutions comparable to those of the Muslim community.

Religious Knowledge in Javanist Pasuruan

During the colonial period government policies forbade religious education in public schools except as an after-school extracurricular activity; even after school it was tacitly discouraged (Noer 1978:26). Barred from public schools, Pasuruan's Muslim community opened private schools to promote religious education. In addition to the long-established boarding schools, after 1920 Muslims opened day schools *(madrasah)* for Islamic instruction. These allowed a much larger portion of the lowland population to participate in religious education. Curriculum standardization in these schools was facilitated by the greater availability of printing presses and cloth paper in the last decades of the nineteenth century. The new printed books replaced the expensive palm-leaf books *(kropak)* that had been the primary medium of instruction in the early nineteenth century.

The diffusion of print technologies coincided with the spread of reformist ideas on the importance of popular religious education. In the early nineteenth century, fluency in Muslim scripture had been, to borrow a notion from Jack Goody (1968), a "restricted" literate skill, used to affirm Muslim holy men's monopolistic control of ritual prerogatives. By the end of the nineteenth century reformist ideas (influenced by Middle Eastern movements) had taken hold even among Java's traditionalist Muslims. This remarkable development was due above all to the brilliant work of K. H. Hasyim Asy'ari, the founder of Nahdatul Ulama. Hasyim Asy'ari had studied for years in Mecca, where he had come under the influence of the Egyptian modernist Muhammad Abduh (Dhofier 1982). Although he rejected the antimystical reformism of modernist Muslims, Hasyim Asy'ari emphasized Qur'anic study and doctrinal purification. The *pesantren* he founded at Tebuireng, East Java, in 1899 eventually trained most of East Java's prominent Muslim leaders and permanently transformed the form and meaning of Muslim religious education (Dhofier 1982; Woodward 1989:136).

Pasuruan's Javanists lagged far behind their Muslim counterparts in their effort to build institutions for the standardization and dissemination of religious knowledge. There was one small Taman Siswa school in urban Pasuruan. Founded in Jogjakarta, Central Java, in 1922, the Taman Siswa organization sought to combine European-style education with (non-Muslim) Javanese philosophy and arts (McVey 1967). In theory, then, it was designed to serve as a rival system to Muslim and Dutch schools. Pasuruan's Taman Siswa, however, had a negligible impact on most of the regency's Javanists. The school was expensive, and its students were recruited from among the families of government bureaucrats. Furthermore, most of Pasuruan's Javanist community lived far from the Taman Siswa school, forty kilometers to the south in the southern highlands. For these rural people, there was no institutional counterpart to the expanding system of Muslim schools.

Religious education in the southern highlands continued to take the highly segregated form it had for centuries. Formal instruction was restricted to a handful of ritual specialists *(dhukun)* accorded the privilege of studying the prayer corpus associated with Javanist ritual; the vast majority of villagers knew little or nothing of this material (Hefner 1985:189). The lack of emphasis on popular religious instruction was due in part to the lack of any educational infrastructure in this region. But it was also due to ideas of religious knowledge recognized in Javanist tradition, concepts dramatically different from those of reformist Islam.

Among the latter, Qur'anic study came to be regarded as an essential rite of passage for all males. Although the majority of village youths could not afford to enter a boarding school, most could spend some time in Muslim day schools or evening religious classes. Most eventually mastered the minimal skills of reading and reciting the Qur'an. The transmission of Muslim religious knowledge was thus an eminently public affair. Instruction took place in large classes open, in principle, to all males; in some instances, too, particularly after 1920, separate classes were held for girls. Advanced students were enjoined to demonstrate their skills in Qur'anic reading contests, holiday recitals, household rites of passage, and other contexts that brought prayer and religious education into the center of village life.

There was no such tradition of public knowledge among Pasuruan's Javanists and no institutions for its standardized inculcation. For Javanists, the most important forms of religious knowledge were those known as *ilmu (ngelmu* in Central Javanese dialect). *Ilmu* is esoteric knowledge par excellence, mastered in private and, by its very nature, not amenable to public instruction. Its efficacy depends on the spiritual condition of its bearers. Owners of *ilmu* must be strong enough to control and channel its force (see Anderson 1972). In this sense *ilmu* has little to do with doctrines, creeds, or other things that might be taught in a prepackaged, modular fashion. It deals with invisible powers and provides the practical skills to control them. It is not designed to serve as the doctrinal basis for admission to a rationalized religious community.

Javanists often contrast *ilmu* with *ilmiah* or, roughly translated, exoteric knowledge of the visible world. *Ilmiah* is most clearly seen in achievements like Western science (see Keeler 1986:81), as well as in mundane enterprises such as industry and agriculture. In some spheres practical techniques based on *ilmiah* merge indistinguishably with the occult skills of *ilmu*. But most of what counts as real religious knowledge is identified as *ilmu*. In principle, access to *ilmu* is socially restricted because it deals with dangerous forces. The restriction is justified, therefore, on the grounds that people must be protected from esoteric things that can harm the weak or uninitiated.

This is the most widely heard explanation of the nature of Javanist religious knowledge and of the reasons for secrecy in its transmission. From a sociological perspective such a restrictive concept of religious learning clearly transforms ritual knowledge into a monopoly good. Not surprisingly, there are other, more practical reasons why specialists might wish to restrict access to their lore. Throughout the southern highlands, village *dhukun* traditionally held a recognized public role. Their position was almost equal in prestige and economic reward to that of the village chief. In most communities there was just one such specialist per village, although there were often lesser *dhukun* for childbirth, healing, love potions, and other needs. Each village had only one official *dhukun*, however, and he was responsible for performing the spirit invocations required in household and village rites *(slametan)*.

These ritual activities were a lucrative source of income. In Hindu-Javanist communities, for example, the *dhukun* could earn several times his yearly agricultural income in three days of ritual service during the annual Karo festival (Hefner 1985). Though their services were required less often and their payments were more modest, the *dhukun* in Muslim-Javanist villages were also paid for every wedding, village festival, blessing of the dead, or other rite in which they were required to invoke the guardian spirits *(roh bau rekso)* of the village. Only after worship of these high deities could one address the spirits of deceased relatives (Hefner 1985:110).

Dhukun in the southern highlands thus enjoyed greater benefits than their counterparts in areas of Java where orthodox Muslims had undermined similar communal traditions, driving Javanist ritual out of the public arena and into the privacy of the home (see Geertz 1960:95). The consequences for the social economy of Javanist knowledge were, nonetheless, severe. *Dhukuns'* interests in maintaining their lucrative ritual monopoly reinforced the general Javanist tendency to view religious knowledge as a restricted good. The village *dhukun* inherited his role from his father, and he alone studied its rich ritual detail. The texts of his prayers were preserved on palm-leaf manuscripts *(kropak, lontar)* passed from father to son and shown to no one else. Although it was part of a communal ritual tradition, then, this religious knowledge was almost entirely secret (see Anderson 1972:43; Geertz 1960:88; Keeler 1986:81). Nowhere in Javanist social life was there an institutional counterpart to the Qur'anic study so central to Javanese Islam. Popular Javanism was premised on a dual economy of knowledge, segregating priestly from popular knowledge.

Nineteenth-century Dutch visitors to the southern highlands were frequently struck by the consequences of this social organization of knowledge. Many commented that villagers were "cautious" and "cryptic" (van Lerwerden 1844:67) when asked about religious matters. Rather than responding directly, villagers quickly referred all questions back to the village priest (Domis 1832:329). In part, no doubt, this was a sign of social deference toward the village *dhukun,* and of defensiveness vis-à-vis outsiders. But the attitude also underscored the fact that there was a better consensus among villagers on matters of ritual authority than there was on Javanism's creeds.

The Struggle for Popular Identity

After Indonesian independence in 1949, Muslims failed to achieve their goal of transforming the Indonesian republic into an Islamic state *(negara Islam)*. Shocked by their failure, many turned their attention to religious education. "The slogan was, as it were: teach the people who want to be called Muslims what it means to be Muslims" (Boland 1982:191). In so doing the Muslims succeeded in leaving their mark on national educational policies. For example, early in the new republic, the government required all Indonesians to profess faiths that recognized a single God with a prophet and scriptures. Until 1962 this restriction meant that only Islam, Protestantism, Catholicism, and a radically reformed, monotheistic Buddhism were sanctioned as national religions. After 1962 a reformist variant of Hinduism also won legal recognition (Boon 1977:240).

As with the tribal religions of Eastern Indonesia (Atkinson 1983; Volkman 1985), these policies left Javanists in the disquieting position of professing beliefs that the government regarded as illegitimate. In the eyes of the Muslim-dominated Department of Religion, these beliefs failed to meet the criteria of true religion—monotheism, scriptural revelation, prophets, and routinized ritual. With only minor qualification, these criteria for what constituted religion were derived from Islamic notions of religion *(agama)*. This was not a coincidence. As Boland

(1982) has emphasized, this and the requirement that all citizens have a religion represented, in effect, a compromise between the nationalist-dominated government and the Muslim opposition.

An equally dramatic concession won from the government by Muslim advocates was the requirement that religious instruction be mandatory from elementary school through college. Though implemented through public schools, responsibility for the educational policy lay with the Department of Religion. Under the pre-1965 Sukarno government, the department was dominated by officials from Nahdatul Ulama. This fact helps to explain why the policy on religious education was so unevenly applied during the first years of Indonesian independence. Through 1965 Nahdatul Ulama adopted an opportunistic attitude toward the government. In the mid-1950s they broke ranks with Muslim modernists in the Masyumi party and supported the embattled Sukarno in exchange for their monopoly over the Department of Religion. In addition to allowing them to influence religious policy, this arrangement also gave them rights to the patronage emoluments of the department. They exercised their privilege vigorously, staffing the Department of Religion with party members from the ministry all the way down to subdistrict offices.

This strategy had unintended consequences for the administration of religious education in public schools. In areas like lowland Pasuruan the new educational policy was warmly received. For Muslims, mass religious education was a logical step in their longstanding effort to revitalize popular religion. The teachers recruited for the program, moreover, had ties to Nahdatul Ulama, making the government program all the more welcome.

In Pasuruan's southern highlands, where most of the population was Javanist, however, the Nahdatul Ulama monopoly on department bureaucracy undercut efforts to implement the mandatory program for religious education. The majority of officials in southern highland villages were affiliated with the Indonesian Nationalist party. They made no secret of their antipathy for Nahdatul Ulama, and they openly resisted its instructions for religious education in grade schools. They were assisted in their efforts by high-level Indonesian Nationalist party officials in regency government. These bureaucrats sought to counter Nahdatul Ulama influence by establishing Indonesian Nationalist party chapters in the southern highlands and helping local officials there to resist the new educational policies. In line with this strategy they instructed Javanist village officials to reject candidates put forward by the Department of Religion for teaching posts. Rather than accepting orthodox teachers, they were told to use existing Javanist teachers to provide religious instruction or to bring in the village *dhukun* to do so. In the politicized climate of the 1950s, *dhukun*s had come to recognize the importance of educational programs and were willing to talk in public schools. Javanism had finally found an organized voice.

Regency-level officials of the Nationalist party (known from its Indonesian name as the PNI) provided logistical and material support for other Javanist initiatives. They organized religious associations for the upland Hindus and for Javanist Muslims, composed and printed religious pamphlets, and sponsored political rallies. Their efforts infuriated Nahdatul Ulama leaders. Several called for the outlawing of upland rites and for compulsory Islamic instruction. Most of the uplanders, they argued, called themselves Muslims, and government policy provided no option for Javanists to educate their children in unacknowledged beliefs. Nahdatul Ulama leaders claimed that even the upland Hindus should be required to undergo Islamic education. After all, they said, the uplanders practiced circumcision, just as Indonesian Muslims did (Hefner 1985: 144). This proved they were Javanese rather than Balinese, the critics argued, and to be Javanese is to be Muslim.

Despite the protests of Nahdatul Ulama officials, religious education in the southern highlands remained in the hands of local officials. With the cooperation of Indonesian Nationalist party sympathizers in regency government, Javanists systematized and standardized a body of doctrine for transmission in public schools. The cultural rationalization entailed in this development was stimulated by the intensifying rivalries between Muslims and Javanists, played out through the vehicle of government.

Religious Education under the New Order

The events following the abortive leftist officers' coup in Jakarta the night of 30 September 1965 shattered the apparent stand-off in Pasuruan between lowland Muslims and upland Javanists. This and subsequent developments benefited the Muslim drive for religious education and brought that of the Javanists to an end.

The coup and related army rebellions were crushed in a few days (Mortimer 1974:413–417; Crouch 1978:97–157). Shortly thereafter, combined Muslim and army forces launched attacks on Communist strongholds, rounding up and executing cadres of the Indonesian Communist party, whom they blamed for the Jakarta coup. In Pasuruan, Nahdatul Ulama was reported to be at the forefront of the killings, launching attacks even before the army intervened in the campaign (Hefner 1990). Eventually, other social and religious organizations joined the anti-Communist assault as well (Report 1986:136). A few weeks after the attempted coup, most of the Indonesian Communist party cadres in lowland Pasuruan had been killed.

In the nationalist-dominated highlands there was at first no violence.

Another two months would pass before Communists in this region would be rounded up for execution. When the campaign did occur, it was carried out not by local villagers but by an alliance of Muslim student groups and army leaders from outside the region (Hefner 1990). The bloodshed terrified the Javanist population. Many regarded it as not just an attack on Communists, but the first step in a larger assault on the Javanist population as a whole. Rumors circulated that after the Communist party was destroyed, nationalist leaders of Javanist persuasion would be next. Except for several unfortunate individuals caught by lowland gangs early on in the violence, however, the upland killings were confined to Communists, and the Javanist nationalists were spared.

Developments in the aftermath of the coup nonetheless dealt a fatal blow to efforts in the southern highlands to institutionalize Javanist religious instruction. Muslim interests, conversely, were advanced, because now even Javanist children were required to receive instruction in orthodox Islam. At first sight this might seem paradoxical, given the well-known hostility of the post-1965 "New Order" government toward Muslim political parties (Anderson 1983b). Muslim parties had worked closely with the armed forces in the anti-Communist campaign, and many believed that Islamic influence would grow in the new government. As the New Order consolidated power, however, it became increasingly clear that the government had no intention of making genuine political concessions to the Muslims.

A few years after the destruction of the Communist party, the military-dominated government moved to restrict the power of the old political parties, including Muslim ones. Shortly after the 1971 elections the parties were merged into two umbrella organizations. One was Muslim, the other an even more unwieldy amalgam of nationalist, Christian, and regionalist parties (Ward 1974; Samson 1978:210). Candidates from both parties were screened by government officials. Army representatives also meddled in party congresses to influence the selection of party chiefs (Hering and Wilis 1973:6). Parallel with its antiparty initiative the government launched its "functional" party, Golongan Karya (GOLKAR), to which all government officials were required to profess loyalty. This effectively ended the last remnants of political pluralism in government (Ward 1974:32–71; Anderson 1983b).

Although such initiatives were correctly perceived as eroding the power of the political parties, including Nahdatul Ulama, the impact on Islamic religious education was less clearly negative. Early in the New Order the Department of Religion was also "depoliticized." Its new minister was recruited from the ranks of the government party GOLKAR, not the Muslim Nahdatul Ulama, and its staff were required like all state employees to profess allegiance to the government party (Emmerson

1978:96). In Pasuruan a few stalwart followers relinquished their jobs rather than renounce their membership in Nahdatul Ulama. But many others did not. Indeed, several Nahdatul Ulama leaders quietly counseled that it was best to work from within the government rather than give up all influence in the department. While forced into the government party, most of these bureaucrats remained strongly committed to Nahdatul Ulama–style Islam.

Similar developments indicate that while the power of Muslim parties has declined, the cause of Islamic education has not. In the mid-1970s the Department of Religion saw its budget swell (Emmerson 1978:96). The precise consequences of this development have undoubtedly varied throughout Indonesia. From some reports, however, it is clear that as long as organizations steer away from "political Islam," government officials in Muslim regions of the country are willing to support programs for Islamic revitalization (Ecklund 1979:260). East Java is one such region in which officials have proved willing, indeed eager, to support Muslim efforts. For example, in the early 1970s the military *bupati* (regency head) of Lumajang, just to the southwest of Pasuruan, called for a program of mandatory Qur'anic study for the entire population (Ward 1974:82). Astoundingly, he did so in a regency in which a larger percentage of the people are Javanists than even in Pasuruan. At the provincial level, similarly, East Java's Department of Religion has earned a reputation quite unlike that of its Central Javanese counterpart, as a vigorous supporter of programs for Islamic revitalization *(dakwah)*. As Labrousse and Soemargono (1985:224) have detailed, the Department in East Java commands a force of some sixty-five thousand teachers, preachers, and bureaucrats, "constituting a well implanted network in rural society and thus a line of transmission as quantitatively important as that available to the Army, the Ministry of the Interior, or National Education."

A key feature of ministry policies in East Java has been to identify "weak" areas and target them for special Islamic programs. Not surprisingly, one region that has received the most such attention has been the Javanist community in Pasuruan's southern highlands, along with neighboring portions of the Tengger mountains (Labrousse and Soemargono 1985:222). Although in Old Order days the Nahdatul Ulama–dominated ministry might have dreamed of launching educational assaults on these "weak zones," the political tensions of the era made this impossible. Indeed, as noted above, regency officials in other offices militated against Islam, supporting Javanist educational efforts. Today, many of the officials supervising Islamic programs in these once-Javanist regions are former members of Nahdatul Ulama. Had they tried to carry out their campaigns in mountain communities a generation ago, they would have been denounced as Muslim spies. Today they are viewed as representatives of the GOLKAR government. In this instance, then, the "depoliticization" of the Department of Religion has served the interests of Muslim education.

Other developments have similarly enhanced the role of Islamic education. Since 1966 Javanists have no longer had the option of withdrawing their children from Islamic courses as was allowed before 1965 (Boland 1982:196; Noer 1978:37). The related arrangement of looking the other way as Javanists instructed children in what Muslims regarded as heterodox beliefs has been entirely suppressed. The religious teachers in Muslim Javanist communities are now graduates of Islamic teacher-training schools. These institutions grew enormously under the New Order government—showing, again, that government officials were willing to make concessions to Muslim interests as long as they steered clear of "political" Islam (Boland 1982:197). The result has been that in areas like the southern highlands, the quality and orthodoxy of Islamic instruction have increased dramatically. Indeed, in a few Javanist communities, regency officials have gone so far as to build *madrasah* in Javanist communities, in one instance over the strenuous objections of the local village chief. When no students enrolled in the school during its first month of operation, regency officials threatened to cut off aid to the village. Faced with the loss of patronage resources, village officials gave in, pressuring reluctant families to send children to the new school.

With the Javanist option eliminated, Javanist parents face a dilemma. The only way to get their children out of Muslim religious classes is to identify them as adherents of some other religion—Catholicism, Protestantism, Hinduism, or Buddhism. This was the option chosen by Javanist Hindus in the highest reaches of the southern uplands. They had never regarded themselves as even nominally Islamic, however, and for them it was thus easier to make common cause with Balinese Hindus (Hefner 1985:247). A few dozen Javanist Muslims—formerly followers of an antiorthodox religious organization with ties to the Indonesian Communist party, whose leadership was massacred in 1965 (Hefner 1987)—also adopted Hinduism, even though their ancestors had been nominally Muslim. In Central Java, reports indicate that an even larger percentage of Javanist Muslims have chosen to convert to Hinduism (Lyon 1980).

As a number of scholars have emphasized (Noer 1978:44; Dhofier 1978:49; Koentjaraningrat 1985:317), however, the majority of Javanists still identify themselves as Muslims, however much they may resent what some Muslim politicians did during 1965–1966, and however much they cling to Javanist beliefs. This is the situation of the majority of Javanist Muslims in Pasuruan's southern highlands. With the exception of the upland Hindus (who never were Muslim) and a handful of other converts, Javanists there have been unwilling to repudiate Islam. As a result, their children receive Muslim religious instruction in elementary schools. The quality and intensity of this Islamic education had no counterpart either in colonial times or in the early years of the Indonesian republic.

Conclusion

The long-term consequences of these changes for Javanese religion depend upon a broader array of social forces than can be addressed here (see Raillon 1985; Tamara 1985; Hefner 1987). Nonetheless, viewed from the perspective of religious education, the overall pattern in Pasuruan is clear. For more than a century, Muslims have pioneered the effort to standardize, disseminate, and, in a word, "rationalize" popular religion. Education has been central to this campaign. The process has been driven neither by an abstract impulse toward rationalization, nor, as some modernization theorists would have it, by a general disenchantment with traditional religion. Rationalization here responded to a more specific set of social concerns. It was made compelling by the contest to redefine popular identity and reorganize social life. The struggle continues today and leaves its imprint on politics and popular religion.

In the nineteenth century, Muslim educational initiatives were spurred by a crisis of community and authority. The crisis was provoked by social dislocation and popular alienation from collaborationist native rulers. In the lowlands of the Pasuruan regency, Islam came to provide the terms for a posttraditional identity that bridged the ethnic divide between Madurese and Javanese. The institutional foundation for this social revitalization was the Muslim boarding school.

At the beginning of the present century, political changes provided the driving force for the further expansion of Muslim schools. Building on this educational network, Sarekat Islam rose to prominence in the 1910s; Nahdatul Ulama followed in its wake. Both organizations attacked Javanist traditions and placed religious education at the center of their political programs. Despite the opening of a small Javanist school in urban Pasuruan, there was no equivalent mass initiative in the Javanist community. Javanist education was confined to the village and organized around a strict and hierarchical differentiation of ritual specialists from their client population.

With independence, it looked at first as if the Javanist community might finally establish institutions for religious education. Officials in the Nationalist party provided logistical support for Javanist initiatives. They wrote pamphlets, sponsored associations, and held rallies to mobilize Javanists against their Muslim rivals. By comparison with some areas of pre-1965 Java, in fact, Javanist efforts in Pasuruan achieved impressive results. They stopped the Muslim advance into the southern high-lands and provided Javanism with an institutional face.

Events during 1965–1966 destroyed these fledgling initiatives, leaving the field clear once again for Muslim education. State policies designed to depoliticize Islam have, at least in the educational sphere, played to the Muslim advantage. In the interests of domestic security, the state has vig-orously promoted religious policies that had no counterpart in colonial times and were laxly enforced before 1965. The result has been an erosion of local control over religious affairs and, conversely, the opening of rural communities to national forces. Indonesia's diverse minority religions have been obliged to conform to state-mandated models of religion. The history of these models reflects the profound accomplishment of the Muslim com-munity. Muslim influence is evident in the requirement that all citizens profess a civil religion and the stipulation that all civil religions conform to proto-Islamic criteria for what constitutes religion.

There is a larger, comparative lesson in this example. Benedict Ander-son (1983a) and Ernest Gellner (1983) have both emphasized that nation-state development everywhere involves "the replacement of diver-sified, locality-tied low cultures by standardized, formalized and codified literacy-carried high cultures" (Gellner 1983:76). In so doing, the nation-state—and its associated complex of industry, markets, and media—demands new forms of political and moral community, capable of speak-ing to the realities of a greatly expanded world. Benedict Anderson has argued that nationalism in the West proved so effective in responding to this demand that the dawn of nationalism was the "dusk of religious modes of thought" (Anderson 1983a:19). He maintains that the concept of the nation was possible only with the demise of religion's "axiomatic grip on men's minds." This required the "gradual demolition of sacred language," with its claim to absolute truth; it resulted in a search "for a new way of linking fraternity, power, and time meaningfully together" (Anderson 1983a:25, 40).

The case studies in this volume suggest that this "despiritualization" thesis does not apply to much of modern Asia. In East and Southeast Asia modern development has not extinguished religiously imagined communities. On the contrary, the growth of the state, the penetration of markets, and the expansion of national media have all stimulated reli-gious activity and pushed religious organizations into the struggle to define what the nation should become. This and other Asian examples suggest that the widespread assumption in many theories of moderniza-tion that development invariably disenchants religious communities is premised on Western historical circumstances (and a somewhat idealized understanding of them at that), not the contemporary world as a whole. A comparative theory of religion and modernity remains to be written.

There is a second lesson in these Asian examples. The essays in this volume indicate that religious developments in East Asia differ from those in Java and Muslim Southeast Asia as a whole. In East Asia high ethnicity was an integral part of premodern political culture, and it remains a critical ingredient in religious developments today. Religion in modern East Asia shows the powerful influence of high-ethnic ideals. In insular Southeast Asia, however, the premodern state failed to establish a stable environment in which high ethnicity and endemic religion could effectively resist the advance of exclusive world religions. Slowly but surely, these religions—Islam most particularly—have succeeded in promoting a cultural vision that banishes ethnicity from the definition of true religion. The outcome was not inevitable. In Java the cultural module for a high-ethnic religion was developed early, but the political machinery for its enduring dissemination was not. Elements of the high-ethnic tradition survived, but in modern times their religious role has come under attack by a resurgent Islam.

Ernest Gellner (1983:41) has emphasized that Islam has always had built-in organizational proclivities toward reform. In Java the development of the nation-state has only reinforced this organizational disposition. As in all of developing Asia, the process of modernization has resulted in the displacement of locality-tied cultures by more national images of community. With its organizational anomie and aversion to doctrinal canonization, the Javanist community was ill prepared to take advantage of this process. *Santri* Muslims, by contrast, showed themselves preadapted for the change. The result is not surprising: contrary to East Asian trends, religion in Java has seen a weakening of high-ethnic influences and a strengthening of the transethnic idioms and institutions so characteristic of "world religions."

PART II | RESHAPING RELIGIOUS
PRACTICE

4

Religion and Ethnic Politics in Malaysia

The Significance of the Islamic Resurgence Phenomenon

SHAMSUL A. B.

The Symbiotic Relationship among Ethnicity, Religion, and Politics in Malaysia

The Malays, who are Malaysia's indigenous population, have claimed to be 100 percent Muslim—at least constitutionally, though not necessarily in reality. For at least three decades now, they have dominated Malaysian politics. United Malays National Organization (UMNO), the Malay-Muslim party, has been the dominant partner in the ruling party coalition since Malaysia's general elections in 1955. It has provided the powerful Malaysian federal cabinet with at least 60 percent of its ministers, including all the prime ministers and deputy prime ministers, since then.

In short, Malay-Muslim politics has been at the center of Malaysian politics since the establishment of modern electoral government in the country (see Funston 1980; Means 1970; Milne and Mauzy 1978, 1986). Although the political position of the non-Malay, non-Muslims has often been described as peripheral, it is an indispensible periphery that has never been taken lightly by the center. This is evident in the historical development of the ruling party coalition, which before 1972 was called the Alliance (with two non-Malay, non-Muslim parties as partners to UMNO) and later was expanded and renamed the National Front (with some ten non-Malay, non-Muslim parties as UMNO's partners). While compromises within the National Front (NF) have strongly favored UMNO (read Malay-Muslim parties), enough is usually offered to the other coalition partners (read non-Malays) to enable the NF to mobilize a substantial share of the non-Malay vote as well (Mauzy 1983). The continued Malay-Muslim domination of the parliament, and hence Malaysian politics, has been guaranteed by an electoral system heavily weighted in favor of the predominantly Malay-Muslim rural constituencies against the non-Malay urban constituencies (Rachagan 1984). In turn, the Malay-Muslim bias in the electoral system guarantees National Front success only to the extent that UMNO is the dominant party in the Malay-Muslim community.

Because a Malay-Muslim political party has exerted such influence in shaping not only the political life of Malaysians but also their whole social existence for such a long period, inevitably whatever takes place within Malay-Muslim politics—or for that matter within the Malay-Muslim community as a whole—has wider sociological implications. In this context religion, Islam in this case, is much closer to the center of national politics than, for instance, in Indonesia, which demographically has the largest community of Muslims in the world (150 million).

Therefore, the significance of the phenomenon of Islamic resurgence in Malaysia must be understood as both an ethnic and a political phenomenon. It has transformed Malaysian society, implicating both Muslims and non-Muslims, reoriented its politics, and pushed Malaysia—despite its small size, location outside the Middle East, multiethnic structure, and poly-religious character—to the center of the Islamic social movement, economic innovation, and political activism in the world today. Even though Malaysia's Islamic resurgence has unique characteristics, it is also a localized version of the worldwide phenomenon (see Barraclough 1983; Federspiel 1985; Funston 1981; Gunn 1986; Lyon 1979; Milner 1986; Noer 1975; Regan 1989; von der Mehden 1980).

This chapter examines the phenomenon of Islamic resurgence in the context of Malaysia's ethnic politics. An outline of the origin and organization of the Islamic resurgence movement in Malaysia, by no means monolithic, is followed by a description of the ideologies, strategies, and activities of the various groups within the movement and the accommodative reactions by the government. The next section examines the nationwide social implications the movement has had upon the wider Malay-Muslim community and the non-Malay, non-Muslim social groups. The conclusion briefly examines the redefined relationship between religion and authority that has taken place in Malaysia since the emergence and widespread influence of Islamic resurgence.

The content of this essay is based upon two major sources: the findings of previous studies on this subject matter and my own experience both as a participant in the formative stage of the movement and, later, as an observer.[1] Through a creative use of these sources, I will advance an explanation of how the Malaysian rural populace has been brought into the sphere of "Islamic revivalism," formerly very much an urban-based phenomenon.

The Malaysian Islamic Resurgence Movement and Its Internal Divisions

In Malaysia, as in many other Muslim countries, Islam has become the major ideology for political dissent as well as legitimation of authority since its arrival in the thirteenth century (Ellen 1988; Roff 1985). During the precolonial era, for example, Islam was the fundamental tool for the traditional Malay chiefs' authority in setting themselves up as sultans, each with his own empire, in the midst of the dominant Hinduized states of the Malay Archipelago. During British colonial rule Malay nationalism was triggered and sustained by Islamic reformist ideals (Roff 1967). Islam became the vehicle through which Malays in general challenged the British-controlled Malay aristocracy. Immediately after World War II, during the interregnum period of near anarchy, Islam was a crucial rallying factor in the formation of cult movements for the self-protection of Malay-Muslims against non-Muslim Chinese threats of physical violence (Stockwell 1979).

When Malaysia achieved independence in 1957, Islamic ideals found a new political platform in Partai Islam, the Pan-Malayan Islamic party popularly known by its acronym PAS (Funston 1980). As Malaysia moved into the 1970s, after the racial riots of 13 May 1969, which resulted in the pro-Malay affirmative action policy known as the New Economic Policy (NEP),[2] PAS joined the ruling party coalition. Thus the Malay-Muslim community lost its main channel through which not only Islamic ideals but also political dissent could be expressed. Islam, progressive as ever and within a redefined political scenario, then reemerged as a cohesive force orchestrating demands for political change, bringing together elites and mass elements, but taking an apparently apolitical form, the Islamic resurgence movement. In popular local parlance the movement is known as "the *dakwah* movement." (*Dakwah* is an Arabic word meaning salvation, including evangelical activity.) Through this new social movement, popular energies and moral enthusiasm were expressed to such a pitch that the government wanted "both to condemn and co-opt it" (Kessler 1980:11).

The emergence of the resurgence movement in the early 1970s was initiated mainly by Malay-Muslim university students who were educated in the Western secular tradition (Muhammad 1987; Muzaffar 1987; Nagata 1984; Anwar 1987). Their renewed interest in Islam grew from the interplay of a set of circumstances, mostly local but some international in origin. In the global context Islam began to occupy center stage during the Middle Eastern crisis in the mid-1960s and later strengthened its presence in the international politico-economic arena during the oil crisis of the early 1970s (which shattered the myth of the economic invincibility of Western powers). But it reached its height in the late 1970s during the Iranian revolution. Since then not only academics but also Western mass media have paid special attention to anything Islamic (Hussain 1988). Against this general international atmosphere Muslims from all over the world became "conscientized" (see Chaiwat Satha-Anand's chapter in this volume) to the "importance" of Islam not only as a possible alternative to Western civilization, then perceived as suffering a decline, but also as an ideological framework for practical actions, in a manner akin to liberation theology. The Malay-Muslim community in Malaysia, especially the students, was also affected by this worldwide development. However, specific local factors contributed to the emergence of the resurgent movement among these students.

Since 1971 the government has imposed a series of restrictions on student activities through the newly introduced Universities and the University Colleges Act, 1971 (UUCA 1971). The act prohibited university students or any of their organizations from affiliating themselves with or expressing support, or sympathy for, or opposition to any political party (read opposition party) or trade union. Anyone who contravened these provisions was liable to a maximum fine of a thousand Malaysian dollars (about four hundred U.S. dollars) or six months' imprisonment. The curbs severely reduced the many social welfare projects for rural Malay-Muslims that Malay-Muslim students had conducted through a number of student organizations they controlled. As a result, many of such organizations embarked on *dakwah* projects of various types. With restrictions imposed on political participation, Islam easily became the safe avenue through which students could air their grievances, fulfill a need to serve society, and find relief from the pressures of university life and urban living.

The draconian 1971 act did not deter students from demonstrating against a number of cases of alleged peasant hunger and poverty. More than eleven hundred students, nearly 90 percent of whom were Malay-Muslims, were arrested; those arrested included the charismatic student leader Anwar Ibrahim. Subsequently, in 1975, the act was amended to prohibit students or student organizations from maintaining or collecting any funds. Assemblies of more than five persons and publishing of any documents without prior permission were also prohibited, but regular daily and weekly prayer congregations among Malay-Muslim students were allowed. Such restrictions only served to further enhance the Islamic cause, then evident in the politicization of the weekly and daily prayer congregations of Malay-Muslim students. The *dakwah* movement was not then publicly known, and the government, having to contend with student agitation over socioeconomic issues, did not perceive Islam as a threat to its control of student activities or as a channel through which a challenge to its authority could be expressed. Sociologically speaking, therefore, the mass involvement of Malay-Muslim university students in Malaysia's *dakwah* movement coincided with the decline of secular "student power," a most influential force in Malaysian politics in the 1960s and the very early 1970s (Muhammad 1973).

Consequently, the new movement began to shape its vision and strategies for action around a central contention: the rejection of secular, West-ern-oriented education and Western-style modernization, both of which were viewed as no longer able to provide solutions to the ills of society. Although the movement as a whole is not a monolithic one, this view informs the central ideology of the different groups within it (Muham-mad 1987).

In the wider Malaysian context the movement's emergence coincided with the political decline of PAS, the Islamic-based Malay opposition party that had championed the interests of the poor Malay peasant class for more than a decade. When PAS joined the National Front ruling party coalition in 1972, a political vacuum was created. Therefore, it was not surprising that the *dakwah* movement was then perceived by many observers (Jomo and Ahmad 1988) as the replacement for PAS, although this was never its expressed intention.

The movement as a whole did provide an alternative ideological framework to that of PAS, although both took the teachings of Islam as the basis of their beliefs and way of life (Jomo and Ahmad 1988:860–862). These beliefs can be summarized as follows. Islam as a comprehen-sive way of life is integral to politics, state, law, and society. Muslim societies have failed because they have departed from this understanding of Islam by blindly following Western secular and materialistic ideologies and values. The solution to this failure is to go back to the original teach-ings of the Qur'an and the Prophet Muhammad, in order to bring about an Islamic and social revolution. Western-inspired civil law must be replaced by Islamic law, considered the blueprint for Muslim society, as a precondition for the creation of an Islamic state. Finally, while Westerni-zation should be rejected and condemned, modernization as such should not—meaning that science and technology should be accepted, so long as they are subordinated to Islam in order to avoid the infiltration of West-ern values.

The members of this new religious movement were high school, col-lege, and university students, graduates, and young professionals. Resid-ing mainly in the urban areas, they formed the social group most recep-tive to this alternative ideological framework. They ranged from highly qualified graduates in the natural sciences of the English-medium West-ern institutions of higher learning to those educated in Islamic theology and jurisprudence from Middle Eastern colleges. Some of them were upper- and middle-class urbanites and others were from poor rural vil-lage families. None fit the stereotype of the so-called Islamic fundamen-talists—uneducated, antimodern, fringe lunatics, social misfits, power hungry (Nash 1984)—so often portrayed in countless reports by the Western press and Western academic literature (Said 1978).

The Islamic resurgence in Malaysia is not a monolithic movement.

Those involved in this movement have ranged from the moderate to the radical, from progovernment to antigovernment, and from the upper crust to the lower stratum of the society. Undeniably, some individuals who did not become members and actively participate in any of the identifiable groups within the movement nonetheless returned to strict religious practice. They remained the silent sympathizers of the movement and have often have been conveniently grouped by analysts as members of the movement. The longstanding Sufi groups, such as the *naskhsyabandiah* school, have also sometimes been hastily and mistakenly categorized as one of the recently formed *dakwah* groups.

The first movement to come on the scene and the most influential on all university campuses was Angkatan Belia Islam Malaysia (ABIM), the Muslim Youth Movement of Malaysia. Its main message was the importance of Islam as a self-sufficient way of life that holds the key to all human beings' universal problems. ABIM also recognized the weaknesses of human beings and thus their varying degrees of commitment to Islam. To ABIM the ritualistic aspects of Islam were of secondary importance. The men usually wore Western-style shirts and pants. Women, however, usually wore the *purdah,* an outfit that covered them from head to toe, sometimes veiling the face.

ABIM was interested in what it called the "conscientization process"— that is, developing its own and the outside world's critical thinking and awareness into a more progressive outlook on the issues and problems that beset society rather than actively participating in mainstream politics (Zainah 1987:45–48). Therefore, within the framework of calling on all Muslims to return to the teachings of the Qur'an and on non-Muslims to understand a society built on Islamic principles, ABIM called for the introduction of Islamic economic, legal, and educational systems; an end to corruption and abuse of power; the protection of basic political freedoms; a guarantee of socioeconomic justice; and rejection of the capitalist and socialist systems as alternatives.

ABIM was a very popular *dakwah* group throughout the 1970s, controlling all the student unions on local campuses. Its role as an activist group was to challenge the government, university authorities, and other "secular" student organizations, and to chart a new Islamic path for student activities. Anwar Ibrahim, its charismatic leader, enjoyed popular support even outside ABIM and among the members of PAS. He was once the president of the World Assembly of Muslim Youths. His visibility also led to his being detained without trial by the government from 1974 to 1976 after leading the massive student protests in 1974.

Despite his oppositional role Anwar Ibrahim was persuaded to join UMNO. He rose quickly in UMNO ranks and is presently the minister of education, an important position within the National Front–controlled government. ABIM's unchallenged position as the most important *dakwah* group in Malaysia, however, was seriously undermined following his "defection" to the ranks of the "infidel" government, which was seen by many students as a betrayal of the Islamic struggle. ABIM lost credibility among the *dakwah* students because not only its chief but also a number of its top leaders left to join UMNO (Jomo and Ahmad 1988: 853–860).

In the early 1980s a group popularly known as the Islamic Republic Group (IRG) emerged and took over the control of the student unions from ABIM (Anwar 1987:35–36). The origin of this group can be traced to an organization called Suara Islam (The Voice of Islam) founded in the United Kingdom in 1975 by a group of Malay-Muslim students. Most members of Suara Islam were studying for their undergraduate degrees in the natural sciences and were fully sponsored by the Malaysian government. IRG was a splinter faction from Suara Islam. Its main intention was to establish an Islamic republic in Malaysia through direct political participation in Malaysian mainstream politics by creating a political party to be called the Islamic Revolutionary Party.

The leaders of the IRG, on their return to Malaysia, did try to establish a revolutionary party, Parti Negara Islam Malaysia (Islamic Nation Party of Malaysia). Their application was rejected by the Ministry of Home Affairs without explanation. In 1982 a few of the IRG leaders, to test the water, ran in the general elections as independent candidates. When they failed to obtain more than 5 percent of the total number of registered voters in each constituency, they lost their deposits. A year later a power struggle took place within the main opposition Islamic party, PAS. A group of more religously committed Young Turks emerged as the winners, and some IRG leaders took the opportunity to join PAS. One of them is currently the youth leader of PAS.

In 1983 IRG won all elections on university campuses.[3] The group's strategy in the elections was to form small, secret cells among the students. It called for the establishment of a total Islamic order in Malaysia to replace the secular "infidel" government. The core leadership of the new order would be provided by the students. The university authorities accused the IRG of trying to establish an Islamic Republic in Malaysia à la Iran, but this was vehemently denied. It was quite clear, however, that the IRG represented the *dakwah* students whose new commitment to Islam was now translated into political activism of a type never advocated by ABIM. This group received much support and guidance from PAS leaders, professors from the Islamic Academy of the University of Malaya, and other university teachers in the various faculties of natural sciences in local universities who had been actively involved in Suara Islam and the IRG in the United Kingdom. The influence of this group is still very strong on local campuses; at present it controls four of the seven student councils of Malaysian universities.

The third *dakwah* group on university campuses is aligned with the Jamaat Tabligh, a Delhi-based missionary organization aimed at renewing the spirit of Islam through personal contact and the example of its missionaries. It is, thus, a campus branch of a larger, noncampus-based *dakwah* organization. This group is much less open than other *dakwah* organizations; it emphasizes rituals and requires all its followers to undertake evangelistic activities for at least a few days each month. Tabligh is an exclusively male organization and thus spreads its message on campus only among the male students, preaching from room to room. It has been the least influential *dakwah* group on the local campuses.

The fourth *dakwah* university-based group, also a branch of a larger, nonuniversity-based group, is associated with Darul Arqam (House of Arqam), a movement named after a companion of the Prophet Muhammad who had offered his house as a hideout for the Prophet to plan the first Islamic revolution. It has three headquarters, the biggest of which is in the east coast state of Pahang, peninsular Malaysia. Founded in 1969, the movement believes in an "Islamic lifestyle" that entails emulating the behavior pattern of the Prophet Muhammad in the conduct of everyday life. For instance, the followers lead an austere communal life, sleeping on double bunks in crowded dormitories and eating from big aluminum trays piled with food, sharing each tray among four or five members. Women and men are totally segregated; the former wear a black or green *purdah* and the latter a green (Islamic color) robe and a turban; the men also sport a goatee. In putting Islam into practice as a way of life, Darul Arqam is actively involved in running various educational projects (religious schools), social projects (clinics and hospitals), and economic projects (minimarkets, manufacturing *halal* or religiously permitted food products).

As in the parent organization, male and female Arqam followers at the universities seem more interested in increasing their religious knowledge about Islam than in pursuing political agendas. They are also involved in voluntary social welfare projects in the urban and rural areas. They refrain from making comments or political statements on the ills of society. Although they do not control any student organization on any of the local campuses, the group is still very active in trying to "re-Islamicize" Muslim students. They certainly have attracted more followers within the campus community than the Jamaat Tabligh group.

There are at least two other important *dakwah* organizations without followers on the campuses. One is known as Pertubuhan Kebajikan Islam SeMalaysia (PERKIM; The Islamic Welfare Association of Malaysia), the other as Pusat Islam (Islamic Center). The former has been a self-financed organization functioning mainly as a missionary body active in trying to convert non-Muslims, mainly Chinese, to Islam and in looking after the welfare of the new converts through special education and economic support programs. In the wake of Islamic resurgence in Malaysia, its role has been highlighted as many foreign wives—mostly Europeans—of Malay-Muslim cabinet ministers, high-ranking government officials, and executives of private firms became openly involved in PERKIM's missionary activities and received widespread media attention.

In fact, PERKIM has the authority to issue a special conversion certificate to all new converts, male or female, to allow them to marry Muslim Malaysian citizens, which in turn qualifies them to become permanent residents of the country. More significant is that once a non-Malay, non-Muslim has been converted to Islam, endorsed by PERKIM, and married to a Malay-Muslim, he or she has often been socially accepted as an "honorary Malay." Such individuals, and especially their children, have been categorized as Malays. This entitles them to receive benefits from the NEP, the government's pro-Malay affirmative action strategy. PERKIM thus has an important complementary role to Pusat Islam, vis-à-vis the *dakwah* movement, in the context of the government's effort to Islamicize Malay society. This role has been highlighted in the mass media by both PERKIM itself and the government.

Pusat Islam was established in the early 1980s with the professed aim of conducting missionary campaigns within both the government and the wider Malay-Muslim community to challenge the ever-increasing popularity and influence of the other *dakwah* groups in Malaysia, whether inside or outside colleges and universities.[4] Pusat has also been the government's watchdog, keenly observing the activities of other *dakwah* groups. It has been funded entirely by the government and placed under a cabinet minister attached to the prime minister's department. Its establishment has to be seen as both an accommodative and "combative" reaction by the government to the development of *dakwah* activities, despite the existence of the longstanding and well-established Departments of Religious Affairs in each of Malaysia's states.

Pusat has also organized special programs for Malaysian students abroad, where "nests" of the *dakwah* movement exist. It sends out religious officers attached to the various Departments of Education in the United States, the United Kingdom, Australia, and elsewhere to observe and to communicate directly with "vulnerable" students to discourage them from joining the overseas branches of ABIM, IRG, Arqam, and Tabligh. On local campuses Pusat finances and helps to organize many of the Malay-Muslim students' religious activities and trips overseas, usually in cooperation with university authorities (which represent the government's interest; all the universities in Malaysia are fully government-funded institutions). Although the *dakwah* students from the various groups have often boycotted such activities, "secular" Malay-Muslim students continue to support them.

In the public sphere Pusat Islam has been responsible for organizing large-scale religious campaigns through the electronic media (mainly television), extolling the virtues of Islam and the need for the *umma* (the Muslim community) to become less materialistic and return to "Islamic ways." For this purpose specially designed "religious awareness" courses have been conducted at the grassroots level to "reeducate" the rural Malay-Muslims. It could be argued that Pusat Islam (read government) has brought the rural populace into the *"dakwah* sphere," which was formerly an urban-based phenomenon. In this sense, Pusat Islam has played an important role on behalf of the government to propagate, nationwide, the government's version of *dakwah*. It has therefore become not only a *dakwah* organization but also one that oversees the activities of other *dakwah* groups.

In the Malaysian context Islamic resurgence has obviously entailed the intertwining of religion and political authority. The movement must be understood in the context of Malaysian ethnic politics, the NEP, and the underlying class tensions that existed within both the Malay-Muslim community and the non-Malay, non-Muslim community. The impact of Islamic resurgence on the wider Malaysian society, among both the Malay-Muslims and non-Malay, non-Muslims, must be examined closely. To date, except for a study by Ackerman and Lee (1988), most analysis on this subject has focused on the Malay-Muslim community. In the next section of this essay I shall examine the impact on both Muslims and non-Muslims.

The Impact of Islamic Resurgence on the Muslim and Non-Muslim Communities in Malaysia

Islamic resurgence in Malaysia has occupied center stage in the social life of Malay-Muslims for about two decades now. Because of its close relationship with Malay politics and the national government, its impact has been felt equally by the non-Malay, non-Muslim communities (Barraclough 1983; Lee 1988). Within the Malay-Muslim community the phenomenon has had its greatest transforming consequences, some literally visible and the rest articulated within the whole spectrum of the believers' everyday activities, among the urban middle class. The Malay-dominated rural populace, which at the nascent stage had been almost unaffected by the resurgence, is now seeing the full brunt of impact, if not from the *dakwah* groups, then from the government itself, through Pusat Islam and its Islamicization programs. Islamic resurgence has now become countrywide.

Considering the impact of Islamic resurgence among Malay-Muslims raises the following questions (see also Muhammad 1987; Anwar 1987). First, what is the commitment of the *dakwah* students after leaving the universities, and what kind of influence do they have in their workplaces? Will they remain *dakwah,* or will they free themselves from this commitment when confronting the "secular, materialistic, and infidel" environment? Second, since the government has also been actively involved in its own program of Islamicization (Mauzy and Milne 1983–1984), a direct reaction to the whole *dakwah* movement motivated by a somewhat different set of reasons and aims, to what extent has the government's version of *dakwah* really been accepted—both in combating what the government has termed deviationist tendencies of the *dakwah* movement and in convincing the public that its version is the *correct* one?

The visible presence of young Malay *dakwah* students and professionals in major Malaysian institutions, their mobility, and their sheer numbers have had a widespread impact on the Malay-Muslim community.[5] Besides the change to more "Islamic" dress, there has been a decline in social interaction between the sexes. At religious talks, whether held at home or at public places, men and women gravitate to their own segregated sections of the room. In some cases they are divided by curtains or movable partitions, and the women are hidden at the back part of the room, out of sight of men and the male speaker.

Today, a large number of Malay-Muslim secretaries and officials in many government offices have become *dakwah*. Religious talks are organized regularly at prayer times, often during office hours. The *dakwah* office workers assemble in the *surau,* a small prayer room found in each office. In the private sector, whether in factories or offices, a similar pattern can be observed. *Surau* are common in electronics factories, which today employ mostly female Malay-Muslim workers. Some cynics, especially those in management within the private sector, have commented that being *dakwah* at office hours has its advantages—for example, reducing working hours without risking a wage cut.

Despite such comments this new religious environment at the workplace, in private and public sectors as well as in private homes and public places, has provided a setting conducive to the *dakwah* graduates' continuing their commitment and engaging in missionary activities. For example, many older and senior colleagues of the graduates have confessed that they feel ashamed to be seen at their desks instead of in the *surau* at prayer times when their younger colleagues are performing their rituals. Annual office parties or dinners have either become alcohol-free or been abolished. These are small changes, but they slowly create a new kind of atmosphere and new rules of behavior and social interaction, dictated by the *dakwah* way of life and values, at the workplace.

Muslims observe a set of strict dietary rules. Among Malay-Muslims

in Malaysia, the sphere of food taboos has now extended beyond not eating pork to not eating anything cooked by non-Malay, non-Muslims.
The new norm is, "If in doubt do not consume." The reason is that non-
Malay, non-Muslims often consume pork or use alcohol in their dishes,
and they cook these foods in a set of pots and pans that, after being used,
are not "religiously cleansed." Whatever is cooked and served from these
utensils is *haram* (religiously forbidden) and hence to be avoided by
Malay-Muslims. As a result, the non-Malay, non-Muslims now have
fewer opportunities to get to know their Malay-Muslim office colleagues
in informal gatherings at their homes unless they are willing to hire special caterers to prepare Muslim foods, and this can prove too costly.[6]

There has also been increased public demand, especially by Malay-
Muslims, for rigorous control over *haram* and *halal* food. Much attention is paid to the use of meat-based gelatin in jellies and ketchup, as well
as lard and alcohol in confectionery and other food products, whether in
fast-food chain outlets or supermarkets. Hence the acquisition of a *halal*
certificate is now mandatory for non-Malay, non-Muslims involved in
the food business, as it is for those involved in importing meat from
abroad. The sign *ditanggung halal* (guaranteed permitted to be con-
sumed by Muslims) is prominently displayed on the signboards of many
restaurants, big hotels, and eating places that have a large Malay-Muslim
clientele but belong to non-Malay, non-Muslims.

In sum, Malay public life is now being redefined on the basis of the
dakwah understanding of Islam, as university life has been transformed
over the last two decades. Instead of uniting the Malay-Muslims, however, the *dakwah* phenomenon has divided them. There now exists a
social division between the *dakwah* Malays and the "secular" Malays.
The "holier than thou" attitude of the *dakwah* students alienates other
Malays, who often try to disassociate themselves from the former. Not
only do the "secular" Malays fear the influence of the *dakwah* Malays,
but they also often feel guilt about not being good Muslims. After their
conversion the *dakwah* members strive to lead a new life—no more
drinking, partying, and mixing freely with members of the opposite sex
—which demands isolation from "secular" former friends. Thus, the
opportunities for the two sides to socialize diminish, and communications between them are slowly reduced to exchanging *salaam* (the cur-
sory religious greetings). In some cases this has led to the development of
animosity and open confrontation between the two groups, such as boy-
cotting each others' ordinary social activities. The division between these
two groups has been gradually carried over into the political sphere, both
inside and outside party politics.

The division has wider ramifications not only for the relationship
between UMNO and PAS but also within UMNO, which now has its

own *dakwah* group led by the minister of education, the charismatic ex-ABIM leader Anwar Ibrahim. Many believe that Anwar's presence in the ministry has provided the protection the *dakwah* students need, thus guaranteeing their entry into the job market, as well as helping to sustain the movement's influence.

The UMNO-led government, in an attempt to curb what it called the deviationist tendencies of the *dakwah* movement, has made a number of amendments to the penal and criminal codes, giving itself wider powers to act against whatever it perceives as a threat to "national security and unity" coming from the religious movement. The non-Malay, non-Muslims are uneasy about these amendments to the civil code which, of course, affect them too (Ackerman and Lee 1988:160–161).

The non-Malay, non-Muslims already resent many other related issues, such as the restriction on the allocation of land for churches and temples and control over the building of shrines and temples. There have also been incidents in which Muslim deviationists who do not necessarily belong to any of the *dakwah* groups desecrated temples, incidents leading to violent deaths. These events and circumstances have been seen by the non-Malay, non-Muslims as territorial encroachment by the Malay-Muslims. Such negative reactions, which can be traced indirectly to Islamic resurgence, have been further compounded by recent developments within the Malay-Muslim community.

The food taboos and the *surau* have accentuated the divide. That Malay office workers can take time off at prayer times to pray at a specially provided space engenders a feeling of dissatisfaction among non-Malay, non-Muslim workers. They perceive that they have to work longer at their desks, and they feel deprived because they are not allocated special space to conduct their religious activities, even if they officially request it.

Non-Malay suspicion of *dakwah* activities now extends to the government, whose Islamicization programs are treated as part of an undifferentiated trend toward wider Islamic activism in the country (Lee 1988). Whether non-Malay, non-Muslims are aware of the divisions within the Malay-Muslim community is no longer an important issue, because they have now developed a heightened sensitivity to the defense of their religious rights, which include ethnic and nonethnic aspects (Ackerman and Lee 1988:59).

Non-Malay, non-Muslims feel that their ethnic identity is being threatened with the rise of the *dakwah* missionary activities, even though most of these activities have been directed to "re-Islamicizing" the Malays. Chinese, Indian, Iban, Penan, and Kadazan have become more conscious of their ethnic identities—hence the call for a stronger intraethnic solidarity (see DeBernardi in this volume). In nonethnic terms, they feel an urgency to establish alliances among non-Muslim religions irrespective of ethnic group—hence the setting up of a national council for the heads of the non-Islamic religions in response to the perceived Islamic challenge. In short, the indirect consequence of intra–Malay-Muslim rivalries has been the mobilization of non-Muslims, despite the great differences among them. Although this development has not yet spilled over into the political sphere, it is often alluded to by the non-Malay political parties, including those in the ruling party coalition.

That the ethnic fears raised among non-Malay, non-Muslims by Islamic resurgence have often been channeled into the religious arena (Ackerman and Lee 1988:55–60) is shown by an increase of religious revivalism among the various religious groups (such as Christians and Hindus). Such revivalism cuts across ethnic lines. Although this has taken place rather unconsciously and has been generated by other, additional factors including class, many non-Malay, non-Muslims have now retreated into various religious activities as convenient alternatives for ethnic expression. For example, on local campuses many groups of non-Malay students belonging to various religious faiths have requested special facilities and sought permission to conduct their religious activities openly.[7] Such activities have been conducted on the campuses before, but mostly on a smaller scale and more quietly. Now that they are larger and more visible, they often stimulate intervention by university authorities or by the *dakwah* Malay students. Religion has become a major political issue in student election campaigns. The heightening of non-Malay, non-Muslim religious consciousness on the campuses can be seen as a direct response to both the dominance of *dakwah* student groups in campus politics and the university authorities' support of the "secular" Malay-Muslim students' religious activities.

The relationship between the *dakwah* Malay students and the non-Malay, non-Muslims is said to be much better than that between the former and their "secular" Malay counterparts. Perhaps it is easier for the *dakwah* students to conduct a "normal" discussion on Islam with non-Muslims than with Muslims, because the areas of common interest and sharing with the latter have shrunk. Besides, the *dakwah* students feel it is their duty, part of their religious mission, to explain Islam and their new commitment to the religion to non-Muslims.

On the whole, it is clear that the social impact of the *dakwah* movement will be sustained, especially in religious and ethnic polarization. The decline of social activities involving Malays and non-Malays does not augur well for a multiethnic society like Malaysia. Even though religious tolerance still prevails, there is much concern among the non-Malay, non-Muslim population about how much more pressure the *dakwah* phenomenon will exert in effecting changes in social and political life and how far the government is willing to accommodate them in its Islamicization policy.

Conclusion:
The Unity of Religion, Authority, and Ethnicity in Malaysia

Throughout the Islamic world the development of modern states, capitalism, education, the media, and other institutions of modernity have altered the bases of communities. These changes have, in turn, engendered crises of tradition rooted in the secularization of modern consciousness (thus the expected demise of Islam), in which modernity has exchanged shared values for excessive individualism and mutual responsibility for personal preference, resulting in what could be called the "demoralization of discourse." In these circumstances religion, often despised as oppressive to the human spirit and thus expected to suffer a slow death, now persists, in a redefined sociopolitical scenario, as the bearer of what humanity cannot do without, namely, a sense of community and tradition.

The emergence of the Islamic resurgent movement in Malaysia, and elsewhere, has to be understood in the social milieu described above. Many observers predicted that Islamic revitalization in Malaysia was nothing more than a temporary phenomenon that was likely to give way to the inexorable forces of modernization and secularization. But this has not been the case. Islamic political and moral force has not diminished but has instead reached another stage of intensive development in Malaysia.

This is not difficult to understand, as Islam in Malaysia is not only a "religious factor" in the larger community and social struggle but also an "identity marker," especially in the ethnic sense. Therefore, the struggle is a self-conscious and sustained effort to construct a sense of self and create new moral parameters around communities, in both ethnic and religious terms.

Since the resurgence of Islam, the significance of the religious factor in Malaysian ethnic politics has reached a level and intensity never before witnessed (Shamsul 1983), mainly because the government, which has been dominated by Malay-Muslims, has to contend with the challenges and widespread influence of the phenomenon. The government has introduced and implemented its own program of Islamization, a major part of which involves public media campaigns and the introduction of specific religious activities and strategies. To a lesser extent, but by no means less significantly, the government has also introduced special legislation to curb Islamic activities.

The overall outcome has been a redefinition of the social and political life of all Malaysians. In intraethnic terms within the Malay-Muslim community, Islamic resurgence has transformed through heightened Islamic consciousness the way Malays from all walks of life, in urban as well as rural areas, live their everyday lives. It has also brought some changes in the ground rules of Malay politics, especially within UMNO, which sees the need to have its own "Islamic" component and high-profile Islamic activities. Finally, it has created a social dichotomy of "religious" versus "secular" within the Malay community as a whole.

One could argue that at present it has become increasingly difficult to speak of Malaysian Islam as a unitary force; rather, like the overall religio-cultural landscape of which it forms a part, Malaysian Islam is characterized by disagreements, debates, and fragmentation. Admittedly, the Islamic resurgent movement of the 1970s and 1980s has experienced some success. However, it has also confronted numerous difficulties in developing its programs and maintaining momentum and credibility in the face of competing claims of a disparate collection of movements and groups, all claiming to speak for and on behalf of Malaysia's Muslims as a whole.

In interethnic terms ethnic polarization has become clearer and more significant, affecting not only mainstream politics but also everyday social relations and interactions. Concern over the threat to their religion has led non-Malay, non-Muslims to join forces, thus heightening their religious sensitivity. Since they form about half the total population, their predicament is not that of a minority group and ought to be taken seriously.

The Islamic resurgent movement in Malaysia and its modernist agenda is not so much concerned with a desperate search for a satisfying identity or with adjusting raised expectations to existing socioeconomic realities but with determining how universal values are modified and reworked for the fulfillment of state aims. The role of the Malaysian state in the remodifications and remolding of these values has at least two important consequences, particularly for the Malays and their religion (Islam). First, it helps to intensify the localization of Islam within the Malay community. Second, it generates new patterns of Malay this-worldly attitudes toward the non-Malay communities. Thus, state influences on religious weltanschauung have had serious effects upon intra-Malay relations and Malay–non-Malay relations.

NOTES

1. Between 1970 and 1974 the main external link of Malaysia's resurgent movement was not with the Middle Eastern or South Asian countries but with Indonesia. This was especially true of the stream initiated by Malay-Muslim stu-

dents that later became Angkatan Belia Islam Malaysia (ABIM, the Muslim Youth Movement of Malaysia). The relationship between the Malaysian and Indonesian Islamic student leaders was very close indeed. In fact, between 1971 and 1973, a number of "special religious courses" were organized by the National Association of Malaysian Islamic Students (NAMIS) with the help mainly of Indonesia's Himpunan Mahasiswa Islam (Muslim Students' Association). Some activities were conducted in Malaysia by the Indonesians, and a few groups, consisting mainly of those who were identified as potential leaders, went to Indonesia to attend one-month courses. I had the opportunity to participate in the one-month course in Indonesia. Before that I was a reporter for NAMIS's monthly newsletter and that of the National Association of Malaysian Students. When I began my career in academia my active participation in these organizations declined considerably.

When ABIM was set up in 1971 and later established Yayasan Anda, a private secondary school to provide continuing education to the mainly Malay-Muslim dropouts from the government education system, I served as one of its voluntary part-time teachers. It was thus that I participated in the formative stage of the resurgent movement. After 1976 my "participation" in the movement became mainly that of a detached researcher.

2. The New Economic Policy (NEP), launched in 1971 in association with the Second Malaysia Plan (1971 to 1975), was formulated mainly as a strategy to avoid bloody racial clashes, such as the one in Kuala Lumpur, Malaysia's capital city, on 13 May 1969. Since the 13 May racial riot was perceived as an expression of Malays' "unhappiness" about their economic position, the NEP has often been described as "a pro-Malay affirmative action" policy. On paper the NEP clearly favors Malays, but in practice non-Malays have also greatly enjoyed the fruits of this policy. This is because Malays depend on non-Malays, especially Chinese, for expert advice and guidance in the commercial world, a world that the Malays have not dominated since European mercantilistic powers established a hegemonic presence in the fourteenth century.

3. I had the opportunity to observe the activities and interview student leaders of ABIM and IRG between 1976 and 1979 and between 1983 and 1988. Both groups dominated student politics in the University of Malaya and the National University of Malaysia for more than a decade. From this constant contact I have gathered a substantial amount of information on these groups' organization and performance.

4. Pusat Islam has recruited a number of academicians from the faculty of Islamic studies at the National University of Malaysia as its permanent staff. Through them I have been able to learn in greater detail about the activities of Pusat. Pusat is actively publishing and distributing propaganda materials for public consumption. The availability of these materials and firsthand information from my former colleagues at Pusat have enabled me to discuss Pusat's crucial role in the government's Islamicization program.

5. I taught at the University of Malaya from 1973 to 1976 and have since 1976 been teaching at the National University of Malaysia. In this capacity I have constant interaction with past and present students from both universities. This firsthand experience and contact have enabled me to observe from close quarters

how they have lived their everyday lives. Part of the information obtained from this contact is presented here.

6. Many of my non-Malay, non-Muslim friends from local universities have openly complained regarding the expensive, specially prepared menu they must provide whenever they host dinner parties that many of their Malay-Muslim colleagues agree to attend. Friends in the private sector, too, complain of such expenses but note happily that they get reimbursed by their employers for their "entertainment expenses."

7. I have been consulted by a number of non-Malay, non-Muslim student leaders from my university on matters such as securing official permission to get rooms to conduct religious gatherings and writing introductory letters for these student groups to seek donations outside the campus.

5 Historical Allusion and the Defense of Identity

Malaysian Chinese Popular Religion

JEAN DEBERNARDI

Penang Chinese popular religion is linked to ethnic awareness both as a diacritic of ethnic identity and as a symbolic medium through which self-awareness may be constructed. The idioms of popular religion are dramatically effective in the formulation of social and political attitudes, and the contemporary political situation of the Malaysian Chinese finds expression in these idioms. Rituals and their associated myth-histories both capture and formulate attitudes toward ethnic and other rivals, and the practice of popular religion is permeated with historical allusions that may be invoked to comment on contemporary social issues and situations. In taking inventory of historical process, historical myths effectively image the Chinese community in relation to other ethnic groups, projecting the complexities of a pluralistic society outward.

In demonstrating the connection between ethnicity and religion, I will focus on the experiences of the Penang Hokkien Chinese, the community with which I did ethnographic research in 1979–1981.[1] My primary research community was a town in the center of Penang Island, but my investigations took me to all parts of the island in a study of temple organizations, temple fairs, and spirit mediumship. In the course of that research, I interviewed temple committee members and participants at a broad spectrum of temple fairs and religious events and conducted intensive interviews with five spirit mediums.

Local religious practices, far from being merely traditional remnants of Chinese culture, are a central means to the Chinese community's awareness of its own history and identity. Events of the ritual cycle are frequently linked with historical narratives that imagine and express ethnic and subethnic identities. These narratives are historically layered, connecting the community with its roots in China, with the period of British colonialism, and with the experience of being an ethnic minority in Malaysia.[2]

Sahlins has observed that in periods of cultural conjuncture (as when Captain Cook first visited Hawaii), there is a "working-out of the categories of being and things as guided by interests and fitted to contexts" (1981:72). In this chapter I analyze three historical myths, recounted to me by spirit mediums, that represent a working-out or stocktaking of the relationship of the Hokkien Chinese to the ethnic and political "other." The first historical myth legitimizes the Hokkien Chinese appropriation of worship of the Lord of Heaven; the second imagines Chinese relations with the British (who colonized Malaysia from 1786 until 1959) as a war of opposing spiritual forces; and the third represents Chinese relations with the Malay community in ritual practices and in a myth-history that provides a parable for Chinese-Malay accommodation. I will first provide background on the Penang Hokkien community, then turn to a discussion of the relationship among religion, ethnicity, and the state in contemporary Malaysia.

Religion and the State in Malaysia

The quest for a unified national culture has taken its toll on the Chinese minority in Malaysia, who feel themselves increasingly marginalized in a variety of domains. They live in a state wherein the Malay language is now promoted as a language of unification and education and Malay claims to cultural and national hegemony are strongly reinforced. For example, Yap Ah Loy,[3] the nineteenth-century Chinese Kapitan (leader) of the tin mine area chosen by the British colonists as their main administrative center, was long considered by Malaysians as the founder of Kuala Lumpur, the present-day capital. The Chinese community honors him in a temple in Kuala Lumpur, and biographies recounting his heroic exploits in the tin mine wars abound. About 1980, however, the history textbooks were rewritten, and a Malay, Raja Abdullah of Klang, is now officially designated as the founder of Kuala Lumpur (Carstens 1988). Hegemony in these matters is clearly located outside the Chinese community.

The Hokkien Chinese community of Penang originated in Fujian province in southeastern China, whence Hokkien Chinese have migrated in recent centuries to Taiwan and many countries in Southeast Asia, including Thailand, Malaysia, Singapore, Indonesia, and the Philippines. The Hokkien Chinese have frequently been under colonial or nonlocal rule and perhaps as a consequence are associated with a tradition of aloofness from the state. However politically disadvantaged overseas Chinese communities may have been, their members have frequently enjoyed economic success in the colonial context. In Southeast Asia in particular they have flourished as a mercantile class. In Malaysia they were ruled by the British in what came to be a quintessentially pluralistic state, and they are now a somewhat uneasy large minority in the Malaysian state.[4]

The Chinese minority in Malaysia is diverse, including members of three major dialect groups: Hokkien, Cantonese, and Hakka.[5] Hokkien Chinese are the majority of Chinese in Penang, and the Hokkien dialect serves as a lingua franca in that community. Members of different dialect groups no longer wage territorial battles, and speakers of different dialects now intermarry, but an awareness of subethnic group divisions persists (Mak 1980, 1981). Social diversity among Malaysian Chinese is also a legacy from the colonial education system, and generational differences have resulted from the reform of that system. Educated, middle-aged Chinese are graduates of two distinct educational streams, English-medium and Mandarin-medium. The younger generation, educated in a school system that is now primarily Malay-medium, is increasingly fluent in Malay. In this context, shared religious practices, language (Mandarin), and history are crucial aspects of the "invention" of cultural and ethnic community for Malaysian Chinese.

Members of the Penang Hokkien community appear to mistrust state political authority and often express a strong preference for settling matters within their own community, avoiding the intervention of the state. At the same time they communicate a strong sense of pride in their cultural heritage. This pride finds important expression in their stubborn loyalty to Chinese-medium education, in the often-expressed desire to pass Chinese culture on through the medium of language, and in active participation in the events of the ritual cycle.

In the period of my field research, Penang Chinese promoted the use of Mandarin in public contexts (political meetings, speeches and songs at temple banquets, transactions in stores), following the lead of President Lee Kuan Yew of Singapore, who sought to erase dialect group distinctions in Singapore by promoting a unified national language. At the same time Chinese guilds and associations in Penang and elsewhere in Malaysia proposed to establish a "Merdeka University" (Freedom University) in which Mandarin would be a medium of education for the Chinese population. This proposal was put forth partly in response to the quota system in the national universities, which reduced the admission of Chinese students from 49.2 percent in 1970 to 36.6 percent in 1975. The political opponents of Merdeka University criticized its Chinese supporters for "cultural arrogance" and an unwillingness to adopt the Malay language as the lingua franca of Malaysia (Aliran 1979). Ultimately the proposal was turned down.

Religion is another area in which Chinese pride is expressed and a sense of cultural unity constructed. This pride finds expression in broad-based support of the "popular religious" events of the festival cycle, including temple fairs. The Hungry Ghosts Festival, for example, is celebrated during the seventh lunar month in market areas in every part of

Penang. This festival is now coordinated by a central committee that has successfully mobilized community participation in ritual events, as well as successfully raised funds for community projects such as construction of a hospital and the Chinese Town Hall. In the words of one of the organizers, the Chinese have "taken peasant customs which are behind the times and transformed them into an alliance and a progressive symbol" (DeBernardi 1984:25).

By contrast with educational institutions, religious institutions have been, until recently, relatively untouched by state intervention. State control over political dissent has contrasted with a relative freedom of religious expression. As Ackerman and Lee observe:

[P]olitical developments of the 1970s have severely limited the opportunities of overt non-Malay dissent. The expression of non-Malay ethnicity via political symbols has become too much of a liability for any lasting public effect. However, the political constraints imposed by the government have until recently left relatively unhindered the development of ethnic sentiments within the non-Muslim religions. (1988:59–60)

The notion of religious unity bears scrutiny. Since the Malayan Constitution of 1957 was promulgated, Islam has enjoyed special status as the official religion of Malaysia. At the same time Malay ethnicity has been linked to the enjoyment of special privileges. A "Malay" was initially defined as "one who speaks the Malay language, professes Islam and habitually follows Malay customs." The privileged ethnic category was later broadened to encompass non-Malay indigenous groups who together with Malays were termed "sons of the soil" *(bumiputera)* (Andaya and Andaya 1982:302). Ackerman and Lee have also observed that in comparison with Malay-Muslim unity, "the non-Malay population is religiously and politically fragmented. The Chinese and Indians of Malaysia adhere to Christianity, Hinduism, Islam, Buddhism, Taoism, and other religions" (1988:6). At the same time they assert that a number of new religious alternatives are emerging in the Chinese and Indian communities and that "the political and religious events of the last decade have ineluctably channeled the direction of non-Malay ethnic expression into the religious arena" (ibid.:60). I would endorse the latter assertion while challenging the former.

Ackerman and Lee have focused analysis on new religions that have emerged in recent years, but Malaysian Chinese popular religion is also a lively avenue for ethnic expression. These authors (and others) err in describing Chinese popular religious practice as "fragmentary" by contrast with congregational religions. As I have argued elsewhere (DeBernardi 1992), the Chinese festival cycle coordinates a number of events organized in time and space rather than by doctrinal unity or congregational commitment. Each event of the ritual year has a time and place, and these events celebrate a range of events viewed as having complementary functions and as forming a totality.

For Malaysian Chinese, membership in a congregational religion does not exclude participation in the events of the ritual cycle. The wife of a strict Mahāyāna or Theravāda Buddhist might still make offerings to ancestors or visit a god possessing a spirit medium to consult about a child's inexplicable fever. A Christian who accompanied me to a temple fair made a direct link between popular religion and Chinese identity when she shifted her point of personal reference from "we Christians believe that . . . " to "we Chinese believe that . . . " when discussing popular religion.

In the 1970s and early 1980s, the vitality of Chinese popular religion, especially in Malaysian urban communities, was striking and much commented upon by Chinese and non-Chinese alike. Viewed from the perspective of ethnic politics in Malaysia, the most obvious answer to the question "Why this revival of religion?" was that the Chinese were responding to Malay nationalism with a "reactive nationalism" (Smith 1981:36) of their own. Through participation in the events of the lunar cycle, in particular in communitywide festivals that gathered enormous crowds for collective worship and processions, Chinese and Malaysians had a means to assert their strength, pride, and a hoped-for ethnic solidarity.[6]

Chinese themselves date the revival of Chinese religion to the May 1969 racial riots involving Chinese and Malays. In the aftermath of these racial riots, a New Economic Policy was launched with a primary goal of economic advancement for the Malay community through a variety of means, including expanded educational opportunities and rectification of "the inter-ethnic imbalance in the ownership and control of wealth in the country" (Jomo 1986:263). The "Malay first" policies are the source of much bitterness in the Chinese community. Events have unquestionably led to an increased awareness of ethnic divisions and have intensified loyalty to practices which express ethnic distinctiveness.

The upsurge of both Islamic fundamentalism and popular religious activities among non-Muslims gave the government some unease over possible challenges to the political order and raised fear of interethnic strife. Chandra Muzaffar observed at a 1984 seminar held in Kuala Lumpur that

> religious polarization is going to be . . . dangerous because it is essentially a channel for reinforcing ethnic identity. After the politics of language of the 60s and 70s, religion is being used to propagate ethnic identity in the new atmosphere here. Religion has become the new channel, the new conduit for transmitting ethnic fears and insecurity. (Putra et al. 1984:124)

While Islamic revivalism was a particular concern, during the early 1980s researchers in the prime minister's office who conducted an extensive study of religion in Malaysia were among the many puzzled over the mushrooming of cults and shrines in the Chinese community.

In 1983, following this state-initiated research, the state instituted new policies that placed religious organizations under stricter regulation, establishing controls on the building of shrines and temples. Penal and criminal codes were also amended to give the government wider powers in controlling religious dissent (Ackerman and Lee 1988:58–60). As Ackerman and Lee observe, the latter law was primarily aimed at controlling Islamic fundamentalist groups. While Chinese popular religion was not the primary target for government control, it was not above suspicion. In particular the longstanding association of popular religion and secret-society activities frequently arouses government mistrust.

Religion and World View

Chinese popular religion in Malaysia is an index of minority ethnic identity; at the same time, it expresses a world view that potentially provides followers with a holistic interpretation of the human condition. In Hardacre's terms, "To delineate a world view is to specify how a group of people understands itself to be related to the physical body, to the social order, and to the universe, and to show how its members think, feel, and act on the basis of that understanding" (1986:8).

The Hokkien Chinese world view is expressed in ritual practices that celebrate a range of spiritual beings, the most basic of which are gods, ghosts, and ancestors.[7] Wolf has observed that "the most important point to be made about Chinese religion is that it mirrors the social landscape of its adherents" (1974:131). In this view ancestors are kin, ghosts strangers, and gods bureaucrats, in a tripartite division that simultaneously classifies spiritual and human domains. In the supernatural bureaucracy localities are placed under the protection of gods who are petitioned and honored much as political superordinates would be (Ahern 1981a:94).

In this world view there is tension between a symbolism of universalism and human unity on the one hand, and of human and spiritual division and antagonism on the other. A fundamental premise is that human beings are universally the same: although they are divided by language and religion, they share a single biological nature regardless of race. The differences, it is noted, are human made and should not distract one from the deeper fact of a shared humanity. By contrast, differences between male and female or between child and adult are seen as rooted in "nature," and Chinese are taught by their religious specialists that to avoid social—indeed, natural—chaos, they must respect these natural contrasts.

A discussion of this topic was offered by an informant, a spirit medium born in China, whom I interviewed in 1980. I was told by the temple committee member who introduced us that Mr. Khor had once been a famous medium for a well-established group of the triad secret society, but his fame had fallen away. He compared the beliefs of the Three Religions of China—Daoism, Buddhism, and Confucianism— with Christianity and Islam, which he described as the religion of the "black people" (meaning the Malays). He contrasted the universalism of the world religions with the factionalized religious field found in practice in Malaysia and vehemently criticized those who would use religion as a basis of social conflict:

> *There are many deep doctrines. The Three Religions are not divided. Religion does not call men to destroy: this is done by men. They don't follow the law.*
>
> *[They say]: "Now I want to do it. This is more true, that's not true."*
>
> *Inside, all religions are the same. These things are done by men. The god doesn't ask you to be like this. The religion doesn't ask you to do this. Buddhism, Daoism, Christianity, all call you to follow the law. Men call you to do this, to do that, they belong in order to find excitement. It's like that. It's done by men, not gods.*
>
> *[The gods say]: "If you want to believe, come."*
>
> *If you want to believe, you call a god to descend. If you believe in Buddha, Buddha descends. If you believe in Jesus, Jesus descends. He doesn't call you, no. Does he come down to save you? No! Men save you. We men save ourselves.*
>
> *[Men say]: "You say your god is more powerful. No! Mine is more powerful. Yours is not true."*
>
> *These things are done by men. If we are like this, then things will be forever splintered. The gods of Chinese religion do not call men to be like this. These are the faults of men. Our minds are too cunning; our hearts don't obey. Your mouth says this, but it's not in your heart.*
>
> *The black race understands, but we don't understand. You ask the Malays [he switches to speaking in Malay]: "If you want to be a Haji [a Muslim who has made the pilgrimage to Mecca], what do you need? If you want to be a Haji, what must you take?"*
>
> *"Your heart. If your heart walks on the right path, then you can pray and become a Haji. Otherwise you will not meet Allah."*
>
> *These things cannot be seen.*

The religious practice taught by this spirit medium emphasized control of the human heart in accord with the *dao* ("path" or "way") and a human moral order harmonized with the order of nature.

The universalistic ideals of Chinese religious teachers are, however, contradicted in practice. Religions often divide groups despite the potential ideological basis for unity. Penang Chinese popular religion is filled with the symbolism of social opposition transposed to the spiritual plane. The spiritual world of the Penang Chinese is territorially divided, a world of hierarchically ranked, potentially clashing spiritual influences that must be placated using the appropriate ritual forms. Religion provides not only a field in which community is imagined, but also a field in which one's enemies are given images—be they imperial soldiers, British colonial officers, or Malay magicians. It is here that the multiethnic social world of the Penang Chinese is reflected and interpreted.

Religion and Autonomy:
The Lord of Heaven and the City of Willows

Let me now consider more closely the imagination of community in Chinese popular religious culture. Before turning to discussion of three contemporary Chinese Malaysian historical myths, I will discuss the relationship between religion and polity in colonial Malaya and will explore a famous historical myth that was fundamental to the invention of community by the so-called secret societies. The secret or "black" societies were voluntary associations that once virtually governed overseas Chinese communities in Southeast Asia; in the Straits Settlements (which included Penang), conflict with the British colonial government led to their suppression in 1889. As I will discuss, echoes of their ritual practice are still heard in contemporary Penang Chinese religious culture.

The Penang Chinese invention of community through ritual performance and collective memory has its roots in southern China. There, voluntary associations in which ritual played a key role functioned as mutual aid societies in defense of local interests. In Southeast Asia the most visible such group has been the Triad, an association (or perhaps more accurately a network of associations) founded in Fujian province in 1761 or 1762 (Murray 1993). The historical myth central to the initiation ceremonies of the Triad declared their intent to overthrow the Qing dynasty and Manchu rule and reestablish the Ming dynasty and Han Chinese rule (Blythe 1969:19–21);[8] recent scholarship, however, demonstrates that these groups are best understood as associations that provided a network of nonkin connections for mutual aid and protection, often in frontier communities (Murray 1993; Ownbey and Somers-Heidhues 1992). These groups were brought from southern China to

Southeast Asia, where Triad and Triad-like groups were powerful as voluntary associations central to the self-governance of immigrant Chinese communities (Blythe 1969; Freedman 1967; Trocki 1990). The officers of the secret societies were called on to adjudicate community disputes; often too they served in the position of "Kapitan China," intermediary between the British colonial government and the Chinese community in a form of indirect rule.

The ritual practice of the secret societies was highly effective in communicating the boundaries of the local Chinese authority structure to immigrant Chinese. W. A. Pickering, the British "Protector of Chinese" in the Straits Settlements from 1873 to 1889, noted with alarm that the immigrant Chinese were not even aware of the colonial government, so they went instead to the secret societies when they had problems (Jackson 1965:61–62). Central to the visibility of these societies was their conduct of initiation rituals to induct all new immigrants into the secret societies, sometimes under coercion. New members swore oaths of blood brotherhood at complex rituals of initiation in which symbols drawn from Daoism, Buddhism, and Confucianism were interwoven (Ward and Stirling 1977). In these rituals, they agreed to treat their fellow members with hospitality and regard for their well-being and to unite in their mutual protection.

In the early days of the Chinese Protectorate, Pickering was invited to observe a five-hour initiation ceremony in which seventy new members were admitted to a lodge in Singapore. He observed that

> the novitiates were subjected to an impressive, prolonged, complicated, and awe-inspiring ordeal which left them in no doubt about what they were committing themselves to and the seriousness of the commitment. The Government made no such formal and effective claim on an immigrant's loyalty. (Jackson 1965:76)

Pickering countered the influence of the secret societies by introducing a process for meeting new immigrants to the Straits Settlements on their arrival and informing them of their rights under British colonial rule—a bureaucratic rite of passage.

In the Triad rite of passage, language and ritual together were used to demarcate social boundaries, separating insiders from outsiders, friends from enemies. The vocabulary of Triad initiation ceremonies, for example, exalted moral virtues—loyalty, filial duty, honesty—and oaths were administered to guarantee their fulfillment. Members swore not to steal from each other, or to cheat each other, or to covet one another's wives. Signs were devised to allow members who were strangers to secretly identify themselves to one another in public. By contrast, it would appear that stealing from nonmembers was legitimate, and the rich slang vocabulary of the Triad attests to the range of predatory activities allowed, from piracy and theft to murder[9]—but only against outsiders (Ward and Stirling 1977, 1:130). In 1889 the secret societies were suppressed in the Straits Settlements, following a murder attempt on the life of Pickering (Blythe 1969:219–220).

Triad ritual took as one theme the retelling and reenactment of a distinctive historical myth that links the foundation of the society to political mobilization against the Qing dynasty. Chesneaux's summary retells the tale succinctly:

> Some seventeenth-century Buddhist monks of Shao Lin Monastery, in Fujian province, offered the Manchu emperor their support against a rebel tribe from Central Asia, the Eleuths. The emperor in question was the first of the usurping dynasty, that is, a Qing. These war-like monks aroused the jealousy of a courtier, their monastery was destroyed by order of the emperor, and all but five of them were massacred. After a long series of adventures involving rebel generals, horse-dealers, and Buddhist deities, the five monks had a mystical experience in which the words of the legitimist slogan, *Fan Qing Fu Ming* [Overthrow Qing and Return to Ming], were revealed to them. They took refuge in the town of Mu Yang, the City of Willows, and founded there within the Market of the Great Peace (Tai Ping) a secret society, the Triad. (Chesneaux 1971:16)[10]

Chesneaux accepts the view that the Triad was formed in political opposition to the Qing dynasty and observes that the ritual framework of the Triad was a means to create "a system of rules and political conventions as complete as the ones they opposed" (Chesneaux 1971:8).

The Triad initiation ritual drew historical precedent from the dramatic story of a sworn brotherhood that led a successful dynastic rebellion. The social rebels celebrated in the *Romance of the Three Kingdoms* initiate their alliance against the ruling dynasty as follows:

> Together the three men went to Chang Fei's farm to talk further. Chang Fei proposed: "Behind the farm is a peach garden. The flowers are at their fullest. Tomorrow we must make offerings there to Heaven and Earth, declaring that we three join together as brothers, combining strength and purpose." To this Liu Bei and Guan Yu agreed.
>
> The next day they prepared their offerings, which included a black bull and a white horse. Amid burning incense the three men performed obeisance and spoke their vow. . . .
>
> The oath sworn, Liu Bei became the eldest brother, Guan Yu the second, and Chang Fei the youngest. When the sacrificial ceremony was concluded,

they butchered the bull and spread forth the wine, gathering three hundred youths in the peach garden, where they drank themselves to sleep. (Lo 1976:7–9)

In traditional Triad ritual, allusion is made to this event, as for example in the following prayer, which is part of the initiation ceremony:

We pray and beseech the Gods of Heaven and Earth, and more especially Liu Bei, Guan Yu and Chang Fei, who formerly pledged fraternity in a peach garden. We will obey heaven and act righteously in order to overturn Qing and restore Ming; our faithful hearts will not alter and we will never change. (Ward and Stirling 1977, 1:61)

Guan Yu, deified as the God of War and Commerce, is a patron deity for Triad members, one who frequently possesses spirit mediums in contemporary Penang, performing martial arts feats and occasionally engaging in magical healing.

Let me turn now to consideration of a contemporary historical myth that in my estimation is linked allusively with the Triad foundation myth recounted above. One of several communitywide festivals in Penang is worship of the Lord of Heaven on the ninth day of the first lunar month. The Penang Hokkien Chinese offer distinctive worship to the Lord of Heaven on the evening of that day by setting up a three-level altar in front of their residence or business, an altar decorated with tall stalks of sugar cane. In so doing they perform a ritual that historically was the prerogative of the emperor, who represented all Chinese people as their high priest. This ritual image of community wholeness is thus at the same time a communal declaration of its direct reliance on Heaven (rather than on the intercession of the emperor) for deliverance from their enemies.

I collected two versions of this historical myth, the first told me by a temple committee member who at one time had been a spirit medium:

In the old days the people were praying to all sorts of deities. The minister of the emperor thought of an innovation. There was an emperor on earth, so there must be one in Heaven. He suggested that they must start praying to him with a tall table. All the other emperors followed him in doing so.

In the Hokkien community the province was raided and there was no place to go. The people ran to a sugar cane plantation and prayed to heaven for their lives to be saved. On the ninth day of the first lunar month the enemy passed by without discovering them. Now there is a thanksgiving ceremony on this day.

Another spirit medium in telling me this historical myth added that "the Jade Emperor had greater power than the emperor: it was he who saved them."

Another version of this narrative was performed by a spirit medium in trance, possessed by the god entitled "The Elevated Venerable Gentleman" (Mandarin: Tai Shang Lao Jun). Tai Shang Lao Jun is in fact none other than Lao Tse, the author of the classic philosophical work the *Dao de jing*. The story was delivered dramatically, in the style of a Chinese opera performance:

> *This is a story from China, this is from Chinese history. When the Golden Horde came to China, they were very fierce, they were very bad. They had no learning, and they were uncivilized. They feared nothing. When they came, they were very cruel. When they came, the Hokkien had no strength with which to combat them. So the people tried to run. There were battles too in Amoy, in the Eastern Mountain [Fujian], do you understand? The Golden Horde came and fought in Amoy, soldiers came, and when they came the people of Amoy refused to mix with them, so the soldiers fought to kill them. It was difficult to evade them.*
>
> *The people of Amoy retreated to this place, their misfortune was great, how to find a way? They came to a river next to a sugar cane estate. The story says that at this place there was a monk following the* dao. *The people found him there in his meditation hut, but there was no space to hide there. Even if they hid in the temple, there was no protection. So this person, who was like a Lohan [a Buddhist deity] chanted a long chant; he chanted and transformed the fields into tall sugar cane.*
>
> *The soldiers came to the temple, but seeing that there was no place to hide there they left. When they left, the people returned to thank the monk and to pay their respects to him in the temple. They found that the meditation hut had vanished, and knew then that the hermit was extraordinary, a heavenly king. So when the people gave thanksgiving for having been saved, they put up an altar with sugar cane. It has come to us like that. Do you have any other questions? Tai Shang can explain for you.*

In all versions, Hokkien worship of the Lord of Heaven originates in a dramatic act of divine deliverance from their enemies.

According to C. K. Yang, in the Qing dynasty (A.D. 1644–1911) the state had declared "a strict monopoly over the performance of rituals in the worship of Heaven, thus keeping others from sharing the same privilege" (1961:183). In practice of course this regulation was difficult to enforce. This prerogative was appropriated from the emperor by the Hokkien Chinese when they directly offered their allegiance to the Heavenly King who rescued them in their time of need (DeBernardi 1986:64–66).

The ritual process of overseas Chinese is, in contrast to Thai royal rituals (Tambiah 1976) or the Balinese theater state (Geertz 1980), not the exclusive property of a royal elite enacting its distinction to an audience of the less privileged. However, in the invention of community in the overseas context, popular religious culture has appropriated indices of power and ritual forms that were once the property of an imperial elite and that now confer authority on a community and its leadership. Ritual performances derive weight from connection to a Chinese past, a past made present in the ritual/narrative performance of historical myths (DeBernardi forthcoming).

The Triad historical myth was long regarded as a statement of political resistance, even while Triad groups were known to have no active political agenda. It is perhaps more accurate to view these historical myths as statements of political autonomy and the groups formed as societies that made claims to authority through rituals performed in a symbolic space that placed these groups and their leaders (rather than the emperor and his scholar-bureaucrats) at the center, mediating between heaven and earth. In so doing these groups also represent their wholeness, for in Chinese popular religious culture totality is represented by the conjunction of heaven, earth, and man, the "triad" of forces that gives the Triad (or "Heaven and Earth Society") its name (DeGroot 1977 [1866]:8–10).

Both Triad initiation ceremonies and worship of the Lord of Heaven involve the symbolic appropriation of the prerogatives of an absent China. In nineteenth-century Malaya dislocated Chinese immigrants lacked both the oppressive authority and the protective jurisdiction of China, but they recreated its moral boundaries in a new land. In contemporary Penang disaffection with the Chinese state (and a long moribund dynasty) is no longer the issue, but rather knowledge of a common history and awareness of shared identity. For contemporary Malaysian Hokkien Chinese this awareness is generated by the shared myth-history of salvation by heavenly intervention and by the simultaneous performance of the ritual of worship of the Lord of Heaven by all members of this dialect group on the ninth night of the lunar calendar.

Spiritual Conflict: The British and the Goddess of Mercy

While the worship of Heaven and its associated myth-history constructs a sense of community wholeness, other ritual practices and myth-histo-

ries interpret disorder through a symbolism of spiritual division and conflict. A striking use of religious symbolism to represent intercommunal
rivalry may be found in an account of a geomantic battle between Chinese and the former British colonial rulers, which was offered as a comment on the complexities of my situation as a researcher. This historical
myth was told in the course of an evening at a spirit medium temple,
recounted to me by the god possessing the spirit medium, whose words
were reinterpreted by the temple committee members present.[11]

The spirit medium was possessed by the Vagabond Buddha, Ji Gong, a
trickster figure known for his quick wit (DeBernardi 1987a). This temple
associated itself with the Triad tradition in its ritual practice and was
unquestionably a "black" or "secret" society. I offer a synoptic account of
the event.

> Vagabond Buddha: *Heaven and earth's clouds have seven layers.*
> *Some people say that man went to the moon, but it is not true. Man*
> *only went to the outside.*
>   *All gods are true. At some temples that you've been to, people*
> *don't want to talk to you because they are afraid that you are a*
> *Christian. You've been to many temples now. Is this true?* [I assent.]
>   *Man can break the law of earth. The British were good at this,*
> *and they sought to destroy the geomantic balance of the Chinese.*
> *The stone lions at the Goddess of Mercy (Kuan Yin) temple used to*
> *dance.*
> Interpreters: *Under British rule, the Chinese were very prosperous*
> *and controlled the entrepôt trade. The geomancy of the Goddess of*
> *Mercy temple of Pitt Street helped the Chinese, and people like Yeap*
> *Chor Ee [a Chinese millionaire] would go to the Goddess of Mercy*
> *and pray to her before speculating on sugar, and he would always*
> *profit. The British were very jealous and tried many ways to combat*
> *the Chinese. So the British consulted their own spirit medium and*
> *tried to find a way to destroy the prosperity of the Chinese, to make*
> *it so that when the Goddess of Mercy spoke, she wouldn't speak the*
> *truth, she would give false answers when the businessmen went to*
> *ask.*
> Vagabond Buddha: *So the British dug a well in the temple and*
> *installed a clock to block the view of the Goddess of Mercy so that*
> *she could not see clearly. But instead of blocking the Goddess of*
> *Mercy they killed the two lions. In the old days, the lions would*
> *dance at night, they would run down to the seaside and drink water.*
> *But now they are dead, they can no longer dance. The Goddess of*
> *Mercy took care of the clock. It has four sides, and the angle facing*

the Goddess of Mercy always breaks down. It has been repaired
numerous times, but it never strikes correctly at twelve. It always
strikes before or after.

Chinese-British relations in British Malaya have sometimes been described as a war of competing colonialisms; here they are given image
as a war of competing geomancies, and economic rivalry is transposed to
the realm of spiritual battle.

This retelling of an event in Penang's myth-history epitomizes the British as jealous rivals who launch a disruptive attack on heaven (the tall
clock) and earth (the well), the very forces that Chinese ritual practice
(including the ritual practice of the Triad) seeks to harmonize. The
attack on Chinese geomantic forces is neutralized by the Goddess of
Mercy, but some harm is sustained. Still, the outcome of the attack suggests that Chinese spiritual power, represented by the Goddess of Mercy,
is higher than that of the British.

In the narrative context of its retelling, this historical myth has further
implications. The Vagabond Buddha offered the story to me as an explanation of why people at certain temples would not share information
with me: "People don't want to talk to you because they are afraid that
you are Christian." This historical myth both epitomizes in vivid images
the conflict and rivalry between British and Chinese and provides a basis
and explanation for mistrust of the Christian "other," a mistrust extended
to the ethnographic "other" intent on studying Chinese popular religious
culture.

The story of the stone lions is as well a narrative of place, and this too
enters into the social construction of shared identity. The story derives
impact from a temple setting that is a potent symbol of community; at
the same time the narrative adds to that image of potency. In contemporary Penang the Goddess of Mercy is a key symbol of community for the
Penang Chinese, and the Goddess of Mercy Temple (of which this myth-
history is told) is widely known and widely attended. When a new Chinese "Town Hall" was built in the early 1980s, the newest community
center was situated beside this temple, which is perhaps the oldest. And
in a recent geomantic battle the Chinese community responded to the
construction of a state mosque in Penang by developing a plan to build a
huge statue of the Goddess of Mercy, taller than the new state mosque,
beside a major Mahāyāna Buddhist temple. This controversial move was
politically opposed by those who interpreted the imposing statue as a
challenge to the Muslim population, but the builders proceeded and the
project was completed (though in a compromise the statue was not as tall
as originally planned).

Datuk Worship and Chinese-Malay Relations: The Trishaw Rider and the Red *Datuk*

The story of the stone lions gives vivid form to the interethnic rivalry of British and Chinese in colonial Malaya but has no contemporary ritual counterpart. By contrast, Malay ethnicity is given a more thorough interpretation in Chinese popular religion in Penang. In the trance performance in particular, the impersonation of Chinese gods and Malay spirits dramatically expresses cultural stereotypes of Chinese and Malay, male and female, old and young.

In its most basic form spiritual conflict enters into the explanation of illness. Spirit mediums are consulted when illness or anxiety besets an individual and recovery does not follow a normal course. In such cases it is suspected that the ill person has "collided with" or "offended" a spirit. Often the spirit is a *datuk*,[12] a spirit resident in a tree or rock, usually conceived of as ethnically Malay. Other times the person is judged to be the target of black magic. The cure in either case is to invoke more highly placed spirits to mediate on behalf of the afflicted individual.

Worship of Malay *datuk* spirits is a common practice among Penang Chinese, reflecting Southeast Asian influence. The practice is derived from the Malay worship of *keramat*, sacred places or persons (Winstedt 1977 [1924]). *Datuk* spirits include both nature spirits—snake, crocodile, wind—and deified spirits of the dead. Some are dangerous and unforgiving spirits, others are benevolent and helpful. These spirits, some resembling Chinese earth gods who are territorial protectors, are imagined as ethnically Malay and offered Malay foods (never pork), fruit, flowers, and camphor incense. According to one spirit medium, Muslim Malays no longer worship these spirits, so instead they help the Chinese, who honor them with offerings and acts of respect.

In worshiping *datuk* spirits the Chinese show awareness of cultural characteristics that distinguish Malays—costume, diet, Islamic religious practice, black magic, musical forms—even though certain of those practices, in particular costume and cuisine, have been adopted by Chinese and thus do not serve to maintain ethnic boundaries in everyday life. Exceptions include the practice of Islam and especially the Muslim prohibition on eating pork, a key boundary maintainer.

Datuk spirits play a role in the explanation and cure for certain afflictions. As mentioned previously, they are said to cause ailments and disturbances that fall under the general category of spiritual collisions, *qiong diok* in Hokkien. This means "to collide with," and it is compared with human interactions in which a social error causes someone to be angry and take offense. Since *datuk* spirits are everywhere, precautions against incurring their wrath must be taken. For example, children are taught to make the act of respect with their hands representing a *kowtow* after they have urinated outside. However, it is not hard to offend a *datuk* inadvertently, and the consequences can be severe. A nine-year-old child who retrieved a kite from a tree fell ill and died soon afterward. The interpretation was that he had offended a *datuk* spirit living in the tree and that the spirit had taken revenge.

Chinese Malaysians also consult *datuk* spirits, usually through a spirit medium, to undo the effects of Malay black magic, a function that *datuk* spirit mediums in Penang share with Thai Buddhist monks. Two sorts of black magic were ascribed to Malays: magic intended to do physical harm and love magic. In these practices, as in the historical narratives, interethnic tensions are given supernatural expression. Thus a woman spirit medium expert in dealing with *datuk* commented that "Malays use charms to hurt people. They give them things to eat . . . these charms are called black magic" (Hokkien: *gong tau*) (see Gimlette 1975 [1915]). She also observed that Malays were notorious for working love magic: "You can tell that someone has cast a spell over you, or your friends can tell, if you are giving many things to a person, go to seek them out often, or think about them often." To remedy such afflictions, Chinese Malaysians approach a *datuk* spirit rather than a Chinese god.

Paradoxically, Chinese ghosts are occasionally worshiped as *datuk* spirits. The situation of one such *datuk* is an illuminating commentary on Chinese-Malay relations. In this account, told to me by the Datuk Aunt, the paradoxes inherent in such worship are explored:

> *A long time ago, in the period of the Japanese occupation, there was a man named A-Qeng, a trishaw peddler. He used to ride his trishaw to Tanjong Bungah to eat pork dumplings, and there he was killed by a Japanese bomb and became a* datuk *spirit. He then "lived" in Tanjong Bungah, in a tree behind the house of So Ju Deng [a rich Chinese]. He's there because he died there, and now his spirit resides together with the Red Datuk.*

The Datuk Aunt visits a spirit medium at the Tai Shang Lao Jun temple, a medium who was normally possessed by the Snake Datuk. But this time A-Qeng enters his body.

> *A-Qeng said to the medium: "Don't you remember me? We used to eat pork dumplings together, at the same coffee shop! We used to eat together, in a thatch-roofed coffee shop in Tanjong Bungah. I know that things are hard for you now, so I've come."*
> *The medium asked, "Can you help me? Can you give me something?"*

*And A-Qeng, who was China-born, said, "Wei! (Sure!). I'll write
a number for you," and he gave him lottery numbers to sell. Then
the medium asked him what he wanted in exchange. "I want to eat
pork dumplings," he replied. So he was given pork dumplings to eat.
But after he had eaten them, he had to rinse his mouth. "Otherwise,"
he said, "the Red Datuk will scold me and press me into the mud."*

Chinese believe that if people are deprived of their normal life span,
then they must stay at the place of accidental or violent death until their
preordained day of death arrives or until they can capture another spirit
to replace them. This situation, however, is unusual. A-Qeng, rather
than being placated as a Chinese ghost might be, is regarded as a *datuk*
spirit.

The story is a rather neat parable for Malay-Chinese relations. A-
Qeng died a violent death on Malaysian soil, at the hand of an enemy
common to Malays and Chinese alike. Because of his death in Malaysia,
he becomes, in a way, integrated with his adopted territory. In death as in
life, he is side by side with the Muslim Malay, and in his new residence
with the Red Datuk he must abide by Islamic law to avoid offending his
neighbor. But he retains a sense of his Chinese identity, a fact revealed by
his linguistic habits (use of *wei*, which marks him as China-born) and his
craving for pork.

Worship of *datuk* spirits by Chinese is a way to express respect for
their adopted homeland and its residents, natural and human, as well as
their own sense of difference from and sameness with Malays. At the
same time the presence of Chinese *datuk* spirits is symbolic evidence that
the Chinese community considers itself rooted to Malaysian soil.

The assumption that the Chinese form of worship can be extended to
deal with spirits found in Malaysia, who are treated as if they were
Malays, is an assumption of human commonality and of the universality
of the distinctions made by Chinese among varieties of gods, ghosts, and
ancestors. It also includes an implicit assumption that harmonious social
relations can be assured if one knows the proper gestures of respect for a
person or spirit, and this involves knowledge of their culture. Lack of
harmony can be attributed to inadvertent neglect of the rules for polite
interaction or to ignorance of the rules governing the behavior of the persons or spirits in question. As Ahern has pointed out in her study of Chinese popular religion in Taiwan, "interpersonal ritual . . . often utilizes
whatever ways of acting people see as most effective in controlling other
people in everyday life" (1981a:16), often taking its logic from the political sphere. In the worship of Malay *datuk* spirits, the spiritual world
clearly provides a model for dealing with different sorts of human beings.

Conclusions

In the Penang Hokkien community, heaven—the symbol of wholeness and unity—is celebrated in a ritual commemorating the historic unity of the Hokkien Chinese. By contrast, a symbolism of division and conflict, which explains disorder and misfortune, is realized in ethnic terms. Social differences are inventoried and encapsulated in historical myths that imagine the Hokkien Chinese in relation to the ethnic "other." The associated images—of heaven, of the lions at the Goddess of Mercy temples, of the Chinese trishaw rider who must live with the Muslim Malay —lend image to political attitudes. These images, infused with meaning, stand as potent figures of community identity and distinctiveness in opposition to the ethnic and political "other."

Once these images have been lent weight through ritual reenactment or narrative performance, they stand as condensed images of complex ideas and attitudes. The allusive mention of story titles, historic persons, or events may then replace full narration in ordinary discourse, in an expressive, epitomizing conversational poetics. For example, the week after the Vagabond Buddha taught me the story of the stone lions at the Goddess of Mercy Temple, I interviewed an English-educated Chinese Malaysian teacher who was well known as a numerologist. In response to a question about the patron deity of an important temple, he began to recount a story, then abruptly said, "The lions at the Goddess of Mercy Temple used to dance," and changed the subject. This time the story was not told; rather he alluded to the stone lions to remind himself of the spiritual rivalry and enmity between Chinese and Europeans and refused me the knowledge that I sought.

The use of historical myths and allusion in discourse resembles the Apache moral narratives described by Basso. There, didactic stories used to criticize delinquent individuals are linked to named locations in the physical landscape. After the story has been told, the landscape itself serves the guilty party as a reminder of the breach of moral values, and "mountains and arroyos step in symbolically for grandmothers and uncles" (Basso 1984:43).

Chinese sites may similarly "step in symbolically" to invoke a defensive political stance. An example is the use of temple space to conduct a political rally in 1987 and the government's response to this rally. The political issue was the government's appointment of teachers whose primary training was in the Malay language as administrators to Chinese-medium schools. This event precipitated protest from the Chinese community, interracial tension, and finally a strong government backlash. According to an article in the *Bangkok Post*:

> What got the authorities upset was the meeting held early in October at the Tian Hou [Queen of Heaven] temple in Kuala Lumpur, attended by representatives of Chinese guilds and associations, political parties in the government and opposition, and interested parties to draw up a plan of action. Why, asked the Prime Minister, Datuk Seri Mahathir Mohamed, was it necessary for them to meet at a temple?
>
> Parallels were drawn by the Chinese community to the meeting of the Buddhist monks at Shaolin temples in China in the 17th century that paved the way for the overthrow of the Ming [sic] Dynasty. Groups met to consider a shutdown of Chinese businesses before the November 1 rally, later banned, and the concerted action planned could only have made the outlook more tense than it was. (Pillai 1987)

Comparison of the planned shutdown with the gathering of monks at Shaolin temple to overthrow a dynasty is an indisputable allusion to the Triad tradition of secret society–led political resistance. And Mahathir's question—Why was the meeting held in a temple?—was entirely appropriate. Soon after this meeting, the government acted to "defuse racial tensions" by arresting politicians, closing three newspapers, and banning public rallies.[13]

The Hokkien use of popular religious symbolic media to formulate and express political attitudes has deep historical roots. For example, *The Romance of the Three Kingdoms*, a classic Chinese novel which recounts the overturn of a dynasty by social rebels, is steeped in such an idiom. Moss Roberts comments on the classical charter for rebellion presented in that novel: "The retributive power of the people is rarely manifested overtly in feudal China; it is shown through charms, cures, jingles, omens, and the like. However potent, mass sentiment is largely latent and may manifest itself as a supernatural force" (Roberts in Lo 1976: xxiv). The religious "dramas" improvised by Chinese spirit mediums, such as the story of Kuan Yin and the stone lions or the dramatization of the trishaw rider's discomfort in living with the Muslim Malay, can be regarded as attempts to formulate and influence mass sentiment, using a supernatural idiom, to pass judgment on the human moral world.

But why is "mass sentiment" expressed in this covert and allusive fashion? Answers might be found in political climates that discourage dissent and rules for social interaction that discourage direct confrontation of social superiors. In normal social interaction, Chinese "give face" to elders and figures of authority by not challenging their authority directly; they seek instead indirect means to express dissent and criticism (DeBernardi 1987b). Metaphor, allegory, and myth may be used to construct social commentaries that are nonconfrontational and indirect, incomplete until the hearer draws out their implicit meanings. Moreover, these artful forms of framing social commentary are frequently more memorable than blunt statements of fact. Fernandez points out that the politician who labels his opponent a "jellyfish" will find his words remembered far longer than one who criticizes his opponent for "caring too much for his self-image" (Fernandez 1986:9). If the metaphor is also a religious symbol—the Goddess of Mercy, the God of War—it is likely to be a powerful magnet for sentiment.

I have considered the historical myths as a form of conversational rhetoric, but they are at the same time a form of historical thought. Chinese popular religious culture transmits in ritual practice and historical myth the memory of past experience, and narration renews a sense of participation in an invisible community uniting past and present. As Valeri observes: "In the end, by allowing a society to communicate with its image in time triumphing over time, its history (which includes its defining rules and their effects) constitutes that society and makes it endure" (1990:162). This use of history is culturally ordered (Kelly and Kaplan 1990; Sahlins 1985): as a form of historical thought, Penang Chinese historical myths are continuous with the classical historical chronicles and popular historical novels of China, edifying tales that taught (and still teach) the lessons of the past (Granet 1959 [1926], 1:200–216; Owen 1986).

At the same time the events of the historical myths demonstrate that culture is historically made. These narratives tell of the Hokkien experience of cruel barbarian invaders, an absent imperial bureaucracy, jealous colonial rule, and accommodation to the norms of Malay society. Chinese popular religious culture may draw an ethnic boundary in a multicultural society, but it also retells the events of a local history deeply rooted in that society. In this mythic history interethnic and political battles are transposed to a spiritual plane. The Hokkien Chinese (or their spiritual allies) are not unequivocal victors in these encounters: the Hokkien people retreat from pursuing barbarian troops and are passively protected, the Goddess of Mercy cannot wholly protect her territory against the geomantic attack launched by the British, and Malay *datuk* spirits must be accommodated and placated. But in every case the spiritual realm provides allies in a world divided by interethnic conflict and rivalry, and the stories told take inventory of historical process and event, allowing the Penang Chinese to better know themselves.

NOTES

This chapter was first prepared as a paper for the conference "Communities in Question: Religion and Authority in East and Southeast Asia," sponsored by the Joint SSRC/ACLS Committees on Japan, Korea, Southeast Asia and China,

Hua Hin, Thailand, 4–9 May 1989. I have benefited from the comments of Jane Goodale, Christine Gray, Cornelia Kammerer, Raymond L. M. Lee, Victor Nee, and Joseph Russo, as well as from the editorial suggestions of Laurel Kendall, Charles Keyes, and an anonomyous reviewer for the University of Hawaii Press.

1. The research on which this article is based was funded by fellowships from Fulbright-Hays and the National Institute of Mental Health.

2. Many anthropologists have analyzed (and sometimes critiqued) uses of the past in the construction of national or political identities, including Anderson (1983a), Geertz (1973c), Gellner (1983), and Hobsbawm and Ranger (1983), who suggest the symbolic importance for new political units of forging links to the (sometimes invented) past.

3. Throughout this essay, I have taken the liberty of replacing diverse romanizations of Mandarin words with pinyin. However, I have left proper names in dialect in their conventional romanized forms.

4. Recent population statistics for Peninsular Malaysia report that Malays comprise approximately 56 percent of the population, Chinese, 35 percent, and Indians, 9 percent.

5. Western scholars follow the Chinese in describing the regional languages of China as "dialects"; however, as Ramsey points out, "they are as different from each other as French from Italian and, when taken together, are probably more complex than the whole Romance family" (1987:16).

6. Ahern (1981b) notes a similar phenomenon in Taiwan, where Hokkien and Hakka Chinese have been ruled by a Nationalist government dominated by mainlanders. Here, she suggests, Taiwanese resist the government-proposed simplification of the Thai Ti Kong Festival because "offering Ti Kong has become a vital marker of Taiwanese (Hokkien and Hakka together) ethnic identity" (1981b:423).

7. Penang Hokkien ritual practice in this respect closely resembles that of Taiwanese Hokkien, as described by Feuchtwang (1974), Jordan (1972), Sangren (1987), Weller (1987a), and Wolf (1974).

8. There is a rich secondary literature on the Malaysian Triad, written primarily by Western colonial officers and scholars (Blythe 1969; Schlegel 1956 [1866]; Stanton 1899; Ward and Stirling 1977 [1925]; Wynne 1941).

9. While the terms have changed, this slang register may be compared with the "antilanguages" of concealment used by contemporary Chinese secret societies (DeBernardi 1987a).

10. According to some Chinese historians, the monks were anti-Manchu even before the war against the Eleuths and only joined that effort to infiltrate the imperial army. The burning of the monastery in this reconstruction is explained as a result of the Manchu/Qing discovery of their conspiracy (Chesneaux 1971:16).

11. In the colonial period the Singapore and Penang Chinese communities, like the Hong Kong Chinese, disputed with the British over construction plans that threatened existing geomantic configurations (Yeoh 1991; cf. Freedman 1969). This historical myth may have had its source in conflicts that arose in Penang when plans were made to develop the land between the Kuan Yin temple and the sea.

12. The term *datuk* is borrowed from Malay, and literally means "grandfather, a senior." It is used in Malay as a title of respect; it also refers to the tutelary spirit of a sacred site or *keramat*.

13. A government White Paper investigating the causes that led the government to invoke the Internal Security Act lists as one threat to security the Democratic Action party leaders' allegations that "the Government practised a policy of one race, one language, and one religion aimed at making Malaysia an Islamic state," thus "eroding the status of the cultures of the other communities" (Kertas Perintah 1988:8).

6

Capitalism, Community, and the Rise of Amoral Cults in Taiwan

ROBERT P. WELLER

The Eighteen Kings temple at the northern tip of Taiwan comes as something of a shock to anyone familiar with Chinese popular religion. The temple has grown in the last decade from a simple roadside shrine for unidentified bones—the sort that sits unattended and almost unnoticed all over the countryside—to one of Taiwan's major temples. At its peak in the early 1980s it backed up traffic on the northern coastal highway for several kilometers, and it still attracts thousands of worshipers each week. While clearly within the traditions of popular worship, the temple inverts and even perverts much standard ritual procedure. The scale of its popularity alone is odd: such temples to unworshiped ghosts almost never grow large. Worshipers normally do not touch images of deities, but here they urgently stroke two large bronze dogs. Typically worship takes place during the day, but here it reaches a peak in the small hours of the morning. Nearly all other Chinese deities are honored with sticks of incense, but the Eighteen Kings prefer burning cigarettes. In spite of its apparently bizarre features, though, this is clearly not a new religion. It is instead a new proportioning of everyday religion, a reflection in a funhouse mirror that has magnified previously lowly, unworshiped ghosts to rival the gods themselves.

The transformation of the Eighteen Kings temple is a small part of a general development in Taiwanese religion closely related to changes in the nature of the Chinese state and economy. The recent flowering of the Eighteen Kings in Taiwan is a reminder of the way late imperial China's uncomfortable connections between bureaucracy and commerce were just as strong in religion. The new proportioning of religion today is less a structural break than a repositioning of values that had always been implied by some aspects of Chinese religious practice, even as they were being denied by others. The very existence of an avowedly amoral, individualistic, and grasping cult like this emphasizes a commercial and competitive side to Chinese religion, which is paired against the more bureaucratic and Confucian model that has generally been better described. "Amoral" here refers primarily to a popular perception that these deities do not care about normally accepted morality—they will grant immoral wishes as happily as moral wishes. While I am drawing in part on I. M. Lewis's discussion of "amoral marginal cults" in Africa (Lewis 1971), the term also encourages comparisons with the role of capitalism in transforming precapitalist moralities, often in ways perceived at the time as amoral. Such deities, for example, offer a strong initial resemblance to the more clearly immoral devil worship by miners and rural proletarians in Colombia and Bolivia that Michael Taussig (1980) has discussed. In his analysis, capitalist profit appears to make sense only as part of a pact with the devil. Some people, for instance, are said to baptize money instead of a baby (to the eternal damnation of the child); the fetishized cash continually steals more money, reaping the unearned profits of sin.

Both Taiwan and South America thus offer cases wherein a changing social formation has emphasized elements of traditional religious practice that resonate with the amoral and competitive aspects of capitalism. Taussig sees this primarily as a protest against the capitalist exchange-value economy pushing out earlier values of reciprocity based on a use-value economy. His analysis helps clarify one facet of capitalist economic experience in Taiwan—the competition, greed, and lack of community values as imagined in ghosts. Yet his explanation will not work fully in Taiwan (and may be arguable in the Latin American cases as well); Taiwan before 1970 was in no sense a use-value economy. In addition, other sides of Taiwanese religious behavior, even of these ghosts, clearly celebrate the free-for-all economy. The relation between religion and economy is more complex than just an anachronistic protest against new kinds of social relations.

This essay will also discuss how the current boom in such religion is related to the inability of the modern secular state to influence religious values, let alone supply alternative value systems of its own. In contrast to Weberian predictions of the death of religion in the modern state, recent changes in Taiwan have allowed a blossoming of religious values. These have responded better to changing identities than to any conscious effort of the government. The coincidence of the timing with Taiwan's economic boom and the emphasis on avowedly amoral and individualistic goals clarify the close ties between these specific religious practices and the rapid development of small-scale entrepreneurial capitalism in Taiwan. This new proportioning of religion has both reflected and affected the questioning of identity that has accompanied Taiwan's dramatic political and economic transformation of the last decade.

Dollars, Death, and Dogs

The Eighteen Kings play a wild variation on the standard themes of popular religion. Popular worship typically centers on two primary categories of beings: gods and ancestors. From neighborhood earth gods to the patron gods of whole districts, gods protect community interests, and the community takes responsibility for their temples and major rituals. Ancestors define the world of family and lineage. Finally, there is a residual category of beings who fall between categories: ghosts. Ghosts, in the most broad sense, are simply dead souls (as are gods and ancestors), but the term refers particularly to the dead who live in loneliness and hunger because no one will worship them. This happens particularly to people who die before marriage, die by suicide, or die unbeknownst to their relatives. Ghosts can sometimes become gods (through promotion) or ancestors (through spirit marriage with the living), but they generally remain in a liminal category à la Mary Douglas (1966)—ill-defined and dangerous (see Weller 1987a:65–66; Yu 1988). In the Durkheimian terms that characterize most of the literature and fit the data very neatly, gods are bureaucrats; ancestors are kinsmen; and ghosts are beggars, bandits, and strangers, who fall into no proper social category. The latter are asocial and individual (Wolf 1974).

Ghosts receive offerings in several contexts. Occasionally, a specific ghost may command worship because it is making someone ill. More usually, people worship ghosts as a generic and anonymous group in rituals conducted by large temples during the seventh lunar month (see Weller 1987a). In these rituals the temple hires priests to provide spiritual alms on behalf of the community for these pitiful beings, a form of ghost welfare. Ghosts often have tiny temples of their own, at which they receive offerings during the annual ghost ritual or when supplicants have specific requests. Such temples typically originate when people discover unidentified bones or bodies—during road construction or on a battlefield, for example. They build a small shrine to house the bones. As a rule these shrines are comparatively tiny; the largest might hold half a dozen adults, and many more are too small for humans to enter. No committee or individual takes responsibility for them (unlike the elaborate arrangements that run god temples), although communities or individuals may occasionally repair a deteriorated ghost temple. The temples contain no images of ghosts, but usually just a gravestone and an incense pot. Many invoke the Earth God (Hokien, Tho-te Kong; Mandarin, Tudigong), among whose responsibilities is protecting the living from the dead.

Ghosts are much weaker beings than gods, and most people thus prefer to make their requests at temples to gods. Yet gods generally behave as upright and moral beings, in spite of the "spirit money" (cheap paper burned to serve as money in the supernatural world) they require. There are entire categories of requests that they will not even consider. Most gods will not help gamblers or people with illegitimate business requests like prostitutes and gangsters. Ghosts, on the other hand, are desperate.

They will grant any request at all, and their temples typically sport banners reading *iu kiu pit ieng* (all requests shall be answered). They are usually referred to as *Iu Ieng Kong* temples, a shortened form of the slogan, meaning Lord Who Grants All Requests. Although many sorts of people might occasionally worship at these temples, they are considered the special arena of the lower strata of society, whom the ghosts are especially willing to help, and whose lives the ghosts also reflect most closely. There are probably thousands of such temples in Taiwan, although their small size and lack of organization make a census of them impossible. They rarely develop beyond the level at which they begin—small roadside shrines that see only an occasional supplicant.

The Eighteen Kings

Until recently, the Eighteen Kings temple was exactly such a minor ghost shrine. Typical of such temples, there are no historical records of its beginnings. Its current popularity has further led to a burgeoning of competing origin stories. Everyone agrees, however, on certain basic features of the story. The temple is situated at the northernmost tip of Taiwan, a coastal fishing area. At some point, probably about a century ago (but in the seventeenth century according to one version), a fishing boat washed ashore. The boat was badly battered, suggesting storm and disaster in the Taiwan Strait. It contained the dead bodies of seventeen men, along with a dog that had somehow remained alive. The local fishermen who found the boat had no way of identifying the bodies; the wreck may have been blown over from the mainland. The fishermen proceeded as one normally proceeds in such cases in Taiwan: they buried the bodies in a common grave on a cliff overlooking the shore, thus creating a new and quite typical ghost temple. The dog, however, makes this story a little different from most others. This dog was outstandingly steadfast and loyal to its masters. According to some versions, it insisted on jumping into the grave with the bodies, until the people finally buried it alive. According to others, it starved itself to death in front of the new grave and was finally buried along with the men. The dog is thus the eighteenth of the Eighteen Kings.

Informants in the area remember the shrine from the 1950s and 1960s as a simple gravestone and incense pot. The grave itself was so old and unkempt that it had lost its characteristic rounded form and was just a bit of flattened earth. Soldiers on coast guard duty occasionally worshiped there, and an old woman (now rumored to have made a fortune from the temple) swept up once in a while. Even by the low standards of a ghost shrine, the Eighteen Kings temple was not very important or active.

The transformation of the temple began in the early 1970s, when Taiwan began construction of a nuclear power plant near the grave. Construction of the plant required shoring up the cliff overlooking the sea, and in the process the Eighteen Kings shrine was to be buried. Because construction in Taiwan frequently turns up old bones, construction sites are known to suffer from problems caused by ghosts, and construction workers regularly make offerings to appease them. This construction site was no exception. According to informants today, an unusually high number of "accidental" injuries and even a few deaths occurred. The most alarming event, in current versions of the story, came when the crane, looming just over the shrine, on the verge of destroying it, inexplicably froze. The large number of accidents and the crane problem finally brought construction to a halt. Workers and local inhabitants wanted the temple saved; the government wanted its power plant finished quickly.

In the end the government and project managers decided to "respect local customs" by rebuilding the temple. The original grave was fixed up and preserved in a small underground chamber, while a large temple was built directly above it, on the new higher ground level. The rebuilt temple contains an exact replica of the underground grave, directly above it, plus an additional wing with wooden images of the Eighteen Kings. Rebuilding the temple marked the transformation of the Eighteen Kings —both a physical transformation into an inordinately large ghost temple and a spiritual transformation into a group of beings with unusual efficacy. They had, after all, made the government itself do their bidding. Just as important, they did this in front of thousands of workers who came from all over the island and thus set the stage for unprecedented growth in popularity.

The rebuilt temple that resulted contains a number of odd features stemming from its ghostly origins, the peculiarities of its reconstruction, and the creative promotion of the weird by its worshipers. The temple is many times the size of an ordinary ghost shrine but retains the basic iconographic markers of such shrines. In particular, it lacks the curved eaves and decorated roof that enliven even a lowly god temple (or a magistrate's residence in imperial times). Nor is it worthy of door gods, or even real doors. People sometimes call these shrines "three wall temples" because they have no front wall. Most importantly, the grave itself remains a critical site for worship. Yet the temple has also taken over one of the most important elements of god worship—the use of wooden images of the deities. The higher-ranking stage in the left half of the temple has an altar arrangement typical of a god temple. The god images sit at the far wall, fronted by an altar table and two incense pots. The only reminder of their ghostly nature in this section of the temple is an extra god. The sharp-eyed (but probably no one else) notice that images of the expected seventeen men and one dog are accompanied by one extra image. This is Tho-te Kong, who is there to keep the ghosts in line.

The god imagery emphasizes that these are extraordinarily powerful ghosts, but the temple is not trying to disguise its ghostly origins. In addition to the ghostly temple construction, the artificial grave itself, built over the original site, dominates the stage at the right side of the temple. This fake grave is at least as important a center of worship as the god altar. Enthusiasts of the temple, however, insist that the most powerful portion is the original grave, now in a basement room. Supplicants enter the room by a dark staircase at the back of the building. Although most people seem to know about it, there is a happy fiction that the underground chamber is something of a secret and that only the real insiders know this esoteric place of power. In the eyes of its patrons, the chamber is a bizarre and unique feature of this temple, a case wherein the necessities of reconstruction have reinforced the weirdness of ghosts. The original grave is directly below the fake grave and looks just like its copy, with the same mosaic-covered mound. The gravestone remains at the edge of the original cliff, but now faces a wall instead of the sea. What passes for an incense pot sits in the normal position just in front of the gravestone, but because of the peculiar construction of this temple—the gravestone was originally at the edge of the cliff and thus now abuts a wall—the incense pot is now crammed between wall and grave, and worshipers can only approach it by squatting or crawling in the dirt and leaning over the grave. This is by no means a respectful posture, as when pilgrims approach a god temple on their knees. It is instead an awkward and dirtying movement that seems appropriate to making apparently immoral, or at least amoral, requests to a dog and some unidentified corpses under the ground. The contrast with normal offerings, even to ghosts, is striking. Even ghosts normally receive offerings above ground from standing supplicants.

The Eighteen Kings are especially efficacious at night, and worship reaches a peak in the small hours of the morning. Like worshiping on one's knees underground, this is an inversion of normal practice that emphasizes the contrast between the ghostly nature of the Eighteen Kings and the gods. Night is the period when ghosts are strongest, and their perceived amorality fits the general image of nighttime activities—sex, crime, gambling, and various illicit endeavors. Most normal ghost worship, however, takes place during the day. This is partly for convenience and partly for safety, since people usually prefer to avoid strong ghosts. The Eighteen Kings, however, are powerful enough that people want to approach them at their most awesome time. These approaches are dangerous, however. If the Eighteen Kings grant a request, they *must* be repaid (usually with donations to the temple), or disaster will ensue for all involved. A more mundane danger also characterizes the place at night and reinforces the overall image of the temple: it is known as a haven for pickpockets and purse snatchers, who come both to worship and to earn a living.

The centrality of the dog adds to the temple's atmosphere of disreputability. Although the dog is just one of many images on the altar, and the two life-sized bronze dogs that flank the fake grave do not have their own incense pots, dogs nevertheless are the center of much ritual attention. The table in front of the altar is filled with images (as in other temples) that people place there, but they are almost invariably little ceramic or metal dogs, not images of the human ghosts. The office at the side of the temple, which sells paraphernalia—charms, banners, books, even an Eighteen Kings movie soundtrack tape—specializes in cast dogs, and many of the banners feature dogs. Most striking, even shocking by the standards of most Chinese worship, is the treatment of the two bronze dogs by the grave. Avid worshipers rub various parts of the dogs' bodies to bring good fortune, and they rub protective amulets on the animals to empower the charms. Late at night, during the temple's peak hours, the dogs seem covered by a swarm of fondling hands as bodies crowd to get at the images.

People occasionally worship animal images in Taiwan, but this very physical, almost sexual stroking of the dogs is unusual. The very use of dogs, rather than the more common turtles (or foxes in other parts of China), is odd. While this particular dog is purported to be a simple allegory for loyalty, dogs in Taiwan are generally associated with unclean sexuality as much as with higher virtues. Seaman describes a story of a woman using a black dog fetus to poison a man, the use of "black dog blood" as a euphemism for menstrual blood (also an ingredient in magic charms), reference to ladies' men as black dogs, and destruction of a supposedly evil Black Dog Demon cult (Seaman 1981:392–394). The combination of loyalty with sex and danger in the images of this dog further strengthens the underworld associations of the temple.

The act of worship itself reinforces the off-key atmosphere. Above ground, large incense pots waft clouds of smoke as they are filled with sticks of incense, typical of any major temple. Below ground, however, as supplicants crawl around to reach the awkwardly placed "incense" pot, they do not place sticks of incense, but instead erect burning cigarettes by thrusting them into holes drilled in the concrete pot. This is a very unusual use of cigarettes in Taiwan, one I had never seen before. People sometimes offer whole packs of cigarettes at the annual ghost festival, but not as a substitute for incense. Cigarette smoking is widespread, especially among men, in Taiwan. Yet it is also viewed as it once was in the United States—a little bit wrong, and not really appropriate for women, children, or religious people. It would be very disrespectful to offer a cigarette to a god. The contrast between cigarette and incense again emphasizes the inversions that typify this temple and contrast the Eighteen Kings with gods.

People at the temple could not explain where the custom of using cigarettes came from, but it seems to be spreading. In the summer of 1988 I saw a similar use in a restaurant in the city of Tanshui in northern Taiwan. This restaurant had a small altar near its cash register, like many small businesses. One of the images on the altar was a statue of the Cloth-bag Monk (Budai Heshang). The Cloth-bag Monk, a fat, jolly character with a big bag draped over his shoulder, is a minor figure on many family and small business altars. The cloth bag is filled with presents and cash which, like Santa Claus, he hands out to little children. He strongly resembles popular images of Maitreya, the Buddha of the next age, and many people say he is in fact an incarnation of Maitreya. He is not normally an important object of worship in his own right, but he is the sort of symbol of easy wealth falling into one's lap that proprietors of small businesses in Taiwan like.[1] This particular image, however, with its chubby cheeks and big grin, had a burning cigarette hanging out of its mouth. Somehow the cigarette transformed the smiling, fat monk into a stereotypical sneering, overweight hoodlum. I have also heard of people who bring dog statues back from the Eighteen Kings temple and worship them by placing burning cigarettes in their mouths.[2] The tie between these two apparently divergent uses of tobacco, from eighteen dead bodies to the Buddha of the future, is the idea of easy money and the amorality of earning it. Both the Eighteen Kings and the Cloth-bag Monk can be seen as sources of unearned wealth, and the cigarettes are a reminder that unearned wealth tends to be not very moral wealth.

The alleged constituency of the temple again connects profit with a lack of morality. People describing the temple invariably point out how popular it is with gangsters, prostitutes, gamblers, and similar people. The pickpockets who frequent the temple are not just taking advantage of the big crowds; they are there to worship as well. This type of constituency is the standard group associated with ghost temples—the sort of people whose requests proper gods would ignore. Although this image fits the general atmosphere of the temple, it cannot be true in practice. There are simply far too many people at the temple to be limited to these underworld types. In addition, images and amulets from the temple adorn the altars and cars of a great many people in Taipei. It is clearly very popular with taxi drivers and other small businessmen who have legal sources of income. The temple management insists that people who come to ask questions of the gods represent a cross section of the population. The temple is thus frequented not so much by gangsters and gamblers as by ordinary people who are attracted to the sort of temple appropriate to the underworld. They see their own needs as best filled by a temple not too punctilious about issues of morality.

Related Cults

The Eighteen Kings temple is an extreme case, but it nevertheless grows out of a general pattern of religious resurgence that began in Taiwan about two decades ago. Statistically the watershed seems to have occurred in the early 1970s. This time is also significant as the beginning of Taiwan's period of stunning independent economic development. Government figures on numbers of popular temples are very unreliable; many temples do not register legally, and many others, especially small shrines to neighborhood earth gods or unworshiped ghosts, are too small to be picked up consistently by even a more determined census. Nevertheless, the statistical bias should be roughly consistent from one year to the next, and government figures show trends over time that should be reliable. After having decreased slowly over the years since the end of the Japanese occupation in 1945, both the absolute number of temples and the number of temples per capita increased significantly after about 1970. The numbers of registered temples grew from 2,930 in 1956 to 6,251 by 1980, an increase of approximately 113 percent. Temples per capita increased 18 percent over the same period, with a steep rise beginning around 1972 (Qu and Yao 1986:657).[3]

The popular religious tradition is not growing evenly, however. Certain features of it have expanded more than others. The primary growth areas in popular religion since about 1970 have been in the most individualistic portions of the cult, rather than in those that most emphasize family or community. The ancestor cult and major community god temples are holding their own, even increasing, but the striking growth has been in worship involving gods who are approached through spirit mediums or involving ghosts.

Spirit mediums *(tang-ki)* who provide advice and perform cures while possessed by various gods have long been popular in Taiwan. Some major community temples have spirit mediums attached to them, but most mediums work out of private, unregistered altars, usually in their homes. Most of the work of these mediums is utilitarian: they cure the sick, find lost objects, pronounce on the probable success of a business venture, and so on. They are not tied to the communal interests of major temples dedicated to gods. The potential for lucrative rewards from the great popular demand for spirit possession has led a number of mediums to leave community temples and open up their own altars, as well as creating the great increase in the number of the privately owned spirit medium temples (Li 1988:7–8).

At the same time more and more different gods are appearing on these private altars. Community temples usually feature one primary deity, often captured in many images. Other gods may appear on secondary altars or in minor positions on the main altar. The horde of different gods on private spirit medium altars—as many as forty or fifty different images—reinforces the utilitarian functions of such cults. With each deity having its own specialty, these temples can meet the needs of a wider variety of clients, just like a shop that expands its selection of wares (Li 1988:11–13).

Ghosts *(kui)* are the other major growth sector, and they are even more clearly tied to utilitarian and individualistic needs. Ghosts have always represented interests beyond the usual communal boundaries of family and neighborhood. As unworshiped deaths they have no broad social ties. If they did, someone would worship them, and they would not be ghosts. Desperate for worship, they will grant any wish in return for a bit of respect. The ritual offerings themselves individualize ghosts. For example, at the major annual ritual to propitiate ghosts, incense is offered in individual sticks thrust into food offerings; ghosts do not get the communal incense pots that honor gods and ancestors.[4] Spirit mediums and ghosts both reinforce a trend toward utilitarianism and individualism within the resurgence of Taiwanese popular religion (Li 1988).

The Eighteen Kings temple itself is just the latest in a series of like cults. At least three similar temples preceded the Eighteen Kings in popularity during the last twenty years. The others tended not to share the systematic inversions of the Eighteen Kings temple, but they all centered on the graves of ghosts and their willingness to grant disreputable requests. One temple honors a general named Li Yong, who was killed fighting aborigines during the nineteenth century. He is perhaps the least ghostly of the group, but still his violent death far from home marks a basic similarity to other ghosts. The second temple commemorates a sort of Robin Hood figure named Liao Tianding. Liao was a thief during the Japanese occupation who was very generous with the poor. The authorities could never find him, but he was finally murdered in his sleep by a brother-in-law who wanted the reward. The third temple houses the remains of a mainland soldier who robbed banks with great success and supposedly used the profits to support a friend's child. He was arrested and shot by a firing squad. All these temples honor figures who were beyond official control and who are willing to help people at the bottom of society. As ghosts, they are more flexible about honoring requests than are proper gods.

The growth and transformation of ghost shrines is not new. A number of temples that now appear as ordinary god temples began as ghost shrines, whose transformation stemmed from their reputations for great efficacy (Harrell 1974). As such temples succeed, their ghostly origins recede. The new development in ghost temples in the last two decades, however, differs in retaining strong ties to the world of ghosts. The graves are prominent, offerings are appropriate to ghosts, temple structure resembles an overgrown ghost shrine (no curving eaves, no door gods), and the beings worshiped are especially happy to honor the sorts of requests that gods would refuse to recognize. The critical change is that these temples insistently retain their ghostly appeal, not acceding to orthodox morality the way they must to become god temples.

While these ghost temples have grown disproportionately large and powerful in the last two decades, ghosts have also played a major role in an illegal lottery that has swept Taiwan in the last few years. The lottery has various versions, but people refer to it generically as "Everybody's Happy" *(dajia le)*. Everybody's Happy depended originally on Taiwan's national lottery, which chose three numbers to share the seventh (and last) prize. The odds against winning any of the prizes in the national lottery, as usual for such lotteries, were astronomical. In the original form of Everybody's Happy, people bet on the last two digits of the seventh-place prizes, and the odds of winning on a single bet could thus be as high as three in one hundred. Anyone could organize a betting pool by photocopying sheets of paper with boxes numbered 00 to 99 and taking one bet per number. The amount of the bet varied with the pool and could range from a few dollars to very large sums. When enough bets were placed (usually when at least fifty of the numbers had been taken), the pool was closed. If not enough bets were taken or if none of the numbers won, the organizer would return all the money; if one or more people bet on winners, the organizer would take a ten percent cut and divide the rest among the winners.[5] Bettors could join any number of pools and bet on more than one number within a pool. Organizers *(zutou)* could organize any number of pools. This led to the phenomenon of betting specialists; the largest caught was said to have more than seventeen million New Taiwan dollars on hand (more than half a million U.S. dollars).

The ease of organizing a pool and the lack of any centralized organization running it made Everybody's Happy almost impossible for the government to control. Officials tried altering the national lottery (and finally canceled it), but people always found new ways to play. Many games are now tied to the Hong Kong lottery; even tour buses play, using the last two digits of the license plate of a passing car. A 1987 police report (Jiang 1987:1) estimated that three million people were betting on the lottery. Bets were often very high, and one of the reasons for the interest was the excess of capital in Taiwan in the last few years with very few routes for investment. As labor costs have gone up, many people have been afraid to invest in new labor-intensive enterprises, yet they have had neither the resources for capital intensive industry nor the opportunity and knowledge to invest abroad. Combined with the great success of Taiwan's export economy, the result by the mid-1980s was unproductive use of capital—passive investments in land or stock for people who saw no plausible alternatives. The illegal lottery provided a similar form of investment, riskier but with a much greater profit for winners and far more fun than other investments.

Like any good investors, many players of Everybody's Happy tried to reduce their risk, in this case by getting an idea of the winning numbers in advance. Religion provided one of the most popular means for learning numbers. Numbers came from two types of sources: deities could give indirect hints about numbers (through patterns in incense smoke, for example), or they could communicate the numbers directly, often through spirit possession. As a rule, however, temples to more respectable deities would have nothing to do with such activities. Instead, people would ask ghosts or marginal deities who do not really fit the standard bureaucratic model, like the lowly earth god Taizi Ye (a small child turned god), Sun Wukong (popularized in the West as the mischievous Monkey), or Ji Gong (the meat- and alcohol-loving Buddhist monk) (Hu 1986). Small and large ghost shrines were even more involved, and there were close ties with ghostly death. People spent the night in graveyards hoping to be inspired by dreams; and according to widespread rumor at least, people went to traffic accidents to see what number the position of the bodies resembled or to get the numbers of the license plates. High community gods, on the other hand, would refuse to give such information or would give false numbers to punish people who asked. Only gods known for bucking the system, and especially ghosts, would cooperate with these requests for help in an illegal activity.

As a result privately run possession cults have increased, and larger ghost temples have experienced an economic boom.[6] Temples suggesting numbers would usually be ambiguous, offering up three or four digits that could be combined into nine to sixteen two-digit numbers. With each number having three chances to win, and more numbers generated by people watching incense smoke or candle drips, the odds of a temple's coming up with a winning number were very high. A temple that helped a winner would see more and more business come its way. In addition, winners had to repay the favor they were granted, especially if it was from ghosts. Ghosts grant requests only in return for payment, and winners had to present the temple with donations of cash or gold medals or arrange for outdoor opera performances, puppet shows, striptease shows, or movie showings in front of the temple. Some ghost temples had a ten- to twenty-day waiting list for puppet show performances (Hu 1986). Unsuccessful temples, in contrast, suffered serious consequences. Newspaper reports described smashed earth god images washing ashore at a river bend, apparently the result of angry revenge from disappointed worshipers (Hu 1986). As in the capitalist marketplace, there is a possibility of great gain or loss for both parties, and successful performance counts for more than traditional values or social ties.

Profit and Morality

The last twenty years in Taiwan have seen the increasing prominence of a set of ideas and ritual acts that encompass ghosts, dogs, cigarettes, private spirit mediums, and an illegal lottery. The themes that unite this set are a general perception of amorality, at most a kind of utilitarianism, and a narrowing of focus from family and community down to the individual and his or her private needs and desires.

This focus on individual profit over social ties of family and community stands in marked contrast to the perceived official morality of gods and ancestors. People may compare gods to officials, but they think of them as paragons of officialdom, far better than the petty and corrupt bureaucrats of late imperial (and, to an extent, modern) times. Ahern, for example, writes of many informants who compare gods to parents instead of officials, in spite of the obvious bureaucratic symbolism in the gods' dress, temples, and manner of worship. One person, for example, denying that offerings to the gods were like cash gifts to petty officials, argued that "offering things to the gods is just like taking a gift to one's host. A stranger won't necessarily help you no matter how nice a gift you bring, and a good friend will help even if you bring nothing at all." Another, making the same point, said, "It is only necessary to do good deeds and burn three sticks of incense and they will be enormously happy. A god is a being with a very upright heart. He is fair and just, rewarding without favoritism" (Ahern 1981a:99). The fee-for-service Eighteen Lords stand markedly against this image of traditional morality.

Dealings with ghosts need not be immoral in Chinese terms; one can make the same requests to ghosts as to gods. The difference is that the ghosts grant requests just for the economic reward, while the gods require accepted morality and are less mercenary about payment. The physical association of the Eighteen Kings temple with pickpockets, the rumored appeal of its ritual netherworld to the secular underworld, the dogs and their associations with black magic and sexuality, and even a fat Buddha with a cigarette hanging out of his mouth continually reemphasize the disreputable implications of the cult. It offers none of the appropriation of official state morality that is the mainstay of ordinary community god temples, nor does it offer to reclaim an earlier set of Confucian or Buddhist values like many of the new religions in Taiwan (see Jordan and Overmyer 1986). In addition, the cult serves only the needs of individuals. The very definition of ghosts rests on their existence apart from any normal social ties. Requests to this cult are thus uniformly individualistic: for profit in the lottery or in gambling or for success in business enterprises (not necessarily legal).

There is nothing startlingly new about profit-oriented and self-serving motives in Chinese religion. The proper morality of gods and ancestors has been the strongest current, both in Western studies and in much Chinese writing, from the imperial steles commemorating the promotion of morally strong gods to the pious texts read at ancestral halls. Yet the commodity- and individual-oriented undercurrent, relatively unconcerned with problems of morality, has always flowed beneath the surface. Hill Gates discusses the example of reimbursement of the celestial treasury, a funeral ritual that repays the loan of life with interest by burning piles of spirit money. This simulates the circulation of profit-making capital, treating life itself as a commodity (Gates 1987:266–274). Maurice Freedman provides a different kind of example: in the specialist system of geomancy, which includes siting graves for the benefit of offspring, one brother may manipulate the burial for his own benefit, even to the detriment of his other brothers. In this kind of geomancy "the accent is put upon the paramountcy of selfish interest, the subordination of forebears, and private action," while in ancestor worship it rests "on the supremacy of the common good, the dominance of ancestors, and collective behavior" (Freedman 1966:143).

While ghosts typically did not reach the glories of the Eighteen Kings, they also formed part of this undercurrent—asocial beings willing to enter into any bargain to improve their own position. The Eighteen Kings and related cults push us to take a more serious and systematic look at such features of late imperial religion. Here, however, I will instead address a more immediate problem: why has this undercurrent suddenly pushed to the surface in the Taiwan of the last two decades? I will argue that the answer lies both in the nature of state control over values and in the particulars of Taiwan's economic transformation.

Evil and the State

The recent growth in Taiwanese religion relates in part to the failure of the government or any other group to succeed in providing new values. The Weberian religious revolution, wherein new national, civic values would replace religion (e.g., Geertz 1973b; Bellah 1965:202–203), never took place in Taiwan. This has been especially true in the last few years, since the death of Jiang Jingguo (Chiang Ching-kuo).

The great success of economic development in Taiwan has particularly sharpened the problem of values: the capitalist market usually presents itself as an amoral phenomenon wherein commodities are qualitatively equated through money and have no ties to systems of social relations. Polanyi described this as the subjection of labor to the laws of the market, which was to "annihilate all organic forms of existence and to replace them by a different type of organization, an atomistic and individualistic one" (1944:163). Taussig's more recent description of Colombia describes similar changes, where "communality and mutuality give way to personal self-interest, and commodities, not persons, dominate social being" (1980:26). These critics of capitalism emphasize only one aspect of the capitalist transformation and to an extent idealize the communal harmonies of precapitalist social life. Yet they point to one of the most important transformations of the new economic system.

Many political leaders, from religious fundamentalists to environmentalists to neoconservatives, try to fight this perceived loss of communal values. Taiwan's Nationalist party government has been no exception, hoping to bolster its legitimacy and to make Taiwan a vault to preserve Chinese culture from communism. The media were tightly controlled, and critical voices generally treated as seditious. From the schools to the legislature, one heard attempts to enforce a value system of filial piety writ large, a system in which the proper respect of children for parents and wives for husbands paralleled a filial respect of citizens for the state. Children learned the Twenty-four Acts of Filial Piety in school, and an occasional gruesome child actually performed one (like cutting off some flesh to serve as medicine for a sick parent). People were expected to stand for the flag, even at the television sign-off; quotations from President Jiang were interspersed with television advertising; and annual rituals at the Confucian temple were revived. While the success of this project is unclear, there is no doubt about the attempt.

Yet the last decade, the last few years particularly, has seen a remarkable loosening in the extent of state attempts to control mental life. As in Eastern Europe, the new openness has shown just how shallow the old official values were. A chorus of competing voices has replaced the old monotone. This general political loosening has been accompanied by public revelations of corruption and abuse of power by the Jiang family and their followers. Accusations range from abuse of family connections to making personal profits from government investments. The models of the Philippines and, to an extent, South Korea have further encouraged people to feel able to question authority. The periodic chaos that breaks out in legislative bodies furthers the feeling that the state no longer truly represents any clear values.

The Everybody's Happy lottery provides a minor example of this. In addition to getting winning numbers through popular ritual, rumor held that there was also a secular alternative for those who knew how to get

it. Members of the Bamboo Gang, a kind of Taiwanese Mafia, had allegedly been involved in the murder of Jiang Nan, a Chinese-American
scholar working on a biography of Jiang Jingguo that powerful members
of the Jiang family found politically threatening. When publicity about
the case broke, according to the story, members of the government paid
off the mob for its silence by publishing in the newspaper a coded indication of the last two digits of the winning lottery number, in advance of
the drawing. Those who knew how to read the code could make a fortune. This "newspaper method" of getting lottery numbers rivaled religious methods in popularity. It indicates a total lack of confidence in the
honesty of the government, especially because the lottery drawings were
televised and obviously random (Qu 1987:30–31).

Attempts at Control

The idea that Taiwan's government failed to impose a new value system
may seem odd for a country that has had a single ruling party (which
learned political organizing at the hands of the Comintern), a powerfully
ideological education system, strong control over all media, and few
qualms (until recently) about crushing dissent. Yet even the more thorough controls that preceded the current relaxation failed either to create
a new and shared value system or to eliminate many alternatives. Real
political alternatives, until recently, were suppressed, but ideas and values never relied on political parties alone, and religious ritual is one of
the areas over which the government has had very little control. I have
discussed elsewhere (Weller 1987b) the failed attempts at control over
ritual, even when the government (or any of its predecessors in Taiwan)
has been more willing to exercise force. The problem is especially difficult for the current state, which is secular and publicly committed to liberal values like freedom of religion. Unlike its control over education, the
media, or politics, the government has very little direct institutional control over religion. There is no priestly hierarchy that can be forced into
particular interpretations of ritual and doctrine, nor is there any real
platform for preaching revised interpretations. At the same time the
political costs of repressing popular ritual altogether are too great, especially because the secular government does not see religion as a real
threat. None of this stops government officials from trying, but it has
kept them from having much success.

   One local temple, which was trying to get government approval for
construction, wrote a history of its god meant to be palatable to the state
(see Weller 1987a:53). It described the god as a Song dynasty hero who
had fought against the northern "barbarians" who conquered China.
This era of history is politically popular with the government in Taiwan,

referring metaphorically both to Sun Yat-sen's anti-Manchurian rhetoric (the Manchus were also northern "barbarians") and to Taiwan's holding out against the mainland. The temple management knows this tale, along with occasional tourists who pick up a brochure, but it is largely irrelevant for most of the people who worship there regularly. It is an interpretation without an audience.

The tremendous popular success of the Eighteen Kings temple and the lack of any firsthand historical sources concerning it have made it, too, an object of conflicting interpretations. The version closest to the government's is a television soap opera that aired at the height of the temple's popularity. Of all the media in Taiwan, television remains the most closely controlled. While the numbers and variety of newspapers have burgeoned in the last few years, there remain only three television stations, which are tightly regulated. The soap opera tells the history of the founding of the temple, supposedly based on a dream by the producer, Zhang Zongrong, an avid follower of the temple (see Zhang 1985). As the soap opera told the story, the seventeen dead bodies that washed ashore were Ming loyalists from Fujian province, fleeing to Taiwan in the seventeenth century to escape the Qing armies and join Koxinga's resistance in Taiwan. They were killed in a storm.

Although there is absolutely no historical evidence for this story, and some reason to doubt the early date, it has the advantage of making the temple politically correct. Just like the story about the Song loyalists, the Ming loyalists fleeing to Taiwan make a convenient metaphor for Taiwan's current position, and the government has promoted Koxinga as a way of making a local hero a symbol of national loyalty.

Especially today, however, the government has neither the institutional ability nor the will to eliminate all alternative interpretations. The tremendous commercial success of the temple has made for many competing interpretations, in addition to the popular ones inherent in the ritual discussed earlier. The most important of these is a movie that appeared when the temple was at its height of popularity. The movie celebrates the popular image of the temple—the Eighteen Kings support gamblers, strip the clothes off innocent bystanders during a chase scene, and even help a hit-and-run killer against his victim, who is haunting the killer's family. The movie itself pushes at the moral limits of Taiwanese society, with sex and partial nudity right at the border of censorship. If the film is in part a cheap attempt to capitalize on the commercial success of the temple, the attempt is fully in keeping with the greedy and amoral image of the temple it celebrates.

Competition for control over the profits from worshipers has also led to alternative interpretations. The temple itself now has a booklet identifying some of the Eighteen Kings by name and claiming them as ancestors for local members of the Lian family (Lian and Lian 1985). When asked, however, the people handing out the booklet actually tell the more usual and plausible story involving a boatload of unidentifiable corpses. Still another variation comes from the "fake" Eighteen Kings temple. This twin to the "real" temple, built in 1986, is a few kilometers closer to town than the original temple. It is a fairly transparent attempt to siphon off traffic from the original temple, whose management is understandably angry about the competition. The new temple's reinterpretation is small but critical. They adopt the usual story but argue that the bones were lost before a grave temple was constructed. The legitimacy of the original temple thus rests on having had a priest "collect the souls" *(shou-hun)* into the grave, a process that the new temple has repeated at the new site.

Like officially sponsored reinterpretations, these local and plainly self-serving versions of the story have not been very successful. The strongly decentralized nature of popular ritual in Taiwan prevents anyone from exercising real control over interpretation. The result has been a multitude of voices, all of them essentially secondary to the pragmatic activities in the temple itself. None of this is a high priority for the government, but it illustrates the general lack of consensus around values. If anything, the Eighteen Kings in action affirm the lack of shared values in the society, certainly a lack of shared Confucian values. If the lack has been caused by the rapid social transformations of the last few decades, and especially the last few years, it has not been remedied by the government, in spite of repeated attempts. While decades of firm control over information and education helped eliminate alternative political voices, they also helped rob the government itself of legitimacy. People may not have heard other versions of the world, but they knew that the one version they were receiving was bent to particular purposes. The political relaxation of the last few years, the opening to new voices, has been a cacophony of competing interpretation.

It should have come as no surprise that the official ideology of patriotism and loyalty to the state was quickly questioned in a country where differences between Taiwanese and mainlanders posed immediate ethnic problems and an alternative government across the Taiwan Strait raised questions about political legitimacy. For religion, the problem was further exacerbated because the secular government could never make a case for legitimate interference, nor did the decentralized nature of religious organization allow for much direct intervention. Religion, especially under the very loose political and clerical control it has typically had in China, is inherently open to multiple interpretations. This is even more true for a carnivalesque religion like the Eighteen Kings, where no one has clear authority to impose an interpretation and the ritual itself is filled with innovative and complex possibilities. Symbols seem saturated with different possible interpretations. The ability to reinterpret in areas where the government does not have firm institutional control naturally restricts the possible success of conscious mystification and cultural domination by the state. Islam under the shah of Iran, for example, shows the limits on the cultural power of a far more dominating state than Taiwan.

The State and Values

Taiwan faces the paradox of a modern, powerful state that has seen the resurgence of religious values it does not fully share. The Eighteen Kings challenge neo-Weberian predictions of the death of religion in favor of civil, nationalist ideologies (as do data from many other countries).

One possible answer to this modern combination of a strong modern state with growing religious ideologies may lie elsewhere in Weber. Of his three ideal types of authority, the modern, rational, bureaucratic type relies least on any kind of shared values beyond acquiescence to the rule of law (Weber 1978:217–225). Legitimacy in traditional authority rests on a shared system of custom and traditional values; in charismatic authority it rests on belief in the sanctity or special character of the individual leader (ibid.:215). Only bureaucratic authority gains its legitimacy from what claims to be an abstract system, created by human intention for pragmatic ends. Values certainly continue to exist, and to an extent underlie the system of law, but they occupy a far less central position in creating an ideology of bureaucratic legitimacy than for the other types of authority. The new religious growth in Taiwan and other modern states reflects a need for meaning that these states cannot meet, in large part because their legitimacy is no longer explicitly based on a shared set of traditional values. Implicitly, many values continue to be shared, but these are less the product of the active interference of the state than of the entire social formation.

Economy and Identity

The lack of a state value system and the malleable interpretations available for a cult saturated with possibilities made space for an Eighteen Kings temple that abandons community for individual, god for ghost, and official for gambler and gangster. The role of the state, however, does very little to explain why the cult takes its particular form. The reasons behind the upsurge in this particular kind of religion lie in the broad economic and social changes of the last few years.

The Eighteen Kings and related cults are individualistic and utilitarian. Like traditional ghost worship, these cults have no ties to communities the way god temples do. They do not receive systematic community financial support, nor do they perform rituals on behalf of any community. Even the cigarettes for the Eighteen Kings are individual (like the single sticks of incense stuck in food offered at the annual ghost festival) compared to the massive piles of incense and combined clouds of smoke in more standard, shared incense pots. Exactly the same trend characterizes the increase in spirit medium altars that has been the other leader in Taiwan's resurgence of popular religion. Such altars serve individual clients rather than communities, and the massive numbers of gods on them allow more individual needs to be satisfied (Li 1988:11–13). God temples have not fared badly during the last two decades in Taiwan, but the really remarkable growth has been in these much more individualistic cults. This religious embodiment of individualism has grown most at precisely the same time as Taiwan's small enterprise-based capitalism has thrived. The relation of the individual to the marketplace in capitalism, along with the associated breakdown of many communal and particularistic ties, has been recognized since Marx on commodity fetishism and Durkheim on anomie. The growth areas in popular religion are tied directly to the changing economic experience of the last twenty years.

These new developments in the traditional ghost cult also imply that success in wealth is capricious and a little corrupt. Several informants described this as a new respect for *piancai*, literally meaning "biased wealth" and originally a term from divination. It refers especially to unearned wealth, and it sums up the attitudes in gambling, playing the illegal lottery, or making offerings to the Cloth-bag Buddha (to whom one informant referred as the God of Biased Wealth). Its special popularity in recent years stems in part from real economic experience of the market. Any market is to an extent capricious and unpredictable, especially for the small entrepreneurs and investors who have created much of Taiwan's growth. The situation was especially bad, however, in the late 1980s because many people felt that small, labor-intensive enterprise would no longer be profitable in Taiwan, yet saw no plausible alternatives. The result was a huge increase in relatively unproductive investment—a booming stock market, skyrocketing land prices, the thriving illegal lottery. Profit appears less a product of hard work and smart decisions, and more a result of luck, greed, and connections. This unpredictable, tooth-and-claw side of the economy is always there, but it has become more visible with the recent crisis of economic confidence.

The Eighteen Kings' perceived amorality, along with their catering to individual and utilitarian needs, fits this view of the economy as a place wherein success has less to do with good social relations than with self-interest and competition against other members of the community. One episode in the movie *The Eighteen Kings* describes a gambling incident that illustrates this. A young gambler needs to make a lot of cash in a hurry and asks the Eighteen Kings for help. They respond by leading him to a book that describes how to use the umbilical cord of a newborn infant as a talisman. It warns, however, that such a use of the umbilical cord will permanently damage the fate of the baby. Conveniently, the man's wife has just given birth to a daughter, whose umbilicus he steals to the protests of the mother and wails of the daughter. The tactic is a great success (except, perhaps, for the baby, who is not followed further in the film). As in the case of the baptized Colombian money, the Eighteen Kings will sacrifice even family morality for profit.

The increasing commodification of religion itself, especially of these cults, further emphasizes profit over community or family morality. Commodification is nothing new in Chinese religion, in which temples have asked for donations, specialists have sold their services, and people burn paper "money" to spirits of all descriptions. These cults, however, have pushed the profit motive to new heights. Tremendous fortunes have been made from the Eighteen Kings temple in just a few years. While the main source of income is donations in thanks for requests granted, the temple also charges for parking and even for use of the toilets—a level of petty greed that other temples have yet to match. The modern media have added a new dimension to temple profitability: extensive news, soap opera, and film treatments of the temple have been as rewarding for the temple as for the media. The fake temple (and, according to rumor, a new branch temple in Kaohsiung) further emphasizes the profitability of the enterprise. Hardly anyone mentions the fake temple without mentioning greed in the next breath. People think the temple is efficacious, but that need not imply that the temple management is motivated by anything other than profit. The spirit mediums who are growing just as fast in popularity are open to the same kinds of criticism. Even believers know that trance can be faked and that spirit-medium altars are businesses like any other. Their profit motivation is not new; the tremendous popularity of such activities is.

Conclusion

This new ghost cult in Taiwan has thrived on the transformation of the island into a modern state and a capitalist economy and at the same time has helped determine how people have understood and experienced that transformation. The Eighteen Kings suggests some more broadly applicable processes. First, modernizing states based on bureaucratic-rational legitimacy may actually promote the growth of religion, in ironic contrast to most early predictions. The modern state itself is not in a strong position to create a value ideology—an explicitly worked-out system of values that might substitute for religious ideology. A secular state has problems even addressing some of the issues with which religion deals, like the meaning of death or the problem of evil.

Particularly since the deaths of the two Presidents Jiang, Taiwan has relied very little on either the personal loyalty of charismatic authority or the shared acceptance of unquestioned values in traditional authority. The widely shared idea that lottery numbers are fixed to benefit gangsters is a minor but telling example of this problem. Various revelations about corruption during the Jiang years have further worsened the situation. All of this has set the stage for the resurgence in popular religion in the last two decades and for the peculiar popularity of the amoral ghost cult in the last few years.

While the government may be unable to create a secular value ideology to replace religion, broad changes in the economy and society generally have been redefining values in relatively implicit, unconscious ways. China has long experience with a commercial economy. This is especially true in Taiwan, whose economy has been directed toward exports for more than a century. The Japanese occupation gave many Taiwanese experience as workers in a commodity economy; the Nationalist period has allowed many to become small entrepreneurs. Yet the impersonal competition of the market, with all its implications of individualism and utilitarianism, has become a more powerful influence on values over the last two decades than ever before. The economic uncertainties of the last few years, when labor-intensive small business no longer seems so profitable, have intensified the feeling of competition and unpredictability in the market. The amoral ghost cult is only one way of dealing with this set of circumstances. It grows out of that part of popular religious practice that resonates most closely with individualism instead of community, utilitarianism instead of family or community good, and an unpredictable, amoral market instead of a clear set of shared morals.[7]

This opening up of popular religion under the modern state also suggests generalizations about the dialectic between social formation and religion. The economic experience of the last two decades, and especially the relative insecurity of the last few years, have bent traditional religious practice in new directions. At the same time, however, those practices have given Taiwanese a partial way of making sense of their new experiences. The development of the ghost cult has played up a theme of individualism and greed that had always been a religious undercurrent; ghosts were always the least important of the beings worshiped, and if gods and ancestors received offerings of spirit "money," the relationship was still never strictly one of fee for service. Late imperial popular religion, like the late imperial economy, contained both a respectable bureaucratic component and a less controlled, more freewheeling informal sector.

Analysis of such change often sees religion as either an accommodation to the new system or a form of cultural resistance. Peter Berger (1988:8–9) and Li Yih-yuan (1988), for instance, have argued that popular images of Chinese gods provided a model of loyalty and cooperation that was preadapted to modern capitalism. On the other hand, Taussig's analysis (1980) encourages us to look at such ritual as a damning image of all against all, without any shared moral community. The two possibilities seem contradictory, but the rise in Taiwan's ghost cult in fact plays up both at once. The Eighteen Kings celebrate the market and encourage people in it, yet they also condemn it as an amoral beast, red in tooth and claw.

Both images have a long history in China, but both have also responded to and helped shape Taiwan's recent economic development. Yet they also show the adaptability of the culture itself, reshaping religious worship over the last two decades in dialogue with rapid economic change. No reduction of the richness of religious practice to a simple comment on the economy will capture all the possibilities. The rise of the ghost cult ties closely to economic change, but there is no close symbiosis between capitalism and religion here. The aura of evil and greed that surrounds these new temples indeed offers a potential critique of capitalism, but it also suggests an adaptation to it. These changes in part set the stage for future developments.

NOTES

I would like to thank Hsiao Hsin-huang, Hsü Chia-ming, Hu T'ai-li, Li Yih-yuan, and Yu Guanghong, all of the Institute of Ethnology of the Academia Sinica, for the help and information they provided. I am also grateful to Hill Gates, John Shepherd, and David Schak for sharing ideas on this while I was in the field.

1. The symbolism is usually fairly crude. Many people simply glue the character *fu* (wealth) to their cash register at every new year; stylized images of old coins are also very popular.

2. One informant claimed that burning cigarettes stood on end are used to bring ghostly spirits down to *die xian* (bowl spirit), a sort of Ouija board in which three players hold a bowl that moves across a sheet of paper printed with characters, spelling out messages. Ghosts typically motivate the bowl and behave generally like weak versions of ghost temples, granting requests for information about winning lottery numbers and the like.

3. Although both Buddhism and Daoism share in this growth, quite a different pattern prevails for Christian sects (see Qu and Yao 1986).

4. See Weller (1987a:60–74) for a fuller analysis. On other occasions, including worship at small ghost shrines, individual worshipers do use a combined incense pot.

5. There are a great many variations on the theme. For details, see Qu 1987:21–31.

6. In her important study of such cults in the Taichung area, Hu T'ai-li (1986) cites evidence that the numbers of temples seeking to enter the Daoist Association almost tripled in 1986 compared to the annual rate for the previous six years and that the number of spirit medium altars applying for such registration quadrupled at the same time. Similarly, the number of officially registered Ji Gong temples increased from 12 to 120 between 1981 and 1986. She also gives many examples of ghost shrines that have become extremely popular, sometimes seeing up to ten thousand worshipers at a time. One, reminiscent of the Eighteen Kings temple, commemorates convicts put to death during the Japanese occupation. They are worshiped with dog meat, cigarettes, and betel nut—all considered minor vices.

7. Just as important, however, has been another kind of religious reaction— the rapid growth of moralistic, spirit-writing cults. These cults make extensive use of spirit mediums who write commentaries, often on classical texts. Much like the conservative American search for "traditional values" that may never have existed, these cults provide politically conservative, backward-looking sets of values. While the spirit-writing cults provide alternatives to marketplace values, the ghost cults simultaneously celebrate those values as rewarding and criticize them as lacking morality.

7

A Rite of Modernization and Its Postmodern Discontents

Of Weddings, Bureaucrats, and Morality in the Republic of Korea

LAUREL KENDALL

Old Style Wedding Out of Style
Korea House Shows What It Was Like

Wedding ceremonies in the traditional Korean style are as hard to observe in today's cities as to find a knot-haired gentleman in his horsehair hat on a Seoul street.

—*Korean Republic,* July 1962

Traditional Wedding Ceremony Convened by Rigid Rules
Old Style Fast Disappearing

—*Korea Herald,* 11 February 1968

Traditional Wedding Enacted for Tourists

—*Korea Times,* 3 June 1973

The various peoples of today's world conduct their wedding rites in accord with their ancient customs and this is a way of maintaining their national pride. Even though we also have a traditional wedding ceremony replete with the spirit of our ancestors, we shun it, calling it "old style" (kusik). This decay of national pride and tradition can only be considered a cause for distress.

—*Our Traditional Wedding Rite*
Ministry of the Interior, 1986

Traditional Weddings on the Rise
Young People Have No Stomach for Quick, Impersonal Ceremonies

—*Tonga Ilbo,* 4 May 1987

A style of wedding rite regarded in the 1960s and 1970s as "old style" *(kusik)* and disappearing, a curiosity performed for tourists, has been revived in the 1980s as "our traditional wedding" *(uriŭi chŏnt'ong hollye).* The "new style" *(sinsik)* of the 1960s and 1970s, then per-

ceived as a mark of progress, is now sometimes denigrated as "the Western-style wedding" *(sŏgusik hollye)*. The oppositions, "old style"/"new
style" and "Western"/"our tradition" reflect two distinct moments in
recent Korean history. The former clothed social and economic aspirations in Western dress. The latter celebrates a uniquely Korean triumph
of the will as measured by the gross national product of a newly indus-
trialized country and acknowledged internationally in the choice of Seoul
as the site of the 1988 Olympics. But Korean weddings provide more
than a lens refracting the times or a measure of shifts in the popular
mood (cf. Hobsbawm and Ranger 1983:12). In the eyes of the state and
in popular opinion, such rituals are, in and of themselves, vehicles of
morality and of personal and national identity.

A government publication criticizes commercial wedding halls for fostering extravagance and thereby fomenting social discontent (Naemubu
[Ministry of Interior] 1986). Journalists opine that the superficiality of
the modern ceremony contributes to Korea's rising divorce rate (*Redi
Kyŏnghyang,* 23 October 1985:261) even as the prototypical Western-
style wedding is seen to correlate with an even higher divorce rate in the
United States (*Chosŏn Ilbo* [Yi Kyu-t'ae], 4 May 1983). Bureaucrats
have claimed state hegemony over both the new style and revived traditional weddings, imposing a discourse of political slogans upon the less
explicit stuff of popular ritual, but their efforts have been only partially
successful.

This essay explores the links among ritual, morality, national identity,
and state jurisdiction through an examination of the form and content of
the two styles of wedding and how they have been encouraged or circumscribed by bureaucratic effort. The discussion leads us into the past in
search of precedents and back to the present for an appreciation of how
that past has been selectively interpreted and reinterpreted. It leads us
outside the boundaries of organized "religions" and into a realm of symbolically charged and emotionally compelling activities that are nonetheless religious and nonetheless representative of religious life within the
East Asian world.

Antecedents and the Definition of Religion

As in China, the premodern Korean state was the moral arbiter of social
and ritual life, defining "good, rich custom" as that which, by Confucian
measure, fostered the morality and well-being of the people (Deuchler
1980:82). Like anthropologists, but for far longer, Korean Confucians[1]
have regarded ritual as both an expression and instrumental affirmation
of significant relationships and values (cf. Geertz 1973c:114). The anthropologist is content to cast an ethnographic gaze through the lens of

ritual, but the Confucian bureaucrat has never been a passive voyeur. Reforming officials in the service of the newly established Chosŏn dynasty (1392–1910) used the rites outlined in Neo-Confucian texts as rituals of and for a virtuous society, essentially different in their premises of kinship, gender, and decorum from the world of their ancestors.

Specifically, the family rites *(karye)*, procedures for coming of age *(kwan)*, weddings *(hon)*, funerals *(sang)*, and ancestor veneration *(che)* were prescribed for the *yangban* nobility, members of elite families who, by birth, claimed various prerogatives of status, including the right to sit for the civil service examination and hold public office (Deuchler 1980: 82–83).[2] Originally intended for the households of the office-holding elite, family rites were eventually imitated as both virtuous and prestigious activities until customs of the *yangban* class came to signify a "Korean" wedding, funeral, or ancestor rite, recounted today in folklore and film to evoke a ubiquitous national past. In particular, attempts to reconcile Chinese-derived wedding rites and Korean marriage customs provoked considerable argument for several generations until a distinctive "Korean" wedding emerged (Deuchler 1977, 1980, 1987; Kim 1969 [1948]; Peterson 1983; Wagner 1983; Yi 1977).[3]

Although Chosŏn period Korea may be accurately characterized as a "Confucian society," household ritual practices were not "Confucian" to the exclusion of all Buddhist or folk religious elements. The four rites did not include procedures for the protection of home and community through the veneration of local spirits, placation of the restless dead, petitioning divine authority to circumvent misfortune and gain blessings, or exorcism of malevolent forces.[4] These activities might be loosely characterized as "popular religion," although participation in specific activities and styles of performance was qualified by class, region, and gender.[5] As in China, much of religious life thus fell outside the Confucian gaze, a gaze that stopped short at the women's quarters and sometimes turned its own blind eye in time of illness or personal misfortune (Kendall 1985a:30–33). The scholar-bureaucrat's encouragement of "good rich custom" did not constitute "religious conflict" insofar as the term connotes complete and contending world views. The Korean kingdom discouraged, without ever effectively suppressing, religious practices it deemed to be socially deleterious as lewd, fraudulent, or extravagant. Common targets of the scholar-bureaucrat's sporadic disapprobation were the ritual activities of women, shamans (usually women), peasants, and monks (Yi 1976 [1927]; Ch'oe 1974:49–51). By contrast, millennial sects—and by extension, early Christian activities—were deemed seditious and consequently targeted for destruction (Shin 1978–1979; Clark 1986:5–6).

Above all, the scholar-bureaucrat and the more ordinary community patriarch were secular ritualists, neither ordained clergy nor members of an organized religion. They wielded their authority over mundane and ritual matters on the basis of their perceived virtue, learning, knowledge of correct procedures, and social standing. This secular ritualist quality of the premodern Korean elite, and early iconoclast reponses to it, would yield a new synthesis in the Republic of Korea. In the early decades of this century, Korean reformers faulted the conservativism and empty ritualism of the past for Korea's humiliation at the hands of foreign powers and for the shame of colonization by the Japanese empire (Robinson 1988, 1991). By the late 1920s, members of the moderate Cultural Nationalist Movement recognized that folk traditions could provide symbols of Korean identity and national pride and that an understanding of Korea's "old culture" was essential to the construction of a reformed and strengthened society (Janelli 1986; Robinson 1988). While progressives had rejected the notion that it was the business of the state to practice ritual, they retained the idea that it was the business of a learned elite to pass judgment on the proper conduct of ritual and the appropriateness of custom. The cultural nationalist project would come to fruition, decades later, under the presidency of Park Chung Hee (Pak Chŏng-hŭi) (1961–1979)[6] when, in the name of national development, the government embarked upon campaigns to eradicate superstitious and wasteful ritual practices (by its definition) while simultaneously promoting the preservation of folk custom as national heritage.

Uncoupled from its conservative past and from a specific body of ritual practices, "Confucianism"[7] is now selectively propagated as an ideology promoting social harmony, patriotism, and education. In modern dress, it provides one locus of a Korean identity that cuts across all contemporary religious affiliations. Korean Christians or active lay Buddhists are likely to spout Confucian homilies about filial piety and to see in them attributes that define "Koreans" as against "Westerners." The notion that ritual is a vehicle of morality has clear, if less frequently acknowledged Confucian roots. Heated discussions about the proper conduct of weddings engage a broad spectrum of the public, whatever their religious affiliation, insofar as these rituals are a ubiquitous Korean practice. Ultimate concerns, such as the living's accountability to the dead, are expressed in a variety of religious contexts including the family rites for funerals and ancestor veneration, Christian worship (Harvey 1987:164–165), shaman rituals for the dead, and secular protest rituals that borrow upon the form of shaman rituals, as described by Kwang-ok Kim (in chapter 8 of this volume).[8]

James H. Foard's notion of endemic religion, developed to grapple with a similarly amorphous field of religious activity in Japan, is useful here. Foard characterizes endemic religion as a "standardized set of Japanese rituals for the annual and life cycle, which might be seen now as the religious dimension to the Japanese way of life, a kind of minimal religious practice that absolutely every Japanese participates in to some degree and which helps bind the Japanese together" (Foard n.d.:2). Participants define these activities as essentially "Japanese" and consequently fitting and proper, rather than as self-consciously "religious." Foard sees endemic religion as an emergent phenomenon, nurtured by mass media imagery and an elaborate commercialization of ritual goods and services.[9] In this volume, Foard suggests that the onion-layered activities commemorating the Hiroshima dead are constructed around a core of Japanese notions concerning the comforting of souls. The imagery of a nondenominational chapel is "Buddhist" because such imagery broadly signifies rites for the dead in Japan.

The notion of endemic religion may be cautiously borrowed for the study of Korean religion to describe a continuing national dialogue about what is fitting, proper, and Korean. The term emphasizes ritual action and indigenous views of that action, rather than its theological taxonomy. It underscores the link between changing ritual activities and evolving notions of "Korean" as representatives of the state attempt to reform family rites and other ritual practices in the name of morality, social welfare, and national advancement without infringing upon "religious freedom."

To the degree that religious freedom is a tenet of the Republic of Korea, the state's jurisdiction over endemic religion is far more ambiguous than the old scholar-bureaucrat's moral hegemony. Where state activities are perceived as religious, the state falters. Plans to commemorate Tan'gun, the mythical founding ancestor, were stoutly resisted by Korea's sizable Christian community. National rites raised the specter of a state religion, a recollection of the colonial government's insistence that Korean subjects pay obeisance at Shinto shrines (Clark 1986:12–13).[10]

Korean bureaucrats do not speak with a single voice on matters of ritual. In the 1970s, when local reformers under the banner of the New Community Movement disrupted rituals, fined and imprisoned shamans, and destroyed local shrines, they found themselves at odds with folklorists in the employ of another government agency, the Bureau of Cultural Properties Preservation (Ch'oe 1974; Choi 1987). In 1986, when the Ministry of the Interior (Naemubu) initiated its campaign to revive the traditional wedding, commercial wedding halls *(yesikjang)* were a specific target. It argued that commercial wedding halls contribute to an unhealthy climate of conspicuous consumption, whereas "wholesome" *(kŏnjŏnhan)* weddings could be performed economically in free public space. The wedding halls were certified by another government agency, the Ministry of Social Welfare (Pogŏn Sahoebu), which enjoyed a cooperative relationship with the national association of wedding hall proprietors.

As the site of these interventions, weddings constitute a significant passage rite, "the one great event of a lifetime," "the putting up of the hair and becoming an adult." The wedding is a social and ritual event totally distinct from the process of registration at a ward office that constitutes a legal marriage in the eyes of the state. But while weddings are something more than secular, they do not draw their primary identity from organized religion. Most Koreans—97 percent according to a 1985 survey— hold their weddings in nondenominational commercial wedding halls (Naemubu 1986:79) and are no less Christian or Buddhist for doing so. Although churches offer Christian weddings and some temples offer Buddhist weddings, these include only minor additions upon the basic structure of the new-style wedding as outlined in the Family Ritual Code (Ko 1982:113–114; Cho et al. 1983:257–259; Ch'oe 1982:77–79). The seeds of this ritual, cultivated by a nascent Korean Christian community, came to signify a new vision of matrimony, a new vision of society.

Old Wedding/New Wedding

The cartoon of the old and new wedding (p. 171) readily illustrates an iconographic contrast of styles. The panel on the left illustrates the older ritual: the groom wears the costume of an antique civil official; the bride wears the crown and embroidered jacket of a palace lady, and her face is painted white and decorated with *yŏnji konji,* auspicious red dots on her cheeks and forehead. The couple is positioned on either side of a ceremonial tray, about to exchange formal bows. In the panel on the right, the antique ceremonial dress is replaced with Western clothes *(yangbok),* the groom's dark dress suit and the bride's white lace dress and veil. The couple stands before the master of ceremonies *(churye),* who addresses them from behind a pulpitlike podium in a tableau that resembles a wedding ceremony in a Christian church. As a distinguished secular figure—a teacher, politician, military officer, or businessman—the master of ceremonies is more a creature of Parsons than of Durkheim.[11]

The Korean viewer assumes the larger settings for these two rituals. As a family rite, the traditional wedding was performed on the broad courtyard *(madang)* of a traditional Korean home, a space used for threshing grain and drying foodstuffs but transformed on ritual occasions to accommodate a village community of celebrants.[12] The new wedding is performed in nontraditional public space, in a Christian church or public hall or most often, in the minimalist, multistoried block of a commercial wedding hall. Each of the wedding hall's rented chambers resembles a church or public auditorium, with rows of seats broken by a central aisle down which the bride marches, on her father's arm, to Mendelssohn's wedding march. An image whose associations are old, rural, intimate,

Cartoonist's view of "old style" and "new style." Illustration from *Han Sŏk-pong ch'ŏnja mun manhwa haksŭp kyobon* (A cartoon textbook for the Han Sŏk-pong thousand character classic), illus. Hwang In-hwan (Seoul: Samil ch'ulp'an sa, 1981.)

and Korean is thus replaced by an image whose associations are contemporary, commercial, urban, and Western.

Although the head of the Wedding Hall Professional Association (Kyŏrhon Yesigŏp Hyŏphoe) took particular pride in describing the new-style wedding as a uniquely Korean development and folklorists have begun to suggest that it be studied as a "new folk custom" *(saeroŭn minsok)* (MCBCPP 1969, "Kyŏnggi":70), informants identified the new wedding with "Westernization" *(sŏyanghwa)*. There was some confusion about my own interest in wedding hall procedures since many of those I interviewed assumed that the new wedding was identical to American custom. This perception would be underscored by the Ministry of the Interior's campaign to restore the traditional wedding rite "which, as our traditional heritage, is both simple and suited to our national temperament" (Naemubu 1986:n.p.).

The written words in both cartoon panels reveal a further contrast in the substance of the two weddings. The older expression "rite of matrimony" *(hollye)* is written in Chinese characters; the modern gloss "wedding ceremony" *(kyŏrhon sik)* appears in Korean script, now used almost exclusively. Sino-Korean expressions of congratulation, with Korean alphabetic glosses, appear with the traditional image. Signboards in Korean script identify the new-style bride and groom.[13] The new wedding is vernacular, filled with the spoken language of modern Korea. A master of ceremonies announces procedures as the groom and bride enter the hall in sequence and pledge themselves to one another. The master of ceremonies delivers his advice on matrimony and presents the new couple to family and friends, who applaud. Piano music swells for the final recessional.

The ritual language of the old wedding was classical Chinese, the language of scholarship in dynastic times, or rather the language of the old wedding was a language of gestures and procedures performed according to the classical Chinese text of a ritual manual.[14] The wedding proper is contained in the fourth and final rite of matrimony, "inducting the bride" *(ch'inyŏng)*.[15] A venerable officiant would proclaim, in Korean pronunciation of the Chinese phrases of the ritual manual, the sequence of the rite. The groom pledged his fidelity by presenting a wooden goose at the home of the bride *(chŏnanrye)*; the couple greeted each other with formal bows *(kyobaerye)* and marked their oath of union with an exchange of cups of wine *(hapkŭllye)*. In a classic wedding, the groom arrived on horseback, heralded by musicians, and the bride departed for her new home in a sedan chair.

Classic imagery is a function of class. I recall the response of one old country woman to my naive query, "And did your bridegroom come for you, riding on horseback?" "Don't you know that only the rich did that? An ordinary person like me went off in a sedan chair with my clothes tied up in a little bundle." Turn-of-the-century accounts suggest that daughters of the poor were routinely sent to their husbands' households without a lavish feast in their own homes and with little dowry or fanfare (Lay 1913; Moose 1911:168–170). Into the early decades of this century, a daughter of the very poor might be sold away and raised in her future bridegroom's household. Her "wedding" would be nothing more than having her hair rolled into a married woman's chignon before spending the night in her husband's room (Bergman 1938 [1935]:56; Harvey 1983; Kim Taik-kyoo 1964:129–130; Koh 1959:20; Lay 1913: 14; Moose 1911:109–111).[16]

By its very nature the classic wedding rite was a *yangban* custom. It assumed the presence of at least one learned member of the community to declaim the Sino-Korean text and guide the couple through the intricate procedures outlined in the ritual manual. Done well, it required slaves or commoner tenants to perform customary service carrying the bridal sedan chair and transporting ceremonial goods. Even so, by the eve of its disappearance, the wedding rite had come to be regarded as the proper Korean wedding, described in nearly every ethnography, whatever the social composition of the village.[17]

In a series of interviews with newlyweds, their families, and members of the wedding hall profession, I asked why the old ritual had been discarded in favor of the wedding hall. I was told, again and again, that marriage customs had "developed" *(paltal)* with everything else since the 1960s or that Korea is now an "enlightened culture" *(munmyŏng mun-*

hwa) as a consequence of the last century of its history. Specific criticism of the old rite usually characterizes it as long, complicated, and difficult to follow because the procedures are declaimed in arcane Sino-Korean. A ceremony in the wedding hall was considered "better suited to modern life." "The whole society has been Westernized, and marriage just follows other changes in social life." The customs changed "naturally"; "it's the way the world turns"; "this is what present-day society is like."

This vague but abiding sense of inevitability is linked to a more explicit practicality, the notion that new weddings are "simpler." "You just knock it off quickly in a wedding hall," to borrow one young woman's turn of phrase. The wedding hall provides all the necessary services, from the bride's gown and flowers to appropriate piano music. Even the white dress and veil can be vested with the virtue of simplicity. A wedding hall proprietor, with just a dash of earthiness, remarked on the dress's superiority over the complications of antique ritual garb, "All the bride needs is the wedding dress and her panties."

Because the old wedding rite assumed a traditional Korean home as its setting, the more cramped conditions of urban housing were often cited as one reason why city people hold their weddings in commercial halls. The relocation of even rural people's weddings to town and city wedding halls reflects a declining rural community, a consequence, in part, of how country children now live and marry. Wherever possible, they leave the countryside and find their spouses in the towns where they work or study. A fiancé(e) met in the town may even hail from another province. Their weddings bring together diverse, sometimes distant communities of kin and friends for whom a town wedding hall is more readily accessible than a rural village. Public transportation is more frequent, the condition of the roads more reliable, and even casual passersby can quickly point out the location of the wedding hall. Recollections of long and complicated journeys to the bride's village in days gone by occasioned some grumbling.

While romantics mourn the lost conviviality of a country wedding, rural women with still-vivid recollections of hosting one recall the onerous task of feeding all the guests. A wedding meant a feast—sometimes days of feasting—for a steady stream of well-wishers, first in the home of the bride and then in the home of the groom: "Old-style weddings were a bother; you had to feed everyone who came by"; "guests arrived all day, nonstop." A single representative of the household may bring an envelope of gift money to the wedding hall and partake of the celebratory meal in a nearby restaurant, but at a village feast, "the whole family comes by to eat wedding noodles." One woman winced and grimaced as she melodramatically pantomimed her memories of dishing up an eternity of long noodles to an interminable parade of wedding guests. A meal at a short-order restaurant is universally conceded to be easier, even though the hostess supplements this repast with plates of rice cake, meat, and side dishes from her own kitchen, and helpful neighbors labor to keep the several tables covered with heaping platters.[18]

Convenience may account for the emergence of commercial wedding services among an urbanizing population, but it does not explain why Koreans found it necessary to evolve a ritual that was such a profound departure from the old rite. Japanese wedding halls offer a Shinto and consequently "Japanese" ritual (Edwards 1989), and recent efforts to revive the traditional Korean wedding have, for the most part, been commercial adaptations held in public space. Even the arcane ritual language of the old rite was not an insurmountable obstacle to innovation during the recent campaign to revive the old rite. To appreciate why informants describe the new rite as "better suited to modern life," how the state found a point of intersection with those perceptions, and why the now nearly universal new wedding has fallen under criticism, we must consider the distinguishing symbolic content of the new rite and the historic circumstances that engendered it.

The Rise of the New-Style Wedding

The origins of the new-style wedding were both Western and at least mildly iconoclastic. From their writing, the Christian missionaries who introduced the prototype at the turn of the last century saw Christian marriage as an instrument of family reform, "this real marriage of two kindred minds 'whom God had joined' (not bargaining parents without consent of the two parties)" (Winn 1921:21; EWUCCHKW 1977:201–212). The Christian wedding provided a public affirmation of mutual respect:

> There was not one snicker when *he* promised to love and honor her. I liked the ring in his voice and the way he answered up. It took much coaxing on my part to induce her to speak up audibly because for centuries, it has been considered next to a crime for a *saxie* [*saeksi,* bride] to speak on her wedding day. Not only was the entire village present but many from all the surrounding villages. This was an eye opener for them as well as for the bride. (Erwin 1918:74)

Missionary writers, particularly women, were concerned with the manner in which converts celebrated their marriages: "The objectionable features of weddings as observed by non-Christian people are discarded, that which is different but looked upon as desirable is retained by our Christians" (Scranton 1898:295). These early Christian weddings were synthetic: "The bride, with closed eyes, bowed four times. The groom bowed twice; then together these two strangers walked to the chapel where the Christian ceremony was performed" (ibid.:297). Great was Cordelia Erwin's glee when a prospective groom's father told her that he wanted a "strictly Christian wedding with not the least savor of heathenism" (Erwin 1918:73–74). The white wedding dress and veil were also a missionary innovation. Mrs. Scranton thought that the traditionally garbed bride, with her full red skirt, yellow jacket, crown, and thick makeup "too nearly resembled the bright colored pictures we so often see in the temples" (Scranton 1898:297). Cordelia Erwin, for her non-"heathen" wedding, had the women of the bride's family fashion a gauzy white veil, pleated in imitation of the hoods that many women wore for public modesty (Erwin 1918:73–74).

Criticism of the Confucian family system did not remain a Christian monopoly. Early Korean nationalists identified the absence of choice and consent in matrimony as an obstacle to individual development and social enlightenment (Robinson 1988: chap. 1). In the colonial period (1910–1945), participants in the tenuous new culture of an urban middle class would begin to redefine the premises that governed their lives: the role of the family, the status of women, the spatial organization and style of daily life (Michael Robinson, work in progress). This period saw the first attempts to evolve a secular version of the Christian ritual. According to the journalist Cho P'ung-yon:

> The new-style [wedding] seemed simpler and the number of persons desiring it increased. Since it was not permissible to hold a church ritual if one were not a Christian, the wedding profession (*yesigŏp*) developed. The Kumgu Yesikjang and the Minhwa Tang, the first of such enterprises to appear in Seoul, were not actual wedding halls but rather places that rented out wedding dresses, dress suits, and flowers. For the wedding itself, restaurants like the Myŏngwŏl Kwan and the Sikto Wŏn were used. Once the ceremony was finished, the adjoining room could be used as a banquet hall where they served the wedding noodles. As the population increased and with it, the number of marriages, the professional wedding hall emerged. (Cho 1983:35)

Elements of an evolving new-style wedding—the bride and groom's costumes, the master of ceremonies, a procession of the wedding party down the aisle (prohibited under subsequent austerity measures)—were elaborated after the Liberation in 1945 (Yi 1983:1282).[19] The head of the Wedding Hall Professional Association considers the Chongno Yesikjang, opened around the time of the Liberation, to be the first commercial wedding hall that would be recognizable as such today. Yi characterizes the weddings of this period as lavish exhibitions by the *nouveau riche,* the "empty formalities" that the Family Ritual Code of 1973 would aim to counter (ibid.:1274–1275, 1282). In this early period, first-generation urbanites marked their transition between two distinct social realms and identities with a new-style wedding in the city, attended by their friends and associates, and a traditional wedding at the family home in the countryside (ibid.).

The old-style wedding came to represent a rural past that was quaint but also tinged with ambivalent recollections of old-fashioned matrimony. "It was no individual contract, and even today it is a contract between families," states the Korean-language label accompanying a tableau of the old wedding rite in the National Folklore Museum. The association of the Confucian ritual and patriarchal familism is nearly automatic in Korean writing about the traditional wedding: "When you think about it, this ritual was performed in deference to a Confucian mind-set; the parents' face and connections were of greater concern than the two people who were getting married" (*Chŏnt'ong Munhwa* June 1983:5). "Weddings in our country were a consequence of the extended family system. . . . [T]he patriarch regulated all matters . . . of family conduct, and since marriage would have a profound effect upon the family's prospects, it was a major event that absolutely could not be dealt with casually" (Cho 1983:30). "The modern tide of free marriage *(chayu hon)* has been one of the causes of this change from the old ritualistic custom" (Yi 1974:75). Even the Ministry of the Interior's pamphlet advocating the revival of traditional weddings links their near-disappearance to "the collapse of the extended family system" as Confucian ethics faded under the onslaught of modernization (Naemubu 1986:18–19).

The ritual structure of the new wedding celebrates conjugality in symbolic counterpoint to the old wedding's association with family authority. The bride and groom greet each other with a mutual bow, a reciprocal bow of common greeting *(matchŏl),* in contrast to the asymmetry of the bride's excessive prostrations in the Confucian rite (although one etiquette book suggests that "it looks better if the bride bows just a bit more deeply than the groom" [Ko 1982:109]).

During the wedding the bride and groom are set apart as a couple, elevated on a low platform as they stand before the master of ceremonies and vow "to love and honor each other always whatever the circumstances, to revere the elders, and to fulfil all the duties of a faithful husband and wife." The master of ceremonies' remarks, although they often include homilies on filial piety, advise the couple on the course of their new life together: "In my opinion, if a couple does not love each other, then they should not marry, but the marriage vow means love in all circumstances"; "Usually in a wedding ceremony the couple is told 'Love each other' and 'Be happy,' but I will tell you that if one lives sincerely and

diligently, pursuing one's guiding star, then love and happiness will follow quite naturally"; "To use a metaphor, let's say we're boarding a boat.
The husband works the oars and the wife tends the helm, and if they are
both diligent they can easily navigate the vast sea."[20]

The imagery is optimistic and romantic. Both women and men suggested that women want to be married in a wedding dress and veil,
to participate in a romantic image of nascent womanhood purveyed
through the media, as in the West. So pervasive is this image that brides
who have traditional weddings performed in the courtyard of the Korea
House restaurant have the added option of being photographed in a
white dress and veil. The manager of wedding services explained, "This
is how they want to see themselves; it's the one opportunity of a lifetime
to wear a wedding dress." I recall the horror of a village bride when her
father suggested holding a traditional wedding. She sputtered in conster-
nation at the prospect of being powdered and dotted in traditional bride's
makeup; in the end she wore a maternity-cut wedding dress and lace veil.

The celebration of conjugality amid a broad community of kin and
acquaintances is counterposed to older themes evoked in the *p'yebaek*
ritual performed in a smaller chamber immediately after the main ceremony.[21] As the only surviving rite of the traditional wedding, the
p'yebaek marks the bride's incorporation into her husband's family. Conventions of space and costume mark the transition from the new wedding
to an older imagery. The bride is stripped of her white dress and veil and
dons a Korean dress, by custom a gift from her mother-in-law. The wedding hall provides traditional wedding robes for the couple to wear over
their clothing. As in a Korean home, shoes are removed at the doorway
of the *p'yebaek* room, a small space meant to accommodate only the
groom's family. Now the bride offers full, deep ritual prostrations (*k'ŭn-
jŏl*) and libations of wine to each member of her husband's family, who
pelt her long sleeves with dates and chestnuts and enjoin her to "bear lots
of sons." In contemporary practice, even the *p'yebaek*'s symbolic celebration of family authority is at least mildly subverted. Whereas the ritual is
intended to signify the bride's incorporation into the groom's home, the
groom now usually bows together with the bride, greeting the parents as
a new, and in statistical probability neolocal, couple. Even the humbling
bows are softened with gifts of "kow-tow money" (*chŏlgap*) bestowed on
the bride by the groom's kin (Kendall 1985b). Recent reports from Seoul
indicate that it is now possible for the parents of both sides to receive the
couple's bows, a further subversion of the *p'yebaek*'s original intentions.

Some years ago, in a study of proletarian theater in Indonesia, James
Peacock suggested that certain ritual and performance phenomena may
be best understood as "rites of modernization": The symbolic content
and spatial arrangements of action in these events are, to the spectators'

eyes, evocative of "modernity." Participants, as both actors and spectators, are encouraged to empathize and identify with these themes and
ultimately to structure their thoughts and actions in recognizably "modern" ways (Peacock 1968:6–8). This last assertion, that "rites of modernization" function as passage rites bridging the transformation from "tradition" to "modernity," is both controversial and ultimately unprovable.
Yet it is thoroughly compatible with notions of the instrumental efficacy
of ritual implicit in the writings of Arnold Van Gennep, Clifford Geertz,
and, as I have suggested above, in the thinking of Korean Confucians and
their modern heirs. The Korean new wedding can be considered as a "rite
of modernization" insofar as it offered both a vision of "modern" matrimony and more general associations with a way of life detached from the
past. While it would be difficult to prove that participation in new weddings encouraged Koreans to think and act in new ways, there is clear
evidence that Koreans saw their acceptance of the new wedding as a
"modern" thing to do and took the increasing ubiquitousness of the rite
as a measure of "progress" and "development." With the implementation
of the Family Ritual Code of 1973, the state inscribed its own modernizing text upon the new wedding through ironically Confucian prerogatives and logic.

The Family Ritual Code

The Family Ritual Code (Kajŏng Ŭirye Chunch'ik), first promulgated in
1969 and significantly strengthened in 1973, was intended to curb the
unproductive use of time and resources for ritual activities, to do away
with "harmful practices [which] imply nothing more than elitism and
a fruitless waste of energy in the obsessive pursuit of face and, as a consequence, pose many obstacles to modern social life" (Kim et al.
1983:339). The code's emphasis on rational, frugal rituals and its criticism of traditions that impede progress were consistent with the pragmatic optimism of the Park regime and with intellectual currents that
preceded policy. A language of "progress and enlightenment" gained
wider credence through frequent sloganeering, and these became the
words through which many Koreans described and understood the world
in which they lived, the vocabulary my informants used in the early
1980s to explain what was in their eyes the inevitable evolution of the
new wedding.

Elaborate weddings, funerals, ancestor veneration, and sixtieth birth-
days *(hwan'gap)* were the immediate targets of the Family Ritual Code.
Procedures were to be simplified, guests limited, and costs curtailed. The
code regularized the new-style wedding and imposed a time limit on its
performance; reduced the number of guests by banning printed invita-

tions; and prohibited floral displays, feasts, and the distribution of gratitude gifts *(tamnye p'um)* to the guests (Kim et al. 1983). The code was silent on the subject of traditional weddings, although by prohibiting feasts and circumscribing the length of rituals, the framers of the code clearly favored the new wedding.

Commercial wedding halls, as enterprises subject to licensing, were more likely than myriad scattered households to honor the provisions of the Family Ritual Code of 1973. A signboard enumerating the code's "prohibitions on empty formalities and vulgar ostentation" was prominently displayed in the reception room of every wedding hall. A professional association of wedding hall proprietors served as a conduit for directives issued by the Ministry of Social Welfare. When I visited the association's Seoul office in the 1980s, the walls bore posters advocating frugal dowries and the one-child family.

As a self-conscious modernizing agenda, the code drew on older notions of ritual as a vehicle of morality; the elimination of harmful customs *(p'yesup)* would foster a good society. But although the intention of the code and responsibility of the state were to foster "wholesome family rites" *(kŏnjŏnhan kajŏng ŭirye),* the code curtailed practices that had theretofore been esteemed as "propriety" *(ye)* and status-enhancing custom. The authors of the code adopted an intrinsically Confucian gambit; reform becomes a restoration of older, "better" custom (cf. Deuchler 1980:80).

> From long ago, our country has been praised as the East Asian Country of Propriety . . . However, while we have revered propriety to excess, it is also true that we have forgotten the true meaning of our rituals and have the vice of stubbornly carrying out rituals that are only contrived formalities. And so it happens that, bound to ancient ritual forms, we blindly go through the motions of holding family rituals on the authority of "family tradition" and the like, and these harmful practices block progress and enlightenment. (Kim et al. 1983:339)

In appealing to "the true meaning of our ancestors," the code echoes a defense of the Confucian tradition that evolved in response to radical critiques in the early twentieth century. Apologists claimed that the essential truths of the tradition could be distinguished from the reactionary attitudes and practices that had encrusted it over time (Duncan n.d.; Robinson 1991). The selective preservation of custom, in the name of progress and enlightenment, is by no means unique to the Confucian tradition of Korea and China. Geertz's young Balinese, "better Weberians than they knew," would distill "the truly sacred" from a Hindu tradition cluttered with "human customs performed out of blind habit and tradition"

(Geertz 1973:183, 184). Similarly, Indian reformers attacked what were, in their eyes, "objectionable religious customs" as being "incompatible with the 'true' spirit of religion," the "perversions and inessentials" that obscured the genuine Indian core of Hindu practice (Werblowsky 1976: 86, 90–91). The particular ease with which the modern Korean state claimed prerogatives for regulating morality by purifying custom, however, may have antecedents in Confucian statecraft wherein the authority of secular bureaucrats extended to ritual matters. Post-Confucian states have perpetuated this role, regardless of their governing ideology or the religious affiliations of the governed (see Anagnost's chapter in this volume for the People's Republic of China).

Themes struck during the reform of family rites in the 1970s would be sounded again during the campaign to encourage the traditional wedding in the 1980s, a response to a new set of social and political circumstances. The progressive vision of the 1960s and 1970s has been modified, in part by its own achievement, in part by an opening of the opportunity for argument about Korea's place in the world and the significance of being Korean—among many other issues.

Western Wedding/Our Traditional Wedding

By the 1960s village weddings were rural folklore, supplanted in the cities by the commercial wedding hall. By the 1970s the old country wedding was disappearing (MCBCPP 1969, "Kyŏnggyi":70; Sorensen 1981: 122).[22] It now claimed the curiosity appeal of an endangered species. In 1977, during my first fieldwork, I was bustled from my room to join the village women who were rushing to see a bride and groom in traditional wedding dress dismount from a taxi at the groom's family home. My ethnographic curiosity was thoroughly matched by my companions' enthusiasm: "You hardly ever get to see an old-style wedding anymore." I reflected on the irony that the instigator of this foray carried the distinction of being the community's first bride to have celebrated a "new-style" wedding in the early 1960s (cf. Pak and Gamble 1975:163 for this same region). By the 1980s a wedding hall proprietor could note with self-satisfied cynicism that "when they hear that there's an 'old-style wedding,' everyone rushes to see, but they choose 'new style' when it's their own wedding."

At Korea House in the late 1960s, where Korean performing arts were showcased for tourists, and then in the Korean Folk Village theme park from the mid-1970s, traditional weddings were reenacted as entertainment, much as bank holdups and shootouts are performed at American Western theme parks. And like the theme park phenomenon these cultural performances were "nostalgic" as Anthony Brandt (1978) and

Christopher Lasch (1984) bid us understand the term. Nostalgia does not evoke a desired return to the past so much as it underscores one's separation from it; the past remains frozen in an ahistorical reconstruction.

Nostalgia, thus understood, may be an apt characterization of Korean cultural memory in the 1960s and 1970s. Both Chung-moo Choi (1987) and Kwang-ok Kim (n.d.) have described the contradictory cultural policies initiated under the regime of the late President Park Chung Hee. While agents of the New Community Movement attacked "superstitious" local rituals, some of these same events would be preserved under the Cultural Properties Preservation Act of 1962. Key performers, eventually including shamans, would be vested with government stipends to encourage the perpetuation of their art (Choi 1987:65–70).[23] While the Family Ritual Code circumscribed the elaborate rites through which local elites demonstrated their own distinctiveness and superiority, those same elites were mollified through the government's lionization of important Confucian figures and the refurbishing of local shrines dedicated to their honor (Kim n.d.:7–9). Both Choi and Kim see the cultural policies of the Park regime as a cynical attempt to enhance its legitimacy as protector and defender of the national heritage, even as its policy makers initiated profound social and economic changes. The success of these programs, despite—or perhaps because of—their contradictory agendas, reveals something about intellectual moods and perceptions in an era of rapid transformation. As elsewhere, the necessity of "preserving" ritual and custom drew a full stop on the past; "tradition" became a thing to be observed and tended, a measure of modernization, reform, and development, not the living, breathing stuff of daily life.

A member of the wedding hall profession, who described the revived celebrations of the traditional wedding as nothing more than a "good work," nevertheless insisted that I see a performance at Korea House. This advice was echoed by two other wedding hall proprietors on the assumption that a view of the old rite was essential to my education in Korean customs. For them, the past was good to think, but not to do.

But while the new-style wedding has enjoyed phenomenal success as the nearly ubiquitous ritual form, it garners faint praise. Several of the brides and grooms I interviewed told me that to avoid the impersonal chaos of the commercial wedding hall and the streamlined speed of the ritual, they had considered such alternatives as a traditional wedding or a wedding in a Buddhist temple. In the end they had succumbed, with an air of resignation, to the easily accessible, omnipresent wedding hall.

Despite, or perhaps because of, the nearly universal use of commercial wedding halls, their swiftly processed services now provoke unfavorable comparison with the old rite. "Compared with the present day 'new-style' ceremonies cranked out routinely and with great clamor in the wedding hall, how much better is the flavor [of the old ceremony], thick with ancient traditions and far more intimate" (Kim 1983:55). "The wedding hall is as noisy as the floor of a crowded market. The bride enters to the Wedding March from Wagner's *Lohengrin*, the master of ceremonies' remarks are 'the shorter, the better,' and it's done. . . . Young people are looking on the traditional wedding with new eyes" (*Tonga Ilbo*, 4 May 1987:5).

Revival is a necessarily self-conscious process, reinscribing "traditions" by so defining them. In Korea "tradition," embodied in a "traditional wedding," must be reclaimed from across a quarter-century of profound social transformation, where urban memories claim contending visions of a rural past, and where urban lifestyles impose new constraints upon its reconstruction.

The revival of traditional weddings in an urban setting began at approximately the same moment that traditional weddings disappeared from the countryside. From the early 1980s the Ministry of Culture's Bureau of Cultural Properties Preservation has attempted to arrest the utter obliteration of the traditional wedding by encouraging and monitoring performances officiated by ritual experts at the Confucian Academy (Sŏnggyun'gwan).[24] These demonstration rituals were actual weddings with the added function of providing instruction in the correct conduct of the traditional ritual. With such guidance the Society for the Preservation of National Treasures began to offer traditional weddings at Korea House in 1983 (where staged versions of the old wedding had once been offered to tourists). Both efforts were extremely successful. By the end of 1986, twenty-three hundred weddings had been performed at Korea House, with the number rising each year. Bookings were full well in advance of the peak spring and fall marriage seasons (Ko Misok 1987:5). By 1986, when the Ministry of the Interior initiated its own campaign to revive "our traditional wedding," traditional weddings were also offered on the rooftop of the Bando-Chosun Arcade, and it was possible to rent space in the Children's Park or at the Seoul Open-air Theater (Seoul Nori Madang) for this purpose (*Chosŏn Ilbo*, 25 May 1986:6).

The success of traditional weddings at Korea House (now a private restaurant and theater) and at the Confucian Academy rests on a profound rethinking of the old wedding. In accord with the Family Ritual Code and the public's disinclination for extended ceremony, procedures that once required a full two hours have, under the solemn scrutiny of the Confucian Academy, been boiled down to an essential twenty-five minutes. The generally unintelligible Sino-Korean of the ritual manual is, at Korea House, translated into modern colloquial Korean. Korea House also incorporates elements of the new-style wedding: the marriage declaration from the Family Ritual Code, brief remarks by a well-wisher, and a formal presentation of the new couple to the applause of their family and friends. The Confucian Academy performs a purer traditional wedding rite, but suggests the possibility of incorporating a second officiant who follows the primary officiant's Sino-Korean declamations with a pure Korean subtitle. The Ministry of the Interior offers both versions as acceptable models (Naemubu 1986). While the ministry's handbook allows leeway for the inclusion of "local custom," the rites at Korea House and the Confucian Academy are pure and solemn ritual as embodied in the text of a ritual handbook. They eliminate playful elements of custom, the teasing, hazing, and spectator participation that were once a part of an old-fashioned wedding (Rutt 1964:158–190; Chai 1962:95; MCBCPP 1969, "Kyŏngnam":148).[25]

Like the commercial wedding hall, Korea House and the Confucian Academy relocate a "family rite" in rented public space and provide commercial services for the convenience of its enactment: costumes, prepared offering trays, photographs, and a trained officiant. Whereas the officiant at the old rite represented the distinction and erudition of the bride's community and the *churye* of the new-style wedding evidenced the groom's or groom's father's ties to influential persons in the realm of public affairs, the member of the Confucian Academy who officiates at the revived traditional wedding links the ritual to a national historical tradition of Korean Confucianism. Like the wedding hall, Korea House and the Confucian Academy detach the rite from a context of community feasting and relocate it at a convenient node of urban activity, albeit a node replete with self-conscious "traditional" associations. One wedding hall proprietor with an eye for business sighed enviously over Korea House's favorable downtown venue.

In 1986 the Ministry of the Interior initiated its own campaign to "reestablish a wedding ritual that sets a wholesome tone and that, as our national heritage, is both simple and suited to our national temperament" (Naemubu 1986: n.p.) While the directive articulated a newfound pride in national traditions, it also expressed an appropriately Confucian response to harmful custom: "it is feared that the trend toward weddings beyond one's means, which is now so pervasive, hampers a frugal livelihood and fosters social discontent" (ibid.). The directive faults the wedding halls for encouraging consumerism. It faults the "Western-style wedding" for superficiality, for failing to foster a sufficiently solemn and appropriately Korean attitude toward marriage (ibid.:79–80). The superficial content of the new ritual is explicitly linked to runaway consumption, insofar as the new wedding "lays bare the trend toward empty formalities and vulgar ostentation and extravagance that is a contemporary social problem" (ibid.:18–19). Written in a climate of mounting dissent and incipient labor militancy, the directive cautioned that the conspicuous consumption evidenced in lavish weddings precipitates social unrest (ibid., n.p.).

While lauding the efforts of the Confucian Academy and Korea House, the Ministry of the Interior's practical objectives were to discourage the performance of *commercial* weddings and thereby encourage thrift. Free public space would be available in every city and county, as well as costumes, ritual equipment, and a trained officiant (*Chosŏn Ilbo* 25 May 1986:6). But the new-style wedding was not necessarily restricted to wedding halls any more than the traditional rite is incompatible with commercial venues. The new-style wedding can be performed anywhere so long as procedures set down in article 6, section 2 of the Family Ritual Code are honored (Kim et al. 1983:342; Ko 1982:108), and the government has, for the last two decades, encouraged frugal ceremonies held in community halls or agricultural cooperatives. Informants, however, held that these facilities are "for people who don't have much money," an assessment that contributes to their lack of popularity. Two percent of the respondents to a 1985 survey used public facilities, in contrast to the 97 percent who patronized wedding halls (Naemubu 1986:79). Why would couples be more inclined to have a free traditional wedding than a free new-style wedding? The logic of the directive bears scrutiny.

Where the Family Ritual Code of 1973 sought direct curtailment of specific practices, the authors of the 1986 directive speak of a more diffuse climate of extravagant spending on dowries, gifts, and celebration, concerns that have been addressed with increasing urgency in the media and in public campaigns by such organizations as the Korean Mothers' Club and the Seoul YWCA. (The emphasis, in 1973, on excessive communal feasting versus the emphasis, in 1986, on excesses of personal and family consumption speak volumes about changes in Korea over the last decade and a half.) The directive situates some of the blame for extravagant weddings within the new wedding itself; it is a blameworthy practice because it encourages a socially deleterious moral climate, both by fostering extravagance and through its superficiality as a family rite. In sum, the old Korean rite, "replete with the spirit of our ancestors," is morally superior to the Western import.

Whose Traditional Wedding?

The nationalist subtext of the government directive echoed the mood of the moment but failed to claim it completely. The 1980s were a decade of debate, argument, and dissension culminating in what was then hailed as the Democratic Revolution of 1987. Things Korean came to be cast in opposition to things Western, the most obvious targets being postwar American patronage and Western-inspired popular culture. The decade of the 1980s saw the flowering of a culture of dissent that draws its idioms from the traditions of downtrodden peasants and outcast shamans (the *minjung,* or "masses"). Kwang-ok Kim (in this volume) and Chung-moo Choi (1987:chap. 3) provide stunning examples of some of these activities.

The wedding ritual advocated by the code and its prior association with a conservative elite were not universally satisfying to those who would reclaim popular culture. In this same period, weddings, as a corpus of shared acts and symbols, became forums for diverse social statements. "Folk weddings" combine elements of the new-style and traditional wedding with farmers' music. Some wedding hall celebrations have begun to replace Western with Korean dress and classic tunes with Korean folk or protest music. Gender symmetry has been self-consciously encoded into ritual form.

As an example of innovation, the woman's magazine *Redi Kyŏnghyang* carried an account of "a folk wedding performance" *(minsok hollye madang)* heralded as "an experimental wedding performed for absolutely the first time under heaven" (*Redi Kyŏnghyang,* 23 October 1985:260–261). This particular wedding was the creation of a folk-song research society that claimed that its ceremony would strip away empty formality and reconnect with the meaning "contained within the cultural life of the past." Again, the rationale strikes the familiar chord of twentieth-century Confucianism, but the vision of an essential core tradition has shifted. The solemnity of *yangban* rites has been replaced by the music and dance of commoners and outcasts. Like a performance of Korean masked dance drama, this wedding began with a procession of percussive music and ended with all the spectators joining the participants in a joyous dance. Farmers' music *(nongak),* performed with drums, gongs, and cymbals, was combined with elements of the traditional and new-style wedding, an exchange of cups and bows, and a speech by the master of ceremonies (ibid.).

The *Tonga Ilbo* described another "traditionalist wedding ceremony" *(chŏnt'ongjŏk hollye sik)* that combined elements of the old and new rite with the music of the masses (*Tonga Ilbo,* 4 May 1987:5). At least one distinguished folklorist is often asked to officiate at these traditionalist celebrations, and I understand from conversations with students that the inclusion of folk music in weddings has become very popular. The Folklore Research Society has issued a pamphlet "Music for Weddings." Celebratory dancing to farmers' music occurs at wedding receptions even within the national Confucian Academy itself, albeit to the ire of the impeccably *yangban* staff. The protocol officer, whose business it is to officiate at weddings and offer instruction on correct ritual procedure, told me that sound and music, even the performance of congratulatory songs that have long been a feature of the new-style wedding, violate the appropriate solemnity of the event. He bent forward and issued the scathing pronouncement, "Music at weddings is a base-born *(sangnom)* custom."

Advocates of women's rights, who name Confucianism as the source of lingering patriarchal oppression, are uncomfortable with the old rite, which requires the bride to bow once more than the groom in symbolic affirmation of the wife's subordination to her husband. Feminist innovations are evident in some recent enactments of the new wedding in which the bride and groom enter the hall together, rather than the groom first, followed by the bride on her father's arm. The kin of both families may receive the couple's bows during the *p'yebaek* rite (described previously). The master of ceremonies might be the bride's mentor, rather than the groom's, and in a few controversial weddings, the master of ceremonies might even be a woman.

Emphatically Korean elements have also begun to infiltrate the wedding hall. In a minor indication of a larger trend, fashion magazines now show, in addition to Western-style bridal gowns, Korean dresses *(hanbok)* in gauzy bridal white sprinkled with colored flowers to distinguish them from mourners' dress. The fashion revives a bridal costume often seen in the early years of the new-style wedding, a Korean dress and a white lace veil. Lauding the "more wholesome wedding culture" brought into being by youthful innovation, the *Tonga Ilbo* cited a ceremony in which the bridal couple wore Korean dress and entered to drum rather than piano music. The congratulatory song was a romantic piece from a Korean ballad opera (*Tonga Ilbo*, 4 May 1987:5). As the protocol officer of the Confucian Academy told me with a mischievous twinkle in his eye, "Those wedding halls are a business. They'll do whatever makes money."

Conclusion, and Some Comparative Remarks

The "new wedding," when it was new, proclaimed a vision of marriage, family, and urban lifestyles that are now more or less taken for granted. The new wedding served its purpose as a "rite of modernization", and it is now subjected to an indigenous postmodern critique. The "traditional wedding," so defined, implies both a self-conscious, selective reclamation of the past and a tacit recognition of the transformed circumstances in which that past is reclaimed and transacted. Precisely because Korean family rituals are construed as signs and instruments of social morality and because, among them, weddings constitute "the one great event of a lifetime," distinctions between new and traditional weddings—as well as innovations and manipulations of both forms—are not trivial matters of fashion.

State intervention in the name of "wholesome family rituals" is not questioned on "religious" grounds, in part because the significance of the rites for all Koreans transcends denominational identity and in part because rites and morality have long been considered an appropriate concern of the state. But does this mean that the Korean (and by extension the "Confucian") state is always successful in inscribing the rites with its own hegemonic vision of "wholesome family rites"?

Neither the new wedding nor the revival was initially a government innovation, save insofar as venerable scholars, under the auspices of the Ministry of Culture, offered instruction on the old rite of matrimony. Both the Family Ritual Code and the campaign to revive the traditional wedding appropriated concerns already present in the performance of popular ritual—infatuation with "modernization" on the one hand, a nationalistic return to "tradition" on the other—providing a more specific agenda and a more explicit discourse, articulated through national media.

The Family Ritual Code of 1973 did succeed in streamlining wedding hall procedure and in fostering the notion that economies of time, money, and procedure were part of what was "new" about the new-style wedding. The code was successful, for a time, in curtailing feasting, the giving of gratitude gifts, the sending of printed invitations, and other related expenses, although all these practices had begun to reappear long before the code was repealed in the liberal climate of the late 1980s. Beyond this, it influenced the way people thought and talked about weddings as templates for their own immediate history.

The campaign to revive the traditional wedding addressed a more diffuse climate of extravagant weddings by advocating a particular style of ritual in a more economical setting. Whereas the Family Ritual Code could be enforced, with genuine legal sanctions, the later campaign merely encouraged. Whether the traditional wedding will universally replace the new ritual or whether one of the hybrid forms will become the Korean standard remains to be seen. More dubious is the campaign's advocacy of free facilities, generally associated with poverty; for although weddings are construed as rituals of morality, they also signify social status.

The repeal of the Family Ritual Code in the late 1980s reflects a changing political climate in which the South Korean state is more cautious about meddling in the intimate aspects of people's lives, from roof styles to hair length, than it was in the 1960s and 1970s, when development campaigns and anticommunism fueled a centrist state. An appreciation of the "Confucian" roots of the two campaigns described above cannot ignore variations in the contemporary political cultures that bear such tenacious roots in their soil. A final comparison with Anagnost's essay (in this volume) reveals the common seed of some Chinese and

Korean assumptions. It also underscores the very different circumstances in which policies governing ritual, and popular responses to those policies, are transacted in the Republic of Korea and the People's Republic of China today.

Where the South Korean state makes conscious use of Confucian homilies to foster harmony and loyalty, and even the authors of the Family Ritual Code were at pains to cast their remarks within an acceptably Confucian frame, the Chinese state claims a revolutionary rejection of an oppressive past. Nevertheless, Anagnost's discussion of state criticism of excessive ritual expenses, a target of the "civilized village" campaign, sounds strikingly familiar. Precisely because the Chinese state defines "feudal superstition" as an oppositional category, it reads the return of popular religion, including lavish wedding feasts, as an assertion of communal identities against the totalizing project of the state. Anagnost describes a state that wields far greater coercive power and a society in which local identities, embodied in communal ritual, are far more compelling than in contemporary South Korea.

Wedding feasts and festivals honoring local tutelary gods, the sorts of Korean communal celebrations that had their equivalents in Chinese ethnography, fell victim to massive urban migration in the 1960s and 1970s. Where community rituals exist, they are often subsidized by visiting folklorists, while the village wedding feast has been relocated in the short-order restaurant beside the wedding hall. To interpret lavish weddings and extravagant dowries, so often a target of Korean government ire, as in any sense "antistate" would be ludicrous. More often, dissident critics cite these practices as particularly burdensome to the disadvantaged victims of political and economic injustice. As indicated previously, and in Kwang-ok Kim's essay in this volume, symbolic expressions of dissent in 1980s Korea were more self-consciously constructed. Even so, critics from both the left and the right, from within the government and in opposition to it, have viewed extravagant weddings as socially deleterious and consequently as either the proper concern of a virtuous government or symptomatic of the state's moral failure. In either view, ritual remains an appropriate forum for the articulation of Korean social visions.

NOTES

This essay draws on the gleanings of three short field trips supported by research allocations from the Joint Committee on Korean studies of the Social Science Research Council and the American Council of Learned Societies, and the

Richard Lounsberry Fund (1983), the Belo-Tanenbaum Fund (1985, 1987), and the Committee on Korean Studies, Association for Asian Studies (1987). I am grateful to my research assistants in Korea, Kim Eun-shil and Han Jeong-u (1983) and Pak Heh-rahn and Pak Hyon-suk (in 1985), and to the many Korean friends and colleagues who have been willing to talk to me about matrimony. Advice and comment from professors Hae-joang Cho, Dawn-hee Yim Janelli, and Kwang-kyu Lee were particularly valuable. An earlier draft of this essay benefited by comments from Chung-moo Choi, Martina Deuchler, Bernard Gallin, Helen Hardacre, and Charles Keyes. I alone am responsible for its shortcomings.

1. I call this voice "Confucian," but only as a means of linking it to a long Korean intellectual tradition. Cultural clichés, among them the premise that wholesome ritual fosters a wholesome society, claim the power of an internalized reflex. Those who write the policy directives of the Ministry of the Interior and the Ministry of Social Welfare may not regard their texts as "Confucian" so much as a correct and appropriate response to the problems at hand. Members of the government-subsidized Confucian Academy (Sŏnggyun'gwan) and its local branches throughout the country, by contrast, see themselves as authoritative representatives of the Confucian tradition.

2. Capping *(kwan),* the first of the four rites, was usually considered part of the marriage procedure. It disappeared with the topknot.

3. We find an echo of this history in the 1980s as brides and grooms, wedding hall proprietors, journalists, and bureaucrats offer their opinions on the "new-style" or "Western" wedding versus the "old-style" or (revived) "traditional" wedding. Is the ritual compatible with modern Korean life? Is it an appropriate commemoration of present-day matrimony? Are the procedures meaningful or insipid, rational or extravagant? Is the ceremony sufficiently Korean?

4. Scholars refer to these activities as "folk belief" *(min'gan sinang)* or "shamanism" *(musok);* others call them "superstition" *(misin).* In the past, they had no name.

5. Students of East Asian religion follow Europeanists in using "popular religion" to designate beliefs and practices that cut across social class. See Bell (1989) and O'Neil (1986) for discussions of the history and limitations of "popular religion" as a descriptive construct.

6. To be absolutely precise, Park governed through a military junta between 1961 and 1963.

7. Notions of "Confucianism," "shamanism," and "Buddhism" have been reified in common speech and scholarly writing to match the more precise notion of membership in a Christian congregation or "new religion" and to satisfy the census taker's categories of "religious affiliation." Some Koreans report their religious affiliation as "superstition" for lack of a better, less prejudicial term for what they do.

8. Whether respect for the ancestors, as demonstrated through ritual veneration, is merely symbolic or constitutes the "worship" of dead souls has been a point of argument since the advent of Korean Christianity (Pyun 1926; Clark 1961 [1932]: 114–116). Christian communities have gradually evolved their own means of commemorating the dead (Harvey 1987). This discussion has been

internal to Korea's sizable Christian community; the Family Ritual Code did not enjoin the rite of ancestor veneration upon the populace; it merely imposed austerity measures upon the procedures for doing so. This stance is in contrast to the absolute moral authority wielded by the state until the turn of the century; early Catholic converts risked execution for the seditious act of burning their ancestor tablets (Clark 1986:5).

9. See, for example, Walter Edwards' (1989) discussions of the Japanese wedding business.

10. The arguments for and against are remarkably similar to those engendered by debate within Japan concerning the appropriateness of state involvement in certain Shinto practices: Opponents of state-sponsored ritual see it as violating the principle of religious freedom, particularly as applied to a Christian minority (considerably smaller in Japan than in Korea). Advocates claim that these activities are purely "civic," and not "religious" at all. In recent years, amid contestation, the Japanese state has reasserted some of its prerogatives in Shinto practice (Field 1991:chap. 2; Hardacre 1989:chap. 7).

11. While the *churye* evokes the image of a Christian minister, his idealized role as the groom's mentor and adviser to the couple recalls another revered secular figure, the *tanomare nakodo* who presides at Japanese weddings.

While underscoring the secular identity of the *churye,* one should not overlook some attributes of enchantment associated with the role, the notion that his worldly and marital success will have a positive influence upon the new couple's future much as "lucky people" *(tabokhan saram)* were called upon to assist in the old wedding. One distinguished gentleman, many times a *churye,* told me that while he did not wish to boast, nearly all the couples he had assisted had subsequently been blessed with first-born sons.

12. Some champions of cultural revival celebrate the broad, flat *madang* as "democratic space" where celebrants frolic as equals, literally all on the same level.

13. The cartoon comes from a comic book designed to familiarize children with the Chinese characters contained in the first textbook of a classic education, a traditionalist project.

14. Procedures contained in Chu-hsi's *Zhu-xi jiali* (Book of family rites) were modified and changed in Korean ritual manuals to accommodate indigenous practice, most profoundly by conducting significant rites in the courtyard of the bride's natal home, rather than in the home of the groom (Deuchler 1977). The best-known Korean manual was prepared by Yi Chae (1680–1746) (Deuchler 1980:85). Today, etiquette books and household encyclopedias routinely include the rites of matrimony as important cultural information that precedes the advice, cautions, and etiquette associated with present-day marriage.

15. The four rites of matrimony are (1) "requesting marriage" *(ŭihon);* (2) "sending betrothal gifts" *(napch'ae),* which includes "choosing an auspicious day" *(t'aegil),* a designation usually made by the bride's family upon receiving the groom's horoscope *(saju);* (3) "sending bridewealth" *(napp'ye);* and (4) "inducting the bride" *(ch'inyŏng).* The final rite of the *ch'inyŏng* is the bride's salutation to her parents-in-law *(kugorye,* colloquially *p'yebaek),* traditionally performed in

the home of the groom, although now accommodated in a special chamber of the commercial wedding hall.

16. In this same period, according to Sorensen, "Japanese researchers into Korean customary law noted that there was customarily no idea that a marriage was invalid simply because no ceremony was performed" (Sorensen n.d.:31). Clearly, numerous "marriages" took place without the benefit of a wedding ritual.

17. Folklorists conducting a regional survey in South Kyŏngsang province in the 1960s noted that "The *Manual of the Four Rites* (Sarye P'yŏllam) has diffused to farming and fishing villages and there are both instances where the procedures are followed precisely and instances where only the most important points are invoked" (MCBCPP 1969 "Kyŏngnam": 130). In some communities lacking a local scholarly tradition, an elder might shout out the sequence of rites in remembered approximation "due to the fact that there isn't anyone who is capable of proclaiming the written procedure" (ibid.). Kyung-soo Chun describes a wedding on Chin Island where the ritual intentions are clear but the rite's procedures are approximate indeed (Chun 1984: 51–52).

18. Under the Family Ritual Code feasts were illegal until the provision was liberalized in 1985. In my experience, the prohibition was commonly ignored in the countryside near Seoul, although I have heard of instances elsewhere in the country where guests were slipped cash for a meal to circumvent the code (Munwoong Lee, personal communication).

19. Yi also mentions a public Shinto wedding ceremony that disappeared completely, along with all other Shinto practices, after the Liberation (Yi 1983: 1282).

20. These quotations were recorded in the summer of 1983 in "Righteous Town" on the northern periphery of Seoul. Although the sentiments are typical, my assistant felt that these *churye* were provincial and that their speeches lacked the literary flair of *churye* speeches among the urban upper middle class.

21. Although some families still perform *p'yebaek* in the home of the groom, wedding halls provide a separate "*p'yebaek* room," which can be rented for a nominal fee. Chung-moo Choi (personal communication) suggests that wedding halls did not begin to provide *p'yebaek* rooms until the 1970s.

22. When Paul Dredge left Okch'olli in 1974, he was presented with the village's communal set of costumes for the wedding rite. The villagers explained that since it was time to replace the costumes with a fresh set, these seemed an appropriate gift for the departing anthropologist. When he returned to Okch'olli a few years later, Dredge discovered that this time, the wedding costumes had not been replaced. There was no need. All village weddings now took place in a commercial hall (Paul Dredge, personal communication).

23. Chung-moo Choi (1987) has described the many delicious ironies contained within the Ministry of Culture's efforts to "preserve" Korean shaman rituals as an art form.

24. Maintained as a national monument next door to a modern university of the same name, the Confucian Academy once trained promising scholars for the high rungs of officialdom. The site includes the national shrine of Confu-

cius, where the spirit tablets of Chinese and Korean sages and worthies are honored.

25. In the early 1970s I was fortunate to observe a traditional wedding lovingly recreated by a rural troupe of middle-aged folk dancers when one of their number celebrated his fourth marriage. In this wedding, as in earlier accounts but not in ritual manuals, each bow and each cup of wine was negotiated between partisans of the bride and groom. After drinking the wine, the groom was offered some food on enormous chopsticks that retreated from his raised and open mouth, repeatedly, until he baldly snatched some of the food with his hands.

PART III

MODES OF RESISTANCE

8

Rituals of Resistance

The Manipulation of Shamanism in Contemporary Korea

KWANG-OK KIM

If one controls people's memory, one controls their dynamism.
Michel Foucault,
"Film and Popular Memory"

In contemporary Korea traditionally marginalized folk rituals have been revived by young intellectuals under the banner of the Popular Culture Movement (Minjung Munhwa Undong). College students and academic professionals have organized various societies to study and perform traditional arts, and some women in these groups have even willingly apprenticed themselves to shamans as their "spirit daughters" *(sin ttal).*[1] Shamanic rituals have been staged as public performances, while other expressions of folk culture, including masked dance and peasant music and dance, have come to dominate the cultural programs of college festivals. Students feel a compulsion to share in the mood of communitas generated by these cultural activities. At the same time, adoption of folk rituals in the public protests of an antiestablishment movement has become an invented tradition of the 1980s (see Hobsbawm and Ranger 1983).

For the sake of discussion it is necessary to have a picture of how shamanistic elements are adopted in organizing a subaltern people's reaction against state power in contemporary Korea. What follows is a description of a ritual of protest by Seoul National University students on 12 May 1985. The occasion was a celebration of the newly organized student council. Because it was a week before the annual commemoration of the Kwangju Massacre of 18 May 1980, when hundreds of civilians had been killed by the military junta (see below), students had proclaimed the day's events to be a ceremonial declaration of war against the people's enemy, the government.

A Ritual of Violent Protest

Several hours before the scheduled opening ceremony, groups of students playing musical instruments paraded around the campus buildings. Both

195

male and female students wore the traditional white costume of male peasants, with a towel or cloth tied around the head as a headband. Throughout this procession they announced their planned activities for the day and appealed to other students to join them. Students gathered in small groups awaiting the opening ceremony. As the scheduled opening hour approached, the groups became bigger and bigger until they began a ritual pilgrimage with the president of the student council at its head. The leaders wore traditional Korean ceremonial dress, but not in gaudy fabrics and colors. Rather, they wore white clothing with black overcoats *(turugami)*, a simple, dignified costume appropriate for performing solemn commemorative rites.

They were flanked by small banners showing the five cardinal colors used at shamanic rituals. Students followed their leaders shoulder to shoulder, each wearing a headband of one of these colors around their heads. Each college in the university was represented by a different colored headband. The main banner was an imitation of the traditional farmer's banner set in the field when musicians accompanied peasants' labor with percussive music. This time, however, instead of the usual motto Farmers Are the Foundation of the World *(Nongja ch'ŏnhaji taebon)*, the banner read The Masses Are the Basis of the World *(Minjung ch'ŏnhaji taebon)*. All the participants sang recently composed underground songs as they marched. Their procession passed all the main places on the campus, stopping in designated spots to pay homage to or pacify the unhappy spirits supposed to dwell there. In most such places commemoration stones had been erected to honor students who were "sacrificed" in their fight for democracy or to mark the spot where a student had flung himself in suicide to protest against the "unjust" establishment.

The pilgrimage and rites of spiritual pacification were accompanied by various festivities called *kutp'an* (shamanic ground) or *nanjangp'an* (a chaotic marketplace), where participants enjoyed traditional Korean peasant food and rice beer, ignoring all the cultural boundaries of sex and age. Each department set up an open market, and even professors were invited to buy some food while students enjoyed themselves singing and dancing in the traditional farmer's style.

At three o'clock some three thousand students gathered at the ceremonial center, the central plaza of the campus, to perform the main part of the day's "ritual." A table of offerings had been prepared, including a pig's head, dried pollack, steamed rice cakes, rice wine, a pair of candlesticks, and pine needles. At the rear center of the table was the spirit tablet reading *Minju Yŏlsaji Sin* (The Spirit of a Heroic Fighter for Democracy). In front of the table, a smaller table held an incense burner, as at ancestral commemorations *(chesa)*. The spirit was invoked through shamanistic performances as a woman student came out in a white peasant woman's costume and danced, accompanied by drums. After a while, banners representing each participating college were carried out to make a bundle of banners symbolizing that the students had united at the call of the (now descended) spirit. The second part of the ritual was performed in Confucian style: the president of the student council burned incense before offering wine to the spirit. The spirit of the day was a collective representation of fellow students who had died while fighting against the riot police, who had been killed by police torture, or who had committed suicide in protest against the "enemy of the people"—the government. Another students' representative came forward to read the ceremonial paper informing the spirit of what the students wanted to do and requesting the protection of the spirit. At the third stage a shamanic dance was performed to pacify those heroic but unhappy spirits who had been invoked and commemorated. Students prayed for the help of the spirits in support of their fight for democracy, social justice, and the liberation of the oppressed. The ritual dance was also performed to expel the evil ghosts of dictatorship, corruption, torture, antinationalism, and those who would sell their nation to foreign powers. This series of rituals was performed in a very lively mood and in everyday language instead of the sacred ritual vocabulary of Confucian rites. After a series of fierce shamanic dances and plays, the students sang a series of protest songs with great feeling and shouts of political slogans. Finally, the president of the student council burned the ceremonial paper to ash and distributed rice wine and cakes to all the participants.

In high spirits, students rushed down to the front gate of the university where they fought against the riot police. The students were overmatched in numbers, sophisticated equipment, and discipline. The police continuously shot tear-gas cannisters while students threw stones and Molotov cocktails. After several cycles of attack and retreat, the exhausted students ran out of stones and were dispersed by the ever growing numbers of police and the tear gas they were using. Within an hour the campus had become a silent and peaceful world filled with tear gas and pieces of bricks, coughs of professors, and grumblings against the police by the nonparticipating students.

Similar rituals of protest have been routinized, occurring at least once a week in all Korean universities since 1980. Of particular interest here are not the student riots and ruthless clashes with the police per se, but the newly established tradition of adopting shamanistic performance in the ritualization of violent protest. Participants are not believers in the efficacy of shamanic ritual as practiced in Korean popular religion. Most of them are Christians, Buddhists, or Confucianists. Although shamanism is not recognized as a proper religion, Christian leaders and Bud-

dhist priests participate in rituals of protest wherein shamanistic performance plays one of the central roles. I use the term "shamanistic" instead
of "shamanic" because this ritual of protest is not performed by any "professional" shamans, nor in the authentic manner of shamanic ritual.
Rather, students apply elements of shamanic rituals, in the form of performance art, in organizing their rituals of protest.

Factory workers also adopt shamanic elements in their labor disputes.
All the participants wear headbands of one of the five cardinal colors:
red, blue (green), black, white, or yellow. They perform an opening ceremony in the form of a shamanistic rite in which an imaginary protective
spirit is invoked. This is followed by a purifying rite to expel evil spirits—
the spirits of greediness, exploitation, maltreatment, antidemocracy,
antihumanism, antinationalism, and so on. Finally, the protesters join in
a rite to entertain their protective spirits and other restless spirits.

This essay accepts the premise that the political manipulation of ritual
is to be contested between the group in power and those who are alienated from the officially defined political resources. It explores the function
of subcultural groups in creating alternative instrumental ideologies
against the image of community provided by the state in contemporary
Korea. If politics consists of the authoritative allocation of values within
a society, then culture, whether popular or elite, is the locus where those
values, mainstream or alternative, dominant or countervailing, are produced and packaged, modified and adapted for the society. If we define
culture as the structure of meanings through which people give shape to
their experience, and politics as one of the principal arenas in which such
structures publicly unfold (Geertz 1973c:312), a ritual of resistance, as a
cultural construction, must be understood within the context of a political movement.

Focusing on the resurgence of shamanic practices or, more precisely,
the manipulation of shamanistic elements in a political movement, I discuss the process of constructing popular imagery through which folk
ideology challenges the official discourse of the state (Lan 1985). Here
ideology is conceived as either solution or instrument: Ideology as "solution," the interpretive or past-oriented emphasis, tries to make sense of
otherwise incomprehensible situations and events. Ideology as "instrument" maximizes an action orientation, designating both goals and
means for a specific population (Geertz 1973c:218).

Political movements in Korea during the 1980s used ideologies instrumentally, to construct alternative forms of social and political relationships. Rituals of resistance during this period were about the relationship
between ideology as explicit discourse and as lived experience (Comaroff
1985:5). They defined a conflict between the imagined community of the
nation and people's social practice.

Every hegemonic relationship is necessarily a pedagogic relationship (Gramsci 1957:64). Popular memory and historical consciousness are controlled in the form of cultural movements or religious rituals (Thompson 1974, 1977; Merquior 1979; Bloch 1977). This essay deals with religious movements as "cultural modes of production" that generate countervailing points of view. They afford a source of private self-esteem and public status to persons consistently excluded from the political and economic arenas. They are not mere substitutes, but for many people the very source of political activity. People adopt religious rituals as their strategies because such rituals meet their organizational needs, provide legitimacy, and offer mechanisms to achieve solidarity without consensus. More than this, rituals can inspire people to take political action by fostering a particular cognitive world view (Kertzer 1983:56).

In this essay I offer my own understanding of popular cultural movements as a source of rituals of resistance and discuss their significance within the process of sociopolitical change in Korea. Following Gramsci (1957) and Geertz (1973c), we should be cognizant of both the cultural and superstructural realms in which these events transpire. I therefore examine the nature of state power and authority in the context of modern Korean political history; the relationship between religious sectors—Christianity in particular—and the state; and finally, the appropriation of shamanistic rituals as a popular reaction to the political situation.

A brief discussion of Christianity in Korea is a necessary background to the recent appropriation of shamanism by the Popular Culture Movement. Both Christianity and shamanic practices have enjoyed great popularity among Koreans who seek in religion a vision of community that reflects the lived reality of their opposition to the state. Among democracy and human rights activists, the appeal of Christianity as a religion of dissent has lost ground to indigenous popular religion as a self-conscious idiom of protest.

The Political Situation as a Precondition of Religious Movements

Since Korea's liberation from thirty-six years of Japanese colonial rule in 1945, consecutive authoritarian regimes have nurtured an absolutist state drawing legitimacy from anti-Communist and nationalist ideologies. Throughout this period, Koreans have struggled with the task of rebuilding their national identity and economy, both of which were almost completely destroyed during Japanese colonial rule and the Korean War (1950–1953). The government has manipulated people's historical consciousness in order to legitimize and increase its power and authority over the people.

The First Republic (1948–1960) indoctrinated people with fervent anticommunism, anti-Japanese feeling, and enthusiasm for national reunification through complete victory over the Communist north. The government, under the presidency of Syngman Rhee (Yi Sung-man), became a dictatorial and corrupt power group, finally toppled by the student-initiated civilian revolution in April 1960. The Second Republic lasted only a year, until General Park Chung Hee seized power through a military coup d'état in May 1961. The military regime proclaimed its policy to overcome "perennial poverty" and achieve the "moral rehabilitation" of the nation. The new government launched its plans for rapid economic growth and initiated a series of "modernization movements."

The government, however, challenged popular national consciousness by initiating official diplomatic relations with Japan in 1965. Many regarded it as a national disgrace that Park's government sought economic aid from Japan as compensation for its colonial exploitation of Korea. At the same time the government favored Japan by promoting the establishment of predominantly Japanese multinational enterprises in Korea. In addition, the Japanese language was included in the high school curriculum and became one of a select number of foreign languages included in the university entrance examinations.

Intellectuals and college students strongly criticized the government's open-door policy toward Japan. In response, Park's regime denounced their opposition as the typical emotional reaction of Third World people. The government argued that the citizenry should look forward to the future instead of being enslaved by memories of the past and that Koreans should be rational and realistic instead of simple-minded and emotional. Suspicious of the government's ideological stance and worried that Korea's national identity would be threatened by foreign cultural influences, intellectuals, especially of the younger generation, began a movement to revive traditional culture in their search for national identity. The government responded by proclaiming its support of nationalism and the development of a national cultural tradition. A law was passed to preserve national cultural treasures, annual folk arts contests and local folk festivals were organized by the government, and even shamans were encouraged to form a nationwide organization (Choi 1987).

These concessions to traditional culture were minor, however, compared to the forces of modernization that the government had set in motion. Politicians committed to modernization ideology and politically oriented social scientists criticized traditional culture as irrational and inefficient and attacked it as a hindrance to the nation's development. Many traditional practices were either simplified or replaced by those learned from more "advanced" countries (see Kendall in this volume). There were, however, major contradictions in the government position. Elaborating upon the term *minjok chuŭi* (nationalism), for example, the government invented a term *minjokjŏk minjujuŭi* (nationalistic democracy). By this it meant that the state's claim to absolute power and authority should be understood as a consequence of Korea's unique social and historical situation. Thus, while representing itself as a democracy, the government was not to be measured by political theories developed in or modeled after the Western world. While criticizing traditions and values derived from Confucian ideology, it appropriated the very essence of Confucian ethics concerning the relationship between the patriarchal state and its people. Confucian officials of the past, who had sacrificed themselves for the sake of the state, were held up as models of good citizenship. The traditional Confucian virtue of *ch'ung* (loyalty) was given primacy over *hyo* (filial piety), and praise was heaped upon historical figures who had abandoned their obligation to their parents in order to serve the nation. The government criticized those who had rejected a royal offer of a high administrative position because it conflicted with their moral duties toward their parents. These men were even accused of being irresponsible for having squandered their energy and thus deprived the nation of the resolve to combat the encroachment of colonial powers.

The government exploited the term "nationalism" to legitimize absolute state power. Shortcomings of the government were excused in the name of nationalism, and any criticism of the regime was itself criticized as a naive conclusion based on Western theory and lacking any concrete understanding of the Korean reality. Those who voiced such criticisms were accused of being puppets of Western imperialism.

With the success of its economic development plan, the leadership grew confident in its exercise of exclusive power and authority. Bureaucratic authoritarianism (O'Donnell 1973) was the order of the day. However, export-oriented economic development under government guidance also produced problems of business ethics and social morality. More and more voices were raised against the deterioration of human rights and social justice, and antigovernment demonstrations were organized at various levels of society. In response to these protests, the government emphasized the threat of a Communist invasion and played upon people's memories of the devastation caused by the Korean War. In addition to the Anti-Communist Law (1961), a National Security Law was proclaimed in 1972, giving the government the legal authority to punish the perpetrators of any organized activity threatening the social order. Anyone who criticized or protested against the government was charged with being either pro-Communist or antinationalist.

In October 1972, the government proclaimed Urgent Martial Law and the Yushin (Reform) Constitution, which abolished general elections. Under the new constitution, an electorate collegium *(t'ong-il chuch'e kungmin hoeŭi)* was organized consisting of government-nominated people's representatives. This body unanimously elected Park as the eighth president, with the exception of two votes subsequently declared invalid. Thereafter, by issuing many "special" laws concerning national security and stability, the regime banned virtually all political activity against the government.

As a prologue to the October Yushin, the northern and southern regimes issued a joint declaration on 4 July 1973 that they would not invade one another's territory. The southern government prohibited any discussion on the issue of national unification. A new law stated that only the government could handle the issue and that people should obey the government's leadership. A famous children's song about unification was banned. Gradually, the government also stopped using the term "nationalism." Instead, it began to emphasize "security," "stability," and "orderliness" under the leadership of a strong government. Faced by fierce criticism from students, intellectuals, and religious leaders who opposed the dictatorship and the corruption of the regime, the government tried to manipulate people's memory of the past in an attempt to persuade them to recognize the benefits of economic progress and admit the importance of a strong and decisive government.

Although innumerable intellectuals and religious leaders were imprisoned, antigovernment activities and protests expanded at the national level and became uncontrollable. Park was assassinated by the chief of his central intelligence department on 26 October 1979.

On 12 December of that same year, however, a military junta led by Major General Chun Doo Hwan seized power through a coup d'état and arrested prominent members of the military elite who were sympathetic toward civilian politics. On 17 May 1980 the government declared martial law, arrested all politicians and intellectuals who were active in the democracy movement, and banned all manner of political activity. The next day, soldiers killed university students in Kwangju City who were about to organize an antimartial law protest. Inflamed by this incident, the people of Kwangju City protested against the local garrison. The government sent troops into the city where they killed hundreds of civilians until the "riot" was finally quelled on 27 May.[2] Since the incident was plotted by the military junta, not ordered by the president, and since the chief commander of the U.S. army in Korea claimed secret prior knowledge of the military operation, the "Kwangju Massacre" became a rallying point for anti-Americanism and for challenges to the legitimacy of the Fifth Republic after Chun Doo Hwan's unanimous election the following August. In response, the Chun regime coined the phrase "creation of an advanced nation" *(sŏnjin choguk ch'angjo)* in its bid to harness national resolve to advance Korea to international prominence. Rationalizing that it was high time to restore the nation's glorious past and Korea's spirit, the government in May 1981 organized a gigantic festival called *kuk-p'ung* ("wind of the nation" or "way of the nation"). The festival, however, was boycotted by intellectuals and students who understood that the government's intention was to deflect concern about the Kwangju Massacre and to gain public recognition of the regime's legitimacy.

The new regime worked to suppress any criticism of the government's legitimacy and intensified national ethics education with its premise of total submission to state authority. The government adopted a policy of confrontation while demanding that people waive many rights for the sake of national integration. However, people were increasingly revolted by the nepotism, corruption, and lack of political morals exhibited by the power group around Chun. Despite the ruthless riot police and repressive laws, antigovernment demonstrations were organized almost every day throughout the nation. Several college students committed suicide to underscore demands for democracy and Chun's resignation. The U.S. embassy and U.S. Information Service centers became the targets of student attacks.

When Korea was nominated to host the Olympic games, the government, under the slogan Korea in the World *(segyesok-ŭi han'guk),* eagerly opened the nation to an unrestricted influx of foreign cultural elements and encouraged all kinds of so-called international conventions. The government did not officially disapprove of traditional culture, but it did take the position that traditional elements should be assessed by the cultural standards of "advanced countries" and modified to more closely resemble foreign fashions. "Korea-in-the-world-ism" inevitably came into conflict with intellectuals' consciousness of their cultural identity. Since the government did not show any clear sense of cultural identity, its cultural policy led to growing feelings of discomfort and dissatisfaction among the people.

Another serious conflict arose between the regime and the people with regard to the concept of the state. Although the government held that the state and the government are one and the same, in popular regard the "state" refers to a much broader political entity that includes all Koreans, regardless of political or ideological differences. This discrepancy indicates that the people conceive of their state as unbounded by time, as an extension of the past, while the government defines the state as a legal body at a specific moment in time. In this context the people did not regard the Chun regime as the legitimate representative of their state and demanded that the issue of national unification be handled by the people themselves, not wielded by the government as its political tool.

The central issue of antigovernment demonstrations during the period of the Fifth Republic was people's demand for democracy, including a constitutional amendment to restore the right to general elections and the resignation of the illegitimate government of Chun Doo Hwan. The government prohibited all discussion of the constitution and all criticism of the government until the end of the 1988 Olympic Games.

In January 1987, the death by police torture of Park Chongch'öl, a Seoul National University student, threw the whole nation into a whirlwind of anger. Finally, on 29 June 1987, the government compromised with the people by promising that it would allow a constitutional amendment and that Chun would serve only to the end of his term. With the adoption of the new constitution, a general election for president was held in December 1987 and for the National Assembly in February 1988. The Sixth Republic thus came into being.

Secular Authority and Religious Power: Christianity and the State

During the past forty years, there has always been tension between the state and religion. Christianity enjoyed special favor during the First and Second Republics, and it was not unusual for ministers and lay leaders to occupy high-ranking government offices. Since the Third Republic, and especially during the Fifth Republic, church leaders have been divided into two groups. While liberal church leaders have criticized the government for its poor record on human rights and social justice, conservative church leaders who espouse an anti-Communist ideology were invited to join the government as consultants or advisers to deal with the problems of national security and social order. Both factions have therefore been deeply involved in state politics, each in their own way. While the liberal church leaders have played a leading role in the democracy movement, the conservative church leaders have mostly tried to accommodate themselves to the authoritarian government.

The liberal theologians and church activists were criticized as disrupters of social order and as threats to national prosperity. The conservative church leaders have approached political issues primarily on the basis of historical experience: the humiliation and exploitation Koreans experienced as a colonialized people, the deterioration of humanity and freedom under the Communists, and the bloodshed and destruction suffered by a nation at war. The message they preach derives in large part from this series of experiences. It is a message that leads many people to place a high value on state leadership and on conformity to the state-imposed social order as a precondition for economic prosperity and political development.

The liberals have insisted that the role of religion is to enlighten people, to help them liberate themselves from the material yoke and thus enhance their human dignity. But they are outnumbered by the conservatives, who have emphasized that religion should remain separate from politics. For them, the Christian church and the state have found common ground in fervent anticommunism and a strong orientation toward the achievement of secular success under patriarchal leadership.

Conservative Christian teaching has led people to believe that all the hardship that has befallen them is a sign that the Second Advent is imminent and that it will happen in Korea. Above all, laypeople are urged to cultivate themselves to become complete servants of God, and this lesson of submissiveness in the spiritual realm translates into submissiveness in the political realm. Both government and conservative church leaders, therefore, have frequently quoted John F. Kennedy's appeal to "ask not what your country can do for you; ask what you can do for your country."

The tension between church and state was highlighted in 1974 when the government deported Father Sinot, an American Catholic priest, and Minister Ogle, a Protestant pastor, both of whom had been critical of the regime. The government manipulated people's underlying consciousness of nationalism to get support from non-Christians. The public was of two minds about this incident. Government supporters criticized the liberal Christian leaders and activists for having let foreigners interfere in Korean internal affairs. The nationalist mood became fashionable again when U.S. President Jimmy Carter, a Christian, criticized the deterioration of human rights in Korea. People engaged in hot debate on the issue of whether they should abandon national self-respect by letting foreigners interfere in the name of democratization or should protect their national identity and autonomy.

The government was partly successful in encouraging conservatives to suspect that Christian leaders had become the puppets of foreign powers, and this gave rise to criticism of the church activities and liberal theologians. Many religious leaders in antigovernment movements, such as Park Hyong-gyu, Ham Sok-hon, and leading figures of the Korean Student Christian Federation, were arrested and imprisoned on the charge of "being pro-Communist." "Antinationalistic" elements were thus "purged" by an alliance of the government and the conservative church.

The conservative church leaders gained political influence through these actions. At the same time, because of their involvement, the church became subordinate to state power. Since the late 1970s the conservative church leaders have been involved in state politics in a new way, organizing meetings and rallies with significant political implications. These included prayer breakfasts for the nation and its leader, mass religious rallies on the model of Billy Graham's evangelical rallies, and overnight prayer rallies for national security and prosperity for which millions of people were mobilized. The government permitted the use of government-owned facilities and provided logistical support. The opposition political parties, in contrast, were not allowed to use those same facilities. The government viewed these events, which were extensively covered by the world press, as opportunities to exhibit Korea's economic achievements and also to demonstrate that there was freedom to organize mass meetings. Furthermore, the meetings showcased the government's popularity with the general population and especially with Christians.

The 1988 Seoul Olympic Games provided more opportunities for cooperation between the state and religion throughout the 1980s. In response to the government's message—"The world's eyes are always upon us. Let's show them our advancement and maturity"—Christian leaders, even some who had been critical of the government, appealed for cooperation between the people and the government for the sake of national fame. The government needed the assistance of the Christian community with its experience of organizing giant international rallies.

At this time, many church activists were still in prison, and the Christian Broadcasting Station was under strict governmental control with respect to programming and sources of income, as a lesson for its previous "negative" attitude toward the government. Still, Christians were generally favored by the government as long as they cooperated. The Far East Broadcasting System, another Christian broadcasting organization that has kept its distance from politics, was allowed to broadcast. The Christian Academy, established by Minister Kang Won-yong, primarily with funds from a German Christian mission during Park's regime, once functioned as a center for liberal church activists but changed its political stance to collaborate with the government. Its director was invited by the president to join the advisory committee for national problems. Many Christians were actively involved in designing and conducting the opening and closing ceremonies of the Olympic Games. The international academic conference to celebrate the Olympic Games was also organized and run by the Christian Academy, although it was held in the name of the Korean people with money from the government.

In sum, the Christian community has constructed a self-contradictory image. Christian churches have achieved a "miraculous" expansion through their cooperation with the authoritarian regimes. While the conservative church leaders have emphasized "nationalism," for them the term means national pride and prosperity. They can identify with the government because both emphasize anticommunism and middle-class aspirations as the ideological basis of their hopes for secular achievement (Kim 1988). Through their cooperation with the authoritarian government, they have been able to build up their religious authority to compete with the secular power of the state, but the basis of their authority remains within the frame of the state. In this regard their "nationalism" is seen as a political tool of the dictatorial government, and because of this, leaders of popular movements for democracy are suspicious of the church leaders as a whole. Although the liberal church leaders have been prominent in calling for democracy and social justice, as advocated by intellectuals and students, they also came under suspicion when people raised the issue of nationalism and antiestablishment ideology because of their elitist attitudes and their connections with foreign missionary organizations.

Ritual of Resistance: Shamanism and Popular Movements

Those who oppose state authority have been deprived of opportunities within the formal political structure and have become politically alienated. Rejecting the established political structure, these people try to build up their politics from the grass roots. The exploitation of all political and economic resources by a coalition of power-oriented technocrats has produced antiestablishment groups called *chaeya-in* (the out-of-power opposition).

The *chaeya* group comprises people from diverse sectors of society: intellectuals of various religious backgrounds who were ousted from their previous professions and those who are forbidden by law to take any public position because of their antigovernment activities. This political movement has been carried out in alliance with leaders of various social and cultural movements on the grounds that they fight for the economically deprived, socially marginalized, and politically alienated. College students and intellectuals who are dissatisfied with social injustice, deterioration of human rights, political and economic immorality and corruption, and ambiguous national identity join various sociocultural movements directly or indirectly.

Some among the *chaeya* once expected religion to provide the space for such antiestablishment movements but were discouraged as the established religious communities came under the control of the state. These people, therefore, began to seek other mechanisms by which they could express their ideological orientation and carry out protest movements. "Cultural movements" were organized to express *minjung ŭisik* (popular consciousness), and religious elements, especially those drawn from shamanism, have been adopted to express that consciousness effectively. They adopted *madang kuk* (open-air folk drama) and shamanistic ritual performances called *kut*. These nationalistic performances began to fill the programs at student festivals.

College students initiated movements searching for national identity and cultural tradition as a counterhegemonic response to the political use of folk culture by the Park regime (Choi 1987:75). Several such movements were organized in opposition to the normalization talks between

Korea and Japan and the government-initiated modernization movement at the end of the 1960s. Instead of so-called elite culture, based on Confucian ideology, the students embraced folk culture. Masked dances, farmers' dance and music, and rituals performed by shamans were favored, both in performance and as objects of scholarly study. In 1965, as a protest against the establishment of diplomatic relations with Japan, several Seoul National University students—including the most outspoken dissident, poet Kim Chiha—staged a satirical drama patterned on the *minjok ŭisik ch'ohon kut* (a shamanic ritual to invoke the national consciousness). The drama employed the structure of shamanic ritual in the style of the masked dance drama (ibid.:71).

At first these movements were mainly carried out by college students with an interest in discovering and protecting the cultural tradition against foreign elements. Soon these cultural movements began to be systematically organized by professional art producers and became more politically oriented. Recognizing the importance of performing arts as a political tool, they developed and spread shamanistic performance and open-air drama combined with various performance arts including peasant music and dance.[3] In 1972 students at Seoul National University again performed a shamanic ritual to invoke the spirit of the April Revolution in a demonstration against the dictatorship. Since then shamanistic performances have been regularly adopted by students in their demonstrations. They invited professional shamans to teach them their ritual process and applied it to their rituals of protest. Thus they brought shamanism into the actual arena of political resistance. No longer constructing shamans as living in the past under the rubric of "tradition," these young radicals have reinvented themselves as modern shamans (Kim Seong Nae 1989:221).

Because of their nationalistic political orientation, the cultural movements have received increasing support from intellectuals who have challenged the legitimacy of the regime. In the judgment of these intellectuals, the government's idea of social and cultural transformation contradicts the people's perception of national cultural identity. The contemporary situation, therefore, is seen as an extension of the history of exploitation and oppression by the elite and foreign powers. In this context folk culture provides the people with a traditional outlet for expressing discontent and a source of ideological production for the cultural movement (Pak 1989:348). Criticizing the new elite as an alliance among the old elite, military officers, and civilians from industry and business, dissident intellectuals seek the driving force of history in the culture of humble people. Resistance and revolution by peasants or the historically oppressed have become major subjects for the performing arts as well as in academic debate among activists.

From the mid-1970s through the 1980s antigovernment movements
have adopted programs developed by cultural movement organizations
for their mass demonstrations. They revived the issue of nationalism,
arguing that it was essential to recognize the ethnic and cultural homoge-
neity of the south and the north and to declare Korea's political and cultural independence from all foreign interference. These steps, they
believe, are most urgently needed as a precondition for national reunification. Because open debate of such issues is disallowed by the national
security law and the anti-Communist law, the movement's leaders have
turned increasingly to shamanistic rituals in their antigovernment rallies.

Why are elements of shamanic practice adopted in people's ritualization of resistance? First, "shamanism" can be regarded as a native religion, while such "major" religions as Christianity and Buddhism are of
foreign origin. In this regard shamanism is chosen as a symbol of the pure
Korean cultural tradition. Second, since shamanism has been branded by
the state as a superstition and not a "proper" religion, it is identified with
the alienated space that is negated by the official discourse of the state.
While many lay leaders of Christian and Buddhist communities have
been connected with secular power, no *mudang* (shaman) is connected
with such power, and no socially established figure is known to have a
connection with the shaman community. Furthermore, the purported
underlying ideology of shamanism is utilized to proclaim marginal people's direct confrontation with absolute state power. Shamanism is based
on the belief that human beings can communicate with superhuman
beings and secure their help to solve worldly problems. In the world of
shaman and client, there is no supreme being comparable to the Christian God, and the character and abilities of spirits and gods are more or
less the same as those of human beings. People approach gods and spirits
much as they approach life (Kendall 1985a:22). Therefore, unlike Christianity, which teaches a total submission of man to God, shamanic practices provide people with the notion that one interacts with superhuman
beings in the same way that one interacts with mortal humans: through
negotiation, compromise, bribery, and fights. This provides an ideological basis for the struggle against absolute power and state authority.

Shamanic rituals are usually open to everyone, regardless of sex, age,
and social status, although there are some rules that exclude polluted
persons on some occasions. Adoption of shamanic elements in the ritual
of resistance symbolizes the participants' aspirations to equality and fraternity among themselves and their struggle for a new polity in which fair
distribution of political resources and opportunities is realized. In performance, and in contrast to a Christian service, the mundane words of
everyday life are used; most of the discourse between the shaman and
spirits is the same as that between the shaman and onlookers. Shamanic

rituals are performed in the mood of the market; the language is vulgar, coarse, and unrefined, the type of language used by illiterate people in their everyday life. This usage of "marketplace language" (Bakhtin 1968) secularizes the communication between human and spirit, transforming superhuman beings into human beings. People can thus enjoy direct contact with these spirits and deal with them on an equal plane. The audience at a shamanic ritual participates at every stage of the process with emotional responses: sighing, nodding, shouting, and encouraging, as the shaman expresses the grievances of client and spirit and negotiates with or fights with the spirit on behalf of the client.

Participants in a political drama in the form of shamanistic ritual attempt to secularize absolute state power, demystify state authority, and ridicule bureaucrats, whom ordinary people cannot even imagine overtly criticizing. More than that, through such dramas the popular discourse becomes formalized and legitimized by the magic power of "shamanism." Participants in the shaman's ritual performance go through a special "emotional experience of a new world" (Geertz 1973c) in which they can solve all human existential problems such as economic poverty, unfairness and inequality, exploitation and oppression, or agony and depression.[4] Performing a political discourse in the form of shamanistic ritual, organizers of the ritual of protest induce people to experience the sacralizing of their ideology while they demystify state authority.

Here one may note that student protests partake of an international form of performance art in their use of dance and that their adoption of dance is perhaps more significant than their adoption of shamanic elements. It is, of course, true that dance through its sophisticated esthetic body movements expresses and conveys one's inner feelings and thoughts. Given this, however, one may also point out that communication between the performer and audiences can be fully attained only when there exists shared cultural meaning or, more precisely, a conceptual framework by which cultural codes are manipulated politically in certain social contexts. And, I believe, in the context described above shamanism provides this. In other words, the fact that it is a "shamanistic" dance and not simply a piece of performance art enhances its dramatic effect. Dance constitutes an integral part of all shamanic rituals in Korea. Therefore, the audiences in this context of shamanistic political ritual also take the performance of dance as religious gesture and are able to read the messages conveyed thereby. If it were simply a piece of performance art, the audiences would need special knowledge to understand its meaning. As a shamanistic dance, however, communion between the performer and audience is, I believe, more easily and effectively achieved, shamanism being a basic cultural code shared consciously or unconsciously by the participants.

Because of the potent political symbolism underlying these performances, the proliferation of such performances in contemporary political movements can be understood quite independently of the actual religious affiliations of those who organize and participate in these events. The manipulation of shamanistic rituals as a new "tradition" can be seen most explicitly in antigovernment demonstrations by college students and political dissidents and in organized labor disputes in which a powerful discourse of contestation is provided.

Shamanistic Ritual for Park Chongch'ŏl

In January 1987 a Seoul National University student, Park Chongch'ŏl, was killed by police torture. After the police secretly informed the student's family of his death, his body was cremated, and his father strew the ashes over the Imjin River. Except for the victim's uncle, who was allowed to attend the cremation, no one saw Chongch'ŏl's body. The police asked his family to remain silent. His death was disclosed in February through the confession of a young doctor who had been called to the torture chamber by the police.

Students then organized their own funeral ceremony and performed the ritual for purifying the soul, despite the government's prohibition of any open reaction to the incident. On a bright day in May, students gathered at the central plaza of Seoul National University. After the usual preliminary ritual procession flanked by banners, farmers' musical troupes, and shouted political slogans led by students in traditional white costumes with black Korean overcoats, the day's main shamanistic ritual to purify and console the miserable spirit began. The centerpiece of the day's ritual was a shaman's dance performed by Professor Lee Aejoo (Yi Ae-ju) of the University. Her dance depicted Chongch'ŏl as the good son of a poor family and as a sincere student who wanted to serve the nation and the cause of social justice. In a woman's traditional white costume of coarse cloth, partly torn and stained with blood and the marks of sticks and whips, Professor Lee performed a fierce dance for about half an hour to describe why and how Chongch'ŏl was killed and to release his soul from lingering grievances and agony.

She moved, sometimes slowly and sometimes briskly, twisting her body, hopping, lingering as though Chongch'ŏl had been exhausted by the electric shock administered by the interrogating police, stretching her body with fists in the air in protest against social injustice and dictatorship, and finally falling to the ground to depict the miserable death of an ordinary and innocent student by the monstrous "fascists." All the participants were moved, weeping, shouting in anger and fury against their imagined enemy. At that moment all present, including the secret police and foreign news reporters, shared the ethical message of the ritual.

The emotional climax came when the dancer could not control her fury and sorrow any longer, burst into tears, and shouted, "Farewell, Chongch'ŏl. Your father has nothing to say," as the victim's father had cried out when he threw the ashes into the river on a cold winter day with neither relatives nor friends by his side. The words, spoken in the father's local dialect, were interpreted by the crowd to mean that the father was warned by the police not to say anything about the death of his son. With these words, the father indirectly expressed his grievance and protest against the huge, monstrous, invisible body of the state. All the onlookers burst into tears. Then, students spontaneously began to sing an underground song in a low tone and sad mood:

> It's a long time since I forgot you;
> It's a really long time since I stopped calling you;
> Only the thirsty memory remaining in my burning heart writes your name
>   secretly.
> With a burning thirst, with a burning thirst,
> I write your name:
> Long Live Democracy!
> Look! The green memory of our freedom is being revived.
> The blood-stained face of our friend is coming back
> With a burning thirst, with a burning thirst:
> Long Live Democracy!

After this solemn moment the dancer began to move little by little, depicting the resurrection of the spirit. Finally, the self-appointed shaman danced with joy, and the students accepted that Chongch'ŏl's soul was consoled, that he had been freed of agony and resentment and was now a happy spirit. Resurrected as a proper spirit and as a guardian of human rights, he would now guide and support his fellow students' fight against tyranny.

The ritual form described above is an artistic rendering of a *chinogwi kut,* a shamanic ritual to console or suppress a vengeful or unhappy ghost, or *nŏkkŏli kut,* a shamanic ritual to call back a drowned or wandering soul. If one dies in an abnormal way as a suicide, murder, or accident victim, one's soul cannot find peace in the afterworld but remains a restless and consequently baleful presence in this world. Since it is full of resentment at its miserable death, a soul of this kind will eventually become a hungry ghost or an evil spirit to haunt people. Therefore, a shamanic ritual is needed to send such a soul to the afterworld as a properly pacified spirit. The ritual process consists of several stages: A shaman tries to locate the unhappy soul. Through the mouth of the possessed shaman, the invoked soul says everything that it wants to express to the living. At this stage, autobiographical stories are told in various forms and tones. Exposing grievance against the unacceptable cause of its death, the soul laments its miserable life after death. The soul's accusations may engender curses and protests from the spectators, while the shaman tries to reconcile the soul to its fate. The soul is consoled with the offerings it has demanded. Then the shaman helps the soul to free itself of any lingering problem and sends it safely and happily to the afterworld. Through this ritual performance, an individual's death becomes the death of a community, and through the soul's rebirth into the afterworld, the whole community is regenerated (Bloch and Parry 1982).

Chongch'ŏl's soul remained a potentially dangerous ghost because he died young in an abnormal and violent way. The dance depicted the stories that would be told by his soul and the things he would tell family and friends when speaking through the shaman. Organizers of the shamanistic dance named it *param maji kut* (a shamanic ritual to greet the wind), explaining that now was the time to greet the rising of a new wind, which the masses had been awaiting for such a long time. Chongch'ŏl's soul was bringing the wind of hope for the masses' victorious fight against antinationalism, neocolonialism, and the antidemocratic "fascist" state.

The Funeral of Yi Hanyŏl

Despite the ever-increasing demand for democratization and the people's resentment against the government following the death of Chongch'ŏl, President Chun announced on 13 April 1987 that any kind of debate concerning a constitutional amendment would be banned. He warned that any violator would be punished under the National Security Law. This announcement ignited more fierce criticism and demonstrations against the government and reaffirmed people's demand for political democratization and a constitutional amendment. Many proclaimed that the only way to save the nation from chaos was to change the constitution so that people could choose the president directly and thus legitimize any government. Encouraged by the "Professors' Declaration," college students and antiestablishment activists organized nationwide protest demonstrations, which were joined by many ordinary people and opposition party members. The government retaliated against these activities, ruthlessly applying the National Security Law.

In late May, in the midst of a fierce clash between students and riot police at Yŏnsei University, a student at the university, Yi Hanyŏl, was hit by a tear-gas cannister; he died two weeks later. The whole nation was aroused by this accident. To prevent the same sort of government cover-up and secret disposal of the body that had occurred in the case of Chongch'ŏl, students surrounded Hanyŏl's corpse. The funeral was organized by antigovernment organizations as a "national funeral" for a heroic fighter against tyranny. It was open to the public, and students from all parts of the country came to the funeral in the central plaza of Yŏnsei University. The citizens silently paid homage, expressing their resentment of the government and support for the students' fight against it. Government officials and members of the government party who tried to visit the funeral site to offer condolences were pushed away by students. Only members of the opposition parties were allowed to pay their respects.

Attended by more than one million people from various religious sectors, the event had the scope and grandeur of a state funeral. Although Hanyŏl was a Christian and the university is a Christian institution, the funeral mixed elements of the Confucian rite and shamanistic ritual. Thousands of banners bore political slogans, and funeral functionaries wore traditional mourning costumes according to their ritual ranks and roles in relation to the deceased.

The highlight of the funeral was the shamanistic rite to send the soul to the afterworld and to give him resurrection. This ritual also included a dance by Professor Lee. She came out wearing a blood-stained traditional white dress of an ordinary woman. Her dance described Hanyŏl's life, but more emphasis was given to the depiction of the history of humble and poor Koreans who have been oppressed and exploited successively by traditional feudalism, Japanese colonialism, American imperialism, and the succession of "fascist" regimes in alliance with foreign superpowers. At the climax she depicted Hanyŏl's death. Demoralized by fear, agony, torture, and despair, she slowly fell to the ground and remained silent and motionless for about five minutes. Then Hanyŏl's sister burst into a cry and shouted, "Hanyŏl, Hanyŏl, wake up, wake up. Your friends are here, waiting for you to wake up." This was followed by the participants' weeping and shouting, "Hanyŏl, get up! Hanyŏl, come back!" The shouting spread like a huge wave. Little by little, in response to the mob's shouting, Hanyŏl (the dancer) began to move and, at last, was restored to life. He was resurrected! All the participants cried with joy and all at once the musicians began to play joyful songs. The exhilarated crowd, bearing the bier of the dead student, began its march toward the center of Seoul.

When they reached the roundabout outside the university, the procession halted for another shamanistic rite. This rite was to send the soul peacefully to the afterworld. The shaman, Professor Lee, once again appeared and depicted the agony and resentment of Hanyŏl and then danced to console the restless spirit. Finally, she plunged herself into a ten-meter-long white cloth called *nŏktari* (bridge of the soul), which symbolizes the bridge between this world and the netherworld. She rushed into the center of the cloth, and as she violently ran forward, her body tore the cloth into two parts. Hanyŏl's mother and sister and some other relatives fainted on the street, and students shouted, "Farewell, Hanyŏl," waving their banners amidst the sound of drums and gongs. In the evening he was buried at the graveyard in Kwangju where victims of the Kwangju Massacre are memorialized as heroic fighters for democracy.

Participants said that the dance and the other events of the day were not simply a funeral for Hanyŏl but, more significantly, a ritual to declare war against the government and to symbolize the eventual victory of the citizens over the state. The invocation of Hanyŏl's soul was understood as his rebirth and thus the resurrection of the spirit of the masses against the dictator and exploiter. The ritual dance of the soul's entering the afterworld via the soul bridge was also interpreted by the students as a symbol of the victory of the masses. According to the participants, leaving behind this world of rotten politics and immoral capitalism, Hanyŏl went to the world where these vices and crimes are purged. Lee Aejoo, the dancer, and her collaborators called the dance *ssŏng-p'uri kut* (a shamanic ritual to resolve anger), saying that it was the time to solve all kinds of anger, not only personal grievances or vengeful grudges, but the anger of the masses that has been heaped up to the limit. Therefore, the people should stop passively lamenting or seeking personal resolutions, but should throw away anger by becoming more active and militant.

Just three weeks after the *chinogwi kut* for Chongch'ŏl and the nationwide violent antigovernment demonstrations that followed, Chun's government yielded. Roh Tae Woo (No T'ae-u), then the representative of the majority party and Chun's designated successor, issued "Roh's declaration," nullifying President Chun's prohibition of constitutional debate. Hanyŏl's funeral was held within days of the government's "surrender."

Presidential Election Campaign

The constitution was amended and in December 1987, for the first time in eighteen years, a general election for the presidency was held. Along with Roh Tae Woo of the ruling party, three main figures, Kim Young Sam (Kim Yŏng-sam), Kim Dae Jung (Kim Tae-jung), and Kim Jong Pil (Kim Chong-p'il) also registered as candidates. General opinion criticized the three Kims' greediness for power and demanded that they decide on only one candidate to defeat Roh. To exert moral pressure upon these three candidates, and to publicize their political message, the allied front of *chaeya,* students, and radical intellectuals registered Paek Kiwan, recently released from prison, as the candidate for the masses.

In contrast to the other four candidates, Paek was a refugee from North Korea and a child of the poor. His grandfather collaborated with the independence fighters during the Japanese colonial period, and as a consequence Paek received only an elementary school education. As a self-identified "nationalist," he had been an outspoken critic of Park's and Chun's regimes and had played a leading role in antigovernment activities.

During the election campaign each party tried to mobilize as many people as possible for its campaign rallies because the number attending was regarded as an indicator of the degree of support. As a mobilization strategy, popular singers and dancing teams were asked to entertain the participants. Notably, the major parties, including the government party and the main opposition parties, employed Western-style pop singers and female cheerleaders, while supporters of Paek utilized folk culture including shamanistic performances and masked dance. Although the candidate himself was a Christian, he wore traditional Korean clothes in public, and shamanistic performances were held before, during, and after his campaign rallies.

The most impressive rally was held at the former campus site of Seoul National University in downtown Seoul, still a popular gathering place for students. Whereas the rallies of the major parties were held in 5.16 Plaza in Yŏŭido, named after the military coup by Park Chung Hee in 1961, this rally symbolized both a civilian challenge to the military-based regime and a nationalist challenge to those politicians preoccupied with Western cultural imperialism.

The rally was organized mainly by college students and carried out in the fashion of a student rally on the campus. It began with farmers' dances and musical troupes. Tens of thousands of students gathered, carrying banners of various colors with them. They sat in the street singing underground songs and shouting political slogans. Meanwhile, side roads and alleys were filled with more than three hundred thousand people of all social sectors. Students and peddlers sold soft drinks and snacks with satirical names such as dictator's coffee, corruption coffee, comprador's coffee, antinational hot dog, and antidemocratic hot dog. As each new group arrived with its own band and banner identifying its college, all those already there greeted the new arrivals with drums and gongs and songs.

After a purification rite the candidate went up to the platform in traditional dress and began his address. His speech was full of satire and jokes in the manner of an old-fashioned oratory contest at a rural marketplace. He didn't say much about his policies, but he sharply criticized the dictatorial government in common language and expressed the people's hope for victory over the "fascist" group. As he ridiculed the government, the crowd burst into laughter and clapped. His speech was interrupted by singing and the shouting of antigovernment slogans by the audience.

The festive mood escalated into one of exhilaration as Professor Lee Aejoo, by then publicly referred to as *kyosu mudang* (professor shaman) —jokingly by students and disparagingly by members of the ruling party

—began a shamanistic dance in the twilight. Surrounded by torchlight, she performed a new dance called *haebang ch'um* (dance for the liberation), which invoked all national *wŏnhon* (spiteful souls) and released their grief and sorrow in order to achieve the joyful victory of the oppressed over the tyrannical government and foreign powers. This was followed by another dance, *t'ong-il ch'um* (dance for national unification), which was in turn followed by students dancing, as people usually enjoy *mugam* (dancing in shaman's dress) during a pause in a shamanic ritual. On finishing the dances all the participants marched in a festive mood to the city plaza, with the candidate and the dancer on a small truck at the head. The white clothing and torches in the darkness and the dancing and singing of prohibited songs in front of City Hall provided the participants with the ritual experience of subversion. The procession resembled a cluster of villagers following a shaman performing a series of exorcisms. As riot police surrounded the crowd and were about to attack, the shaman, Professor Lee, came forward to confront the police. Both the police and the people were astonished by this unexpected act of bravery by a woman. In the tense silence Paek stepped forward and warned the police that uncontrollable chaos would result if the police attacked the people, and the consequences would be the responsibility of the police. The police stopped, and the people sang the national anthem before shouting, "Long live the national unification, long live the world of the masses." In a wave of applause, the shaman calmly disappeared into the nearby subway station to go home.

Conclusion

The contradiction between the images of national community borne by the state and the people has widened through the transformational process of the past forty years. The discrepancy is between the state ideology and the people's perception of lived reality. While the government achieved its so-called miraculous economic development, enabling people to escape chronic poverty and enjoy "modern" life, people refused to recognize the government's achievements; instead, the tension has become so intense as to generate violent protest.

Even the brief historical outline in this essay reveals that resistance came from three main sources of discontent. First, the national economic development program, carried out mainly through the alliance between the government and some privileged business monopolies, deprived people of open and fair access to political and economic opportunities. As a result there appeared a wide gap between the haves and have-nots: the rich became richer while the poor became poorer. Second, the enforced restructuring of the population transformed former agricultural producers into low-paid labor in the industrial sector, thus indenturing them to state monopoly capitalism. Finally, the enforced disruption of a long-established cultural system muted its challenge to economic and political legitimacy. Radical sociocultural change, the feelings of relative deprivation of those who have failed to adapt to the newly emerging situation, and the deep and wide gap in economic advancement are sources of growing discontent and social instability.

The imagery of dispossession, of loss, of longing for the restoration of a lost world of their own was a constant pulse in the literature, oral tradition, and rhetoric of the nationalist movements. But loss was not the only cause, nor was it sufficient to make the great, brave leap into violent resistance seem the only available option (Lan 1985:121). In the imagery wrought from the process of resistance, all three sources of discontent reappear. Together, they express two powerful desires: to regain the lost world of their own and to restore the people's lost control over their lives. Much of this imagery is driven by and forged out of memories of what life had been like, of how society had been organized, of the freedoms that had prevailed before the arrival of the foreign powers. The people have been through a historical process of colonization in which the government has been either the mediator or the agency.

Religion lends a space for the oblique expression of otherwise inexpressible political discontent. Radical intellectuals and political dissidents began to construct their space through the manipulation of shamanism. According to them, Christianity can contribute to democracy and human rights only within limits because it teaches, as the ultimate means of human emancipation, a total submission to God. Because in Christianity the line between God and secular state authority very often becomes blurred and because the majority of Christian leaders have advocated a proestablishment ideology, dissidents claim that they must turn to shamanism for the elements with which to produce a powerful counterideology.

Compared to Christianity, shamanism is based on the belief in communication between human being and superhuman being. Invocation and possession, singly or in tandem, are the most important features of its ritual. Shamanism provides the people with a profound symbolic language. Most of all, it gives people the "spirit" of resistance. They can "invoke" their own significant spirits and thus transform them into the bearers of their political message. They invoke the spirits of students, factory workers, and nameless masses killed by abnormal causes and translate them into political rhetoric: the resurrection of nation, restoration of history, return of subaltern people, and reconstruction of popular space. All this has been rejected or lost through colonialism, capitalism, foreign domination, and modernization. As spirit possession is a cultural construct for a dialectic play of identity formation (Crapanzano 1977), shamanistic ritual process attempts to replace a reality imagined by the state with the people's own imagined reality.

In other words, shamanistic rituals of resistance bring popular discourse into established space and thus let people construct their own symbolic community. This is attempted not through a total dependence upon God as in Christianity, but by creating a comradeship with spirits in a festive mood. Although the construction of a symbolic community is accomplished through such idioms as a revival of the soul and a recalling of history, it would be a mistake to characterize the shamanistic ritual as a revitalization movement. The invention of tradition (Hobsbawm and Ranger 1983) is a selective construction of the past which resonates with contemporary influences (Cohen 1985:99).

Most of those who are active in producing shamanistic ritual in protest movements are college graduates and students. These nonproletarians, though not bourgeoisie, utilize the form and content of a religion that has traditionally been practiced by socially marginalized people in an attempt to create or restore the world of subaltern people. In this regard the use of shamanistic ritual—of dance, song, and spirit mediumship—in the struggle for popular liberation is a *bricolage* whose signs appropriate the power both of the populace and of the objectified intellectuals.

Dissenters need their own language, through which they both stigmatize the establishment as lacking legitimate power and cultural nationalism and legitimize their own counterculture. Shamanism is a source of language because of its power to invoke and dramatize. Through this, violence and resistance become sacred, and people construct their own space for a popular reappropriation of their history (Comaroff 1985) in which national unification, cultural identity, and popular democracy are accommodated. Through the magic power of shamanism, ahistory becomes history, the muted are given voice, and a private space becomes the public space.

NOTES

1. [Not only does this phenomenon contradict the scholar's traditional disdain for the shaman, but apprenticeship is usually seen as a reluctant and painful surrender to the will of the spirits (Kendall 1985a:63).—Eds.]

2. [Some place the unofficial death toll at a thousand or more.—Eds.]

3. For more about the open-air drama in the context of cultural movements, see Chae and Yim 1982; Kim 1988).

4. For recent anthropological studies on Korean shamanism, see Chang 1982; Ch'oe 1981; Choi 1987; Kendall 1985a, 1988; Kim Seong Nae 1989.

9 The Politics of Ritual Displacement
ANN S. ANAGNOST

In 1983 the *Fujian ribao* (Fujian Daily) reported the success of a countywide antisuperstition campaign in Zhangzhou county that had suppressed 308 temple cults. The cult organizers were all arrested or forced to submit to self-criticism and reeducation, and their temple buildings were redesignated to uses officially defined as "healthy." With regard to this spatial expropriation, the newspaper account described the action in statistically precise detail. Seven of these temples were converted to school dormitories, twenty-five to childcare centers, fifty-four to recreation centers, sixteen to television-viewing centers, and nine to youth clubs, and a number of small roadside temples and shrines were converted to rest stops and rain shelters (*Fujian ribao*, 7 October 1983).[1] In a similar campaign in 1986, a survey of Wenling county in Zhejiang province revealed the presence of more than five hundred temple buildings that had been illegally repaired or built, more than half of which had appeared since 1984. Most of these were dismantled and converted to approved uses that included housing for "five-guarantee households" *(wubaohu)*, collective warehouses, wayside pavilions for rest stops, or recreational places for the masses (*China Daily Report*, 11 March 1986:K3).

What is immediately apparent about this appropriation of temple buildings is not just its legitimation in terms of turning "wasted" space to good uses. Its importance as a signifying practice is affirmed by the level to which it descends. Even the humble earth god temples *(tudigong miao)*, which guard the precincts of most rural villages and which embody the minimal units of ritually defined space (often no larger than a phone booth), are not exempt from this transformation into secular space. The state-Party apparatus displays here a meticulous concern in its official designation of these smallest of ritual sites as "wayside pavilions," an authorial conceit (defined here as a "strained figure of speech") that demonstrates the need for a symbolic language that can superimpose itself upon the hierarchy of ritual places in such detail as to displace completely local practice. The uses to which these transformed spaces are put are also carefully selected. They define activities that announce the onset of a "socialist spiritual civilization": education and healthy recreation.

These accounts are representative of many, appearing in the early post-Mao period, that depict the overt confrontation between the Chinese socialist state and local communities over ritual practice. Throughout the 1980s the policing of popular culture, although increasingly more relaxed, has not disappeared completely. Some practices have been granted more latitude, but the state generally continues to regard popular religion with suspicion. Whatever ritual practice the Party disvalues is included within the negative designation of "feudal superstition." This category, however, is far from fixed; how it is defined, what practices are included in it, and its strategic deployment in political discourse all follow the prevailing political wind blowing in the context of wider cultural debates that concern the discursive construction of "modernity" and the Party's practices of self-representation throughout the post-Mao period.

This chapter looks at what I call the "politics of ritual displacement," which refers to this contestation for ritual space and control over how ritual practice is represented. During the often violent political campaigns of the Maoist period, such politics were far more unforgiving, allowing the forcible seizure and destruction of ritual places by agents, whether Red Guards or local activists, acting within an aggressive modernizing project. Although this campaign mentality has subsided, its methods persist, whether as implicit threat or explicit intervention. In either case feudal superstition continues to be a potent signifier of "backwardness." Its elimination affirms the universal, homogenizing values of a modernizing state over the disparate, unassimilable meanings of local cultures, even in cases where the "little traditions" are encouraged to reinvent themselves.

As we shall see in the following discussion, local party organizations often attempt to extirpate "superstitious" practices in campaigns that are highly ritualized, appropriating the sites of popular ritual and converting them to purposes that it defines as "healthy." Temples and shrines are turned into schools or community centers; images of gods and spirits are burned; and ritual practitioners abandon their vocations to become publicists exposing the fraudulent claims of their former practice. The rituals of the state-Party, therefore, reinscribe the local landscape within its own totalizing order. They define spaces swept clean of the twin evils of ignorance and poverty and affirm the Party's undisputed leadership in a narrative of progress toward a "disenchanted," rational world that promises "modernity" and abundance.

Operating oppositionally to the Party's own ritual forms are local practices that reclaim what has been "lost." The tremendous resurgence of community rituals in the post-Mao period reinvents the local traditions that have been suspended in a totalizing symbolic order. The ritual definition of community is performed through processions that honor local deities, circumscribing spaces that are ritually cleansed of evil influences. In marking the boundaries of inherently local spiritual jurisdictions, these processions reinscribe the landscape with a qualitative "difference," disrupting the homogenizing order of the Party and undermining its self-definition as a transcendent authority. The temples and shrines, which are the symbolic centers of these ritual demarcations, become once again the vehicles of local memory that restore to local communities a sense of place marked by the singularity of their history and their ritual traditions.

On both sides, the contestation for what can be called "mnemonic sites" is engaged through rituals of displacement.[2] These sites, which thereby become the vehicle of the struggle, are actual physical places where temple buildings stand or were known to have once stood or even locations within domestic space where altars to gods or spirits are placed or were once placed. The rituals of the state and of local deities compete with each other to inscribe these sites with their own meanings, at times in a relationship of mutual exclusivity, at other times in a relationship of uneasy accommodation. In this contestation for symbolic space, however, we see that the relations of power between the state and local authority are always proximate and never final; they are continually renegotiated in the context of local politics as well as in the larger context of debates concerning national identity as well as the changing import of central policies.

Set within the shifting context of these larger issues, the battle against feudal superstition is not one that is simply won or lost but continues as the recurring site of a longstanding struggle between the differing symbolic orders of the state and local communities. What needs to be explained is why, in a battle that never seems to achieve any final resolution, popular ritual remains such a powerful domain in the discourse and practice of the Party. I will argue that the Party appropriates the space of local ritual to define itself and make itself visible as a palpable force in society. Ritual practice provides a "surplus value" expropriated by the state for its purposes of self-representation. This representational impulse may indeed outweigh the importance of the ostensible goals of these campaigns as disciplinizing interventions into everyday life. Their significance may be more at the level of how the state "imagines" itself than at the level of the real. Moreover, the contested space of ritual has entered into the heated cultural debates of oppositional intellectuals increasingly through the decade of the 1980s, so that the surplus value of what the Party excludes becomes in turn the raw material for a cultural politics that challenges the Party's monological authority.

In this chapter I begin by tracing the location of "superstition" in the discourse and practice of the Chinese socialist state and show how, as part of a modernizing project, campaigns to eradicate superstition have differed in the specific historical trajectories of modernizing nations elsewhere. I then explore how "feudal superstition," as an oppositional category, is intrinsic to the Party's self-definition and then place this process of self-definition in the changing context of the post-Mao economic reforms. I follow with a discussion of the strategies and tactics of symbolic displacement as they are deployed by the Party and by local ritual practice.[3] Finally, I discuss how the Party's dependence on oppositional categories to define itself also invests these categories with the potential to express counterhegemonic sentiments and to what extent these expressions offer resistance to a totalizing ethos of power.

The Modern State and the Decline of Magic

The antagonistic position of the post-Mao state toward popular religion continues in some ways the tradition of the modernizing state in China since the early twentieth century (Duara 1990). Under socialism the political campaigns of the 1960s and 1970s, starting with the Four Cleanups *(siqing)* and the Destroy the Four Olds *(posijiu)*, mark the most repressive period. In the post-Mao period, the state continues to hold a militant line in discouraging popular religion, only to have its efforts mocked by the resurgent vigor of popular culture that has accompanied the economic reforms. The resurgence of ritual practice in a time of relative prosperity betrays the thesis that economic development and the imposition of a technical rationality of production is accompanied automatically by the decline of magic. Modernization theory "forgets" or occludes the fact that the "decline of magic" was not a "natural" or automatic epiphenomenon of industrialization, even in early modern Europe. It was a process accompanied by great violence in the retooling of a proletariat for the disciplines of labor in a capitalist reorganization of production (Federici n.d.). Once this process was accomplished in the industrial transformation of the West, the disappearance of a belief in magic was "naturalized" as an inevitable product of the progress of history. Therefore, to understand the present location of "feudal superstition" in post-Mao political discourse, it first must be placed in the history of how a modernizing discourse, originating in the West, was imported to China, and, in the process, became transformed in China's struggle to attain a modernity shaped by the specific conditions of its own history.

The category of "feudal superstition" *(fengjian mixin)* is therefore one of those neologisms borrowed from the nineteenth-century European narratives of progress, entering China by way of Japan. It can be paired oppositionally with "civilization" *(wenming)*, another import of the early twentieth century that has achieved unprecedented prominence in the post-Mao period.[4] However, before the entry of these discourses of modernity, the Chinese imperium had an already developed technology for the regulation and incorporation of popular practices, including folk religion. Duara (1990) suggests that the efforts of the early twentieth-century state to suppress or control popular ritual represent a break with the practices of the imperial state by the former's incorporation of a far more exclusionary modernizing ethos.[5] He notes, for instance, that popular religion was denoted in the Confucian world view as *xie,* which implied a heterodox but alternative set of beliefs. *Mixin,* on the contrary, he sees as a much more pejorative and trivializing connotation (1990:18). While the first designation connotes an elite perspective of moral supremacy, one that also marks class position in Confucian terms, the other poses a more totalizing rupture of a "primitive" world view transcended by science.

This argument suggests that what may at first glance appear as a historical continuity with the Confucian past must be regarded with an appreciation for its specific historical context. The same will be true in comparing present state policies with the early twentieth-century adoption of a Western conception of modernity. Noting these apparent continuities is not sufficient to understand the present discursive location of popular religion in the post-Mao period. Therefore, in tracing the genealogy of the post-Mao state's will to eradicate superstition, I will assume that this recurring antagonism of the state to popular religion must be explained anew and not merely assumed to be continuous with the past. I will, therefore, pay attention to the discontinuities both with the Confucian past and with the state-building efforts of the modern state in China and elsewhere.

In this vein we can start by questioning the notion of a secularized world view as "naturally" emerging from the logic of capitalist production. Federici notes that in early modern Europe the project to eradicate magic was directed at its power to disrupt the newly emerging disciplines of capitalist labor. Magic offered the promise of obtaining one's desires without labor; it was a "refusal of work in action" (Federici n.d.:11). This echoes the argument of the Chinese state, which also associates superstition with the passivity of a body resistant to work. The technical rationality of industrialism imposes a homogenizing regime in which all time and space are rendered qualitatively undifferentiated and interchangeable. Magic disrupts the imposition of regular work rhythms by noting lucky and unlucky days and observing a calendar of ritual celebrations and festive occasions. The decline of magic in the West was therefore accompanied by state violence to remove the intrusive elements of what was becoming increasingly an alien logic, the battle against witch-

craft being the most violent episode. Federici notes that the fathers of scientific rationality applauded this terrorism as necessary for predisposing
the population toward civil obedience. Intrinsic to this process was the
imposition of a new work ethic effected by the application of myriad disciplinary processes that transformed the resistant body of the proletariat
to the "responsible worker, temperate, prudent, proud to possess a
watch" glimpsed by the end of the nineteenth century (ibid.:3).

In his discussion of Meiji Japan, however, Fujitani situates the modernizing state's efforts to eradicate superstition in its conscious will to
refashion the relationship of the Japanese people to their emperor in the
invention of a modern national culture. It was less a project of imposing
a new labor discipline than it was a political mobilization requiring the
active participation of the Japanese people in celebrating a national culture and a reworking of their subjectivity to align it with a national identity. In the name of "civilization" and "enlightenment," the Meiji rulers
employed a kind of "cultural terrorism" that was not seen as violent but
as essentially instructive in the suppression of irrational beliefs. In the
destruction of local shrines and ritual practices, communities were incorporated into a newly invented homogenous national culture. The refor-
mation of everyday life through the disciplinizing practices of the state
"extended the state's reach into the very souls of the people" (Fujitani
1993:101) and transformed them from passive subjects to subjects
actively responsive to political mobilization by the state for national
goals. Clearly, the urgency of this movement, accomplished over a
remarkably brief time, was closely connected to the urgency attached to
the need for national form and the rapid state-building efforts of the
Meiji state.

The early modernizing state in China shared with the Meiji state this
commitment to a profoundly pedagogical project.[6] Duara notes the
power of the modernizing project in legitimating the early state-building
efforts of the Republican era, operating through what he refers to as a
"logic of modernizing legitimation" (1990:74). This logic was closely tied
to a notion of popular sovereignty ideally embodied in a citizenry that
had to be radically refashioned as rational actors in a disenchanted
world. The goals of political mobilization were implicit in this project,
but more immediate was the goal of "remaking the people," a project that
constructed "the people" as not yet ready for direct political participation. This construction of "the people" as unready for political sovereignty legitimated putting a strong centralized control in place and
thereby instituting in China the *longue durée* of the "period of political
tutelage."[7] The campaigns against popular religion during the Republican era simultaneously granted to what was yet a weakly institutionalized state a highly visible agency even as they constructed the people as

backward and in need of strong state supervision. This logic of rendering the state as a visible presence through its pedagogical exertions returns with renewed force in the post-Mao period.

The campaign against popular religion waged by the Maoist state, which began in the liberated areas, was given a discursive construction within the broader frame of class warfare that differed significantly from that given by the modernizing elites of the Republican period. Hinton's account of land reform in Long Bow village describes how popular ritual, as well as Catholicism, was recognized as a suspect domain supporting the political hegemony of the ruling classes. These campaigns were a radical attempt to transform the ideology of the masses by rooting out practices identified as tools used by the ruling classes *(tongzhi jieji)* to blind the masses to their own oppression and to encourage them toward political passivity through a blind acceptance of "fate." Following the establishment of the socialist state, the campaign against feudal superstition continued to be defined in terms of class struggle. With the consolidation of state power, however, this struggle came to be represented as more educative in nature, aimed at refashioning a backward peasantry whose ideology lagged behind the historical development of China's progress toward socialism.

The rhetoric of class warfare returned, much intensified and more antagonistic in tone, during the Cultural Revolution, leading to the widespread destruction of ritual sites by the Red Guards. The campaign against the Four Olds proved to be a highly effective means to deflect the full force of Red Guard fury away from the Party bureaucracy itself and onto an attack against practices identified as holdovers from the feudal past that retained an assumed counterrevolutionary threat. Popular ritual provided a convenient target for attack that was safely removed from the factional political struggles of the time. It was a unifying target, in the sense that the various factions could all identify toward it a common antagonism that facilitated the reassertion of central control in a period of runaway factionalism. The irony of course is that in a period when peasant consciousness was most valued, this construction of a threat posed in the form of the successful manipulation of a "false consciousness" on the part of the peasantry seriously complicates any simpleminded notion of how the Party saw its relationship to "the people." In this instance, the Party bureaucracy may have been reasserting its control by undermining Mao's populist strategy of invoking the authority of the people to bypass the Party's institutional structure. Clearly, we see from this history that the campaign against feudal superstition has not been a continuous process but a fitfully recurring impulse that has resulted in an intermittent and discontinuous policing of practices that must be read, in each instance, within its wider political context.

However, this fitful destruction and expropriation of ritual places did have a cumulative effect. Each foray marked out spaces that were being incorporated into the construction of a national socialist culture. In some senses this secularization of ritually marked spaces effected a homogenization of space analogous to that effected by industrialism, but in this case the sites that bore local meanings were absorbed into the universal promotion of a national socialist culture, related only tangentially to a logic of production, as I will illustrate subsequently. Places were redesignated with a language that glorified the heroic images of mass mobilization of the Great Leap Forward and the militarized imagery of the Cultural Revolution. They were thereby inscribed with a law that derived not from local particularisms but from a national revolutionary culture designed to obliterate difference in a cosmographic reordering of the local geography through the power of naming.[8]

What is important here is Duara's suggestion that campaigns to eradicate popular ritual in China have historically been about power struggles much larger than the immediate stakes in the game. They have almost always accompanied the assertion of state presence in local communities.[9] I will argue that the same is true for the post-Mao period but in ways that must be read as specific to China's present dilemmas. The post-Maoist state has in fact defined itself as in retreat, delegating downward much of its control over production. This delegation has, of course, led to an ongoing renegotiation of power in which the state-Party has marked out other domains in which to reassert its power and is using more subtle means to do so.[10] The violently antagonistic campaigns that were loudly advertised in the early years of the post-Mao reform represented, perhaps, the desperate ploys by local Party leaders to reassert their control just as the economic reforms were undermining their power. The breakup of the collectives seriously damaged the leaders' power to mobilize aggressively against popular practices. The shift toward education and persuasion and the incorporation of antisuperstition programs into more broadly defined programs for economic and cultural development represent a recognition that the crude methods of a "Mao-style" campaign have been superseded by more sophisticated and "scientific" approaches.

As the reform decade of the 1980s continued, feudal superstition continued as a potent sign of backwardness and, at times, depending on the larger political context, as a powerful marker of social disorder as well. As a sign of backwardness it became caught up in the late 1980s with the project of raising the quality of the people *(tigao renminde suzhi)*. This project extends far beyond a directly eugenics discourse to encompass issues of education and the inculcation of the masses with the requirements of good citizenship. For instance, engaging in popular religious practice would disqualify a peasant household from attaining any of the status markers that designate model households, such as the civilized household *(wenminghu)* or the Five-Good family *(wuhao jiating)*. Clearly, by the middle of the decade, the massive mobilizations directly targeting popular religion as their single goal were beginning to give way to more comprehensive approaches in which feudal superstition became just one item in a catalogue of practices defining, by their absence, a state-defined norm of civility in rural villages. Similarly, in the discourse of social disorder that became increasingly audible in the late 1980s and into the post-Tiananmen period, feudal superstition has been a persistently recurring item on the list, although increasingly it appears to be in competition with the appearance of powerful new sources of social disorder that suggest, more evocatively, the incipient corruption of a free market economy: prostitution, gambling, drugs, pornography, and violent crime. This concern for the social order is hardly limited to Party rhetoric; it circulates freely among the general population, for whom the proliferation of legal pictorials *(fazhi huabao)* provides a vicarious astonishment at the effects of easy money on social morality and reasserts the need for strong Party control.

Feudal superstition, therefore, seems to remain a powerful signifier in the symbolic economy of the post-Mao state, but to a degree that transcends any realistic evaluation of its material threat to Party hegemony. Indeed, throughout the post-Mao period, one gets the sense that this battle against magic has become so ritualized that it has itself become transmuted into a sign in a transnational culture of what it means to be "modern." Superstition is disvalued not only because it offends a rationality of production or because it interferes with the authority of a newly reconstituted center, but because it has itself become an unequivocal "sign" of backwardness and underdevelopment that troubles China's attempts to represent itself to the rest of the world as a rapidly modernizing nation. For the state to enter the fray is to offer itself up as a representation of the modern, activist state opposed to all that is irrational, traditional, and local. The question of what the state's intervention into popular practice "does" in its present context is not simply a matter of discipline or even how subjects are produced through these disciplinary practices, but it is perhaps more what this disciplinization is made to signify.

Foucault sees discipline as an invisible technology of power, essential to the production of the modern subject in its Western, normalized, but highly individuated form. In China, however, disciplinary practices are extravagantly visible as ritual; and in the post-Mao context at least, they are intricately involved with how the state represents itself as a palpable force in society. Disciplinization itself is perhaps not the goal, so much as the state feels compelled to represent itself as disciplinizing. This compulsion explains, in part, the obsessive concern that animates the Party apparatus to engage in these rituals, despite the often ephemeral and ambiguous results produced.[11] And yet, these signifying practices also have a material reality when local communities deploy the normalizing values of civility to indicate to the outside world the readiness of their populations to participate in the transnational flows of labor and capital, rapidly transforming large areas of China's coastal provinces.

The Politics of Tradition and Modernity in the Post-Maoist National Culture

In the post-Mao period both "superstition" and "civilization" figure importantly in the Party's identification of itself as leading the nation in a conscious progression toward modernity. As suggested above, both of these categories derive from an Enlightenment notion of history in the Hegelian mode. Duara has suggested that Enlightenment history provided the means by which "non-nations were converted into nations." It simultaneously establishes the primordial basis of national identity as a subject that extends backward to the dawn of history and the notion of the nation-state as a revolutionary rupture that conveys the nation from a feudal darkness to the light of historically conscious progress toward the telos of modernity. Duara suggests that "there is an underlying gap in national histories between the past and the present, a gap that it must conceal or misrepresent in order to contain ruptures in the body of the nation itself" (Duara n.d.:13–14). Nationalist discourse rests uneasily in "the aporia of simultaneously having to be of the past and free of it" (ibid.:14). This tension is readily apparent in the semantic play between culture *(wenhua)* and civilization in the heated context of the cultural debates *(wenhua re)* of the last decade. *Wenhua* here refers to the notion of reclaiming a Chinese essence in the project of moving toward *wenming,* a state of civility closely identified with the advanced industrial cultures of Asia and the West. Indeed, although *wenming* is often identified with Westernization, much popular interest is directed toward Japan and Singapore as two nations that have successfully achieved civility without losing their cultural identity.

Duara further notes that "at the heart of this split in the time of the nation is the concept of the people" (Duara n.d.:16). Intrinsic to the idea of the nation as a deeply historical identity, "the people" likewise retain a primordial identity. And yet to constitute a popular sovereignty that is intrinsic to the "modern state," "the people" have to be remade as part of the massive pedagogical project of the state. This pedagogical project includes not just the formal educational apparatus, but also, as Duara suggests, the creation of a modern literature and the emergence of folklore as a motivated recuperation of the national essence, and, of course, historiography itself.

In the post-Mao period this uneasy positioning between the past and future is omnipresent in people's consciousness as well as in the often contradictory policies for policing the cultural realm. The post-Mao period has seen the recuperation of a tradition that recreates a glorious past that is in some way directly connected to the present. For instance, the fad for building old towns *(fanggujie)* invokes the former glories of China's ancient cities while at the same time providing the foci for the transforming development of a commodity culture. Tradition becomes very clearly a commodity that constructs the glory of the national past but one that must be reinvented in opposition to the Maoist narratives of the unmitigated darkness of the feudal past and sanitized and channeled for the promotion of internal tourism and foreign investment. Ritual places are allowed some presence in this reinstallation of tradition. Temples that are considered to have "development" potential for tourism and to attract overseas remittances are renovated and opened to the public. In designating some temple sites appropriate for development, the state-Party demonstrates its power to police the line drawn between practices that are identified as healthy or as compatible with the development of socialism and those that are not.

The reconstruction of local traditions is highly selective, excluding those elements that remain outside what is officially defined as civilized. The category of *wenming,* therefore, poses the outer limit within which local traditions can be reconstituted. Therefore, the totalizing order of the Party refers to a vague construction of *wenming* and not to a universal cultural order that contains a set cultural inventory. This construction allows even minority cultures to be incorporated; these can then be subsumed within the construction of *wenming* or at least within terms of evolutional progress toward civility. The elements that cross over must be convertible into a currency that can circulate the notion of a national culture, a monumentalization of local traditions in service to the national essence. Nor is the process of exclusion consistent in time or space, as the local Party leadership retains a certain authority to discriminate where the line is to be drawn. More important, the excluded elements do not necessarily disappear but are encompassed within the symbolic order in highly visible ways. Their exclusion, therefore, does not imply their disappearance from representation itself; quite the contrary, they are what makes representation possible.

Out of these practices is constructed an "otherness" against which the Party can exercise its legitimating activism. It becomes the means by which the Party represents itself as deploying energies, as playing a constructive role *(fahui zuoyong),* to demonstrate that it is not parasitic on the social body. Superstition therefore embodies aspects of "peasantness" that the state marks as backward and uncivilized, as the "other" of modernity. Or superstitious practices are made to incriminate the emerging commodity culture as polluting and alien, a sign of the decadence of Western capitalism, against which an alternative modernity can be constructed.[12] Others of these practices embody "excess"—social and ritual display that becomes a "scandal" in the rational allocation of means to state-defined ends. These categories are not always so discrete. Ritual and festive display, for instance, in addition to their status as "waste," also reproduce difference in locally engineered recuperations of the "little traditions" that may threaten to overwhelm the controlled insertion of "tradition" into the symbolic economy of the national culture.

Therefore, although the disruptive potential of popular ritual is clearly recognized, it does not disappear. Rather, it is consistently brought to our attention by the Party's own ideological apparati. The Party expends great energy in a process that is essentially ethnographic; it records and renders into representation the practices it claims to eradicate. The state has its own informants and methodologies that produce texts for interpretation. These take the form of "social surveys" undertaken by local Party branches that serve to expose targets for reform and the self-criticisms written by those who have been identified as "feudal superstition practitioners" and who are required to elaborate in written form the exact nature of their chicanery. But, in a curious way, the Party is dependent on this flagrant display of its own negative categories, because they provide the stimulus that allows the Party, as a tireless combatant, to make itself visible again and again, as a palpable force in society.

The difference between this process of recording and ethnography in the sense usually connoted by Western scientific discourse is, of course, important to note. Ethnography imagines itself recording what is about to disappear as a salvage operation in the face of ineluctable historical forces (Clifford 1986), whereas the descriptive impulse of the Party is directed precisely toward recording what history has failed to transcend so that it may be more effectively displaced. Mullaney (1983) describes a similar "rehearsal" of popular practices through which the state in early modern Europe selected out the pagan practices of local traditions that could not be assimilated into its more universalizing symbolic order.[13]

Nor does this practice operate on the principle of what Alloula (1986), looking at the colonial postcards of Algeria, has called the "ethnographic alibi," which engages in a love of looking at the object constructed from the projection of imperial fantasies onto the other. This principle may be operative in representations of national minority religion and cultures in the Chinese context, but in the discourse of popular religion in general it is difficult to trace its workings.[14] Rather, the representational modes deployed register an alarm, the presence of a scandal, a call to arms intended to mobilize. In this sense these practices point toward dangers more perilous to the nation or the social order. They are not exploited for a nostalgic re-creation of otherness through a richness of detail, nor do they attempt to explain belief in superstition as a logically coherent system except in the most unabashed resort to psychological functionalism.

Indeed, these accounts work by way of "thin description," using recorded detail judiciously to arouse a certain frisson complexly composed of both horror and titillation that is experienced vicariously. These accounts, when read by an urban, "civilized" readership, exert a certain quasi-pornographic fascination. One gets the sense that the world described within is separated from the reader in both time and space, indeed, as if the actions had taken place in "another country" entirely. This is especially true of accounts that report what may come under the rubric of the "sensational crime" that entails violence, sexual depravity, or murder. These accounts therefore attempt to invoke the irrational in a way that will condemn them irrevocably within the Party's enlightenment project, but they do so using extremely economic means.[15] In so doing, they construct the "quality of the population" in terms of a lack that must be filled by the pedagogical agency of the Party.

The representational process is intimately tied to practice at the local level. Responsibility for this mobilization lies with the propaganda arm of the Party organization and its special work groups. In contrast to the campaign mentality of the Maoist era, this work has been increasingly recognized as a long-term responsibility, requiring meticulous attention. In the dissemination of propaganda material, local activists are urged to integrate it with practice, "administering the proper medicine to the disease" (Fan et al. 1987:136). The emphasis of this work is on the selection of concrete incidents to use as examples in propaganda work, work that requires representation:

> Feudal superstition is very stubborn, but it has one fatal weakness: it cannot tolerate exposure. . . . The greatest weapon for eradicating feudal superstition is to use typical examples to dissect and expose its fraudulent and harmful nature. In practice, one must pay close attention to grasping the crucial point, when opportunity presents itself, and then let the facts speak for themselves. Select those examples that can be exposed on the spot, and then use propaganda media to publicize them widely. Only by creating such an influence will the masses receive a thorough education and only then will a powerful attack be launched against feudal superstitious activities. (Fan et al. 1987:234–235)

Here, the representational impulse operates according to a politics of disclosure by which these practices are emptied of any value except for the purpose of negating them.

Definitional Politics

Clearly, the ritual practices subsumed within the discursive construction of feudal superstition work oppositionally to the self-representation of the modernizing state-Party. And yet, as noted above, this category, despite its continuous presence in this symbolic economy, became remarkably more fluid as the reform period gained momentum and began to generate its own contradictions. During this period also, new voices were added to the Party's exclusive authority to represent ritual, although the Party retained the power to constrain this dialogue when it threatened to challenge the Party's political authority. The social sciences, rapidly gaining credibility as part of the renewed value of science in post-Mao Chinese society generally, provided one important arena of debate about religion and ritual; the emergence of officially countenanced religious constituencies provided another. The fluidity of feudal superstition as a category of excluded practices must also be put into the larger context of this opening of discursive boundaries.

How, then, must we define this category? First, gradations have always existed within the general category of "superstition." Not all ritual practices have been marked by the state-Party as equally oppositional to its authority. Distinctions are made regarding how various categories of superstiton are to be handled by Party authorities. Any clear inventory of what is to be categorically excluded and suppressed is difficult because of the residual nature of the category itself. The only constant is that a line must be drawn between acceptable and unacceptable practices. And while this line is always defined as being self-evident and "natural," a tremendous amount of ambiguity surrounds its interpretation. The state appears steadfast in its discouragement of "unhealthy practices," but within the larger political context, the bounds of what is permissible are constantly changing.

This indeterminateness of superstition as a category is not immediately obvious in authoritative definitions of it found in booklets and handbooks guiding ideological work. For example, a booklet written in the early 1980s discriminates three subcategories within the more general category of superstition: religious superstition *(zongjiao mixin)*, the practice of institutionalized religion; common superstition *(yiban mixin)*, the everyday ritual practice of households or communities; and feudal superstition *(fengjian mixin)*, the ritual practice of professional spirit mediums and other practitioners whose services can be bought (Wu 1982:36). In a discussion published five years later, religious superstition drops out, reflecting the newly restored freedom of religion, leaving only the last two categories, which remain largely the same (Fan et al. 1987). For instance, the catalogue for *yiban mixin* covers, as before, the belief in gods and spirits and superstitious activities that are self-initiated *(zifade)* among the masses, such as the observance of New Year's and other annual festivals, worshiping heaven and earth, honoring ancestors, praying to the god of wealth, praying for a cure, making vows, setting up memorial tablets for the dead, making offerings of food and wine, burning spirit money, and so forth. The other category covers the superstitious activities of spirit mediums, geomancers, and other professionals who cheat and harm people for personal gain. Both of these categories of superstitious practice are negatively valued, but not equally so, as illustrated in the following:

> These two categories are not the same in nature. The first is a problem of ideology and understanding among the masses; the activities in the second category are illegal and are crimes. These two categories must be carefully distinguished in how they are handled. But common superstitious belief and activities are also not beneficial to the thought or life of the masses, nor are they beneficial to the social atmosphere or The Four Modernizations. If they are not dealt with, bad elements can take advantage of them for their own purposes, and this would seriously harm the masses and the socialist cause. Therefore, both categories of superstitious activities must be opposed through propaganda and education. (Fan et al. 1987:237)

As already noted, religious superstition has disappeared, to be replaced by a newly valorized category of religious belief removed from under the shadow of "superstition." From 1986 on, religious belief became recognized as an ethical basis for everyday life that was at least as effective as (if not more effective than) socialist ethics in producing good civic behavior.

> After the harm done during the Cultural Revolution *(shinian dongluan)* to the social atmosphere and the Party's prestige, religious tenets and discipline had a beneficial influence when practiced by their adherents. Among a number of cadres and people, those who were religious followers did not hit or curse others; they did not smoke, drink, or fight with family members or neighbors; they did not steal or pilfer, but were relatively honest. Production team leaders would often send them to watch over fields and storage bins. Religious followers were noted as good people doing good deeds, happy when helping others *(zhuren weile)* and not pocketing money they found." (Luo 1987:186)[16]

Yet despite the removal of religious belief from the negative field of connotations attached to the category of "superstition," it still appears to remain under a shadow within the rhetoric of the Party itself. Handbooks for ideological work recommend that religious activities remain under Party surveillance to ensure that bad elements do not use them for fraudulent purposes or to disturb the social order (Sun 1988:156). Moreover, religious believers are still subject to the educative efforts of the Party's ideological apparati. For instance, one discussion suggests: "While explaining why the attitude of the Party and the government differs in the treatment of religion and superstition, it is also necessary to explain to the people, from the standpoint of historical materialism, the laws governing the origin, development, and decline of religion" (Fan et al. 1987:236). Although religion is allowed some value as a viable ethical system at the present stage of China's social development, it is still clearly one that will be transcended by the historical progression of Chinese society toward socialism and a secularized world view.

Despite this cautious relegitimation of religion, the line between it and feudal superstition remains ambiguous. Drawing a line between high and low culture has always been problematic in the case of Chinese popular religion because of the complex interpenetration of popular ritual with the so-called great religious traditions: Buddhism, Daoism, Confucianism, Islam, and Christianity. Indeed, to a large extent these categories are themselves constructed by the state as a strategy of containment that ultimately retains for the state and its authorities the arbitrary power to determine the line between proper and improper practice case by case (Duara 1990:79). At the same time, however, this indeterminateness is problematic for any sustained effort to police the spiritual environment because where the line is drawn in any one instance is very dependent on the current political wind. For instance, official statements are consistent in stating that public subscriptions for funds in support of communal ritual activity are fraudulent practice. And yet, when local officials attempt to intervene, they are not infrequently confronted with ritual participants citing the 1982 constitutional provision for the freedom of religious expression as proof that what they are doing is legitimate. This ambiguity blunts the resolve of the local Party apparati to sustain its ideological position. Moreover, local Party authorities may themselves be co-opted by a popular demand for ritual tolerance, not only by looking away from activities whose status may be ambiguous, but by becoming active participants themselves or, in some cases, assuming leadership positions within questionable ritual activities (Perry 1985). However, when an urgent concern for social order is expressed at the higher levels of the Party hierarchy, the local Party organization must spring into action and clean up the undesirable practices that its erstwhile "laxness" has allowed to accumulate.

Therefore, although the campaign against superstition remains a constant in the Party's ideological program, one does get the sense that the policing of the spiritual atmosphere is not consistently stringent, but waxes and wanes in intensity. In general this intensity has slackened somewhat since the early 1980s, as some forms of popular ritual have gradually crossed the line into legitimate practice. A number of local festivals have been revived with the active compliance of state authorities; temples have been restored, primarily as "cultural treasures" and tourist sites.[17] Therefore, the body of ritual practices that I am calling oppositional is not always as fixed as it is represented. It is a residual assemblage of practices that reflects the controlled reinsertion of tradition in the post-Mao period. In this sense the category of "feudal superstition" has become more and more residual as the state has retreated from direct assertions of its authority and as some forms of ritual practice, forbidden earlier, find some form of accommodation within the official order. However, those ritual practices not so accommodated remain attached to a core of meanings that continue to activate the Party's militant response:

> Feudal superstition is both fraudulent and harmful. It is fraudulent in that it takes advantage of people's ignorance and devoutness to delude and cheat them. It is harmful in that it saps people's morale in the struggle with nature or with the reactionary controlling classes. It paralyzes people's thought, resists scientific knowledge to the point where it entraps and harms people. At the present stage, feudal superstition also produces social disorder and undermines the social atmosphere. (Fan et al. 1987:234)

This statement touches on two important legitimating arguments against superstition. From the perspective of the state's modernizing ethos, superstition renders people passive, impedes their transformation into productive citizens, and prolongs people's suffering when an appeal to science would be more effective. However, a much stronger argument is made in terms of social disorder. The distinction between the two is reflected in the methods used to deal with the problem. People who engage in ritual practice at the level of the everyday are to be handled through persuasion and scientific education. Those who engage in ritual practice for profit, however, fall outside the law and are dealt with much more stringently through arrest and thought reform.[18] At the very least, their crime is defined as the sale of a "fraudulent commodity." If their activities result in physical harm, they can be accused of much more serious crimes. Such an accusation is especially common when magical healing leads to death because proper medical care was not sought. Of even more concern to the state is the use of ritual to spread counterrevolutionary sentiments or the call of sectarian religions to their followers to cease productive labor in preparation for a change in the moral and political order (Munro 1989). This concern with the social order has been increasingly a major arena for the construction of the Party's legitimacy, especially since the spring of 1989. The representation of feudal superstition figures importantly in that discourse.

One of the most important means to connect popular religion to the specter of social disorder is through its association with the market. In the context of the post-Mao reforms, popular ritual has reappeared along with the expansion of the free market. This renewed visibility of folk ritual is not merely coincidental with the expansion of the market, for these domains interconnect in a number of ways.[19] This reappearance of popular ritual poses an inescapable dilemma for the Party's narrative of modernity and progress. If the economic reform is the most rapid route to economic modernization, how is it that it has also produced activities that connote backwardness and ignorance? Increasing prosperity and sophistication among the peasantry have often resulted in an increased interest in ritual display, not in its disappearance. Increasingly, the state finds that the persistence of ritual practice cannot be explained simply as an element of a primordial peasant mentality continually returning to haunt the present. It is now recognized as emerging from the economic prosperity itself, and therefore it has become an issue in the Party's attempts to reconstitute its waning authority in the post-Mao period. The state, therefore, actively seeks this ritual domain as the very stuff of its own self-definition.

How popular ritual figures in this process of self-definition is complex. The campaign against popular ritual is part of a more comprehensive goal to construct spiritual civilization *(jingshen wenming jianshe)* that is intended to parallel economic development, or the attainment of material civilization *(wuzhi wenming)*. The relationship between these two civilizations *(liange wenming)* marks a major reversal in Chinese Marxism in how the relationship between base and superstructure is conceptualized. The material base is accorded a much greater priority than it had in Maoist thought. The economic well-being of the people is now seen as necessary before cultural change can be effected (this is explicitly stated as an antithesis to the superstructural determinism of the Cultural Revolution); yet the superstructure is not without a certain countereffect *(yidingde fanzuo-yong)*. Therefore, Party rhetoric maintains that the material and spiritual spheres must be grasped together *(yiqi zhua)*, especially since the Party acknowledges that many problems in the spiritual realm derive from the economic reforms themselves. Therefore, the material development of society is seen as both the source of spiritual problems and the enabling condition for their conquest—but only when combined with the spiritual guidance of the Party, thereby reinstituting the imperative for the ideological leadership of the Party at a time when it has been brought increasingly into question.

This renewed emphasis on the party's leadership has gained momentum as economic reform has unleashed market forces that have become less and less amenable to state control. The state's interpretation of the reappearance of popular ritual consequently has changed in its emphasis over the decade. In the early 1980s feudal superstition was a "persistent dreg" of a feudal mentality that had reappeared in the despair and anomie produced by the chaos of the Cultural Revolution. In the reevaluation of collective agriculture, the egalitarian policies of the Maoist period were blamed as producing "poverty" and "backwardness" that went beyond the material immiseration of the peasantry to their spiritual impoverishment as well. The belief in gods and spirits had returned because of the failure of Maoism to deliver its promise of wealth and abundance. To a certain extent, this argument remains. Those most likely to engage in superstitious beliefs and practices are said to be rural people with a low cultural level, especially those who reside in mountainous or peripheral areas. They are generally elderly, poor, uneducated, and female (Fan et al. 1987:235). Superstition figures into a semiotic chain of signifiers that mark the divide between those regions that are backward *(luohou),* isolated *(pianpi),* uncivilized *(bu wenming),* and poor *(pinkun)*—the interior—and those coastal areas that are advanced *(jinbu),* developed *(fada),* wealthy *(fuyu)* and civilized *(wenming).* In this play of oppositions, superstition is the "other" of civilization, the essence of backwardness, and therefore an active sign in the discursive construction of the radical reterritorialization of the national economy in its opening out to a global economic system.

In the late 1980s, however, as popular ritual continued to flourish particularly in areas that experienced exceptional economic success, this argument had to be supplemented with one that could explain why superstitious beliefs did not disappear with prosperity. This puzzle has been most prominently discussed in reference to what has become known as the "Wenzhou phenomenon." Situated in a mountainous area on the periphery between two major economic regions of China (Jiangnan and the southeast), Wenzhou has always been anomalous. It has long been famous as a place resistant to state control, harboring all sorts of illicit commercial activities. In the post-Mao economic reforms, Wenzhou's commercial economy has exploded, but so has its ritual activity. This anomaly has become a favorite focus for the discussion of the relationship between material and spiritual development. In Wenzhou the building of elaborate tombs flourishes, and geomancers and spirit mediums have become ten-thousand-yuan households *(wanyuanhu)* (Xu et al. 1988).[20]

The state's ambivalence about whether the Wenzhou phenomenon is also a "model" *(Wenzhou moshi)* suggests how the heteroglossia of alternative models of economic development that have proliferated in the last decade (cf. the Sunan model, the Kunshan model, etc.) all provide, when taken together, a total semiotic system through which debates about the proper path for the development of Chinese socialism get articulated. The Wenzhou case exemplifies the dangers of allowing the untrammeled freedom of the marketplace to overwhelm the spiritual development of society. Wenzhou has therefore come to embody the imperative for the Party's leadership in the ideological realm as a necessary complement to its efforts in the material realm. In recognition of this need, Wenzhou City was the first urban center in China to establish an Office for the Reform of Customary Practices (Yifeng yisu bangongshi) (*Nongmin bao*, 3 March 1987:3).

The Rectification of Names

Every power is toponymical and initiates its order of places by naming them.
—Michel de Certeau,
The Practice of Everyday Life

If names are not rectified, then language will not be in accord. If language is not in accord, then undertakings cannot be completed. If undertakings are not completed, then ritual and music will not flourish. If ritual and music do not flourish, then punishments will not be on target. If punishments are not on target, the people will not know how to move hand or foot.
—Analects of Confucius, 25/13/3

The appropriation of space through the imposition of a technical rationality and through naming is a strategy of displacement, forcefully applied, and often accompanied by political terror. Yet such imposition and naming are represented as actions in which the masses, once they are properly mobilized by the Party, will participate voluntarily. The suppression of feudal superstition takes the form of antisuperstition campaigns that are colonizing forays into the spiritual domain of the community. They disenchant ritual space by reinscribing it into secular terms. This is most blatant in the appropriation of temple buildings for nonritual uses as described in the account opening this chapter.

A similar contestation occurs when monies gathered to fund the renovation of temple buildings or the costs of the rituals associated with them are seized by local officials and used for officially approved uses, such as repairs to the rural infrastructure or scholarships for local schoolchildren. Huang Shu-min reports that the local people refer to these subscriptions as "taxes" (Huang 1989:152). In a report from Zhangpu county (Fujian), the temple activists who collect these funds are represented as forming an administrative structure that displaces state jurisdiction over control of local funds. A group of eight men in a local cult for *wanggong* were referred to locally as "the standing committee of the god" *(pusa changwei)*. They collected 3,000 yuan for operatic performances to celebrate the god's birthday. The brigade leader reasserted state authority in this case by appropriating these funds for repairs to the local water-control system *(Fujian ribao,* 23 January 1983:2).

The process of displacement is not limited to public ritual spaces; it may extend into domestic ritual space as well. In one account, a movement to send off the gods *(songshen yundong)* was launched in a Henan village when a work team of three cadres was sent down from the county level to help a number of households designated as poverty households *(pinkunhu)* improve their material condition. After their initial survey, the work-team members noted that in each case these poverty households had all set up spirit altars in their houses, with a god's image hung on the wall and an incense burner placed in front. The team then conducted an intensive campaign to develop strategies to improve the economic condition for each household. After three months the fifty-odd poverty households had paid off more than 25,000 yuan of debt altogether, twenty-six households had accumulated some savings, and six households had joined the ranks of prospering households *(zhifuhu)*. To culminate the success of this economic transformation, the team conducted a campaign to promote scientific knowledge and expose the dangers of feudal superstition. The futility of worshiping the gods was incontrovertibly "proven" in the wake of this rapid turnover attributed to the Party's activism. The absences in the text taunt us with their refusal to inform us about the auxiliary resources required to engineer such a dramatic display of efficacy—the special loans and access provided, the euphemized forms of state violence deployed to "mobilize" the latent potential of these households.[21] However, in the denouement of the story, we find the once-poor households "voluntarily" removing the spirit images from their walls and bringing them to a public meeting where they are burned in front of the seated work team. This closing tableau, in which the spirit images themselves become burnt offerings to the work team, who sit like gods behind the flame, neatly displaces the everyday practice of domestic ritual when incense is burned for the gods. And lest there be any doubt in the terms of the displacement, the account ends with a poor peasant comparing his five years of worshiping the gods with no result to the three months of Party activism that brought him out of poverty: "The party's policies are stronger than the gods!" *(Nongmin ribao,* 7 October 1986:3). In the competition between the gods and the Party's economic and spiritual agency, the gods simply do not measure up in terms of their efficacy *(ling)*, the traditional measure of a god's worthiness of being worshiped.[22]

This semiotic connection between Party officials and the gods is not purely gratuitous. In cartoons appearing in the official press, the extravagant demands of officials for gifts and free meals are satirized as being like the insatiability of gods for incense and offerings. This association is obviously not intended in the story above, but its co-presence in the political culture has the potential to provide a scandalous reading here of the power of both gods and officials to coerce displays of "voluntary" offerings through fears of reprisal. In this case, the offerings are not the usual currency of "squeeze"—wine and cigarettes—expected by even relatively upright officials. Rather, the performance of offering up one's ritual images speaks to the power of political terror that local officials continue to wield in the post-Mao period and that allows them to produce at least the fiction of outward compliance with Party policies.

This ironic subtext of ritual as insincere performance is also present in another commentary on the subtle contract between gods and men:

> One year when I returned home for the New Year's festival, I saw a number of people burning spirit money and incense. I said jokingly: "At New Year's the ghosts are not allowed to rest. They are so busy collecting paper ash, how do they manage?" My words were overheard by an elderly lady who still preserved her "quintessence of Chinese culture" feet *(guocuijiao)*. She stared at me in fear and trepidation and said: "Be careful that the gods do not get even with you!"
>
> Although this old lady did not answer my doubtful query directly (I am afraid this would have exceeded her intellect), she still scored a lucky hit: the real reason that people worship ghosts and gods is as a precaution against their revenge. They burn rolls of spirit money and incense just to try to bribe the little ghosts and great gods . . . not to abuse their power. Burning incense, kowtowing, and prostrating oneself in worship may simply look pious, but they are really ways of preventing the gods from taking their revenge on oneself. *(Nongmin ribao,* 7 August 1987:2)

This account appeared as a small commentary *(xiaopin)* in the official press. The narrator clearly positions himself outside local practice by marking his language as irony. He is an urban sophisticate who has returned home for a brief sojourn, not unlike the opening of many of Lu Xun's most acerbic short stories (see Huters 1984). The woman is placed into the antithetical position of backwardness, not just by her ritual activity, but by her very physical appearance marked by the preservation of her bound feet. The disdain of the narrator for the woman's intellect is not for her native ability but for her ignorance, although the word used to refer to intellect *(zhili)* can connote a combination of both. The subversiveness of this text, when juxtaposed to the one discussed above, is in its implications of ritual as a performance of the inauthentic self. One defers to the gods as a defensive posture against their potential abuse of power. In post-Mao China this clearly applies as much to local Party officials as it does to the gods.[23]

The ritualized fashion in which these strategies of displacement announce their effects suggests the ephemeral nature of their success. The news stories that report these activities have a certain obsessive quality about them that intensifies with every repetition. The regular appearance of newspaper reports on the dangers of feudal superstition and on successful campaigns in specific locales, especially as the New Year's holiday approaches, suggests a rhythm between relaxation and intensity that has its own annual cycle and that parallels the ritual housecleaning done before the holiday, when the dust of the previous year is swept out the door along with a year's accumulation of evil influences. The alternation between relaxation and intensity also reflects perturbations in the social order at the local level or even at the level of the nation, such as the campaign against the Six Evils *(liuhai),* following the disruption of the Tiananmen Spring.[24] When martial law was declared in May 1989, I was in the Fujian town of Zhangzhou, talking to temple keepers about their freedom to engage in ritual activities openly. One elderly man laughed and said, "Sure, the local officials attempt to keep things under control, but usually only when they are worried about social order" *(Tamen guan shi guan, hen guanxin shehui zhixu de shihou).* At that moment, the concern for social order was not focused on the crowded, twisting alleys of the old town, where most neighborhood and sectarian temples are situated, but on the modern thoroughfares of the new town, where thousands of students, journalists, and other citizens were marching. The politics of the symbolic appropriation of space were being simultaneously worked out in two quite separate modalities.

The fitful and discontinuous manner in which these campaigns are waged and the ephemeral results they produce do not go entirely unrecognized. For instance, a commentary on the ideological practice of the Party organization in an unspecified Henan county suggests that the campaign mentality, spoken of as a wind that blows hot and cold *(guafeng),* is in itself a kind of superstition. The formation of shock troops *(tujidui)* to tear down temple buildings can never replace long-term commitment and meticulous work in disseminating scientific knowledge and a secularized world view. The author decries the use of repressive measures in favor of persuasion and education: "You can tear down the temples with such tactics, but you can never destroy the 'temples' in people's minds." Moreover, the indiscriminate policy of tearing down all temples fails to make distinctions among those temples that are truly associated with superstitious practice, those that are important to the tourist industry, and those that "have an intimate connection to local feeling" *(fengtu minqing)* (*Nongmin ribao,* 16 September 1986:4).[25] This statement reflects both the measured revaluation of "tradition" and the importance of subsuming the eradication of superstition within a broader program of economic development and education, as illustrated in the example from Henan.

Despite this recognition of their limitations, however, the continued use of campaign methods suggests their importance as a signifying practice of the Party. They have become the ritualized expression of the Party's own will to make its power visible. Not only do they represent the state as a civilizing force to the masses at large, but they also reinscribe the political subjectivity of the Party faithful through campaign activities that reanimate a local apparatus grown weary and uncertain of its role in a changing political and economic environment. The reliance of the Party on these fetishized demonstrations of political efficacy suggests the extremes to which it must go in China's present political crisis to make itself "real" even to itself.

Local Memory

> The places people live in are like the presences of diverse absences. What can be seen designates what is no longer there . . . it is the very definition of a place, in fact, that it is composed by these series of displacement and effects among the fragmented strata that form it and that it plays on these moving layers. . . . Haunted places are [after all] the only ones [in which] people can live.
>
> —Michel de Certeau,
> *The Practice of Everyday Life*

In discussing popular ritual as a "return of the repressed," one must deal with a number of issues that have surfaced in recent discussions of the cultural politics of the post-Mao period. Among these issues is the question of how effective indeed was the wholesale destruction of traditional culture during the Cultural Revolution. In locales where the campaign against the Four Olds was most effective, the devastation appears complete indeed. In many areas no temple buildings survived the period. However, the results of this campaign were not everywhere the same; many structures of recognized historical value were preserved, often in the name of prestigious Party leaders. Moreover, even in areas where no temple buildings remain, the assumption that the physical eradication of cultural artifacts has led to a total cultural vacuum is belied by the astonishing resurgence of many aspects of popular culture.

However, in asserting the resilience of a set of practices in the face of organized attempts to obliterate them, I do not want to suggest that "tradition" returns untouched by the political upheavals of the past. Rather I would suggest that, even in cases of the total physical eradication of cultural artifacts, much can be imagined on the basis of a trace and that local traditions are retrievable through the "post-modern arts of memory" that reinvent them, as much as reconstruct them, in the context of contemporary concerns.[26]

In this sense, despite its self-congratulatory accounts of victory in the symbolic sphere, the state is never allowed the last word. The reappearance of local ritual practice is guaranteed, once the fever of the state's missionizing zeal has subsided. The mnemonic sites appropriated by the state are gradually reclaimed for the dictates of local practice. This reclamation by local ritual happens silently, almost invisibly, a slow but insistent decolonization. It begins with the disruption of school discipline resulting from the quiet intrusion of aged grandmothers who burn incense and *baibai* in the midst of classroom activities (*Fujian ribao,* 22 December 1982). Eventually the school, the food-processing plant, or the recreation hall that has been housed there is completely displaced, and the building turns into a temple again. Or the reappropriation of temple buildings may take the form of a more overt challenge to local Party authority, often in face-to-face confrontations between local officials and possessed spirit mediums who demand the return of temple buildings for ritual uses. In Xincuo county (Fujian province), for instance, "a woman spirit-medium said that the god was speaking through her. She ran to the home of the brigade Party branch secretary and threatened him, saying that the god wanted to return to the temple and the food processing plant that was currently lodged there had to move" (*Fujian ribao,* 22 December 1982). The news story goes on to report that temple cults had displaced altogether four primary schools, a commune-operated noodle factory, two food-processing plants, and the cattle pens of a production team. In the economy of its "thin description," this account gives us no clue as to the shifting balances of power that permitted this apparently irrational and foolhardy act on the part of an ignorant woman. The window of opportunity is usually attributed to the laxness of the local Party organization or the backsliding of Party officials.

Here, ritual clearly becomes oppositional in that it reasserts local meanings and local identity against the more universal claims of the state. But although the appropriations of symbolic space by the state may be made in the name of values that are insistently identified as rational and progressive, they are not necessarily any more "utilitarian" in terms of an instrumental logic than are temple spaces. One commentator reports passing the door of a local "cultural station" to discover that its interior was empty of both people and furniture (*Nongmin ribao,* 28 November 1987:4). The question then becomes whether we are speaking here of something that is really an instrumental rationality or something that operates more importantly at the level of signification.

Community rituals in China have always been "about" (among other things) marking boundaries that define ritually protected areas, inscribing a qualitative difference onto the landscape through the elimination of polluting influences.[27] If we consider this process of ritual cleansing along with the eliminative mechanisms of the state to suppress the "noxious winds" of "feudal superstition," isn't there something fundamentally the same about them both? By inscribing both of these practices within the category of social imaginary identifications, we equalize the power relations between them (at least at the level of discourse) by refusing to privilege the rationalist project of the state with the ontological supremacy it claims for itself.

The operation of this dialectic at the symbolic level explains more completely the obsessive intensity of the state in its struggle for recognition by a population that has only partially internalized its power. It is only a matter of time before higher-level authorities start to mutter darkly about the lax attitude and poor morale of local Party officials who must then demonstrate their zeal for the task by reinitiating yet another campaign in response to mounting pressure from above. If these campaigns are the means through which the state defines itself, then despite their apparently fitful and discontinuous nature, their effect is to make visible again and again the practices against which this self-definition is constructed. They always produce successful results. But success is haunted by the return of disruptive elements that stimulate the mechanisms of elimination once again in the periodic alteration between unity and difference. As Lefort suggests, "The campaign against the enemy is feverish; fever is good, it is a signal, within society, that there is some evil to combat" (1986a:298). The contestation for symbolic space is a Bakhtinian politics of the sign in which temple buildings become the sites of a struggle over signification, in which the battle itself may be more important than permanent victory.

Ritual and Antipolitics

At the end of my discussion on the construction of feudal superstition as an oppositional category at the discursive level, I suggested that the Party's dependence on negative categories to construct its own identity also invests them with the potential to express counterhegemonic sentiments. The time has now come to consider this possibility.

In suggesting popular ritual as an oppositional category in post-Mao political discourse, I do not assume any essential political registration for ritual per se. It is merely noting the projection of an oppositional status onto popular ritual by the state's own definitional impulse. My approach to this question aligns with a more general method of reading the "popular" that derives from Gramsci and that is represented by Marxist cultural studies in current theoretical discussions on popular culture.[28] In this view, the domain of the popular has no essential political connotation; its potential for either opposition to or incorporation by the structure of power is dependent on the particular sociohistorical conjuncture in which it is found. One also must be wary of a totalizing reading that would reduce the political potential of popular ritual to being entirely emancipatory or incorporative. The domain of the popular is capable of a more complex articulation with the structure of power that allows both these possibilities to coexist in complex ways.

Whether or not one can call popular ritual counterhegemonic depends on how one defines the latter. The little resistances of everyday life are not readily visible, yet they do subvert the values and symbolic order of a totalizing structure of power. The mere assertion of their otherness prevents the ideological closure that is the aim of any totalizing power. Whether or not these practices are effective in radically changing the structure of power is perhaps beside the point. Their importance is in their ability to disrupt the totalizing claims of power, which are often asserted but seldom, if ever, realized.[29]

Beyond the confrontation at the symbolic level, the oppositional potential of popular ritual can lead to physical confrontation between ritual practitioners and the state. In 1982 the *Fujian ribao* reported an incident that illustrates the violent extremes to which such confrontation can be carried. The Party headquarters of Yuanzhuang Commune had learned of a small group of people in Lingbei Brigade who were preparing for a ritual performance. To be exact, the account, with its characteristic economy of "thin description," reports simply that they were preparing special dragon robes *(longbao)*. That night, the Party committee organized a group of ten or more cadres to put a stop to the preparations. According to the report, the "ringleaders" in charge of the ritual preparations incited resistance to the commune authorities, and a mass of "unenlightened" people from several brigades raised a ruckus at the commune offices. The crowd surrounded the building and charged it four times. They swarmed inside, hurling insults at commune officials, smashing windows and doors. They trashed offices and conference rooms, smashing file cabinets and telephones. They took bicycles, tables, chairs, quilts, blankets, along with other property of the commune, including commune records, and piled them all outside the building, where they set them on fire. Only after repeated warnings from commune officials did the crowd finally retreat from the premises (*Fujian ribao,* 28 January 1982).

If one defines a counterhegemony as an aggressive challenge to the legitimacy of the state to rule, then this incident is clearly not counterhegemonic in that sense. It is perhaps better understood as a reactive form of resistance against the aggressive intervention of the state to suppress local practice (cf. Perry 1985:438). However, the state is likely to read such incidents as counterhegemonic. This is clear in the language used to describe this "insurgency," a mass of "unenlightened people" led by a few unscrupulous "ringleaders" who are unquestionably assigned to a criminal element (see Guha 1988). Ironically, Maoist historiography elevates peasant uprisings as a historically progressive force and documents the potential of popular religion for counterhegemonic movements—thus the state's present concern with sectarian religious movements that transcend communal and kinship solidarities. Leaders of cult organizations fall into a category suspected by the state to be guilty of the much more serious crime of counterrevolution. Syncretic sects often act secretly and do have eschatological beliefs in an imminent transfer of power, and in some cases, if public security documents are to be believed, they may embrace an explicitly anti-Party rhetoric. Syncretic cults have sometimes plotted armed insurrection against the state. Truly these cases must be regarded as counterhegemonic in intent, although their ability to provide a serious political threat to the state is limited (Munro 1989).

We must also consider how ritual has been radically revalorized by other voices unleashed before the Tiananmen Spring. If ritual provides a surplus value of use to the state in its representational machine, then this value in its very visibility within the state's own discourse can be hijacked by a cultural politics that defines itself as oppositional to the party. Popular religion, in its capacity as the antithesis of *wenming*, thereby becomes a reservoir of images that recuperate the grotesque body in a way, not unfamiliar to the readers of Bakhtin, that unseats all that is solemn and dignified. The grotesque body here represents an antipolitics, a refusal of the high moral ground of the state in its definition of *wenming* as the production of ordered, disciplined, productive bodies. The festive grotesquerie of Chinese ritual, the scandalous sex play of big-headed puppets, the cross-dressing and gender ambiguities of ritual opera, all suggest themselves here as the quintessence of popular vulgarity and vitality. The rituals of commensality, banqueting, and drinking to excess that accompany festive occasions in Chinese peasant culture play out a politics of the body that reaffirms the bonds of community, that lies outside the civilizing gaze of the state.

The Chinese film *Red Sorghum* (*Hong gaoliang,* directed by Zhang Yimou, 1987) portrays a notion of presocialist peasant society as yet "intact" from the relentless onslaught of the political rituals of the Maoist state. Images of festive excess—drinking, feasting, and copulation—become the markers of a "spontaneous," prepoliticized body untouched by the disciplinary technologies of the state.[30] These images may be justly criticized as a dream of lost plenitude when the body was not yet alienated from the pleasures of the lower bodily stratum. Indeed, the retrieval of a pristine body from a primordial time when it was not yet marked by a regime of power can only ever be a mythic project. The film constructs a carnivalization of the body that projects a politically powerful counterdiscourse to confront the ubiquity of the state's moral order. The irony, of course, is that these rituals of excess are not just evocations of an imagined presocialist past but are present in contemporary Chinese society in the rituals of big eating and drinking *(dachi dahe).* Such rituals not only pertain to "the people" but penetrate deeply into "cadre culture" as well, where they become intricately implicated with the structure of power in highly localized ways. The grotesquerie of the body thereby becomes an antipolitics, a refusal of *wenming* in action, that challenges the Party's high moral ground not just at the level of the cultural politics of oppositional intellectuals, but in the daily rituals of everyday life. Here, ritual becomes empowered to speak another politics of the body. In this sense the suppression of ritual does not necessarily result in a cultural vacuum, no matter what has been lost in terms of presumed "authenticity." The reclamation of ritual as "something lost" provides a potentially liberating moment when the signs have been "set free" to signify the impoverishment of people's lived reality suspended in the state's monological order. This grotesquerie marks a refusal to be encompassed by the state's presumption to be the sole arbiter of civility. And indeed, what could be more *bu wenming* ("uncivilized") than gunning down unarmed students committed to an ideal of disobedience that was decidedly "civil"?

NOTES

An earlier version of this essay was presented at the conference on "Communities in Question: Religion and Authority in East and Southeast Asia," Thailand, 4–8 May 1989, and was revised in May 1990 and June 1992. I wish to thank the University of Illinois Campus Research Board, the University of Illinois

Hewlett Summer Awards for International Research, and the Stanford Humanities Center for research support. I also wish to thank Jean Comaroff, Laurel Kendall, Charles Keyes, and Louisa Schein for comments on earlier drafts of this paper and the anonymous reviewers of the published volume for comments on this version.

1. This report was of special interest to me as I had observed a lively ritual scene when I visited the town of Zhangzhou in 1981. This ritual activity appeared to be unabated when I returned in spring 1989. For a detailed account of ritual activities in Zhangzhou, see Dean (1986). He was able to observe two Daoist *jiao,* for which he describes the efforts made to revive Daoist rituals that had been unperformed for decades. The local ritual specialists improvised and substituted when they lacked the required texts or had forgotten the proper order.

2. Fujitani (1993) adapts this phrase from Pierre Nora's *lieux de mémoire* (Nora 1989). Fujitani defines "mnemonic sites" as "material vehicles of meaning that helped construct a memory . . . or that served as symbolic markers" (ibid., 89). He would include rituals as well as more concrete manifestations such as statues, monuments, emblems, and symbols within this category. He talks of these sites in the context of building a national culture around a cult of the Japanese emperor during the Meiji period when the regime "found themselves with a fairly meaningless natural terrain, from the point of view of a dominant national memory and discourse" (ibid.:97). China also has its sites that concentrate memory in the representation of a national identity, yet the meaning of these sites is never fixed, but always contested. (See Waldron [1993] on the Great Wall, Hu and Zhang [1987] on Jinggangshan, Wakeman [1985] on Mao's mausoleum, and Su et al. [1988] on the Yellow River.) The creation of public space as part of the nation-building activities of the state also creates arenas of contestation. The occupation of Tiananmen Square by the students in spring 1989 demonstrated that most clearly (Calhoun 1989). The mnemonic sites I am discussing here inscribe memory on a local landscape, and the symbolic authority to do this is an area of contestation between local meanings and a centralizing authority that wants to subsume these local meanings within its own transcendent and universalizing identity.

3. I will follow Certeau (1984) in making a distinction between strategies and tactics that marks the differential relationship of two actors within a relationship of power. Here "strategies" refers to the clamorously visible and invasive practices of a powerful state, and "tactics" belongs to the less powerful (but not powerless) local community, which often engages (although not exclusively) in silent, invisible moves to decolonize ritual space. "Tactics" here closely approximates what usually gets translated as "stratagem" *(ji)* from the Chinese. The deployment of stratagem, a working outside "the proper," is a notion that pervades contemporary Chinese culture and historical memory.

4. In ideological handbooks and in dictionaries, the history of the term "civilization" *(wenming)* is traced back to the classics, where the characters *wen* (writing, ritual, refinement) and *ming* (light, brilliance, clarity) happen to come together—once in the *Book of Changes (Yijing)* and once in the *Book of Histories (Shujing)*. The text then jumps a couple of millennia to Morgan and Engels (Sun

1988:178). The post-Mao period has generated a host of ideological practices that bear this discursive marker, including the promotion of *wenming* language and public behavior (Dirlik 1982; Erbaugh n.d.).

5. See Watson (1985) and Duara (1988) for detailed discussions of these state strategies of incorporation, what Duara refers to as "superscribing symbols."

6. Indeed, Duara cites Ernest Young's work (1983) on the Yuan Shikai administration, which recruited advisers educated in Japan, thus demonstrating once again the importance of a Japanese model of modernity in China's self-construction of a modern nation, a process still evident in present-day discursive practices (Duara 1990:76).

7. This *longue durée* was of course not continuous on the mainland, where the valorization of peasant revolutionary consciousness complicated the pedagogical relationship. The Party recognized the "small producer's mentality of the peasantry," characterized by an egalitarian ethos, as potentially disabling and in need of correction. However, in the recurrent evocation of the mobilizational culture of the liberated areas, "learning from the peasants" provided an effective control over other groups, intellectuals especially, in Chinese socialist society. In contrast, peasant culture has been devalued in the post-Mao period, both in official rhetoric and by the new social values emerging from a growing consumer culture. Meanwhile, in Taiwan, the period of political tutelage continued up to the recent past as justification for the tight hold of the Nationalist party over the democratic process.

8. The appropriation of temple buildings began soon after liberation; but the Cultural Revolution period is generally credited with the most violent repression of traditional practices, especially the Destroy the Four Olds campaign. In Huang Shumin's account, however, Party Secretary Ye insists that the campaign against superstitious practices started much earlier, during the Four Cleanups campaign of the early 1960s, which had a much more profound impact on rural society. He mentions household ancestor worship, especially, as a target for suppression by the local Party organization (Huang 1989:93). Siu reports that ancestral halls were dismantled even earlier, during the Great Leap Forward in 1958 (1989: 124). This intermittent character of the campaign, in which its intensity varied locally as well as temporally, suggests that it had its local politics as well as being part of a more universal national movement.

9. However, Duara further notes that movements to eradicate superstition were deployed instrumentally in the power struggle between right and left factions of the Nationalist party (1990:78).

10. This of course is the position taken by Shue (1988), who argues that the state has retreated but that its goal is to control less in order to control better.

11. Therefore, in adapting Foucault's theory of the disciplinary state to the post-Mao Chinese context, we must amend it to take account of the tremendous importance of power making itself visible in order to construct itself as a subject-writ-large. In taking such a possibility into account, we are perhaps truer to Foucault than we would be if we attempted to assert the universality of his notion of power in the modern state as essentially invisible and individuating in terms of the subjectivity it produces. One must be wary of essentializing a notion of "modernity" as everywhere the same. At the same time, in noting these differ-

ences I do not wish to assume that non-Western modes of discipline are somehow not as "advanced" as our own but to try to understand them within the specific conditions of their production. That is, the battle to eradicate superstition must be placed in the context of contingent historical forces and not reduced to any deterministic notion of history.

12. Especially with respect to the emerging commodity culture in the post-Mao period, it is important to mention that the line drawn between the "healthy" and "unhealthy" commodity is constantly being redrawn so that these categories are not constant. In particular, the Anti–Spiritual Pollution campaign and the Anti–Bourgeois Liberalism campaign of 1987 were periods during which the polluting aspect of "foreignness" was most intensely targeted.

13. This difference raises important questions about how modes of power/knowledge are constructed in the Chinese socialist state and how they may differ significantly from Foucault's discussion of the disciplinary state as it took its form in nineteenth-century Europe. However, this difference may well be in the process of being superseded in the context of the post-Mao cult of positive science and the importation of empirical social science methodologies, even into the realm of ideological work *(sixiang gongzuo)* itself. It is not yet clear what sorts of new modes of power/knowledge this encounter may be producing.

14. See Louisa Schein's (n.d.) discussion of how the dominant culture represents national minority women.

15. Of course, this love of detail is notably present in Chinese ethnography as an academic discipline, especially when the objects of ethnographic description are China's national minority cultures.

16. The phrase "happy when helping others" is strongly associated with the Lei Feng cult. Lei Feng was a young soldier who died while trying to save state property. He is promoted as a model of selfless sacrifice that has been repeatedly resurrected since the 1960s in campaigns to promote socialist ethics to young people. Its use here notes the potential overlap between socialist ethics and religious values.

17. Local festivals that inscribe a sense of place may even be promoted by official authorities as a means of co-opting their potential enriching the national culture through the display of difference (Siu 1989).

18. The line drawn between everyday ritual practice and that of professionals is not entirely unambiguous. I have written elsewhere of the case of a woman spirit medium who offered magical healing to her neighbors in return for small gifts within the bounds of local norms of reciprocity between neighbors (Anagnost 1987). Although her case was not too serious, she was still targeted by the local Party secretary for thought reform and for mobilization as a publicist against feudal superstition.

19. Perry mentions other periods of relative political and economic relaxation, such as the Hundred Flowers campaign of 1956–1957 and the period of reconstruction following the Great Leap Forward, as periods of renewed ritual activity (Perry 1985:423 and 427).

20. The discussion of Wenzhou appears as a chapter in Xu et al. (1988). Although the authorship of this chapter is not attributed, parts appear to be lifted from a longer piece of reportage on Wenzhou by the celebrated reportage writer

Jia Lusheng (co-authored with Wa Lu 1989). For other accounts of Wenzhou's cultural backwardness, especially the craze for elaborate tomb building, see the *Nongmin ribao,* 3 March 1987:3 and 30 March 1987:2.

21. See my "Producing Productive Bodies" (n.d.) for a more detailed discussion of the representational politics of the Party's campaign to combat poverty *(fupin gongzuo).*

22. This argument that the Party policies are stronger than the gods is always presented as immediately obvious and beyond contestation. In practice, however, prosperity derived from the policies of the economic reform do not necessarily preclude a felt imperative on the part of a community to thank the gods for their good luck. See, for instance, Huang (1989:152).

23. See Ahern (1981a) for a longer essay on ritual as a heuristic frame for learning to deal with power.

24. For a discussion of this alternation between relaxation *(song)* and strictness *(jin),* see Schell (1988). At the macrocyclic level, of course, this has been plotted over time in a classic essay by Skinner and Winckler (1969).

25. The official renovation of temples, while it does occur, is selective. In a booklet on feudal superstition compiled for use in ideological work, the final question was, "If beseeching the gods and worshipping Buddha is superstition, then why are temples being preserved?" The answer states that given the freedom of religious belief, temples must be provided for legitimate religious activity. Moreover, some temples were of historical and cultural value and were therefore part of China's heritage that should be preserved. As important tourist sites for Chinese and foreign visitors, these temples also helped to spread recognition of China's ancient culture. Many temples are not being renovated, however, but are being used for other purposes, such as factories, schools, warehouses, and the like. Not all temples are the same, and if a temple building lacks any historical value, there is no need to preserve it. Instead of demolishing temples, however, it makes better sense to convert them to useful ends in a rational allocation of social resources. Temples in rural villages, such as those dedicated to the earth god, the god of wealth, or the dragon god, are not considered as proper places of legitimate religious expression, nor do they have any cultural or historical value. They merely encourage the propagation of feudal superstition and should therefore be destroyed (Fang et al. 1982:171–174).

26. I have borrowed this phrase from Fischer's (1986) essay on the reinvention of ethnic identity. I am arguing against a polarization of the issue of whether or not the late Maoist period was a total rupture with the past. Suggesting that older kinship and communal solidarities have survived does not belie the fact that much change has also occurred and that these solidarities are very much the product of the structure of power relations in the socialist period. In assuming a total rupture, we are, perhaps, granting the state too much power.

27. For ethnographic descriptions of these rituals of communal definition, see Baity (1975) and Schipper (1977).

28. See Hall (1981) for a classic statement of this view. Helen Siu (1989) takes issue with what she considers an overly hasty reading of popular ritual as inherently counterhegemonic. She cites my work (Anagnost 1987) as an example of posing the opposition between state policy and the return of popular ritual in a

mechanical fashion. In fact, she may have mistaken my reading of official discourse on the return of popular ritual as my own reading of popular ritual itself.

29. Siu herself suggests this when she refers to an "aggressive touch of public display that acknowledged the limits set by officials" (1989:123) and that the wastefulness of ostentatious weddings and funerals are seen by political cadres to produce social networks outside the authority and priorities of the state (ibid.:129).

30. I am indebted to an essay by Zhang Yingjin (1990) for this Bakhtinian reading of the film. It is also worthwhile to note that Bakhtin's study of carnival (1968) was written as a veiled protest to Stalin's repression of culture in the 1930s (Holquist 1981).

10 Salman Rushdie in China

Religion, Ethnicity, and State Definition in the People's Republic

DRU C. GLADNEY

In this chapter I argue that the transnational character of a Muslim protest in China that took place at the height of the Tiananmen democracy protest in the spring of 1989 reveals the ways modern religious and ethnic identities are shaped and how local Muslims move within the specific "contours of power" (Yang 1989:26) in Chinese society. These contours are shaped by what Partha Chatterjee (1986) has called the "derivative discourse" of nationalism and religion in China—the definition of what it means to be a member of an identified nationality or officially approved religious group in China. By appealing to these state-imposed rationalizations of religion and ethnicity, Muslims were able to turn these discursive restraints to their own favor.

I suggest that the categories the state assigns in China intimately shape action and reaction. As in Arjun Appadurai's (1986a) study of material commodities, these classifications, or officially designated labels, take on "social lives" of their own, providing another means of hegemonic control and yielding to certain preshaped channels of rationalization. To paraphrase Jean Comaroff (1985:150), through these discursive units of bounded definition the state engages in the "colonization of consciousness." Not only has the state colonized its subject peoples, but by exerting classificatory control over national and religious identities, it has sought to control the ways that people conceive of themselves and act vis-à-vis the state. The protest over "China's Salman Rushdie," however, evidences effective ways in which some people have turned these designated identities against the state into legal forms of resistance.

The Rushdie Ripple: Transnational Islam "Even unto China"

Just before the bloody suppression of the 1989 democracy movement in China, amidst the flood of protesting students and workers who, for a remarkably lengthy moment in history, marched relatively unimpeded across Tiananmen Square and the world's television screens, another, comparatively unnoticed but nevertheless significant, procession took place. It moved between three main points in the city. Starting at the Central Institute for Nationalities, the state-sponsored college that attempts to "educate" some of the most elite representatives of China's seventy million members of minority nationalities, the protest was composed mainly of Hui Muslim students. They were joined by representatives of all ten Muslim nationalities in China, as well as some sympathetic members of the Han Chinese majority.[1] The rather unwieldy procession made its way down the "high-tech corridor" of China's university district in the northwest corner of the city, where Beijing University, People's University, Qinghua University, and a host of other colleges had erupted with innumerable student protesters in the heady days before 4 June. Like those zealous student marchers, this procession was on its way to Tiananmen Square, the Gate of Heavenly Peace, which would soon open onto a hellish nightmare of indiscriminate warfare in the streets of the terrorized city. This procession to the square also made its way along Changan, the Avenue of Eternal Peace, which shortly thereafter was to be renamed Blood Alley by Beijing's citizens. But instead of proceeding directly to the square, it veered south to its second point of destination: the central Oxen Street (Niujie) Mosque patronized by many of Beijing's two-hundred thousand Muslims and the nearby Chinese Islamic Association.

Instead of calls for "Democracy!" and "Freedom!" this protest raised banners that proclaimed "Death to China's Salman Rushdie!" "Respect China's Freedom of Religion!" "Uphold the Constitution!" "Uphold the Party's Nationality and Religion Policies!" "Preserve Nationality Unity!" "Love our Country, Love our Religion!" "Oppose Blasphemy against Islam!" "Allahu Akbar!" (God is Great) and "Ban the Book *Sexual Customs,* the *Satanic Verses* of China!"[2] Unlike the students and workers dressed in their street clothes, these protesters wore the emblems of Islam in China: men donned the white hat by which Muslims are frequently distinguished, while the women, many for the first time, adopted the Middle Eastern–style *hijab,* or head covering (*gai tou* in Chinese), which is publicly worn (in a different style) only in very conservative Muslim areas of China, but adorns Muslim women throughout the Islamic world.[3]

Numbering almost three thousand by the time they reached their final destination of Tiananmen Square, these Muslims, primarily students from the Nationalities Institute, were protesting the publication in China of a book, entitled *Sexual Customs (Xing fengsu),* that they claimed denigrated Islam—just as did *The Satanic Verses,* they said, recalling the book whose publication had evoked charges of blasphemy throughout the Islamic world. *Sexual Customs* was an innocuous description of the history of sexuality around the world, which guaranteed it a strong market in China, where few official books address the subject (see Schell

1989:73–84). Muslims in China would normally pay little attention to such popular literature. They were violently incensed, however, by sections of the book dealing with Islam that compared minarets to phalli, Muslim tombs and domes to the "mound of Venus," and the Meccan pilgrimage to orgies, which were an excuse, the book claimed, for homosexual relations and sodomy—*with camels,* no less (Ke and Sang 1989: 45–46, 74–75, 105–113, 130–131).

The denigration of Islam and of religious practices not thought to be Chinese has a long history in China, and this is by no means the most degrading example. The response this time, however, was the most violent in recent years. In addition to the protest of three thousand Muslims in Beijing on 12 May, the Chinese press reported that more than twenty thousand Muslims marched in Lanzhou, the capital of Gansu, at the end of April, and up to a hundred thousand Muslims filled the streets of Xining, the capital of Qinghai, in mid-May. Smaller protests were reported in Urumqi, Shanghai, Inner Mongolia, Wuhan, and Yunnan.

Remarkably, in another dramatic contrast to its response to the student prodemocracy movement, the state took the following actions in response to this Muslim protest over an insignificant Chinese book. The government granted full permission for all of the Muslim protests,[4] often dispatching police to close streets, stop traffic, and direct the marchers, many of whom were organized by the Chinese Islamic Association, a state-sponsored organization established in the 1950s. In Beijing the police even provided a car for a Hui Muslim professor from the Central Institute for Nationalities to escort the protesting students. At the end of the students' long day of protesting, the state provided buses to bring them back across town to their home universities. Perhaps the state's rapid response was influenced by the visit of Iran's president Ali Khameini, who on 11 May—just one day before the Beijing protest that ignited protests across China—stated that he was in full solidarity with the Chinese Muslims' demands and that despite international outrage the Ayatollah Khomeini continued to maintain his death threat against Salman Rushdie, the author of the allegedly blasphemous *Satanic Verses.*

The state immediately met all the demands of the protesters. *Sexual Customs* was banned, and 13,000,000 copies were allegedly confiscated, with 95,240 copies publicly burned in the main square of Lanzhou; the Shanghai editors were fired and the authors required to make a public apology; and the publication houses in Shanghai and Shanxi were closed for "reorganization."

It is perhaps even more significant that the government decided to be lenient toward Muslims who had gotten carried away in the largely peaceful demonstrations, breaking laws and damaging state property. In a Lanzhou Muslim protest on 12 May, more than two hundred Muslims rampaged through the downtown offices of the provincial government, breaking windows and office equipment and severely injuring the driver of a car suspected of transporting copies of the book. The Public Security Bureau, after a prolonged struggle, arrested thirty-five Muslims, who were detained overnight. However, instead of prosecuting the Muslims, the government released them after an emergency meeting with representatives of the local Chinese Islamic Association, who arbitrated on their behalf (see Gansu Provincial News Agency 1989:59). The pseudonymous authors, whose real names were finally discovered, were rearrested after their release for their own safety. Muslims in Qinghai had offered a reward of 600,000 *yuan* (U.S. $200,000) for their execution. As of this writing, they are in hiding under police protection, Salman Rushdie-style.

Although the protests were briefly mentioned in the Western media (*The Economist* 1989:103; *Los Angeles Times* 1989; *New York Times* 1989), they were portrayed as anecdotal and marginal compared to the significance of the Tiananmen movement. Given that they occurred in the midst of the student demonstrations, hunger strikes, and the visit of Soviet president Mikhail Gorbachev, this is not surprising. What is noteworthy is that the Chinese media covered every detail of the Muslim protests, and the procession in Beijing on 12 May shared the front-page headlines of the *People's Daily (Renmin ribao)* with the student strikes and the Gorbachev visit.

This was not the first time Muslims have demanded redress from the Chinese state. Similar protests over anti-Islamic publications have taken place since the rise of the popular press in China. Löwenthal (1940:242–246) recorded another Beijing incident in 1939, when Muslim protesters wrecked the publication offices of the *Shijie wanbao* and the *Gongmin bao* and forced the Commercial Press, China's largest publishing house, to publish a formal retraction of an article that the protesters found "insulted Muslim womanhood." Pillsbury (1989:6–7) noted that between 1926 and 1936, Han Chinese magazines and newspapers published more than twenty-four articles denigrating "peculiar customs" of Muslims in China. These included such statements as "the pig is the most beloved son of the Muslim gods" and described Muslims as descended from a pig, which they worshiped (the Muslim prohibition against eating pork was described as veneration for their ancestors!). One such article, entitled "Why Muslims Do Not Eat Pork," appeared in Shanghai in 1932 and led to an attack on the magazine's editor and the closing of the publication house. These incidents were not limited to prerevolutionary China, however. The 12 May letter presented by the protesting students contained references to a 1984 Shanghai *Youth News* article and a 1988 *History of Religion* volume published in Shaanxi that was "barbarian and impertinent to

Muslims." The rise of the Muslim nationalist protests against published insults to Islam and its heritage is one more demonstration of Benedict Anderson's (1983a:46–49) argument that the proliferation of print media in Europe gave currency to national and transnational identities, reaching out to isolated groups and individuals. This protest is unique in that it made use of the Rushdie incident as a rallying point for a local concern. The Rushdie case has now been elevated to an international metaphor for local Muslim complaints anywhere, "even unto China,"[5] underscoring the transnationalism of Chinese Islam. In addition, and perhaps because of the international attention given to the matter, including Khameini's support for the Beijing protesters, the Chinese government's response and acquiescence to Muslim demands has never been as thoroughgoing, nor the protest as influential on a national scale.

The state-controlled media, by stressing the legality of the Muslim protests (what Pillsbury [1989:10] noted as their *"protest to* the government," rather than *against* it), sought to juxtapose its legality and rationality against the illegality or chaos *(dong luan)* of the student protests. The students, as an unrecognized voluntary association, were labeled "hooligans" *(bao tu);* unlawful and riotous, they were a threat to the state's order. For that they were met by a military crackdown. The actions of the Muslims, as members of state-assigned minority nationalities believing in a world religion approved by the state, were considered tolerable, and perhaps useful. For that they were smothered with state-sponsored media and assisted in their demands. The difference, from the Chinese state's standpoint, was one of order versus disorder, rationality versus confusion, law versus criminality, and reward versus punishment.

The Making of Minorities:
Nationality Identification in the Chinese Nation-state

The notion of state-sponsored objectification of nationality may be familiar to students of colonialism in other settings. There is a specific link among China's nationality policy, anthropology, and colonialism— one that should give Western anthropologists pause. Until very recently, anthropology in China has been almost exclusively limited to the study of minorities, generally taught and carried out in the nationalities institutes and nationalities research centers rather than in the universities. During the most liberal periods the universities offered sociology as a means of studying social trends and the majority people, the Han, whereas anthropology was devoted to the study of minorities—the traditional British anthropological approach. In China, as is often the case where such derivative disciplinary distinctions are maintained, sociology studies the "we" while anthropology researches the "other." (This may be a factor in the widespread Chinese suspicion of Western anthropologists of China who have sought to study the Han majority, because the traditional role of anthropology is to study the "primitive," which the Han certainly do not see themselves as representing.)

As David Arkush has documented in his description of political turmoil in the life of China's senior social anthropologist, Fei Xiaotong, sociology received the full brunt of the Maoist critique in the late 1950s:

> It was said that bourgeois sociology had been progressive at first, when subverting feudalism, but had lost its revolutionary nature when the bourgeoisie became the ruling class. It had consistently supported the bourgeois capitalist order by justifying its social division, extolling social harmony, and generally depicting capitalist society as just and the highest stage of social development. (Arkush 1981:268)

Anthropology, in contrast, was generally given approval because of its practical usefulness in understanding, incorporating, and by implication, colonizing minorities:

> As for anthropology, it had served imperialism by providing information on primitive colonial peoples, that was used in controlling them. Firth's *Human Types,* which Fei had translated, was quoted to show that anthropologists provide this service knowingly: "Modern anthropology is practical. . . . Colonial governments have known it is important to use anthropology in dealing with aborigines" (Hu 1958). Functionalism, it was said, had not been concerned with explaining origins or the history of systems but with pointing out functions, in order that colonial administrators could handle peoples more effectively. (Arkush 1981:269)

In China, anthropology became "people's anthropology" (Fei 1981), because it concerned itself exclusively with the cultural study of minority peoples, generally ignoring such issues as political economy, social structure, religious authority, and socioeconomic change. So long as they were viewed as tools of the state in dominating the minorities, ethnography and anthropology were in general more protected than sociology. In China anthropology became an important means to a nationalist end: the description and production of an object, the objectified other, a process that Johannes Fabian (1983) discussed as being one of the unintended, but often lasting, results of ethnographic research. After the 4 June crackdown sociology was again banned from Beijing University as being a tool of "bourgeois liberalism." The teaching of ethnology and anthropology at the Nationalities Institute, however, was not as affected by the crackdown. Though both anthropology and sociology departments at the different universities supplied equally numerous students to the square, anthropology was viewed by the authorities as a lesser threat, since by definition it was concerned with the study of the objectified minority "others," not the social problems of the majority subjects.

In the 1950s teams of Chinese anthropologists were sent out by the state to identify the minority nationalities who would be recognized by the newly founded People's Republic (Gladney 1991; Heberer 1989:30–39; Chiang Feng and Tzu Wang 1982). Upon encountering many of these peoples on the Long March, which wound through many minority areas, the leaders of the Chinese Communist party had often bargained for protection by promising affirmative action and favoritism in the new China, including at the outset even the possibility of secession (a promise that was withdrawn after 1934). After the establishment of the People's Republic, these early promises of favoritism were taken seriously by a multitude of peoples who considered themselves "ethnic" and wished to be recognized by the state as nationalities. More than four hundred of these peoples applied to be recognized. Decisions on these applications and final determination of which ethnic groups would be recognized as nationalities were predicated on an interpretation of their meeting the four criteria, first proposed by Stalin, of locality, language, economy, and "culture," as well as on a Marxist application of Henry Lewis Morgan's theory of stage developmentalism.[6] Only fifty-four peoples were finally recognized as "nationalities," the Chinese technical term for which is *minzu* (Fei 1981).

Many of these nationalities, such as the Miao, were actually umbrella groups of several peoples that were told they had to join together as one nationality to be recognized (see Diamond 1988). Other nationalities, such as the Yi, included many groups who were only remotely linguistically related (see Harrell 1990). Others were members of a former (and in some instances multiethnic) state, such as the Tibetans, Mongols, Koreans, Manchus, Dai, and Bai. Some received ethnonyms derived from other nations—most notably from the Soviet Union, which had already categorized several nationalities in Central Asia under Lenin's program in the 1920s, including the Turkic Muslim groups, the so-called Uighur, Uzbek, Tatar, Kirghiz, and Kazak (see Gladney 1990b). Other groups were simply invented on the spot. One residual group of Muslims not identified by language or locality took their ethnonym from a Chinese mistranslation of the Central Asian Muslim Uigur; they became registered as the Hui. Members of this group include a wide range of Muslims speaking disparate languages such as Mandarin, Tibetan, Mongol, Dai, Bai, and Yi—but all simply registered as members of the Hui nationality (see Gladney 1991). The term "Hui" simply meant "Muslim" before the People's Republic was founded, and included all Muslims anywhere (even foreign Muslims could be referred to as Hui). Only later did the term come to designate one particular Muslim nationality as distinct from nine others.

Those peoples who were not accepted as nationalities were included as variants within the Han majority nationality, including the Chinese Jews, the Ku Cong, the Chuanqing Blacks, and a host of others, many of whom have by now disappeared. These people were considered simply *ren* (people), not *minzu*. Hence the Chinese Jews, who according to the Sino-Judaic Institute may now number as many as eight thousand, are merely termed *Youtai ren* (Jewish people) and are accorded no legal status under the constitution. In all, the 1982 census revealed 799,000 members of "unidentified" peoples. Once it became known that the State Commission for Nationality Affairs was beginning to accept applications to become nationalities from previously unrecognized groups, there was an overwhelming surge of requests for recognition. In Guizhou province alone, more than eighty groups totaling 900,000 people petitioned for nationality status in 1981 (Heberer 1989:37–38), but most were not even allowed to be considered. Only fourteen groups have been officially allowed to be considered for recognition, and they are currently under investigation. In January 1989 I was told that the state was no longer accepting applications. While the state drew several groups together into umbrella nationalities, split others, invented some, and denied even more, these nationalities became objectified as bona fide "peoples" over the course of the last forty years.

While many minorities existed in premodern China and were of great concern to the various empires that conquered China, they were generally regarded as "barbarians" to be ruled, not "nationalities" to be incorporated into the nation-state. It is this discourse of nationalism and participatory government (whether actually so is not at issue) that distinguishes the People's Republic from the dynasties—the former claims authority from below, the people; the latter sought legitimacy from above, the heavens, with the emperor, the Son of Heaven, as supreme ruler.

Why would anyone want to belong to a nationality in China? At times there were many reasons not to, but during liberal periods, such as from 1950 to 1958 and since 1979 (perhaps until 4 June), pluralistic policies allowed—even, I would argue, encouraged—people to adopt national identities that were made available by the state.

In Chinese these groups, including the Han majority (also an umbrella group subsuming the wide diversity of Cantonese, Hakka, Sichuanese, Shanghainese, Fujianese, and a plethora of other so-called sub-Han identities under one nationality label), are all known as *minzu* (literally "people" and "clan")—one term that can be loosely translated as nationality, nation, ethnic group, and people. The term is not native to Chinese: the nationality volume of *The Complete Encyclopedia of China* dates its arrival in China to 1903, when it was introduced by the "capitalist Swiss-German political theorist and legal scholar, Johannes Kaspar Bluntschli" (Zhongguo 1986:302).

The importance of having one's *minzu,* or nationality, was most effectively popularized in China by Sun Yat-sen, who was himself influenced by Japanese (*minzu* comes from the Japanese term *minzoku*) and Russian nationalist movements. More important, Sun was an overseas-born Chinese and Cantonese who sought to unify all of China under one major nationality, the Han (effectively masking his own differences from the northerners he was trying to enlist). This creation of the Han as a nationality, a *minzu,* accomplished two things: it set them apart from the internal "others," identified by Sun as the Tibetans, Manchus, Mongolians, and Muslims, who together with the Han majority formed the "five peoples" (*wuzu gonghe*) of the Republic; and it distinguished the Han as one enormous unified nationality in opposition to the imperialist nations, represented by other perceived "nationalities"—such as the British, German, and Japanese—that at the time were carving China up into dominions of extraterritoriality. If China was to successfully modernize and oppose these foreign aggressors, Sun argued, it must unify under the banner of one nationality: the Han, whose past was reconstructed as almost unilineally descending from the Yellow Emperor to the Han dynasty. A multinational state became the ancestor of a unified nationality. By distinguishing the "other" as Tibetan, Mongol, Muslim, and foreigner, the Chinese "we," no matter how problematic and internally varied, began to cohere as a distinct nationality for nationalist goals. Sun, a Cantonese raised outside China who spoke little Mandarin and educated himself in Japan, revealed his concern to assert—and perhaps *invent*—Han nationality in his famous Three People's Principles speech.

> The Chinese people have shown the greatest loyalty to family and clan with the result that in China there have been family-ism and clan-ism but no real nationalism. Foreign observers say that the Chinese are like a sheet of loose sand. . . . The unity of the Chinese people has stopped short at the clan and has not extended to the nation. . . . China, since the Ch'in and Han dynasties, has been developing a single state out of a single race, while foreign countries have developed many states from one race and have included many nationalities within one state. . . . The Chinese race totals four hundred million people; for the most part, the Chinese people are of the Han or Chinese race with common blood, common language, common religion, and common customs—a single, pure race. (Sun 1924:2, 5)

The fervor of nationalism in the early twentieth century was soon felt in China and led to the overthrow of the Qing empire, the brief establishment of the Republic, and finally the People's Republic. Swept up with the new state was the notion of the *minzu*—a foreign term, concept, and tool that proved effective for political control and nation building.[7]

After forty years these nationality designations have stuck, taking on perhaps unforeseen lives of their own and contributing to the resurgence of national identities according to the labels prescribed by the state. These labels are attached to culturally defined contents such as language, religion, and customs specific to the peoples identified by the Stalinist-inspired search for these traits. These traits become "primordialized" in the Geertzian (1963a:105) sense, in which essentialized identities become represented to and by the state. The objectivized depiction of minority peoples in China as good dancers, singers, and sportsmen is a feature of this process well known to travelers in China and of the Chinese state's representation of itself as "multinational." While unidentified peoples have continued to apply for recognition, those fifty-six designated nationalities have functioned legally vis-à-vis the Chinese state. The Muslims demonstrating in the streets of China's major cities protested not only as Muslims, but also as members of the state-assigned Islamic nationalities, in a demonstration of what Geertz (1963a) has called "primordial" politics.

This is illustrated by the means with which Muslims justified their participation in the Salman Rushdie–style protest in China. Several accounts reported that many Muslims felt compelled to take part in the protests because the book was an affront to their identity as members of state-assigned Muslim national groups. In Qinghai the following statement was made to the Xining news service:

> Han Fucai, a Hui leading cadre, said: *As a Hui cadre,* in common with all Muslims, I am extremely angry. The masses have called for punishment according to the law for those concerned with publishing, distributing, and editing this book. This is quite fair and reasonable. (Qinghai 1989:53; emphasis mine)

As a member of the Hui minority, one of ten Muslim nationalities in China, this man felt insulted by the portrayal of Islam in the book *Sexual Customs,* though he himself was a cadre, probably a Communist party member, and undoubtedly not very religious. In an immensely useful circularity, the state-assigned label of identity became the means by which this man's claims were placed before the state.

Confusion in the literature on minority nationality identity in Marxist-Stalinist states, whether Soviet or Chinese, has arisen over the interchangeability of the terms "ethnicity" and "nationality."[8] The failure to make a distinction has seriously muddied discussion of Chinese minorities. The problem lies in the fact that, though they are not always used consistently, English and Russian make clear distinctions among the various terms for people, ethnicity, nationality, and nation, whereas Chinese expresses all these notions with the single derived term *minzu*. Though this term can be glossed as nationality, people, or ethnicity, it is clearly the state-identified meaning of the term that is important to the Chinese. When the Chinese recognize a group as a *minzu*, they are officially conferring nationality status upon that group, whether the group thinks of itself as "ethnic" or not. Western scholars, more influenced by Weberian (1978 [1956]:389) notions of self-ascribed ethnicity, become preoccupied with the appropriateness of the nationality label itself, namely whether the identified *minzu* qualifies as an ethnic group or not, whether by Chinese or Western anthropological criteria there are unrecognized groups who should be officially accepted as nationalities, or whether the state has "invented" ethnicity for some groups (Harrell 1990; cf. Handler's 1985 distinction between nationality and ethnicity). Although there are clear instances in China of unrecognized groups who see themselves as "ethnic" (such as the Chinese Jews, the Ku Cong, or the boat people) and of recognized nationalities that were probably not single ethnic groups before being designated as such (the Hui, Yi, or Uigur), labeling by the state assists the process of ethnic change. The ethnonyms of many of these groups existed before their recognition by the state, but the attachment of the term *minzu* by the state legitimates, objectifies, and in some cases invents these identities. Whether the Hui were an ethnic group before they were identified as a separate nationality by the state in the 1950s is not at issue here; that the Hui and other nationalities certainly see themselves as bona fide ethnic groups today is at the heart of the "race to nation across ethnic terrain," in the phrasing of Brackette Williams (1989:401). In this case, some groups have gone from seeing themselves as "ethnic" to recognition by the state as nationalities, while others have moved from being identified as nationalities to beginning to think of themselves as ethnic groups. My argument is that the discursive categories of identity applied by the state have shaped the contours of this ethnogenesis. The state authorized and legitimated a defined set of categories—which would be accepted, and then used, in resistance to the state.

Rationalizing Religion in China

"Religion" *(zongjiao)* is also a term foreign to Chinese (Gao and Liu 1987:83). It first arose in Japan with the proliferation of Buddhist sectarianism. In the *Chinese-English Buddhist Dictionary,* Soothill and Hodous (1935:255) wrote that *zong* represents the "ancestor, Siddhartha, category, kind, school, main doctrine." Coupled with *jiao* (teaching) it took on the meaning of the central teaching as opposed to the sectarian offshoots, or *zong pai,* of Buddhism in Japan. When the term was gradually reintroduced into China, it came to refer to the central, often systemized, rationalized world religious traditions (see Geertz 1973a:170–192) as opposed to local folk religious traditions.

This distinction between rationalized world religions *(zong jiao)* and local folk traditions was employed by the early Chinese Marxists against the proliferation of those practices that they labeled as superstitious *(mixin),* also a term borrowed from the Japanese (see Gao and Liu 1987:83–88). "Superstition" became sharply differentiated from the world religions, of which the Chinese identified five: Buddhism, Daoism, Islam, Catholicism, and Protestantism (there is no generic term for Christianity in Chinese).[9]

In a debate over religious theory and practice that raged from 1949 to 1966, radical Marxists argued that all religion was superstition and should be discarded in favor of the complete imposition of atheism. These purists cited Mao's position that all religion is a form of oppression of the masses, stated most fully in his 1927 speech "Overthrowing the Clan Authority of Ancestral Temples and Clan Elders, the Religious Authority of Town and Village Gods, and the Masculine Authority of Husbands" (in MacInnis 1972:10–11). Moderates, in contrast, argued that since the oppressive structures of religion had been overthrown, a distinction should be made; superstition should be condemned as feudal; but religion, a worldwide phenomenon of modern society, though thought incorrect, should nevertheless be protected along with atheism by the constitution. The late social scientist Ya Hanzhang best summarized this distinction, which became the accepted policy when the moderates triumphed in 1978, in a *People's Daily* article in 1963:

> Religion *(zongjiao)* and superstition *(mixin)* have their similarities. They also have their differences. All religious activities are superstitious activities. This is their similarity. But not all superstitious activities are religious activities. This is their difference. Among the people of our country, especially people of the Han nationality, such superstitious activities such as fortune telling, physiognomy, and geomancy were quite prevalent in the past. While these, of course, are superstitions, they are not religious, being neither the activities of any religion nor any religions in themselves. (Ya Hanzhang in MacInnis 1972:38)

This approach was further elaborated in a more recent article by the late Ya Hanzhang, who as a Party member and former director of the nationalities research department of the Chinese Academy of Social Sciences, was an avowed atheist. He stated:

> A religion (the three major world religions in particular) has a complete and systematic religious philosophy and religious doctrine. It has well-organized religious organizations, religious bodies, religious systems, religious rites, and religious activities. Religion differs from feudal superstition in many aspects, but the most fundamental one is: Religion is a way of viewing the world, while feudal superstition is a means by which some people practice fraud. (*Guangming Daily,* 20 April 1981, in MacInnis 1989:404)

The distinction between religion and superstition continues today. Despite the reemergence, even explosion, of so-called superstitious activities in the countryside, these practices are still considered illegal, and the state may arrest those involved or crack down on them (see Anagnost's chapter in this volume). Activities associated with the five religions are considered legal, and the state is generally more hesitant to restrict them. At the fringe, however, there is much debate about what is actually religious and what is superstitious. While this debate is constant in the official press and at the local level, it is entirely artificial to traditional Chinese society, using derivative categories of religion and superstition that make invidious distinctions not present in Chinese religious tradition. The Chinese state has traditionally concerned itself with heterodoxy and orthodoxy (and this may be the origin of the current preoccupation), but it never made a distinction of religion or superstition among Daoist, Buddhist, and folk traditions. Anthropologists have documented that Chinese traditional religious practice combines elements from all of these traditions, and Chinese throughout history have made regular use of ritual practitioners from each tradition, depending on circumstance (Weller 1987a:167–170).

In modern China it is incumbent on the practitioner to convince representatives of the state apparatus that what one is doing is really religious and not superstitious, just as a person must convince the state that she or he is a member of one of the fifty-five recognized minorities to qualify for the benefits accorded to minorities in state-sponsored affirmative action programs. Activities normally associated with superstition and restricted among the Han, such as shamanism among the Naxi and mystical expressions of Sufism among Muslims, are allowed to flourish because they are considered expressions of nationality custom permitted under the law. A foreign researcher was recently granted permission to carry out research on shamanistic healing ceremonies among the Naxi in Yunnan; such ceremonies would never be allowed among the Han (though they are of major interest to anthropologists in Taiwan; see Sangren 1987; Weller 1987a). The researcher was later denied access, however, because of fears that she would discover secret herbs the Naxi shamans use and market them in the West for a financial profit. The loss of the real capital of the herbs was a greater threat than the study of the symbolic value of shamanism by this foreigner.

The acceptance of religion, as opposed to superstition, is often justified by reference to the belief in world religious traditions by established nationalities, thus making religion useful, just as is the recognition of these nationalities themselves, in nation building:

> The Party and the State have adopted the policy of freedom of religious belief because religion is a longstanding, complicated matter, concerning millions of people of *various nationalities*. Only by firmly implementing the policy of freedom of religious belief will it be conducive to the stability of the country and the *unity of the nation;* only thus will it be able to fully arouse the enthusiasm of the religious masses so that they will work hard together with all the other people of the country to build a modern, powerful Socialist state with a high degree of civilization and democracy. (Xinhua [New China News Agency], 28 December 1982, reprinted in MacInnis 1989:398; emphasis added)

Categorization and Colonization

One of the most effective means at the state's disposal in "colonizing consciousness" is categorization. Although Michael Hechter's (1975) theory of "internal colonialism" is primarily concerned with economic dependencies and hierarchical divisions of labor instituted by the state over its internal regions, reminiscent of colonial models of appropriation and extraction, there is also a classificatory dimension to internal colonialism that bears on this discussion. Hechter and Margaret Levi wrote:

> [E]thnic solidarity among any *objectively defined set of individuals* is principally due to the existence of a *hierarchical* cultural division of labor that promotes reactive group formation. This kind of division of labor is typically found in regions that have developed as internal colonies. (Hechter and Levi 1979:263; first emphasis mine, second in the original)[10]

In another, albeit completely external, colonial setting, Bernard Cohn (1987) described the "objectification of culture" through the assignment of ethnic labels in the institution of the census in India under the British raj. Cohn argues that many of these labels, such as washerman, though occupation-specific and constantly shifting, "ethnicized" into "objective" identities once they were rather arbitrarily assigned, identified, and quantified by the state in the census—identities that persist today.[11] In the same way, Nicholas Dirks (1987:3–5) has argued that an overessentialization of caste in India ignores its genealogy of growth and decline in communities where caste can be shown to be constantly shifting as a result of the dynamic realignment of power relations. *Homo Hierarchicus,* Louis Dumont's monumental work, is criticized for reifying the constantly negotiated existential phenomenon of caste into an essentialized identity of the "Indian" as such. His critics have argued that the British state contributed to the objectification of caste by stripping away its political power and reducing it to a fundamentally religious identity (see Prakash 1989; Appadurai 1986b:745–761). Indian "hierarchy" is often contrasted with Western "egalitarianism," both orientalist idealizations that may have little do with social reality.

In China the state has played a very important role in the rationalization of these identities through the assignment of categories by which people begin to channel, fix, and gradually rationalize their behavior. I have suggested nationality and religion as two examples of this colonization of consciousness, but there are many others. History, time, art, language, music, and literature are but a few areas wherein the state exercises taxonomic control over what is chronicled, scheduled, exhibited, spoken, sung, written, and published as exemplars of these colonized labels. The traditional importance attached in China to names and naming is evidenced by the Confucian practice of the rectification of names *(zheng ming)* whereby, it is believed, a thing's essence is contained in the name it bears. By attaching official, legal status to the categories of identity, the state has appropriated the traditional role of the literatus in determining the correct names of things. Aesthetic categories are tightly controlled and defined by the state, but I argue that the nationality policy mostly leads to objectification of identities, since nationality is the main category by which one is registered in the state census and receives the authority of the state. The state enumerates and divides its population in cellular fashion; the cells have grown into a living organism.

While we might disagree with how religion and nationality have been defined in China, we cannot dispute the imposition of these labels upon the Chinese people by the state. Just as these policies have been a means of suppression and expression of the Chinese people—often arbitrarily adapting who is defined as a nationality and who is not or which activity is religious and which is superstitious—they have also been turned back on the state in the form of claims. Actions and protests, using the categories created by the state and rationalized accordingly, force the state to make good on at least some of its promises. The fact that Wuer Kaixi, one of the main leaders of the student democracy protest in Beijing, belonged to a Uigur Muslim minority from Xinjiang (his Uigur name is

Uerkesh Daolet) may have been a factor in his influential position vis-à-vis the state authorities, who may have been initially less inclined to suppress him as a member of a sizable Muslim nationality. I have argued elsewhere (see Gladney 1990a) that the involvement of many minorities in the democracy movement, disproportionate to their population in China, indicates the beginning of what Roderick MacFarquhar (1989: 10) has termed the "Tibetanization" of all of China. The categories applied by the state have now been successfully used as a means of resistance against it. By legitimizing these voices with the power of the state's authority, the state is more constrained to at least take note of their demands and not dismiss them as irrational or chaotic. In this sense, the colonized have turned the tables (and their labels) on the colonizers, using the categories as levers against them or, to follow James C. Scott (1987), as symbolic weapons of the weak, empowered through appropriation of the state's own taxonomies.

"Preserve Nationality Unity!"

The call for national unity *(minzu tuanjie)* was one slogan shouted and printed on banners in the Rushdie protest that well illustrates this "label turning." During my fieldwork, Hui Muslims traditionally quoted another popular slogan with a very different meaning, a Chinese translation of a Qur'anic *hadith,* "All Hui under Heaven are one family." The *hadith* originally referred to all Muslims in the wider Islamic *umma,* but it is now taken by the Hui as referring only to the unity of their own people. This saying occasionally arose when I asked Hui informants what was unique about them as a people.

I once caused a famous Hui calligrapher great embarrassment when I asked him to inscribe for me the phrase "All Hui under Heaven are one family." This phrase was criticized during a 1958 campaign against "local nationalism" *(difang minzu zhuyi),* which sought to discourage local ethnic identities in favor of broader national unity (Dreyer 1982:34). Out of fear of later being accused of local nationalism, my Hui artist friend suggested instead that he paint the state's preferred slogan, the one chanted by the Muslims in the Salman Rushdie protest: Nationalities Unite! *(minzu tuanjie).* This slogan, which is intended to encourage all minorities to unite together with the Han majority for the good of the country, serves as an official contradiction of the Hui phrase. It is still prominently displayed in every minority area. A magazine devoted to minority culture bears its name; until recently the slogan graced the main entrance of the Central Institute for Nationalities in Beijing, and it can still be seen on the underside of a five-*yuan* note.

Hence, it came as quite a surprise to me when, during several interviews with Hui informants, the Hui used the same phrase to refer to their own solidarity when threatened by outsiders. To a question I often asked about what they saw as a characteristic of being Hui, several responded: "We Hui nationality are very united" *(Womende Hui minzu hen tuanjie de)*. They thus reinterpreted the meaning of *minzu tuanjie* to be "nationality unity" instead of the plural "nationalities united"—a retranslation perfectly permitted by Chinese grammar, since there are no plurals in Chinese, but completely opposite to the state's original intent. Without changing the Chinese phrase, they have thus radically altered its meaning. This slogan, for many Hui, is now often taken to mean the solidarity of their own ethnic group vis-à-vis other nationalities and the dominant hegemony—a far cry from its official public meaning. In short, the Hui have unconsciously, or perhaps deliberately, substituted the meaning of their traditional Islamic *hadith,* "All Hui under Heaven are one family," for the state's own slogan, Nationalities Unite, by changing the original intent of the phrase to fit their own preferred interpretation. Identified by the state as a nationality, the Hui have now begun to see themselves in ethnic solidarity. These shifts in and appropriations of meaning, tradition, and history demonstrate the dynamism of the manipulation of state-assigned labels to meet local concerns.

The myth of the unity of all the members of the People's Republic as one socialist entity has not been accepted by all its peoples. Instead of being a "body without organs" (Deleuze and Guattari 1987:149), it is as though the separate body parts now wish to go their own ways. Lefort (1986b:279) argues that the idea of the "people as one" is fundamental to the totalitarian vision. In China the state has instituted a policy that allows the possibility, if not the actuality, of pluralism. Though many in China may await the diminution of national difference, as predicted in Marxist and modernization theory, China remains a multinational state. The Rushdie protest has demonstrated that Muslims in China are anything but "assimilated" or "Sinicized" and that they are reasserting their identities in the public sphere.[12]

Salman Rushdie and National Protest in China

Slogans shouted during the Rushdie protests and reported in the Chinese press included "Uphold the Constitution!" "Uphold the Party's Nationality and Religion Policies!" "Oppose Blasphemy against Islam!" "Ban the Book *Sexual Customs!*" The government did all this and more. The book was confiscated, the authors punished, and the publishing houses closed (actions that promptly raised the value of the street copies of the book: a reporter for the *Los Angeles Times* found that some were being sold privately for several times their original price [Pillsbury 1989]). The Muslims, as members of a state-recognized, and to a certain degree state-rationalized, category of nationality (an official *minzu*) and believers in a state-approved religion (an accepted *zongjiao*), could make claims on the state that others were denied. By contrast, voluntary associations, student organizations, and labor unions are generally illegal in China, and, therefore, denied a voice. In its preempted role as colonizer, the state sets the categories and institutions by which its subjects can rationalize their actions. Otherwise, they appear chaotic and illegal. These were precisely the charges the state used to justify imposing martial law and calling in the tanks. The colonial authorities had lost control of their internal colonies.[13]

During the Rushdie protest in Beijing, the Muslim students moved from the Nationalities College to the Open Street Mosque (which is also the site of the Chinese Islamic Association) and finally to Tiananmen Square. Each of these three institutions had been established by the state as a means of controlling and channeling religious and nationality expression.

In the Nationalities College minorities are trained primarily to serve as cadres—future colonial administrators for the state in the minority areas (see Gramsci 1957). This system of nationalities training institutes was one of the few minority policies not adopted from the Russians: it was a holdover from the empire, thus further establishing the genealogical link between China's current nationality policy and colonialism. After the fall of the Qing dynasty, the Manchu Court of Colonial Affairs was replaced by the Mongolian and Tibetan Affairs Bureau (Meng-Zang Shiwu Chu) (*China Handbook* 1947:30, 74, 99; Dreyer 1976:18, 23). Under its jurisdiction was the Mongolian and Tibetan School (Zhipian Xuetang), established in 1909 by the doomed Qing government in an effort to incorporate Mongols and Tibetans into the imperial bureaucracy, since Han migration in the latter half of the nineteenth century had been steadily increasing and encouraged in those areas, a reversal of previous Manchu policy (see Brunnert and Hagelstrom 1912:165–166; Dreyer 1976: 12). The Mongol and Tibetan School (renamed Meng-Zang Xueyuan) was continued under the Nationalists, and many of the future minority nationality leaders trained there became leaders of the Nationalist and Communist parties. The first Nationalities Institute (Minzu Xueyuan) was established in Yenan in 1941 under the leadership of the Mongolian Party members Ulanfu (who became assistant director of the institute in 1943), Kui Bi, and Ji Yatai, all of whom were students at the Mongolian and Tibetan School when they joined the Communist party in 1925. As early as 1950, plans for the establishment of the Central Institute for Nationalities in Beijing were initiated. Today there are thirteen related nationalities institutes throughout China. The State Commission for

Nationality Affairs, which is responsible for all minority-related issues in China, is the last of what Dreyer (1976:30) calls "several reincarnations" of the Mongolian and Tibetan Affairs Bureaus passed on from the Qing through the Nationalist governments. Significantly, the Rushdie protest was initiated by Muslim students organizing within the walls of the Central Institute for Nationalities. The educational institute established by the state to educate, incorporate, and integrate its minorities had become the site of pan-Islamic activism.

The Chinese Islamic Association was founded by the state in the 1950s, along with other religious organizations for the officially approved religions, as a means of incorporating the native religious leadership into the state apparatus. All other religious organizations were banned and suppressed (the Catholic bishop appointed by Rome is still in prison and the Dalai Lama still in exile). The Chinese Islamic Association represents the culmination of several Muslim political activist organizations that appeared in the 1920s and 1930s during what one Hui historian, Ma Shouqian (1989), termed "the Hui people's new awakening" and concern for "national salvation." In the 1950s the state quickly moved to ban all other Muslim political organizations, co-opting them under the umbrella aegis of the Islamic Association. From 1958 to 1978 even traditional Islamic organizations such as Sufi brotherhoods, the Saintly Lineage *(menhuan)* organizations, and other established Islamic orders were generally banned in China, but these have since begun to reappear (see Gladney 1987; Lipman 1989). Until 1983 the Chinese Islamic Association in Beijing was the only organization officially allowed to train future imams, publish Islamic literature, and coordinate Muslim activities like the pilgrimage to Mecca. These functions have since become much more decentralized and mosque-centered, as in traditional China, but the Islamic Association nevertheless still wields tremendous power in its responsibility for overseeing national and international Islamic affairs. Situated around the corner from the Oxen Street Mosque, the oldest and largest mosque in Beijing, the association received the Muslim protesters, and its director made a speech supporting their demands for "upholding China's nationality and religious policy." By traveling to Beijing's largest mosque and the Chinese Islamic Association, the Muslim students made it clear to the state's leaders that their demands were founded in their religious identity, a religion accepted and sponsored by the state, with a national and international audience.

Their final destination was Tiananmen. The students did march past the State Nationalities Commission just off Changan Avenue, where they also read their letter of protest, but their main display was geared for the heart of Beijing. Tiananmen has become the public ritual center of the new Communist state, replacing the former religious center of imperial

China at the Temple of Heaven, whose ancestral rites are now considered to be forms of feudal superstition. The Muslims circled the square, walking past the picture of Chairman Mao suspended above the Gate of Heavenly Peace of the Forbidden City, and engaged in a public spectacle of protest for the assembled journalists and television crews, most of whom were Chinese. There were few foreign journalists in the square on 12 May because the students had called off their protest in hopes of obtaining the dialogue the government had promised them. When it became apparent that the state was unwilling to enter into dialogue with the students' leaders, they called a hunger strike on the night of 12 May and marched to the square the next day, diverting the world's and China's media attention from the Muslim protest.

By leading the procession to the three centers of administration set up by the state—the school, the mosque, and the square—the Muslims were challenging the state on its own grounds, within its own categories. The students were not given this option. It is not surprising that the Muslims, as well as the students, were playing to a world audience through the modern technology of the media. The Muslims' signs were in Chinese, Arabic, and English (most of China's Muslims do not read Arabic and recite the Qur'an from memory), and many of the women covered their heads with Middle Eastern–style *hijab* (perhaps donated by the Iranian embassy) instead of the traditional Chinese Muslim head covering. As mentioned earlier, the support visiting Iranian president Khameini gave to the Chinese Muslims' Rushdie copycat protest was certainly not lost on China's leadership. After the bloody Tiananmen crackdown China's reliance on Middle Eastern Muslim countries as important trade partners became all the more critical when Western businesses withdrew from China out of protest and concern for a stable investment environment. The last thing China wants to do is isolate itself further by antagonizing its Muslim minority.[14] By taking advantage of these shifting international power relations, Muslims in China have turned what was once a colonial policy of nationality and religion, a derivative discourse influenced by Soviet, Japanese, and American nationality theories, into their own avenue of expression. The calls to Uphold the Constitution and Praise Allah were no longer contradictory for China's Muslims. In a deft political maneuver, they had turned the labels of nationality and religion back on the Chinese state, illustrating the reclaimed identity of Islam in the People's Republic and the salience of primordial protest.

Conclusion

Although Muslims have lived in China since the middle of the Tang dynasty (eighth century), they have never been fully integrated or assimilated into the Chinese cultural mainstream. Inhabiting urban ethnic enclaves and isolated villages, attending separate schools, and maintaining their own unique languages and forms of speech, they have been perpetual outsiders inside Chinese society. Salman Rushdie himself, like the Muslims of China, is an eternal immigrant, an internal exile, who in *The Satanic Verses* is engaged through the characters in his novel (particularly Chamcha, who describes himself as a "British citizen First Class") in the struggle for subjectivity, in wresting away from others the objectifying labels that define and circumscribe one's identity. In one remarkable paragraph Rushdie's Chamcha is told how the upper-class whites objectify the immigrant's identity in England: "They describe us. . . . That's all. They have the power of description, and we succumb to the pictures they construct" (Rushdie 1989:168). The Arab literary critic Sadik Al-Azm (1991) cogently observes that in Rushdie's novel, just as in Jean Genet's plays *The Maids* and *The Blacks,* the characters only become objectified "others" through the gaze of a superior "self." By accepting these stigmatized identities, they begin to gain control of the asymmetrical relationship. In *The Blacks,* the black protagonists frequently declare, "We are what they want us to be. We shall therefore be it to the very end, absurdly." Just as Rushdie's Chamcha undergoes the gross transmutation from Pakistani immigrant to devilish monster, the objectivizing process of the minority experience in China has now been accepted, challenged, and promoted in the public sphere, as illustrated by the Rushdie protest.

As "others" inside Chinese society, never fully *Chinese,* always a lesser minority, the Muslims in China have again found their identity in an outside community, the Islamic world. Concerned also not to disrupt profitable relations with that world, the Chinese state dare not antagonize its own Muslims to too great an extent. Such are the precarious conditions of religion and nationality in modern China.

NOTES

For comments on earlier drafts of this chapter, I would like to thank Charles F. Keyes, Laurel Kendall, Dale F. Eickelman, Robert Hefner, and members of the SSRC/ACLS Thailand Conference, especially Ann Anagnost, Jean Comaroff, Robert Weller, and Jean DeBernardi. My colleagues at the Institute for Advanced Study, where the bulk of this essay was written and revised, especially Arjun Appadurai, Nicholas Dirks, Clifford Geertz, and Sherry Ortner, provided numerous helpful comments. Funding for research in China during 1983–1987 was received from Fulbright-Hayes, the Committee on Scholarly Communication with the People's Republic of China, and the Wenner-Gren Foundation.

1. There are ten "official" Muslim nationalities in China, who altogether have a total population of sixteen to twenty million, with the Hui Muslims the most

numerous. The Hui are distinguished by the lack of their speaking any one language, living in any single locality, or sharing any common cultural attribute other than a traditional belief in Islam. This is in contrast to the nine other Muslim minorities, who are members of Turkic-Altaic or Indo-European linguistic subfamilies and many of whom also have significant populations outside China, such as the Uzbek, Kazak, Uigur, Tatar, and Tadjik (see Gladney 1987, 1990, 1991). China has recognized a total of fifty-six nationalities, with the Han designated as the majority (Dreyer 1976; Heberer 1989).

2. For more information on these protests, see the sketchy but fascinating news accounts and radio broadcasts reported in the Beijing China News Agency 1989:52; Beijing New China News Agency 1989:53; China Communication Service 1989:52; China Communication Service, Hong Kong 1989:53; Gansu Provincial News Agency 1989:59; *Huaqiao ribao* 1989:3; Qinghai Provincial News Agency 1989:52; *Shijie ribao* 1989:6; Tokyo Kyodo 1989a:23, 1989b:52.

3. See Chaiwat Satha-Anand's discussion in this volume of the controversy over women's wearing the *hijab* in public schools in Thailand. In China, generally only Muslim women in the northwest provinces of Ningxia, Qinghai, Gansu, and Xinjiang wear the *hijab* in public when they are not performing *salat* in the mosques, and their head coverings generally veil only the hair and neck, not the face. As far as I know, unlike Turkey, Thailand, and even France, in China's conservative Muslim areas the government has not proscribed the veiling of women in public schools since the reforms of 1978. During the Cultural Revolution (1966–1976), however, and more generally since the Religious Reform Campaigns beginning in 1958, all forms of Muslim dress were discouraged and criticized (see Gladney 1991). This protest was distinguished by the participation of large numbers of young Muslim women in veils (for a discussion of Chinese Muslim women in Taiwan, see Pillsbury 1978:651–676).

4. An apparent exception was the uprising in Urumqi, Xinjiang, where Uigur Muslims arrested during the protest in the public square had still not been released up to one year later. This may be due to the proximity of Xinjiang to Soviet Central Asia, where Muslim nationalist movements are a greater threat to Chinese interests. It has led to increased ethnic tension in Xinjiang because it appears that only Uigur protesters were arrested, while several Hui Muslims, who the Uigur claimed first brought the Chinese book *Sexual Customs* to the local Uigurs' attention, were not prosecuted. For Hui and Uigur relations in Xinjiang and intra-Muslim conflict in China, see Gladney (1991) and Forbes (1987).

5. This plays off the well-known *hadith* (saying of the Prophet) "Seek knowledge, even unto China." While much ink has been spilt on the Rushdie incident, and several have noted the transnational implications of the event (Spivak 1989; Taylor 1989; van der Veer 1989), we do not find, even in the recent wide-ranging compilation of the articles surrounding the event by Appignanesi and Maitland (1990), any speculation regarding the possibility of the Rushdie scandal being mimicked effectively elsewhere by Muslims with local complaints, as happened in China, though I suspect this will not be an isolated example. In a recent fascinating paper, the Syrian scholar Sadik Al-Azm traces significant parallels between Rushdie and Rabelais, Voltaire, Joyce, Fellini, and Genet. Rushdie, "as a demythologizer, a demystifier and a dereligionizer" (Al-Azm 1991:37) is not

alone in offending the status quo of his age; he thus becomes a useful icon for other transnational movements.

6. The Sichuanese archaeologist, museologist, and novelist Tong Enzheng in a controversial article published in China (1989) was the first Chinese social scientist to outline and critique the strong influence of Morgan's theory of stage evolutionism on Chinese anthropology. Tong described the almost slavish adherence to the theory in China and illustrated attempts to demonstrate the theory's validity time and again by reference to "primitive communist" customs discovered among minorities regarded as "living fossils," all of which was driven by the desire to prove Marxist nationalist ideology.

7. See Walker Connor's (1984) discussion of the primarily pragmatic and strategic goals of Marxist-Leninist nationality theory, which covers a multitude of inherent contradictions and policy reversals.

8. For excellent recent summaries of Soviet nationality policy and ethnology, see Bromley and Kozlov (1989), Karklins (1986), and Shanin (1989). While the borrowed and limited Chinese term *minzu* conflates the categories of identity, Soviet ethnological vocabulary distinguished in Russian among *ethnos, nationalnost,* and *narodnost* (roughly equivalent to ethnicity, nationality, and "peoplehood"). In the 1960s Soviet ethnology began to move away from essentializing studies of "primitive minority customs" to more processual and historical studies of ethnogenesis and ethnic change, but because of the breakdown in Sino-Soviet relations this change had little influence on Chinese ethnology.

9. In an interview a representative of the Ministry of Public Security responded to a question regarding superstitious and feudal activities:

> According to stipulations in China's constitution, citizens have freedom of religious beliefs. In China, Buddhism, Daoism, Islam, Catholicism and Protestantism are protected by the State's religious policy. Religious believers are allowed to conduct religious activities in religious places. However, all reactionary secret societies and witches and sorcerers are banned and prohibited from resuming their activities. (*Agriculturalists Daily,* 17 April 1987; reprinted in MacInnis 1989:409)

10. For the debate on the usefulness of the "internal colonialism" model, see Cassanova (1965), Eley (1976), Hind (1984), and O'Neil (1980); Gouldner (1978) argues its appropriateness to Stalinism in the Soviet Union, and Verdery (1979) for Eastern Europe, while Friedman (1989) notes the "re-Stalinization" of post-Tiananmen China. Hechter's (1975) theory has certainly been used too broadly, but it provides a useful framework for discussing recent nationalist movements from Eastern Europe to China and the resurgence of primordial politics.

11. Compare also Handler's (1984) discussion of the gradual objectification of Quebecois identity in Canada, which is relevant to current separatist movements.

12. Space precludes a discussion of the importance of the public nature of this event, particularly with regard to Habermas' (1989 [1962]) argument regarding the nature of the public sphere in the development of the nation-state, but the fact that the Muslim protest was directed at all of the major power centers of the government, terminating in Tiananmen Square, indicates the new vitality and assertiveness of Islam in China.

13. To carry the colonial analogy even further, Rey Chow (1991) suggests that the important role of the Western media in China in broadcasting the protest was only allowed because of the tradition of extraterritoriality in China, established by foreigners during the unequal treaties of the 1850s. Few totalitarian regimes would tolerate such live coverage by foreign media of their crackdown on their own civilians; that Chinese authorities did indicates their tacit acceptance of this Western press as not subject to China's own laws. Chow writes:

> Nowadays, instead of guns, the most effective instruments that aid in the production of the "Third World" are the technologies of the media. It is to these technologies—the bodies of the Western journalist and camera person, their voices, their images, their equipment, and the "reality" that is broadcast in the U.S. and then "faxed" back to China—that extraterritoriality is extended, and most of all by Chinese communities overseas who must, under the present circumstances, forget the history of extraterritoriality in Sino-Western relations. (Chow 1990:8)

14. Yitzhak Shichor's (1989) detailed discussion of the "Sino-Saudi missile deal" reveals the importance China places upon its Middle Eastern relations to gain hard currency, and this importance has increased with the decline in Western business after Tiananmen. China relies on many of its Muslim nationals as representatives in negotiations with foreign Muslim countries. It can ill afford to alienate them. The increasing importance of the Muslims in China as mediators in these exchanges may signal their regaining their place as important middlemen on the legendary Silk Road, only in this case it is Silkworm missiles, not fabric, that are being bartered.

11

Hijab and Moments of Legitimation
Islamic Resurgence in Thai Society
CHAIWAT SATHA-ANAND

In early 1988 there was an extraordinary debate concerning Muslims in Thailand. As a result of the so-called *hijab* crisis, daily papers carried numerous articles and letters from Muslims and non-Muslims alike exchanging views on the issue of Muslim dress. Responding to my letter arguing against a columnist's piece that had suggested that *hijab* dress is more of Arab culture than Islamic code (Chaiwat Satha-Anand 1988a), a foreign reader wrote to the *Bangkok Post:*

> The various dresses of these peoples (Muslims) are determined by their disparate cultures. This is not to say that the new radical elements of Islam worldwide are not trying to change this; these fanatics *are* trying to make dress an Islamic issue. . . . When Islamic people [*sic*] use Islam itself in an attempt to have their own way regarding dress, they are taking unfair advantage of the Thai government by escalating their "cause" from a simple cultural matter to a religious crisis. (Slattery 1988)

Another angry letter from a Thai reader asks, "Do schoolchildren and students in Islamic countries demand to dress according to Buddhist, Christian, Sikh, Jewish, etc., religions?" (Pantup Danasin 1988). It is important to note that for Muslims, dressing is an Islamic issue; "these fanatics" may be symptomatic of a people who need to reassert their own identity; and wearing *hijab* in this case at this time is no "simple cultural matter." The second letter, despite its angry tone, raises questions concerning the relationship between a dominant religious group and a religious minority and the way in which the latter is treated by the former. These letters are examples of the kind of debate generated by the *hijab* crisis of December 1987 to March 1988.

This essay examines the way Muslims in Thailand express their Muslim identity in a society in which the majority of people are Buddhists and in which Buddhist rhetoric and symbolism are used extensively by the Thai state. It seeks to construe the dilemma of legitimation when the Muslims appeal to religion as a form of legitimation that supersedes that

of the state. The *hijab* crisis is chosen as a case study through which a
pattern of relationship between the Muslims and Thai society, amidst the
wave of Islamic resurgence that contributes to a new moment of legitima-
tions, can be constructed.

I begin with a discussion on the problematic nature of "Islamic resurgence" and its possible impact on Muslims in Thailand. Then, reasons
for choosing the *hijab* crisis as a case study will be suggested and a
detailed account of this event presented. As this event has generated a
lively debate that touches upon important issues concerning Muslims in a
Buddhist country, the nature of this public debate will be discussed.
Finally, problems of legitimation resulting from this *hijab* crisis will be
analyzed.

Islamic Resurgence

The notion of "Islamic resurgence" is problematic. Two other notions
commonly used in the same vein are "revivalism" and "reassertion." The
former clearly indicates the idea of returning to the past and perhaps "a
desire to revive what is antiquated" (Muzaffar 1987:3; see also Muzaffar
1986:6). The latter term is more complicated. Arguably, "reassertion"
does not convey the idea of a challenge to existing social arrangements.
"It does not even come close to suggesting that dominant paradigms are
being questioned. It merely connotes insistence, insistence upon one's
cause, one's position. It is essentially a positive statement" (Muzaffar
1987:2–3; Muzaffar 1986:5–6). For Muslims, however, the notion of
"reassertion" has one clear advantage: it is a religious concept. The history of Islam can be characterized as a movement of resistance *(al-muqu-
wamah)* and reassertion *(al-takid)*. The latter notion finds its sanctity
in the original conception of Islam, for the Prophet Muhammad was
obliged to practice resistance as a prerequisite for asserting the doctrine
of *tawhid* (unity of God) and its corollaries (Saikal 1987:194; Ayoob
1981).

Some scholars use the terms "resurgence," "revivalism," and "reassertion" interchangeably without taking into account their fine differences
(Ahmad 1983:218–229; Anwar 1987:9). Chandra Muzaffar (1987:2;
1986:5) has pointed out three reasons for choosing "resurgence" over
other terms such as "reassertion" or "revivalism." First, it is a view from
within the Muslim community itself and highlights the growing impact of
the religion among its adherents. Second, it suggests a phenomenon that
has happened before and thereby connects present events with the past.
Third, the term embodies the notion of a challenge and perhaps more
importantly, even a threat to those who adhere to other world views.

Muzaffar also argues that Islamic resurgence as a social phenomenon began more than two hundred years ago. It is normally associated with names such as Muhammad ibn 'Abd al-Wahhab of eighteenth-century Saudi Arabia (the founder of the Wahhabi movement), Jamal al-Din al-Afghani in the nineteenth century, Sayyid Muhammad bin Ali al-Sanusi of nineteenth-century Algeria (the founder of the Sanusiyyah movement), Zia Gokalp of early twentieth-century Turkey, Mulla Hadi Sabziwari of eighteenth-century Iran, and Shah Wali Allah Dilhawi of eighteenth-century India (Muzaffar 1986:6). But it is also possible to argue that Islamic resurgence is a recurring phenomenon. Piscatori, for example, asserts that throughout Islamic history there have been those who have thought of themselves as *mujaddid* (renewers) of Islam. He writes:

One thinks of the agitation surrounding the Hashimiyya in the eighth century; the Carmathians in the tenth; the Fatimids in the tenth and eleventh centuries; the Naqshbandiyya, particularly Ahmad Sirhindi, in the late sixteenth and early seventeenth centuries; Ibn 'Abd al-Wahhab of Arabia in the eighteenth; Uthman dan Fodio of western Africa in the early nineteenth; the followers of al-Afghani, 'Abduh, and Rida, often referred to as the Salafiyya, in the late nineteenth century; and the Muslim Brotherhood in this century. (Piscatori 1986:24)

Examining the examples of Imam Husain, Umar bin Abdul Aziz, Al-Ghazzali, Ibn Taymiyya, Imam Shamil of Russia, and many of the others mentioned above, one can also argue that it is naive and misleading to say that the present wave of Islamic resurgence is a strange phenomenon. Because it emerges out of the recurring conflict between Islam and *jahiliya* (pagan practices or practices resulting from the age of ignorance), Islamic resurgence can be seen as a continuous process throughout the different phases of Muslim history.

In general, Islamic resurgence has been inspired by the following factors: disillusionment with Western civilization as a whole among a new Muslim generation; the failings of social systems based on capitalism or socialism; the lifestyle of secular elites in Muslim states; the desire for power among a segment of an expanding middle class that cannot be accommodated politically because of the prevalence of unelected rulers and limited institutions in Muslim societies; the search for psychological security among new urban migrants; the urban environment resulting from, among other things, the process of development, which has strained the social and political fabric, effecting a turn to traditional symbols and rites as solace; the economic strength of certain Muslim states resulting from their oil wealth; the defeat of Egypt, Syria, and Jordan in the 1967 war with Israel, which resulted in a sense of inferiority based on technological rather than theological inadequacy; a sense of confidence about the future in the wake of the 1973 Egyptian victory over Israel; the success of the 1979 Iranian revolution against one of the most powerful armies in the world (and one backed by major Western powers); and the dawn of the fifteenth century of the Muslim calendar (Muzaffar 1986: 12–22; Piscatori 1986:26–34; ul Haq 1986:343).

These factors have given rise to Islamic resurgence, which assumes two broad forms. One is to fall back upon Islamic tradition as much as possible, believing that any change would be for the worse. The only solution is to hold fast to Islamic tradition and legacy either by withdrawal from the processes of Westernization or preservation of the Muslim legacy in culture, knowledge, and institutions. The other form emphasizes that the preservation of the past is inadequate. A creative, positive response to the Western challenge, an attempt to understand its nature and offer an alternative, is needed. Islamic resurgence must prepare for an all-out confrontation with the challenging powers and offer Islam as the alternative basis for culture and civilization. This kind of response, as seen in the lives and works of al-Afghani, Iqbal, and Shariati among others, has been described as *tajdid* (renewal and reconstruction), a perennial phenomenon in Islamic history (Ahmad 1983:219–220). These Muslim resurgents can be referred to neither as "traditionalists" nor as "fundamentalists" in the generally understood sense of dogma and petrification because they do not simply hold the Islamic principles as "frozen in time in their historical applicability" (Saikal 1987:191).

Despite this broad structural explanation of Islamic resurgence, however, it would be misleading to overemphasize similarities among widely separated phenomena. In fact, one of the most salient features of contemporary Islamic resurgence is that it manifests local features, sectarian differences, and indigenous accents (Saikal 1987:191). Islamic resurgence, like other social phenomena, needs to be contextualized if the relationship between Muslims and the society they reside in is to be meaningfully analyzed. Because contexts differ, the nature of Islamic resurgence in various societies will vary accordingly. In a context wherein Muslims constitute a numerical majority, the portrait of Islamic resurgence will inevitably differ from that sketched in places where they are a minority. Ethnic and religious components also contribute to different features of Islamic resurgence. Therefore, an understanding of Islamic resurgence in Thai society, wherein Muslims constitute a clear minority in a culture vastly different from their own, will shed light on the strategies that the resurgents and the Thai state utilize in coping with each other. Such a process has crystallized in the recent *hijab* crisis in Yala in southern Thailand.

Significance of the *Hijab* Case

In several cases, patterns of relationships between the Muslims and the Thai state have required readjustment. Chief among them were incidents of school burning in the four southernmost provinces from March 1987 until the end of that year (*Islamic Guidance Post* [*IGP*], October 1987:5–7). In another case, a government report stated that eighteen Muslim youths trained in terrorist activities by Libya were returning to carry out terrorist acts in the southern provinces (*Siam Rath*, 2 February 1987). A Narathiwat deputy governor published and distributed a book on Islam that many Muslims considered blasphemous (*IGP*, April 1987). A time bomb was planted at the large Buddha statue in Narathiwat on 24 March 1987, to be detonated at 1:00 P.M., but the authorities successfully defused the thirty-pound TNT bomb three minutes before it was to explode (ibid.). Cases like these were either isolated or lacked a clear religious overtone. Violence, for example, does not occur in everyday life and can be considered an aberration rather than the norm. In this sense these cases can be seen as lacking the strength to generate serious questions about the normal pattern of relationships between Muslims and the Thai state.

The Yala *hijab* case is different. It concerns dress, which is a normal everyday activity. Like many other common human actions, besides depending on economic and climatic conditions, dress is a function of accepted social values and dominant world views. A change in dress can sometimes reflect a genuine change in basic social values. It is not accidental that pictures of Muslim women in their *hijab* or words about *hijab* tend to grace the front pages of publications dealing with Islamic resurgence.[1] Muzaffar (1987:3) points out that the rapid diffusion of what is regarded as Islamic attire among a significant segment of the Muslim female population in Malaysia, especially in urban areas, is the most obvious sign of Islamic resurgence in that country.

Islamic resurgence in Malaysia is by no means monolithic. In fact, it reflects different levels of belief, commitment, and lifestyle. The turn toward Islam occurred through contact and exposure to Islamic ideals, "oftentimes plus pressure from those already in the *dakwah* (to call or to preach) movement" (Anwar 1987:59). In other words, peer pressure can play a significant role in convincing a female Muslim student in Malaysia to change her attire. Therefore, while wearing *hijab* is "the most obvious sign of Islamic resurgence," it cannot be used to assess the extent of religious commitment of those who wear it. In Malaysia, changing into "Islamic attire" is but an outward manifestation; it may not honestly reflect conscious Islamic resurgence, unlike *hijab* in Thai society.

Because they are a minority in Thai society, Muslims in Thailand sometimes try to live the way Thais of other religious persuasions do. Many emphasize similarities rather than differences between Muslims and non-Muslims. Because there are few Muslims at Yala Teachers' Training College, peer pressure is not significant enough to influence female students to put on *hijab;* in fact, to differ from the majority of students is to invite difficulties. Female students who put on *hijab* have had to face numerous obstacles including opposition from fellow students and school authorities. Unlike the Malaysian case, their change of attire does express a strong determination reflecting genuine commitment. In this sense, because Muslims are a minority living in an alien culture, wearing *hijab* in southern Thailand is a better indicator of Islamic resurgence than it might be in other societies.

The high visibility of wearing *hijab* is also significant. Especially when this attire appears in a situation governed by clear regulations, such as a college which normally has its own uniform, it can be read as a direct challenge to existing rules. When these rules are espoused by an institution of higher learning supported by official policy, the students' decision to change their attire effectively calls into question existing rules as well as the institutions behind them. As a result, the dynamism of relationship adjustment between the Muslims and the Thai state becomes crystallized when one analyzes cases such as this. When the Muslims decided to demonstrate in support of the students' decision, the political nature of the *hijab* case, which cannot be separated from the original cultural issue, became apparent.

As mentioned above, the *hijab* crisis received unusual attention from the press. Muslims and non-Muslims alike participated in this public debate. Thai decision makers as well as lower-ranking officials aired their opinions, some more openly than others. The publicity in this case resulted from an amalgamation of factors including visibility, religious overtones (considered sensitive in Thai society), and geographical significance. That this event took place in Yala, one of the four southernmost provinces of Thailand, where the Malay Muslim population is a clear majority and which borders Malaysia, must be taken into consideration. The Thai state always regards incidents in the four southernmost provinces as indicative of a sensitive security problem (McBeth 1986:30–31).

The Malay Muslims of southern Thailand tend to take pride in Malaysia as the epicenter of Islam and view events there positively. Malaysian-based *tabligh* (propagation) groups have ventured into Thailand in the last decade or so to participate in mass meetings organized by their counterparts in Thailand. The impact of Islamic development in Malaysia is also far greater among this group of Muslims in Thailand because they appear identical in dress to, and display other outward religious symbols prevalent among, their neighbors in Malaysia (Farouk 1988:157–168). Despite the impact of Malaysian religious awakening on the Malay Muslims in Southern Thailand, the religious content of the *hijab* issue enables Muslims from all corners of Thai society to consider it more than "another southern problem." This is another reason why the *hijab* issue can be better used to understand Islamic resurgence than other cases such as the planting of a bomb at the basement of the Buddha image in Narathiwat. A discussion of the latter is usually overshadowed by conditions specific to the southern problem such as the historical background of the area, poverty, and separatist movements with their international linkages (Chaiwat Satha-Anand 1987).

Hijab Crisis: An Event

In 1986 a school in Nonthaburi laid off a Muslim teacher because she came to work after the end-of-year examination dressed in accordance with Islamic teachings: she wore a blouse with long sleeves, an ankle-length skirt, and a head covering. The school fired her after issuing an order on 6 May 1986 claiming that she disturbed the "normality" of the school. The woman said that her dressing in accordance with Islamic tradition should be considered an attempt to preserve morality and civilization. She saw no reason for her dismissal (*Sanyaluck,* 10 June 1986).

A similar incident took place in Pattani on 2 June 1986. A Muslim civil servant dressed modestly with her head covered walked into the government house in Pattani to report to work. The governor urged her not to dress in an Islamic way. He told her that he had been serving in the province for ten years, during which he had seen numerous religious people, and that there was no need to cover her head. If she were allowed to dress as she desired, other government officials would want to follow suit. She was eventually transferred to Bangkok (*IGP,* June 1986). These cases show that the bureaucracy had been serious in its response to *hijab* for some time, so when a few female students in Yala decided to put on their *hijab,* the reactions of the Yala college officials were not unexpected.[2]

On 11 December 1987 a group of female Muslim students at Yala Teachers' Training College conveyed a message to the college administration concerning their intention to dress in accordance with their religious beliefs. Three days later three of the students walked into their respective classes in their *hijab* dresses, only to be met with strong reaction from the administration. Some Muslim lecturers pointed out that their dresses were not in keeping with college regulations. Other lecturers threatened that if they did not wear college uniforms they would have to find a new place to study. A week later, twelve Muslim students gave up their college uniforms and went to study in their *hijab.* Some lecturers began to ignore them, while others criticized them severely. On 23 December the college administration announced that some students were intentionally violating college uniform regulations and that therefore the college would be unable to accommodate their demands. Moreover, they claimed, the action of these students was a result of outside intervention. The vice-rector in charge of student affairs met with the Muslim students. He asked them to bring their parents to the college and announced that they would be suspended.

The next day, a pamphlet with the following anonymous message was issued:

> Every religion teaches people to be good, to sacrifice for the benefit of society and not to disrupt peace in society, nor create disunity. . . . Because you misuse education, it amounts to an attempt to sabotage this society. The effects of your actions will definitely be felt in the future! You have lived peacefully for a long time with no problem, haven't you? What kind of a joke are you thinking so that it bothered you now? So much fantasy. We strongly believe that this kind of idea does not belong to students of Yala Teachers' Training College. It is the idea of those who are uneducated, barbaric and irrational.

The Muslims, of course, were furious. Meanwhile, the offending students were barred from their classrooms.

During the first week of 1988, a student in *hijab* tried to attend her classical dance and drama class. Her teacher, apparently annoyed by her dress, asked her to leave the classroom. She sadly complied. Later that day, Ms. Fatima Kaewdamrongchai attended another class. When students who had not previously taken a test were asked to identify themselves, she did so promptly but received no attention. The test questions were distributed to everyone but her. She remained in class until the end of the test. On the same day, 4 January, all students in *hijab* were simultaneously asked to leave their classrooms. They were also barred from using the college library. One of the librarians reported having received "an order from someone in high position" to do so. Another young woman tried in vain to lead a normal student life. When asked to leave her classroom, she requested that she be allowed to study "right outside" her class. The teacher refused and said that "it would be an objectionable scene." Other lecturers reprimanded the students in *hijab,* accusing them of trying to achieve notoriety by wearing such dress. "If you don't want to study," they said, "then leave so that everything will be over." As a result of these pressures, some of the students decided to ask for leaves of absence. On the morning of 7 January, students found six prayer mats, one ordinary mat, and one *telekong* (dress worn by Muslim women during their prayers) near the college dog house. All the Muslim students, both female and male, were furious. They decided to boycott classes altogether as a sign of protest. On the next day, a Friday, they continued to boycott all classes and gathered in their group room, which also served as a prayer room. Other students were taken aback when they heard the sound of a powerful *takbir* three times. After collectively saying *"Allahu akbar"* (God is great), they performed their Friday prayer together.

During the protest, students tried to approach politicians and concerned government agencies for solutions. From Den Tomina, a Pattani member of parliament, they received a copy of an order issued by the minister of education, Mr. Marut Bunnag, asking the Teachers' Training College to accommodate the Muslim students' demand.

On Monday, 11 January, non-Muslim students protested that order. The next day, some students came to class in Thai classical and *likae* dress, colorful costumes worn for traditional performing arts. The protesters demanded that the ministerial order be lifted. Meanwhile, some lecturers continued to consider wearing *hijab* dress a violation of college regulations in spite of the ministerial order.

As if the issue were not complicated enough, the media reported that Mr. Sawai Pattano, then deputy minister of the interior, publicly voiced his disagreement with Minister Marut's accommodating order. He argued that Minister Marut was wrong because compliance with the Muslims' demand violated regulations, which should be applied to all without exception, in addition to creating a breach of national unity.

At the college the non-Muslim protesters insisted that those wearing *hijab* put on uniforms like all the others. The Southern Border Province Administration Center (SBPAC) offered a compromise, urging that *hijab* be worn only on Friday, the *jumma-at* (congregational prayer) day. Muslim students refused this proposal, arguing that there was no religious justification for them to wear *hijab* only on Friday. To do so might be considered *bid'a* (deviant behavior).

The college administration then tried to enforce its regulations step by step. First, the students would be allowed to wear *hijab* for a few more days. Then there would be three official warnings to those who refused to comply with college regulations. After this, students' parents would be called in. Finally, students would be asked not to come to college.

By then Muslims in Bangkok had begun to intervene; many issued protest letters to concerned organizations. On 27 January 1988 the National Security Council deliberated the issue and decided not to allow those who wore *hijab* to go to classes. At a press conference four days later, seven Muslim organizations, including the Muslim Lawyers Association, Muslim Students Association of Thailand, and Muslim Youth Association of Thailand, voiced their support for those who wanted to uphold

Islamic principles in Yala. Some groups sent a letter to General Prem Tin-sulanonda, then prime minister, urging the government to reconsider its stern position. Meanwhile the Office of the Chularajmontri (Shaikh-ul-Islam),[3] complaining that the SBPAC no longer sought their advice, pro-tested the way the situation was handled. Acting on reports that there was going to be a huge protest in the south, the police and the military were ordered to block the Muslims from Bangkok and the southern prov-inces who planned to join the Yala protest.

On 11 February more than ten thousand Muslims protested in front of the Yala central mosque. One day later the crowd was informed that "agents" of the Thai state—the secretary of the Ministry of Education, a representative of the National Security Council, and the governor of Yala —agreed to relax the regulations, allowing the students to wear *hijab* at least until the end of their examinations. The protesting crowd dispersed.

However, on 15 February, when Muslim students in *hijab* came to the college, they were forbidden to enter the campus. College officials explained that this was for their own safety because some student groups were very upset and might do something drastic. In addition, they said, they had not yet officially received word from higher authorities about the relaxation of regulations. Female Muslim students were barred from appearing on campus; a special examination would be arranged for them on 12 and 13 March. The students did not accept these conditions. When they returned the next day, they were barred from all classes.

On 18 February thirteen Buddhist student representatives from the Consortium of Southern Teachers' Training Colleges presented a letter to the minister of education urging him to uphold regulations and order the Muslim women to put on student uniforms before sitting for the exami-nation on 22 February.

When examination day came, all female Muslim students were asked to take the test in a separate room. They requested permission to sit in the same room as their non-Muslim friends, arguing that "this is not South Africa and there should be no discrimination based upon racial or any other factors." The college administration did not grant their request, so twenty male and seven female Muslim students decided to boycott the examination. This led to another mass protest beginning on 23 February. After a few days, the number of protesters in front of the Yala central mosque reached ten thousand. More letters of protest were sent to both the prime minister and the commander-in-chief of the army, General Chavalit Yongchaiyudh.

On 2 March representatives of the Ministry of Education accepted all requests by the protesters to put the relaxation order into practice, to investigate college administrators who failed to follow the orders of the minister of education and the National Security Council, to amend uniform regulations to accommodate Islamic dress, and not to punish the students who had participated in the protest (as well as to provide them a later opportunity to sit for the examination). Upon learning that their voices had been heard by the state, the crowd dispersed. Shortly after the crisis, a deputy minister of education announced that a new College Act was being prepared and would be considered by the parliament in May. This act would contain an injunction allowing a college to pass regulations concerning students' dress in accordance with local needs and cultures. But the parliament was dissolved. The *hijab* case is no longer a burning issue, although its potential to reemerge remains.

The *hijab* crisis at the Yala Teachers' Training College reflects social patterns found more generally in Thai society. Muslim students constitute a minority in the college, which is governed by administrators armed with rigid regulations. A basic question is whether those regulations were formulated to take into account the existence of minority religious groups. If the answer is negative, then questions need to be raised concerning the foundation upon which those regulations stand. Several key issues have emerged from the public debate generated by this *hijab* crisis.

Public Debate on the *Hijab* Crisis

The immediate debate generated by the *hijab* crisis produced two groups: those supporting the right to wear *hijab* and those opposed. Such a categorization is inadequate, however, for a proper understanding of how the *hijab* crisis at Yala Teachers' Training College reflects the nature of Islamic resurgence in the Thai polity. A better way to analyze the different opinions expressed is to examine the nature of the arguments themselves.

Some oppose *hijab* because such attire violates college regulations. The college administrators were the main exponents of this argument. A vice-rector in charge of student affairs pointed out that the regulations of Teachers' Training Colleges are important. If students want to dress differently, then regulations would have to be amended first. Such amendment must follow official procedures (*Chao Thai,* 26 December 1987). One columnist insisted that Muslim students must unconditionally follow regulations. "If they don't want to follow [regulations], they should not come to study. It has nothing to do with religion" (*Daily News,* 4 February 1988). This kind of argument, though simplistic, is usually effective in relegating the issue to the domain of bureaucratic procedures, which the ordinary citizen normally dares not enter.

Another argument opposing the wearing of *hijab* is based upon politics. Mr. Taveesak Srisuwan, a representative of Buddhist students from Sahavidhayalai Taksin, or the Consortium of Southern Teachers' Train-

ing Colleges (consisting of teachers' training colleges in the provinces of
Yala, Songkhla, Phuket, Nakorn Srithammarat, and Surat Thani), went
to Bangkok in February 1988 to persuade the minister of education to
uphold the regulations. He threatened that if the minister failed to accept
his group's suggestion, they too would protest. He argued that the problem of *hijab* dress had already spread to primary schools; left unchecked,
it would spread to secondary schools as well as vocational colleges, ignit-
ing separatist problems. He also emphasized that southern politicians
were involved, as well as a shadowy group calling themselves "Mujahid-
deen who wanted to see the four southern provinces transformed into the
Republic of Pattani" (*Thai Rath,* 19 February 1988). Another "analysis"
published in a weekly magazine pointed a finger at intervention from a
Muslim country that "operated through its cultural office in Thailand."
The article argued that this outside force was using propaganda and sab-
otage to spread its ideology.[4]

Two basic assumptions seem to characterize this political argument.
First, politicians are manipulating already explosive conditions for their
own benefit. Second, a secessionist group may want to manipulate the
situation, posing a serious security issue. In addition, because of the
transnational character of Islam, foreign intervention is always suspected. This type of security-related reasoning points to a deeper set of
arguments that emphasize the benign nature of the Thai state as well as
unity in Thai society.

A Muslim letter writer suggested that *hijab* should be abandoned and
students should return to their uniforms. He argued that religion need
not interfere with accepted social practice. Dressing in accordance with
religious teaching, though morally correct, should be exercised with care
by taking into account the specific local cultural context. Besides, the
Thai state has guaranteed "more than enough" extra rights to the Muslims. He cited as examples religious holidays when Muslim officials are
normally permitted to take up to five days off and the quota system for
Muslim students in the four southern provinces who enroll in colleges
and universities (*Daily News,* 11 February 1988). Another Muslim
argued that *hijab* dress originated in the desert and therefore is not
proper for Thai society. Muslim students should quit their protest
because of the security threat posed to Thailand by Laos in the Rom Klao
incident (*Daily News,* 18 February 1988).[5]

M. R. Kukrit Pramoj, a former prime minister and influential newspaper publisher and columnist, unequivocally promoted the theme of unity
in relation to the *hijab* crisis. He disagreed with students wearing *hijab*
because, he asserted, while Islam is a matter of personal faith, everyone
in the country is a Thai. From time immemorial, Muslims in Thailand
have been dressing like Thais. He said, "It is a pity that this dress issue

will create disunity among the Thais who love one another" (*Matichon,* 23 February 1988). This type of reasoning ignores two basic questions. First, what exactly is the meaning of "Thai-ness"? Is this "Thai-ness" defined by the Thai state? This relates directly to the second basic question: is Thai society as monolithic as many have been led to believe?

Other perspectives on the *hijab* case, especially those that support the Muslims' position, employ a different kind of reasoning from those that make bureaucratic regulations or national unity the fundamental premises of the argument. Some writers simply point to the facts that people are different, that their religious convictions are protected by the constitution, and that as long as wearing *hijab* does not create any problem for Thai society, they should be allowed such religious freedom (Preecha Suwannathat 1988; Narongrit Sakdanarong 1988). Others try to answer the two questions above.

Two prominent academics, taking the nature of Thai society seriously into account, have drawn on deeper reasons for their positions. Chalardchai Ramitanon, an anthropologist from Chiangmai University, points out that religious holiness stems from the use of a symbolic system supported by the faith of the religious community. Religions have several functions: they provide norms for societies, legitimize existing power, and endow people's lives with meaning, among other things. He states succinctly that in a society consisting of peoples of different religious persuasions, it is difficult to create a unified nation, particularly when the state interprets the notion of nation or country by associating it fundamentally with a particular religion. The possibility of conflict is thereby enhanced. He writes: "Being Buddhists is no proof of being Thais. The Burmese and Sri Lankans are Buddhists but they are not Thais" (Chalardchai Ramitanon 1988).

Acknowledging differences in religions and citing the authority of history to support the point that in the past quarrels about religious symbols have easily led to battles as well as to the founding of new countries, Professor Nidhi Eiosriwong, a noted historian, asked: "Will our country disintegrate because Muslim girls who go to schools or colleges dress differently?" He argued forcefully that to push a people to choose between their religious loyalty and their love of the nation is the most unwise thing a state can do. A state with some degree of wisdom would try with all its might to avoid creating such a dilemma (Nidhi Eiosriwong 1988).

These two academics help elucidate the fact that the Thai state tends to ignore basic differences in Thai society. The sociological basis of their argument is helpful to understanding the complexities of Thai society. When serious attention is paid to the sociology of religion, both the limits and contributions of Buddhism as a pillar of the Thai state become apparent. In this sense these professors argue that the foundation of the

Thai state, which many claim to be Buddhism, is not broad enough to accommodate the Muslims in Thailand. Meanwhile, the Muslims' commitment to their religion can effectively call into question the thesis of a unified Thai political community.

The line of reasoning of the Muslims who participated in the public debate in support of the young women who were wearing *hijab* is basically religious. Religious reasoning in this case helps to clarify the kind of sociological reasoning mentioned above. The secretary-general of the Shaikh-ul-Islam Office began his article in a Thai daily newspaper by pointing out that covering a woman's head is a cultural symbol of Muslim women's dress code, not, as many suspect, a symbol of Iranian women. He then cited an oft-quoted verse from the Holy Qur'an which reads:

> *And say to the believing women*
> *That they should lower*
> *Their gaze and guard*
> *Their modesty; that they*
> *Should not display their*
> *Beauty and ornaments except*
> *What (must ordinarily) appear*
> *Thereof; that they should*
> *Draw their veils over*
> *Their bosoms and not display*
> *Their beauty.*
>   (Al-Qur'an XXIV:31)

Using this verse, he pointed out that those who tried to characterize *hijab* as mere tradition were abusing Islamic principles. Islamic dress does not undermine other people's culture, does not violate anybody's rights, does not jeopardize national security or the educational system. Arguing that Islamic injunctions on dress would instead serve as a protection from such evils as rape and fornication, he concluded that those who opposed an Islamic dress code were directly opposing Islam itself (Marvan Sama-oon 1988).

While Phra Khru Thavorn Stakom, a Buddhist monk, claimed that the *hijab* crisis was the result of foreign intervention, especially by Shiites determined to threaten the Buddhists in the society (*Dao Siam,* 16 March 1988), another Buddhist-oriented writer posed a much more fundamental question. "Pagadhamma," a senior *Matichon* columnist, pointed out that the *hijab* crisis was generated by "people who cannot appreciate *dhamma* [teaching, the way] and *dhamma* that cannot reach people." This columnist argued that the state had to understand fundamental *dhamma,* namely, the diversity that exists within any given political community. Regulations formulated without taking into account diverse groups of people who belong to different religious persuasions are not based on *dhamma:*

> It is important not to tolerate any violation of legitimate rights simply because of official regulations implemented by governing bureaucrats who believed that such a singular norm is appropriate, connotes Thainess and will protect it. They forget that there are other Thais who belong to other religions with different norms. It is as if they were determined to press the Muslims to choose between their nation and their religion, although there is absolutely no necessity to make that drastic choice. (Pagadhamma 1988)

Although the columnist's exposition seems to be similar to the socio-logical reasoning of the academics cited above, the reasoning here is basically religious. By pointing out that fundamental *dhamma* accurately reflecting social reality is ignored, the columnist seems to question the claim that Buddhism is a basis for the Thai state. More straight-forwardly, Pagadhamma questions whether the "Buddhist Thai" group who protested against Muslim students wearing *hijab* are real Buddhists; if they are, they should meditate on the Four Noble Truths and show compassion to all. Based on Buddhist-oriented wisdom and compassion, they should not attach too much significance to how people dress and should be able to appreciate those who dress differently. An ultimate question for "Buddhist Thais" should be "In what way does their dressing differently from us affect the extent to which we are Buddhists?" (Pagadhamma 1988). In other words, attachment to a specific uniform sanctioned by the state does not enhance the quality of being a "Bud-dhist," whereas coming to terms with diverse and changing social realities by using compassion and intellect does.

The debate generated by the *hijab* crisis is political. Two kinds of poli-tics based upon two different kinds of reasoning—distinguished by their capability to correspond to diversified social reality—can be identified. They are "bureaucratic reasoning" and "sociological reasoning." I would argue that as a result of its institutional character and rules governing its practice, the former tends to resist change and is less capable of corres-ponding to the dynamism of social reality. The strength of "bureaucratic reasoning" is drawn from regulations enunciated chiefly for governing and security purposes. These regulations, in turn, are implemented by bureaucrats who suspect the governed.[6] When facing problems, those influenced by bureaucratic reasoning have resorted to solutions that include enforcing regulations without exceptions, punishing violators, blaming outsiders for the perceived disruption of social order, even appointing a special committee to pass judgment on Muslim students' dress codes, as suggested by a Muslim member of parliament (*Siam Rath*, 28, 29 January 1988). The *hijab* crisis in Yala is a fruit of such petrification of social reality.

"Sociological reasoning," in contrast, is based upon the sociological character of a given society. It is sensitive to differences among peoples in the society and therefore amenable to critical appraisal of both the bureaucrats who sometimes blindly follow petrified regulations and the foundation on which such regulations rest. Chalardchai Ramitanon's piece and that of the secretary-general of the Shaikh-ul-Islam reflect this kind of reasoning. Unlike bureaucratic reasoning, wherein rules and regulations are of utmost importance, sociological reasoning can and must include local voices on the issues. In the *hijab* crisis, voices of the young Muslim women at Yala Teachers' Training College who chose to brave the controversy indicate that at the fundamental level the incompatibility between these two kinds of politics point to the problems of legitimation:

> In the past, the relationship between the teachers and myself was good, but when I put on my *hijab*, they stopped talking to me. They said: "If you want to dress like this, then go to live in your own country. This is not your country. This is Thailand with the Thai dress code. Go to where you belong!"

When asked whether family pressures were present, another answered:

> There are some. The first day I put on my *hijab*, my brother warned me not to do it because they might think that I am radical. . . . Then he asked whether I was worried that my action would jeopardize the position [of] my other brother who is a soldier in the Thai army because he happened to be my guarantor when I was admitted to the College. I did not know what to do. That night I could only cry. Then I told my mother that if I were expelled from the college, do not feel sad. If I follow their regulations and graduate with a bachelor's degree, are you certain that Allah Almighty would have blessed me when I had not lived in accordance with His Way? . . . I cannot knowingly follow them and ignore Allah's Truth.[7]

One of the Muslim girls who, in her *hijab*, attended a rally in front of Government House in Bangkok in support of the Yala Muslim students, spelled out the case from a Muslim point of view. She said:

> Thanks be to Allah for giving us a chance to participate in this protest. It is clear what a Muslim should do in this case. The *kafir* [nonbelievers] refused to let the Muslims practice their religious duties. They are not opposing us but we regard them as opposing Allah. (All three quotes from *IGP*, 1 April 1988:50)

From these young women's point of view, the *hijab* crisis arose from the fact that the Muslims are now conscious of Islam and want to follow its tenets to the best of their abilities in a state chiefly constituted by non-believers. Their reaffirmed sense of religiosity within the larger context of Islamic resurgence portrays the limitation of the Thai state's legitimacy. It is therefore important to analyze the dynamics of legitimation reflected from the interaction between the Muslims and the Thai state.

Moments of Legitimation

A Buddhist philosopher explained that according to the Buddha, *dhamma* is to be used like a raft to cross over to the safety of *nibbana* (nirvana) but not to carry as a burden, identifying oneself with it and becoming obsessed with a sectarian identity. *Dhamma* is universal, and the religious community or *samanabrahmana* is an essential ingredient of society because it turns people away from evil. As a result, a Buddhist can neither disparage nor discriminate against a follower of another religion without violating the fundamental principles of the Buddhist doctrine. Thus, he concludes: "Within a polity governed by Buddhist principles, the problem of minority rights should not exist at all" (Premasiri 1988:56).

The Thai state is sometimes characterized as a political manifestation of all Buddhist values and ideals based upon Buddhist cosmology. Its rulers are "the very essence and best exponents of Buddhist teachings. The blessings that permeate the land flow from the *baramee* (charisma) of the highest ruling institutions, which are the earthly images of the ideal Buddha himself" (Surin Pitsuwan 1988:188). If such is the case, how can the problems of religious minority rights in Thai society, such as the *hijab* crisis, be explained? A common answer is to point to "the gap between the ideals cognitively acknowledged and how individuals and groups professing these ideals behave in actual life situations." (Premasiri 1988: 55). Perhaps a more enlightening question is not to measure Buddhist society against a set of principles derived from the canon of Buddhism but to examine the way in which Buddhism or its doctrines are partially used in a state that claims Buddhism as one of its revered pillars.

In a study attempting to investigate the interactions of the *sangha* (order of monks) with politics in a situation of sociopolitical change, Somboon Suksamran argues that Buddhism "has long served as one of the most important sources of political legitimation for political rulers." In fact, because of the kind of influence Buddhism has over Thai society in its various dimensions, political rulers "may make use of religious ideas and the *sangha* to legitimate their rule and to facilitate social control" (Suksamran 1982:6).

In the *hijab* crisis, young Muslim women claimed legitimacy for their Islamic dress by citing God's commandment. One problem with a state's using Buddhism not as principle, but merely as legitimation to subordinate sectarian identity to marginal importance is its possible inability to incorporate differences among its citizens. Although the Muslims are Thai citizens, the basis for legitimation of the Thai state with its emphasis on Buddhist rhetoric cannot accommodate their totally different cosmology based on Islam. Realizing this, in times of heightened conflict the Thai state shifts emphasis from its religious-oriented legitimation to rules and regulations. In other words, if the state's basis of legitimacy is dysfunctional, the state will resort to the authority of rules and regulations to govern the citizens' behavior, because in the realm of impersonal regulations differences of identity cease to be of much importance. To rely on Jürgen Habermas's wisdom, the *hijab* crisis embodies a case wherein "supplies of legitimation can compensate for deficits in rationality and extensions of organizational rationality can compensate for those deficits that do appear."[8]

A legitimation deficit makes it impossible to maintain or establish by administrative means "effective normative structures" to the extent required (Habermas 1975:47). Facing a protest by Muslims who based their case on a different type of legitimation, the legitimation basis of the Thai state proved inadequate. To maintain social control under such circumstances, the state used official regulations based upon bureaucratic reasoning. Such reasoning becomes rationality produced and maintained by the bureaucracy for its own sake. This is what Habermas called "organizational rationality," maintaining that "while organizational rationality spreads, cultural traditions are undermined and weakened" (ibid.). In this case, however, "organizational rationality" seems unable to compensate for the legitimation deficits and to weaken the Muslims' cultural traditions, as theoretically anticipated.

A more fruitful approach to the "minority problem" posed by Muslims in Thai society begins with the recognition that Thai society is not monolithic (Chavivun Prachuabmoh and Chaiwat Satha-Anand 1985:22–31). Benedict Anderson has pointed out that the state of old Siam was defined by its center, not its boundaries. Thus different peoples such as the Muslims could be loyal to the monarch yet keep their cultural (read religious) and ethnic identities undisturbed. Elites in the Bangkok area suffered from "historic failures in dealing with the 'minorities' (especially 'indigenous minorities'), indeed in ever really comprehending the problems posed by this group" (Anderson 1978:211–213). In fact, it can be argued that the nation-building phase of Thai society is not yet over. The process is long and quite difficult among the Muslims, especially those Malay Muslims in the border provinces, because of their distinctive culture (lan-

guage, religion) and history (Chaiwat Satha-Anand 1987; Surin Pitsuwan 1988:198). But stating that there are different groups of people in
Thailand with different principles of legitimation, although necessary, is
not sufficient to explain why the *hijab* crisis erupted at this particular
time. One of M. R. Kukrit Pramoj's questions during the height of the
hijab crisis was "Why do Muslim women begin to put on their *hijab* now
although Islam was born more than a thousand years ago?" (*Matichon,*
23 February 1988). The question, in spite of its rhetorical tone, points to
the fact that mere differences of legitimation cannot fully account for the
eruption of such a crisis. It is therefore important to examine the
"moment" when such legitimation is exercised.

Legitimation processes can be separated into two phases or "moments," establishing a referent against which actions can be vindicated.
In the first moment legitimation is based upon the authority of the
referent itself. The legitimation referent is treated as not problematic and
thus becomes an "extra-discursive non-practice-related entity" (Shapiro
1988:26–27). For example, some groups of people claim to be who they
are on the basis of a sacred text or a unique history. Such a basis serves
the purpose of legitimizing their existence. It is not necessary for many of
them to know exactly what the text or that history is about. But if this
kind of legitimation referent is criticized or desecrated, many adherents
will do what they can to "protect" it. In this sense, the referent is not
included in their discussion.

The second moment of legitimation deals with the commentary or set
of commentaries on the referent. "Even if the referent is taken to be
authoritative in principle, its features emerge in a commentary on those
features" (Shapiro 1988:27). Here I would argue that one of the best
forms of commentary on the referent is to put the principles enunciated
by the referent into practice. In so doing the referent needs to be discussed. Some social conditions must serve as prerequisites for bringing
the referent back into the discussion. The revitalization of Islam is just
such a major condition to question the gap between the sacredness of the
text as referent and the importance of practices in accordance with the
teachings embodied in the text. Once the principles are being practiced, legitimation will consequently be strengthened. With a newly
strengthened legitimation, a minority group can challenge the dominant
legitimation. In other words, legitimation of the dominant group will be
seriously challenged when the religious minority group arrives at their
second moment of legitimation.

For a long time Muslims in Thai society lived in the first moment,
using Islam only as a referent to identify who they were. Muslims "practice" their religion: the majority of them do not eat pork; many pray five
times a day. But these practices assume the form of ritual, while the

referent itself becomes "extra-discursive." Religious discussions have rarely sought to question the teachings contained in the referent. In the past, religious conflicts among Muslims in Thai society were not about issues such as the evil of usury or the tragedy of Muslims in faraway lands such as Afghanistan or Palestine, but about the procedure of prayers. In this first moment of legitimation Islam's sociopolitical message, which emphasizes the reunification of religion and public action by asserting the Muslim identity, was not clearly evident. If at times their "practices" as Muslims came into conflict with accepted behavior in Thai society, they compromised. Although many were aware of the Islamic dress code, they continued to wear uniforms sanctioned by their different institutions. The legitimation deficit of the Thai state did not manifest itself, and not only because it was compensated for by organizational rationality. The fact that organizational rationality prevailed meant also that the legitimation basis of groups such as the Muslims was not strong enough.

With the tide of Islamic resurgence sweeping the world, however, Muslims in Thailand have begun to practice their religion in a new moment of legitimation. In this moment Islamic principles are articulated,[9] and many Muslims assert their identity by practicing the newly found principles. The meanings of Islamic resurgence become crystallized not with such phenomena as the success of the Iranian revolution, but when ordinary Muslims unify principles and practices of Islam in their lives against the background of a society largely ignorant of their conviction and somewhat frightened by the seriousness with which they take their religion. In the second moment of legitimation for the Muslim minority, the true meanings of Islamic resurgence emerge, and its potential is tested.

Conclusion

In the *hijab* crisis in Yala a religious minority reacted to a state legitimized by Buddhism. Dress codes may be considered trivial by some, but for Muslims they are a religious matter. When a columnist in a daily paper wrote that "there is no need to heed any god. Living in Thai society, one has to follow the Thai social order regardless of religious denominations" ("Dogmakhua" 1988), it was evident that the problem was deeper than a mere questioning of college regulations. The debate generated by the *hijab* crisis elucidates two kinds of politics resulting from bureaucratic or sociological reasoning. The Thai state, legitimized by Buddhism, relies upon bureaucratic reasoning or organizational rationality when there is a deficit of legitimation. This kind of legitimation substitute would have sufficed if the Muslims in the Thai polity had not arrived at the second moment of their Islamic legitimation. Contrary to the first moment of legitimation, when practices according to Islamic teachings may be easily compromised, the second moment gives rise to assertive practices in accordance with Islamic principles. In this moment Islam ceases to be but a referent to outside discourses and comes alive in the daily practices and discourses on those practices of the Muslims.

An emphasis on moments of legitimation does not mean that the leadership of the protest, the psychohistory of the Muslim students who decided to wear *hijab,* the geopolitics of Yala as one of the four southernmost provinces, intracollege politics, or government policies are unimportant. In fact, some analysts might choose to view this incident by using gender analysis as a framework and argue that *hijab* must be viewed in relation to the desire of ethnic groups to reassert their autonomy through a gendered discourse. Because "masculinization" represents a claim to full humanity, the minority group assert themselves by insisting on female conformity to a restrictive dress code.[10] To look at Islamic resurgence from the framework of gender analysis would necessitate an examination of Muslim male/female relationships in addition to the masculinization attempt mentioned above. The process of Muslims' identity reassertion also involves males. More and more Muslim men wear beards, for example. Many Muslims—both male and female—no longer greet one another with traditional Thai salutations but by the Islamic *salaam.* Here I am addressing the significance of *hijab* at a different level and emphasizing the relationship between the Muslims and Thai society through contrasting sets of legitimation.

Analysis of the significance of Islamic resurgence in the Thai polity reveals the foundation of political actions underscoring different sets of legitimation as well as changing moments of legitimation. Such an analysis sheds meaningful light on the foundational strengths and weaknesses of Muslims in both Thai society and the Thai state.

In *Religion as Critique,* Robert John Ackerman (1985) suggests that major religions always retain the potential to develop a social critique. To provide this possibility, a religion can never be reduced to mechanically understood dogma because in that form it would lose touch with changing social reality. This assertion seems incompatible with the case of the Muslim minority in Thai society because in the *hijab* crisis, the Muslims seem to have returned to dogma and altered their daily practices in accordance with Islamic principles. Did they lose touch with social reality? An answer is not easily forthcoming because there may be more than one social reality. They may have lost touch with social reality as defined by the Thai state, but that is not the only reality. By clinging to dogma, religion becomes for Muslims a critique—not of itself, but of its alien social context. By presenting a different set of legitimation, the Muslims effectively call into question the dominant legitimation used by the Thai state with Buddhism and bureaucratic rationality as its core.

NOTES

1. See, for example, the cover of *Asiaweek* for 27 November 1987 with a lead article entitled "The Islam Question: Malaysia's Changing Society." The second sentence of Zainah Anwar's *Islamic Revivalism in Malaysia* reads: "In the streets in Kuala Lumpur, the capital city, young women covered from head to toe in the loose flowing *hijab*" (Anwar 1987:1).

2. The *hijab* crisis described here is based upon reports drawn mainly from the Muslim press, especially the special issue on *hijab* in the *IGP*, (April 1988:16–26 [in Thai]).

3. The Chularajmontri (Shaikh-ul-Islam) is the officially recognized spiritual leader of Muslims in Thailand.

4. Although the article, "Revealing the Battle at Yala Teachers' Training College" (*Siam Rath Weekly*, 20–26 March 1988:10–11 [in Thai]), does not identify that Muslim country, I believe that Iran is implicated.

5. The Rom Klao incident, a territorial dispute that took place in early 1988 between Thailand and Laos, resulted in hundreds of casualties on both sides.

6. The author of an award-winning thesis written for the National Defense College (academic year 1984–1985) points out that according to a survey done in 1983, 25.7 percent of civil servants in the four southernmost provinces were not happy to work there, while 24.20 percent were indifferent. Some of the reasons given for their dissatisfaction include problems arising out of linguistic and religious differences, as well as concern for their own safety (see Racharak 1984–1985:143–144).

7. These two remarks come from interviews conducted on 12 February 1988 (see *IGP*, 1 April 1988:30–32).

8. In *Legitimation Crisis,* Habermas's major concern was with crisis in advanced capitalism. Nonetheless, his discussion of the problems of legitimation is applicable here, in part because for Habermas the legitimation crisis is "directly an identity crisis" (1975:46). As mentioned previously, Islamic resurgence means, among other things, a reassertion of Muslim identity.

9. On 16 July 1983 the Office of the Chularajmontri issued a series of religious rulings on various issues pertaining to Muslims' participation in Buddhist rituals and state ceremonies. Questions included whether it was permissible for Muslims to stand up during the lighting of incense and candles by the presiding person at official functions; to present wreaths and pay homage to the equestrian statue of King Rama V on the day commemorating his death; and to kneel before the statue of Rama VI during the Boy Scout ceremony. In all these cases the religious rulings are decisively "no." I cannot help but wonder whether such a definitive answer will be possible outside the necessary historical moment (see Surin Pitsuwan 1988:194–198).

10. I wish to thank Professor Helen Hardacre for bringing the possibility of gender analysis of the *hijab* incident to my attention both in a workshop and in her written comments on this essay.

EPILOGUE
Defying Disenchantment
Reflections on Ritual, Power, and History
JEAN COMAROFF

The Lingering Legacy of Evolutionism

The essays in this volume together make an important statement about the nature of religion and society in the late twentieth century. Certain developments in Asia, such as those occurring in Thailand, where the dynamism of capitalist production is rivaled only by the drive of diverse forms of ritual creativity, both within and outside Buddhism (see Chaiwat Satha-Anand in this volume), are an affront to occidental myths of modernity. In classical sociology the "religions of Asia" were often invoked as evidence for a global evolutionary scheme in which Europe emerged as the birthplace of secular reason, itself the sine qua non of modern life. Yet the present essays draw on Asian history and ethnography to assert something very different: that religion and ritual are crucial in the life of "modern" nations and communities, in Asia as elsewhere. They urge us, in collective voice, to distrust disenchantment, to rethink the telos of development that still informs the models of much mainstream social science.

Two issues follow directly from this challenge. The first is that "modernity" has long been equated with secularization in the European mind. And, to the degree that mind has been able to create "modern man" in its image, the equation has been given world currency. Thus, as illustrated in this volume, the governments of new states in Southeast Asia have come to understand "religion" in a particular sense: as living survival of an archaic order, a view that has obvious political implications. In fact, the definition of "religion" now hegemonic in the civil life of the region—religion as an individualized and intellectualized "faith" (cf. Tambiah 1990:5)—is clearly itself a product of the politics of modernization (see Hefner in this volume). A second issue thus follows: if there is ample evidence that such ideologies are contested in local practice, we must learn from this fact. These ideologies must be the subject, not the terms, of scholarly analysis, and it behooves us to rethink the role of religion in society, East and West. If not a remnant of premodern

301

authority, a trace of "traditional" cosmology, what is it? And in what language should we speak of the other sorts of practices discussed in these essays—rituals that, though they fail to fit modernist molds, still seem able to make and unmake local worlds?

These two issues are intimately connected: if our scholarly sense of "religion" is a function of the modernity we seek to analyze, it should not surprise us that seemingly very different approaches—such as Marxism and modernization theory—alike see "faith" as a fetish inhibiting human beings from acting upon the real material world. While such schools of thought are neither simple nor unitary, they share a vision that separates facts from values, instruments from signs, and the secular from the sacred; human history lies in the triumph of the first of each pair of terms over the second. In Durkheim's scheme, for instance, social reality is distinct from its representations, and sociology itself is born of the gradual disengagement of the profane from the sacred, religion from magic, and science from religion. His legacy helped make modernist dualisms into universal definitions, forming a procrustean bed on which subsequent "religious" phenomena were made to lie, however distorting the results. But Durkheim also held that the sacred was everywhere an empowering image of the social; in this sense, he insisted, there was "something eternal in religion"; the faith that enabled people to live and act was destined ever to "pass science and complete it prematurely" (1965 [1915]: 478, 479). Yet for the most part the sociology of religion has focused less on such meaningful practice than on ecclesiastically oriented, juridically defined institutions (Berger and Luckman 1974:102). Such a focus has perpetuated parochial definitions and masked continuities with other forms of social action, such as those performed in the name of modern nationalism—which, as Kapferer notes, "makes the political religious" (1988:1). In a world where, for many, flag burning is sacrilege, it is strange that so few sociologists have challenged the doctrine of disenchantment.

Weber's writings on religion are more complex than Durkheim's, in many respects, but they are no less teleological: "religious and ethical reflections upon the world," he said, "were increasingly rationalized . . . [and] primitive and magical notions were eliminated" (Gerth and Mills 1976:275). Indeed, Weber's particular understanding of this multidirectional "rationalization"—for him, a morally dubious process—has all too easily been reduced to monolithic models of "rationality" by a developmentally oriented social science. Influential "neo-Weberian" schemes have thus purported to measure the progress of non-European peoples on the straight and narrow path from tradition to the modern macrocosm (Horton 1971).

Although Weber, too, had another face, and like Durkheim, a less historicist sense of the animating power of the "supernatural," much of his contribution to mainstream sociology bore heavy evolutionary freight. In this he was a man of his time. In fact, the emerging discourse of social science, so secular in its self-image, fed directly on the telos of Judeo-Christian tradition (Sahlins n.d.); and this was nowhere clearer than in definitions of "religion." In that tradition the longstanding segregation of "prayer" from "idolatry" and "religion" from "magic" became enshrined in the study of comparative sociology by Victorians like Tylor and Frazer (Tambiah 1990:19). But this legacy was also conjugated with the terms of bourgeois modernism, which arrayed religion and magic side by side against secular reason. As otherworldly belief and occult practice, they were alike the stuff of "ritual"—that is, of otiose ceremonial that opposed rational thought and instrumental action. Framed in such teleological terms, the secularization of the modern world was little more than a foregone conclusion.

Imagined Modernities

Although more recent writing in the social sciences is no longer framed in terms of explicitly evolutionary themes, their legacy lingers. There remains a tendency, for instance, to see modernity as a sociohistorical break, reifying its opposition to "tradition" and substituting classification for explanation. These dualisms distract us from seeing important similarities in the fabric of all societies—such as the persistent role of ritual and of organizations built on transcendent authority, godly or otherwise. Thus Anderson's view of modernity as driving a "harsh wedge between cosmology and history" (Anderson 1983a:40) breeds stereotypes of the traditional state as one in which cosmology reflects community and vice versa or of modernity as the alienation from traditional certainties (see the introduction to this volume). Yet surely this is yet another version of the exile from Eden, a myth often substituted for history in the West, where modernity is perceived as the passage from "culture" to "practical reason" (Sahlins 1976). Material progress removes all shelter from the "homeless mind" (Berger, Berger, and Kellner 1973); whether in alienation or angst, we see ourselves condemned to a world of loss without fulfillment, signs without symbols, exchange without use value, rationality without religion (Horton 1967; Taussig 1980; Baudrillard 1981).

This is not the context to argue for a theory of "modern" meaning; I suggest that both Durkheim and Weber give grounds on which to build an imaginative sociology of cosmopolitan culture. Marx also, in his treatment of the commodity as social hieroglyph, provides additional resources for an analysis of capitalism as a signifying system. The essays in this collection give clear evidence of the symbolic richness of the mod-

USE:

∞

ern mind, whether in response to an explosion of market commodities or an atom bomb (see chapters by Weller, Kendall, and Foard in this volume). Nor is such creativity limited to the "developing" fringe of the European world. Yet—and this is the point—stereotypic dualisms make the cosmic chaos of modernity the flip side of traditional order, a contrast all too easily spatialized in terms of the West and the rest. And they generate caricatures that feed off one another rather than generating the more complex empirical realities they purport to describe.

Let us look, for instance, at what we know about cosmology and community in preindustrial states; can the relationship be said, in any unqualified sense, to be one of unproblematic, mutual reinforcement? In fact, the weight of evidence suggests that, despite much variation, such states tended to rest on multiple and competing bases of authority, authority whose inscription in religion was seldom unambiguous and uncontradictory. In a classic, typical account, Wyatt MacGaffey (1986: 171ff.) describes the complex relationship between chief and priest, who formed the double pivot of the highly fragile states of the Kongo of Central Africa. Chiefs, here, were benevolent despots; they had the power of witches, though they were meant to wield it for the communal good. In fact, the contrast between chief and witch was less an empirical one than a matter of moral judgment, often mobilized to discredit rulers and impugn the highest office. Though in normative terms priests were the alibis of royal authority, they also had the sacred power to denounce temporal rulers (if not temporal rule) and to reveal the chief for the witch he really was. Comparative cases of righteous regicide occurred frequently in other African kingdoms (Claessen 1981), as they have done elsewhere in the ancient oriental, medieval, and modern worlds (Grottanelli 1985:32). As Grottanelli notes, the stability of monarchical rule has usually been "grossly overemphasized" by historians (ibid.). In fact, once "traditional societies" are allowed to exhibit agency, even instability, they turn out to have had politics and history all along. Their cosmologies appear less as sacred gardens than as ruling hegemonies—more or less firmly entrenched—that differ from those of "modernity" in degree rather than kind. As Ranger has recently insisted (1993), our assumptions of stability have persistently blinded us to the dynamic role of ritual activity in precolonial societies.

This is not to deny that important sociocultural features distinguish modern from preindustrial states, in Southeast Asia and elsewhere. I do suggest, however, that as yet we have a rather poor understanding of what these features might be. And I would question the analytic value of basing them largely on a problematic relation to the past or in the unprecedented need to "imagine communities"; after all, to return to Durkheim's most profound insight, such imagining is the major creative project of all human societies, large or small—whether by means of rites or written texts. More constitutive of the uniqueness of modern communities must surely be their participation—to a greater or lesser extent —in a global order of commodity production, transaction, and consumption. But even such distinctiveness must be read as a variant of more universal themes in the making of human communities everywhere—that is, the production and reproduction of social persons and collective value. This project requires establishing shared realities that persist beyond immediate space and time; and this is done, even where people imagine themselves demystified, by mobilizing the formal properties of such sign systems as language, poetics, and ritual.

Modern Religion Refigured

These considerations return us to the problem of how we are to characterize religion in society—that is, once we have come to distrust disenchantment. If imagining the social is an eternal project, I have suggested that we have been far too ready to see traditional, face-to-face societies as having a particular genius for this task, a genius rooted in the regenerative religions that were their distinctive feature. Yet as the Kongo case makes plain, even seemingly simple states tend to have complex structures, in which the basis of authority is never unitary. It is the very presence of dual authority, even in the most coherent of polities, that opens the ever-present possibility for conflict and chaos. Evans-Pritchard (1962) argued long ago that even divine kings were not incarnate gods and did not really fuse, in their persons, the sacred and the temporal. The role of the *reth* of the Shilluk of the Sudan, for instance, was a (partially successful) attempt to reconcile the conflicts between the ritual and political aspects of the office. In fact, the *reth* "reigned but did not rule," serving as priest to his administratively active settlement chiefs, in a relationship fraught with political tension and discord. If religion here was action resting on irreducibly sacred authority, its potential for securing social order was also the power to undermine it.

In thinking about the implications of this pervasive capacity, it is Weber who comes to our aid—the Weber concerned less with historicist theories of religion than with universal features of transcendent power. It was he who stressed (Gerth and Mills 1976:245ff.), for instance, that charismatic authority everywhere was "supernatural," by which he meant outside the direct constraints of social institutions; charisma was neither restricted to divine power (at least, in terms of the Western notions of "spiritual beings") nor the preserve of premodern predicaments. In fact, Weber's concern was less the referents of charisma than its modalities. He held, for instance, that the "attitude" of charismatic activity was "revolutionary" (1958 [1946]:250)—by which he meant that it opened up a space from which the established world could be judged and acted on in terms other than its own. Here, then, is a nondevelopmental approach, applicable to religious practice at its most transcendent—an approach at once global in scope, yet historical in implication. It suggests that while charismatic movements are always contrastive in form, they are also historically specific in content. Their potential plays into the character of particular social systems, past and present, emerging wherever thoroughgoing structural contradictions polarize human experience. For charismatics are not respectful of the distinction of "tradition" and "modernity." It should not surprise us, then, that spirit mediums today confront the impact on local communities of global politico-economic forces, that *kamisama* shamanesses in rural Japan "deliver subtle commentaries on gender relations and the manifold anxieties of late capitalist culture" (Schattschneider n.d.). So, after all, do their counterparts in storefront churches on Chicago's south side, if in a different cultural register. But lest these be seen as cases marginal to the modern mainstream, let us remind ourselves of the growing charismatic trend in established churches in late twentieth-century America, not only among "fundamentalists" (still, for some, exiles from bourgeois reason) but also within the "high" churches of Protestant and Catholic orthodoxy (McGuire 1982; Liebman and Wuthnow 1983). The recent upsurge of such practices in the West can hardly be rationalized as mere archaic reactions to the march of modernity.

Religious enthusiasm, then, is in no simple sense peripheral in the contemporary world (we have, in recent years, had "evangelicals in the White House" [Jorstad 1981], not to mention astrologers). Yet true charisma is always in creative tension with temporal power. Prophets are oppositional by their very nature, though their lines of distinction are often subtle, revealing the various ways in which social conflicts crystallize in popular perception. In our present world the focus is not modernity itself but the contradictions inherent in what we gloss as "modern life," including tensions of neocolonialism, commoditization, and a global division of labor that have imposed particular strains on local experience. We can read these patterns in particular prophetic texts: in the critiques of bourgeois liberalism by the American New Right, for instance, or in the message of spirit mediums in Zimbabwe, who separated themselves from an exploitative colonial regime (refusing to use soap, petroleum, cars, and Coca-Cola) yet who allied themselves with a revolution offering material progress (Lan 1985).

In fact, the oppositional logic of charisma often capitalizes on the very dualisms set up by modernist ideologies. As Kwang-ok Kim shows in this volume, the marginalizing of Korean shamanism as "folk ritual" by a "modernizing" state helped reinvent it as mystical "tradition," empowering it to serve as a language of dissent untainted by the establishment and the Christian church (with which it was associated). The "politics of tradition" (see Lan 1985:176) turns the ideology of modernism against itself, distilling the terms of resistance from the exotic "otherness" that is the flip side of secular reason; thus it can often be used, as in Korea and Zimbabwe, by thoroughly modern people in their opposition to established might. Spirit possession, with its implications of unwilled invasion, of bodies seized by superhuman force, violates the model of selfhood central to bourgeois modernism. As such, it may merely confirm the marginality of its practitioners, condemning them to meaninglessness and historical obscurity. But such possession can also provide a critical displacement, its otherworldly authority empowering it to speak innovatively of contradictions in the world from which it comes.

Weber also noted (Gerth and Mills 1976:248) that the very instability of inspired authority limits its political possibilities; to work consistently in the world, the white heat of charisma must be cooled and routinized. Yet if the superhuman becomes too conversant with ruling power, it loses its uncontaminated force, its pristine potential for renewal and resistance. In becoming more worldly, charisma may take on many of the trappings of political authority, molding itself into the "altar ego," so to speak, of the state. This has been the history of all the so-called world religions at one time or another, their universal status being the result of their place in imperial regimes that have waged war with rites as well as rapiers. But the legitimation of state power is often more modest in scale: ancestor cults sanctioned chiefships in precolonial Africa, just as the "new religions" of early twentieth-century Japan can be seen to have endorsed the emperor system in important respects (Hardacre in this volume). Yet in none of these cases can we assume that "cosmology" simply reflected "community" or that it did so in perpetuity. In each case the role of religion in extending hegemony is a historical question, for which counterinstances can be found. Its social conditions must be explained, not presumed a priori.

For if religious institutions can parallel state structures, they can also elude many of the cumbersome constraints of temporal authority. Thus highly routinized movements have the organizational capacity to rival governments at their own game, building states within states, creating diasporas across sovereign borders, and threatening to usurp constituted political functions. Again, the established world religions give classic evidence of this: Christianity in Northern Ireland and Eastern Europe; Islam in contemporary Southeast Asia and beyond (see the chapters by Hefner, Shamsul, Gladney, and Chaiwat Satha-Anand in this volume). But DeBernardi's account of popular Chinese ritual in Malaysia reminds us not to label religions too rigidly as "local" or "universal," "traditional" or "rationalized" (cf. Ranger 1993). Not only do world religions often serve distinctive parochial purposes; movements of seemingly small-scale relevance can have surprisingly widespread appeal. Our own map of universal history often blinds us to the globalizing constructs of others, especially in a "postmodern" climate. The growing identification of African American with Yoruba signs and practices, for instance, draws on the longstanding salience of West African *orisha* as a currency of a trans-Atlantic black identity and history; its recent revitalization reemphasizes a dynamic diaspora that challenges Western cultural orthodoxies, both "religious" and "secular" (Matory n.d; Verger 1981). As "globetrotting evangelists" (Hackett n.d.) from Africa and elsewhere travel the world bearing homegrown revelations on cassettes and videotape, we have to think again about the nature of "local" and "translocal" religions and about the universal "cultural economies" they help to create (Appadurai 1990).

As the age-old history of religious persecution can attest, temporal authorities do not sit idly by if such captivating forces seem subversive. The fate of Theravāda Buddhism in recent Cambodian history (Keyes in this volume) or of Catholicism and Islam in Singapore has too many echoes East and West to list; but noteworthy parallels exist in communities that make little distinction between "religion" and "politics." Thus in the Zande states of the early twentieth-century Sudan, nobles sought strenuously to curb the operation of the international *mani* movement, since its healing rites challenged the authority of the oracles that buttressed their rule (Evans-Pritchard 1976:205ff.). Again, whether or not folk belief separates cosmology from history, very similar processes are observable at an analytic level in superficially different systems. Clearly, the absence of a consciousness of history in *our* cultural terms cannot be allowed to banish other societies to timeless "traditionalism."

In fact, as we move back across the scale from routine to charisma, we find that religious movements are less likely to rival established authority in its own terms than to challenge the very hegemony on which it rests. Movements of prophetic protest may vary considerably in scope: the expansive "regional cults" and witch-finding movements of Central Africa, past and present (Richards 1935; Werbner 1977; Fields 1985; Auslander n.d.) contrast with the operation of localized mediums in every type of society, from contemporary China to colonial Colombia, Nuerland to New York (Anagnost in this volume; Taussig 1987; Evans-Pritchard 1956; Harding 1986). Such groups are animated by powers contesting, at least in certain respects, the ruling lore and logic. At the very least they shed ironic light upon the tenets of temporal authority. If dominant regimes seek to limit the proliferation of power and meaning, prophetic cults defy them by opening new channels to seemingly infinite inspiration. By this token alone they are inherently subversive, for they threaten to denaturalize the ground on which nation-states erect themselves as primordial structures, contesting sovereign maps and mandates (Anagnost in this volume; Comaroff 1985:196ff.; Boddy 1989). Indeed, inspired leaders tend to build communities by reformulating the signs and practices, the bodies and memories, of their followers. And in keeping faith with divine decree, they often slight more mundane masters, refusing to render unto Caesar his tribute, material or moral. These efforts may siphon off a disaffected minority rather than empowering it to engage dominant powers in audible debate. But in an adequately polarized social field they may also crystallize significant and consequential opposition. If nothing else, their ability to engage orthodox authorities in argument keeps them central to mainstream cultural debate: televangelists like Jerry Falwell, Jimmy Swaggart, or Jim Bakker have become the audible others in terms of which the American establishment seeks to define itself in the media, church, and state (Harding n.d.). As such, though they may be seen as embodiments of "unreason," they are peculiarly modern creations.

Inspired movements are especially well equipped to deal with the impact, on local communities, of colonizing forces—whether imperial conquerors or imperious commodities. Again, as early Christianity attests, such prophetic ripostes are by no means a merely modern phenomenon. Neither, I suggest, are these actions just "a defense of tradition" (Introduction in this volume) or a backward-looking attempt to shore up indigenous worlds against external threats. In this respect so-called cargo cults and millenary movements are one with shamanism and spirit mediumship: they draw on charismatic creativity to heal breaches in everyday experience, working innovatively with signs and practices to appropriate the powers that oppress them. More than the ritual "anti-structure" of the early Turner (1969) or even the carnivalesque irreverence of the late Bakhtin (1968; cf. Kelly and Kaplan 1990), these prophetic performances seem freed from the grammar of everyday action. And such freedom can never escape convention altogether. In this regard Taussig has probably overplayed the creative chaos of shamanism (1987). While ecstatic trance and visions set signifers afloat, they do so to effect new constructions and fields of meaning (cf. Rogers 1989). To claim, as Taussig has, that the synthesizing power of mediums is a mere product of systematizing scholarship is to reduce their potential as historical agents. Inspired ritual texts build novel currencies of communication, often resituating elusive, colonizing signs in productive relationship with local symbols and making them *seem,* at least, to be susceptible to indigenous control (cf. Munn 1974; Comaroff 1985:197ff.).

Social observers have tended to take diametrically opposed views of the creativity of such *bricolage,* seeing it as simple semantic repetition (Lévi-Strauss 1966) or pure political invention (Hobsbawn and Ranger 1983). I would argue, however, that it is both—and hence neither. As Weller's account in this volume of Taiwan's "amoral" temple cults shows, such rites both reproduce certain longstanding features of indigenous practice and subtly revalue their meaning and moral valence. Like ritual movements all over the late capitalist world, these cults address the impact of radically diffused and individuated production, of the insecurities of life in a capricious market where greed and luck appear as effective as work and rational choice (see Burdick 1990 on Umbanda and evangelicalism in contemporary Brazil). And while they still cast a critical light on prevailing moral economies, these practices also promise the possibility of getting in on the act, of redirecting some of the largesse to those previously denied it. They thus express the experience of fragmentation that some label the "postmodern" predicament; but they also seek to counter it.

The meaning of such innovative movements is complex, and the fault lines they mark are subtle. Their historical implications lie precisely in their particulars—the way in which they distill and mobilize specific structures of feeling, specific assertions of right and desire in the face of dominant interests and authorities. They do not reduce, in unidimensional terms, to the zero-sum logic of "conservatism" or "resistance," although they probably entail elements of both. They are imaginative efforts to reclaim a runaway world, to make history with a recognizable face.

One way in which to categorize reformist ritual movements is in terms of their relation to the world they address. Among markedly alienated populations, ritual inspiration can form the basis for thoroughgoing encapsulation, groups withdrawing from the world and defying political authority without actually confronting it (see Cohn [1961] for a classic account of the New Jerusalems of medieval Europe; Jorgensen [1985: 124] on Native American movements). Furthermore, such distant defiance can radically challenge the status and authority of constituted governments, drawing down upon its perpetrators the full armed might of the state. Thus the British in colonial Sudan felt compelled to hunt down the Nuer prophet Gwek and destroy his focal shrine (see Coriat 1939; Newborn n.d.), just as the government of the newly independent Zambian state felt it necessary to rout the headquarters of the defiant charismatic Alice Lenshina (Binsbergen 1981:266ff.). In a different context but a similar vein, the civic leaders in late nineteenth-century Chicago felt compelled to harry the utopian leader Alexander Dowie, whose radical

Christian Catholic Apostolic Church in Zion, Illinois, flouted their authority (Harlan 1906).

But charismatic cults also thrive in the thick of society, not only in Accra or Rio de Janeiro, but in London and New York (Brown 1986; Mullings 1984; cf. Boddy 1989). Urban prophets often give fee-for-service antidotes to practical problems, though the relief they offer frequently fails to remedy the deeper contradictions they address (Brown 1986; Mullings 1984; cf. Boddy 1989). Their actions may or may not challenge authority directly. Charismatic cults, unlike more routinized religious movements, are not easily assimilated into organized political projects. But they do provide a dynamism to be harnessed by institutionalized forces, both orthodox and oppositional, forces with which they may move in tandem at least for a time; thus millenarians and mediums have been drawn into more routinized forms of resistance (see Ileto 1979; Lan 1985; Kim in this volume; also cf. Scott 1977). Established authorities have also attempted to capitalize on charisma. Brazilian politicians, for instance, have tried openly to co-opt the élan of Umbanda. Similarly, in the early 1980s the new Zimbabwean leadership sewed images of leading spirit mediums on their banners and flags. But because they march to a different drummer, these movements are never reducible to the rhythm of temporal politics; inspirations remain out of step, their loyalties to worldly power suspect. Thus while Shona spirit mediums may have been fixed on the flag of the Zimbabwean ruling party, they have continued, especially as revolutionary fervor wanes, to seem marginal and dangerous forces; in fact, the new government has come to use the same legal and bureaucratic mechanisms to control them as did its colonial predecessors (Lan 1985:221).

Conclusion: The Relevance of Ritual

One further issue has been lurking at the back of this discussion: In attempting to free "religion" from parochial definition I have treated it merely as portentous action, action in the name of collective values that transcend the temporal and mundane. Such action, I have implied, is ritualized; its power emanates as much from its poetic form as from its ostensibly awesome objects. Ritual, in fact, generates the very force it presupposes. But how? And how salient is an understanding of this process to an assessment of religion in the world?

The sociology of religion in the West has largely been concerned with content, with the referents of thought and action, rather than with the language in which they are expressed. This emphasis is part of the more general tendency to separate reality from its representations and the "message" of social practice from the seemingly transparent media that bear it. Anthropologists have been more concerned with ritual than most, often using it as a loose synonym for religion itself. Yet as Silverstein (n.d.) has noted, they have also been more sensitive to its semantic than its formal properties. Relatively few have been preoccupied with the mechanisms—poetic or pragmatic—that make sacred performances real; with the ways in which signs, objects, and gestures are wielded to inflate charisma and invest present practice with absent potential (cf. Hanks 1984).

The neglect by anthropologists of these formal properties of ritual is part of a more complex history to which I can only allude here (see Kelly and Kaplan 1990 for an excellent overview). Until quite recently, the most influential writing on the topic was resolutely Durkheimian: ritual was treated as "a mechanism that periodically converts the obligatory into the desirable" (Turner 1967:30); rites represented social utilities as collective consciousness (cf. Sahlins 1976:114ff.). This perspective did not preclude quite subtle explorations of ritual symbolism (rites were, after all, the quintessential site of culture). Functionalists even made occasional (and influential) efforts to define ritual in terms of its signifying properties (Turner 1967). But they continued steadfastly to regard ritual (and by implication, "religion") as the sanctification of social structure—as integral to the reproduction of traditional systems beyond the reach of time.

Ritual, in fact, was fetishized in this scheme. It was the "all-purpose social glue" that might cement the slivers of a shattered structure. From this perspective, it was seen to guarantee the coherence of "traditional" societies in which cosmology reflected community and vice versa. The ubiquity of such views beyond anthropology and their resilience in the face of critique suggest that they mirror our own, deeply rooted myths of modernity. Consequently, it should not surprise us that classic ethnographers saw communal rites as a distinctive feature of "small-scale" communities or that "complex" societies were held to be radically deritualized (Gluckman 1966; Turner 1969:202–203). Such conclusions followed tautologically from the very definition of ritual itself: formal behavior directed at "mystical beings or powers" (Turner 1967:19; cf. Tambiah 1990:5). All other modes of conventionalized, symbolically saturated action were dubbed "ceremonial." The narrowness of these established concepts bred overgeneralized reactions; Leach (1968) argued, for instance, that ritual was merely the communicative aspect of all human behavior, a definition so broad that it failed to discriminate rites from any other form of social action.

Within the functionalist mainstream, ritual continued to be seen, for the most part, as "quintessential tradition" (Turner 1967:100); it was judged unlikely to flourish under conditions of instability and change. Although allowed a dynamic role in regulating repetitive processes, it was not recognized as a means of making history. Where ritualized movements inescapably addressed historical forces, they were dubbed "millenarian" and explained as the disjunctive outcome of disintegrating traditional worlds (see, for instance, Gluckman [1963] on Mau Mau; cf. Fields 1985). Only recently, as timeless models of society and culture have at last been discredited, has the historical potential of ritual been acknowledged—the potential not only to comment on culture, but also to change it.

This shift has been occasioned by a more general destabilization of the social sciences and humanities, one that has undermined established disciplines and proprieties. Anthropologists have begun to find history in peripheral societies—and have, in the process, taught Western scholars about historicities other than their own; and they have also begun to move from the margins into the wider world system. At the same time, historians and critics have not only found ritual in the heart of the urban metropole, they have begun to explore the cosmologies and "subcultures" of local communities in the West (Davis 1975; Hall and Jefferson 1976; Hebdige 1979). Ritual has been brought down from its pedestal, dusted off, and put to work in the world, no longer condemned merely to mouth pious sentiments that persist above dispute. In the hands of such writers as Hebdige, ritual has been used to designate any kind of repetitive action whose stylized form is dense with social significance—dance, dress, even deportment. Yet if this is "ritual" in the lower case, there is still the "Ritual" that is set apart, for its practitioners, from everyday time and space: Ritual with ultimate referents. If this is what we wish to imply by "religion," however, we must acknowledge that it is one among other forms of ritual action. It has no simple monopoly over the making of social meaning, for it plays off other, everyday modes of symbolic creativity with which it shares its cultural field.

The practices discussed in this collection are largely Rituals in this second sense. They infuse the present with meaning beyond itself, giving it referents in space-time horizons that exceed mundane existence (Munn 1990). It is portentous action, action that seems to derive its authority from outside the will of those performing it. Its prescribed form places limits on agency, "make[ing] large claims possible" (Kelly and Kaplan 1990:140). But ritual does not only forge meaning through exclusion (Bloch 1989). It is also positively productive, pressing new or enhanced associations and asserting the right to signify the world, even to contest its established definitions or appearances (Comaroff 1985; Lan 1985). Its productivity lies in its capacity to create morally charged experience, to speak with and without words, in diverse sensory registers and through "multiple channels" (Tambiah 1985:60ff.). And while such rites never work with empty signs, always refiguring meanings made in other domains of practice, their poetry intensifies perceptions, invoking new subjects that presuppose new objects. In this sense ritual is intensely pragmatic. It not only makes and remakes its actors, but can also call on them to make and remake worlds. Its modes are indispensable to the forging of "culture" and "society," in the modern world as in any other. Ritual, in the end, defies disenchantment.

WORKS CITED

Ackerman, Robert John. 1985. *Religion as Critique.* Amherst, MA: University of Massachusetts Press.

Ackerman, Susan E., and Raymond M. Lee. 1988. *Heaven in Transition: Non-Muslim Religious Innovation and Ethnic Identity in Malaysia.* Honolulu, HI: University of Hawaii Press.

Adas, Michael. 1979. *Prophets of Rebellion: Millenarian Protest Movements against the European Colonial Order.* Chapel Hill, NC: University of North Carolina Press.

Ahern, Emily Martin. 1981a. *Chinese Ritual and Politics.* Cambridge: Cambridge University Press.

———. 1981b. The Thai Ti Kong Festival. In *The Anthropology of Taiwanese Society,* ed. Emily Martin Ahern and Hill Gates, 397–425. Stanford, CA: Stanford University Press.

Ahmad, Khurshid. 1983. The Nature of Islamic Resurgence. In *Voices of Resurgent Islam,* ed. John L. Esposito, 218–229. New York and Oxford: Oxford University Press.

Akiba Tadatoshi. 1986. *Shinju to sakura: Hiroshima kara mita Amerika no kokoro* [The pearl and the cherry tree: the heart of America as seen from Hiroshima]. Tokyo: Asahi Shinbun.

Al-Azm, Sadik J. 1991. The Importance of Being Earnest about Salman Rushdie. *Die Welt des Islams* 31 (1):1–49

Alexander, Jennifer, and Paul Alexander. 1979. Labour Demands and the "Involution" of Javanese Agriculture. *Social Analysis* 3:22–44.

Aliran. 1979. *The Real Issues: The Merdeka University.* Penang, Malaysia: Aliran.

Alloua, Malek. 1986. *The Colonial Harem.* Minneapolis: University of Minnesota Press.

Amara Pongsapich and Noppawan Chongwatana. 1988. The Refugee Situation in Thailand. In *Indochinese Refugees: Asylum and Resettlement,* ed. Supang Chantavanich and E. Bruce Reynolds, 12–47. Bangkok: Chulalongkorn University, Institute of Asian Studies.

Anagnost, Ann. 1987. Politics and Magic. *Modern China* 13 (1): 40–61.

———. n.d. "Producing Productive Bodies." Ms.

Andaya, Barbara Watson, and Leonard Y. Andaya. 1982. *A History of Malaysia.* London: Macmillan.

Anderson, Benedict. 1972. The Idea of Power in Javanese Culture. In *Culture and Politics in Indonesia,* ed. Claire Holt, Benedict Anderson, and James Siegel, 1–67. Ithaca, NY: Cornell University Press.

———. 1977. Millenarianism and the Saminist Movement. In Benedict R. O'G. Anderson, Mitsuo Nakamura, and Mohammad Slamet, *Religion and Social Ethos in Indonesia,* 48–61. Melbourne: Monash University.

———. 1978. Studies of the Thai State: The State of Thai Studies. In *The Study of Thailand,* ed. Eliezer B. Ayal, 193–247. Athens, OH: Center for International Studies.

———. 1983a. *Imagined Communities: Reflections on the Origin and Spread of Nationalism.* London: Verso.

———. 1983b. Old State, New Society: Indonesia's New Order in Historical Perspective. *Journal of Asian Studies* 42:477–496.

———. 1991. *Imagined Communities: Reflections on the Origin and Spread of Nationalism.* Revised edition. London: Verso.

Ando, Hirofumi. 1969. A Study of the Iglesia Ni Cristo: A Politico-Religious Sect in the Philippines. *Pacific Affairs* 42 (3): 334–345.

Anwar, Zainah. 1987. *Islamic Revivalism in Malaysia: Dakwah among the Students.* Petaling Jaya, Malaysia: Pelandok.

Appadurai, Arjun. 1986a. Introduction: Commodities and the Politics of Value. In *The Social Life of Things: Commodities in Cultural Perspective,* ed. Arjun Appadurai, 3–63. Cambridge: Cambridge University Press.

———. 1986b. Is Homo Hierarchicus? *American Ethnologist* 13 (4): 745–761.

———. 1990. Disjuncture and Difference in the Global Cultural Economy. *Public Culture* 2 (2): 1–24.

Appignanesi, Lisa, and Sara Maitland, eds. 1990. *The Rushdie File.* New York: SUNY Press.

Arkush, R. David. 1981. *Fei Xiaotong and Sociology in Revolutionary China.* Cambridge, MA: Harvard University Press.

Asiaweek. 27 November 1987.

Atkinson, Jane. 1983. Religions in Dialogue: The Construction of an Indonesian Minority Religion. *American Ethnologist* 10 (4): 684–696.

Auslander, Mark. n.d. Inversion and Appropriation in Modern Ngoni Witchfinding. Ms.

Aymonier, Etienne. 1883. Notes sur les coutumes et croyances superstitieuses des Cambodgiens. *Excursions et Reconnaissances* 16:133–206.

———. 1900–1904. *Le Cambodge.* 4 vols. Paris: Ernest Leroux.

Ayoob, M., ed. 1981. *The Politics of Islamic Reassertion.* London: Croom Helm.

Bailey, Frederick. 1974. *Stratagems and Spoils.* Oxford: Blackwell.

Baity, Philip C. 1975. *Religion in a Chinese Town.* Taipei: Orient Cultural Service.

Bakhtin, Mikhail. 1968. *Rabelais and His World.* Helene Iswolsky, trans. Cambridge, MA: MIT Press.

Barraclough, S. 1983. Managing the Challenges of Islamic Revival in Malaysia. *Asian Survey* 23 (8): 958–975.

Basso, Keith. 1984. Stalking with Stories: Names, Places, and Moral Narratives among the Western Apache. In *Text, Play, and Story: The Construction and Reconstruction of Self and Society,* ed. Edward M. Bruner, 19–55. Prospect Heights, IL: Waveland Press.

Baudrillard, Jean. 1981. *For a Critique of the Political Economy of the Sign.* St. Louis, MO: Telos Press.

Beckford, James A. 1987. New Religions: An Overview. In *The Encyclopedia of Religion,* ed. Mircea Eliade, 10:390–394. New York: Macmillan.

Beijing China News Agency [Beijing Zhongguo Xinwen She]. 1989. Publication Ban Sought. Reproduced and translated in Foreign Broadcast Information Service (FBIS), *Daily Report—China,* FBIS-CHI-89-092, 15 May:52.

Beijing New China News Agency [*Beijing Xinhuashe*]. 1989. Government Bans Book. In Foreign Broadcast Information Service, *Daily Report—China,* FBIS-CHI-89-150, 15 May:53.

Bell, Catherine. 1989. Religion and Chinese Culture: Toward an Assessment of "Popular Religion." *History of Religions* 29 (1): 35–57.

Bellah, Robert N., ed. 1965. *Religion and Progress in Modern Asia.* New York: Free Press.

———. 1970. *Beyond Belief: Essays on Religions in a Post-Traditional World.* New York: Harper and Row.

Benda, Harry J. 1983. *The Crescent and the Rising Sun: Indonesian Islam under the Japanese Occupation, 1942–1945.* Leiden: Foris Publications.

Benda, Harry J., and Lance Castles. 1969. The Samin Movement. *Bijdragen tot de Land- en Volkenkunde* 97:19–94.

Berger, Peter L. 1967. *The Sacred Canopy: Elements of a Sociology of Religion.* New York: Doubleday.

———. 1988. An East Asian Development Model? In *In Search of an East Asian Development Model,* ed. Peter L. Berger and Hsin-Huang Michael Hsiao, 3–11. New Brunswick, NJ: Transaction.

Berger, Peter L., Briggitte Berger, and Hansfried Kellner. 1973. *The Homeless Mind: Modernization and Consciousness.* New York: Random House.

Berger, Peter L., and Thomas Luckmann. 1974. Sociology of Religion and Sociology of Knowledge. In *The Social Meanings of Religion,* ed. William M. Newman, 99–110. Chicago, IL: Rand McNally.

Bergman, Sten. 1938 [1935]. *In Korean Wilds and Villages,* trans. F. Whyte. London: John Gifford.

Bernardini, Pierre. 1976. L'Implantation caodaïste au Cambodge an 1969. In *Asie du Sud-Est Continentale. Acts du XXXIXᵉ Congrès International des Orientalistes,* ed. Pierre-Bernard Lafont, 1–6. Paris: L'Asiathèque.

Binsbergen, Wim M. J. van. 1981. *Religious Change in Zambia: Exploratory Studies.* London and Boston: Kegan Paul International.

Bitard, Pierre. 1966. Le Monde du sorcier au Cambodge. In *Le Monde du Sorcier,* ed. Serge Salneron, 305–328. Sources Orientales 7. Paris: Ed. de Seuil.

Bizot, François. 1976. *Le Figuier à cinq branches: Recherche sur le bouddhisme Khmer.* Publication de l'E.F.E.O., 107. Paris: Ecole Française d'Extrême-Orient.

————. 1980. La Grotte de la Naissance: Recherches sur le Bouddhisme Khmer, 2. *Bulletin de l'Ecole Française d'Extrême-Orient* 67:221–274.

————. 1981. *Le Don de soi-même: Recherches sur le bouddhisme Khmer 3.* Publications de l'E.F.E.O., 180. Paris: Ecole Française d'Extrême-Orient.

Bloch, Maurice. 1974. Symbols, Song, Dance and Features of Articulation: Is Religion an Extreme Form of Traditional Authority? *European Journal of Sociology* 15 (1): 55–81.

————. 1977. The Past and the Present in the Present. *Man* 12 (2): 278–292.

————. 1989. *Ritual, History and Power: Selected Papers in Anthropology.* London: Athlone.

Bloch, Maurice, and J. Parry, eds. 1982. *Death and the Regeneration of Life.* Cambridge: Cambridge University Press.

Blythe, Wilfred. 1969. *The Impact of Chinese Secret Societies in Malaya.* London: Oxford University Press.

Boddy, Janice. 1989. *Wombs and Alien Spirits: Women, Men, and the Zar Cult in Northern Sudan.* Madison, WI: University of Wisconsin Press.

Boland, B. J. 1982. *The Struggle of Islam in Modern Indonesia.* The Hague: Martinus Nijhoff.

Boon, James A. 1977. *The Anthropological Romance of Bali: 1597–1972.* Cambridge: Cambridge University Press.

Boua, Chanthou. 1991. Genocide of a Religious Group: Pol Pot and Cambodia's Buddhist Monks. In *State-Organized Terror: The Case of Violent Internal Repression,* ed. P. Timothy Bushnell, Vladimir Shlapentokh, Christopher K. Vanderpool, and Jeyaratnam Sundram, 227–240. Boulder, CO: Westview.

Brandt, Anthony. 1978. A Short Natural History of Nostalgia. *Atlantic Monthly* 242 (December): 58–63.

Bromley, Julian, and Viktor Kozlov. 1989. The Theory of Ethnos and Ethnic Processes in Soviet Social Sciences. *Comparative Studies in Society and History* 3:425–437.

Brown, Diana De Groat. 1986. *Umbanda: Religion and Politics in Urban Brazil.* Ann Arbor, MI: University of Michigan Press.

Brunnert, H. S., and V. V. Hagelstrom. 1912. *Present-Day Political Organization of China,* trans. A. Beltchenko and E. E. Moran. Shanghai: Kelly and Walsh.

Bunchan Mul. 1982. The Umbrella War of 1942. In *Peasants and Politics in Kampuchea, 1942–1981,* ed. Ben Kiernan and Chanthou Boua, 114–126. London: Zed Press; Armonk, NY: M. E. Sharpe.

Burdick, John. 1990. The Progressive Catholic Church in Urban Brazil's Religious Arena. Ph.D. dissertation, City University of New York, New York.

Calhoun, Craig. 1989. Tiananmen, Television and the Public Sphere: Internationalization of Culture and the Beijing Spring of 1989. *Public Culture* 2 (1): 54–72.

Carney, Timothy Michael, comp. and ed. 1977. *Communist Party Power in Kampuchea (Cambodia): Documents and Discussion.* Data Paper no. 106. Ithaca, NY: Cornell University, Southeast Asia Program.

Carstens, Sharon A. 1988. From Myth to History: Yap Ah Loy and the Heroic

Past of Chinese Malaysians. *Journal of Southeast Asian Studies* 19 (2): 185–208.

Cassanova, Palo Gonzalez. 1965. Internal Colonialism and National Development. *Studies in Comparative International Development* 1 (4): 27ff.

Certeau, Michel de. 1984. *The Practice of Everyday Life.* Berkeley, CA: University of California Press.

Ch'ae Hŭi-wan and Yim Chin-t'aek. 1982. Madangguk esŏ Madanggusŭro [From Madanggeuk to Madanggut]. *Han'guk Munhakŭi Hyŏndangye* [Contemporary stage of Korean literature]. Seoul: Ch'angjakkwa Pip'yongsa.

Chai, Alice Yun. 1962. Kinship and Mate Selection in Korea. Ph.D. dissertation, Ohio State University.

Chanda, Nayan. 1986. *Brother Enemy: The War after the War.* San Diego: Harcourt, Brace Jovanich.

Chandler, David P. 1979. The Tragedy of Cambodian History. *Pacific Affairs* 52 (3): 410–419.

——. 1982. Songs at the Edge of the Forest: Perception of Order in Three Cambodian Texts. In *Moral Order and the Question of Change: Essays on Southeast Asian Thought,* ed. David K. Wyatt and Alexander Woodside, 53–77. Monograph Series, no. 24. New Haven, CT: Yale University Southeast Asia Studies.

——. 1983a. *A History of Cambodia.* Boulder, CO: Westview.

——. 1983b. Revising the Past in Democratic Kampuchea: When Was the Birthday of the Party? *Pacific Affairs* 56 (2): 288–300.

——. 1983c. Seeing Red: Perceptions of Cambodian History in Democratic Kampuchea. In *Revolution and Its Aftermath in Kampuchea: Eight Essays,* ed. David P. Chandler and Ben Kiernan, 34–56. Monograph Series, no. 25. New Haven, CT: Yale University Southeast Asia Studies.

——. 1986. The Kingdom of Kampuchea, March–October 1945: Japanese-sponsored Independence in Cambodia in World War II. *Journal of Southeast Asian Studies* 17 (1): 80–94.

——. 1991. *The Tragedy of Cambodian History: Politics, War, and Revolution since 1945.* New Haven, CT: Yale University Press.

——. 1992. *Brother Number One: A Political Biography of Pol Pot.* Boulder, CO: Westview.

Chandler, David P., and Ben Kiernan, eds. 1983. *Revolution and Its Aftermath in Kampuchea: Eight Essays.* Monograph Series, no. 25. New Haven, CT: Yale University Southeast Asia Studies.

Chang, Y. S. 1982. Shamanism as Folk Existentialism. In *Religions in Korea,* ed. E. Phillips and E. Yu, 25–41. Los Angeles: California State University Press.

Chao Thai. 1987. 26 December (in Thai).

Chatterjee, Partha. 1986. *Nationalist Thought and the Colonial World: A Derivative Discourse.* London: Zed Books.

Chau Seng. 1962. *L'Organisation buddhique au Cambodge. (Culture et civilisation khmères no. 4).* Phnom Penh: Université Bouddhique Preah Sihanouk Raj.

Chesneaux, Jean. 1971. *Secret Societies in China in the Nineteenth and Twentieth Centuries,* trans. Gillian Nettle. Ann Arbor, MI: University of Michigan Press.

Chiang Feng and Tzu Wang. 1982. *Zhongguo Shaoshu Minzu* [China's minority nationalities]. Beijing: People's Publishing Society.

China Communication Service [Zhongguo Tongxun She]. 1989. "Sex Habits Book" Causes Controversy in Beijing. In Foreign Broadcast Information Service, *Daily Report—China,* FBIS-CHI-89-092, 15 May:52.

China Communication Service, Hong Kong [Zhongguo Tongxun She, Xiang Gang]. 1989. Writer of "Sex Habits" Has Been Suspended for Examination. In Foreign Broadcast Information Service, *Daily Report—China,* FBIS-CHI-89-092, 15 May:53.

China Daily Report. 1986. 11 March.

China Handbook, 1937–1945. 1947. New York: Macmillan.

Cho Ki-hong et al. 1983. *Yeron* [Treatise on propriety]. Seoul: Songsin Women's University.

Cho P'ung-yŏn. 1983. *Honin kwa kyŏrhon* [Matrimony and marriage]. *Chont'ong munhwa* 6:30–35.

Ch'oe Kil-sŏng. 1974. Misin t'ap'ae taehan ilgoch'al [A study on the destruction of superstition]. *Han'guk minsokhak* 12:39–54.

———. 1981. *Han'gugŭi mudang* [Shaman in Korea]. Seoul: Yŏlhwadang.

Ch'oe Sang-su. 1982. *Kajŏng mansa pogam* [Comprehensive household compendium]. Seoul: Sangnok Ch'ulp'an Sa.

Choi, Chungmoo. 1987. The Competence of Korean Shamans as Performers of Folklore. Ph.D. dissertation, Indiana University.

Chŏnt'ong Munhwa. 1983. June (in Korean).

Choson Ilbo [Choson Daily News]. 1983. 4 May (in Korean).

———. 1986. 25 May.

———. 1987. 25 May.

Chow, Rey. 1991. Violence in the Other Country: China as Crisis, Spectacle, and Woman. In *Third World Women and the Politics of Feminism,* ed. Chandra Mohanty et al., 81–100. Bloomington, IN: Indiana University Press.

Chun, Kyung-soo. 1984. *Reciprocity and Korean Society: An Ethnography of Hasami.* Seoul: Institute of Social Studies, Seoul National University.

Claessen, H. J. M. 1981. Specific Features of the African Early State. *L'Uomo* 5:3–29.

Clark, Charles Allen. 1961 [1932]. *Religions of Old Korea.* Seoul: Christian Literature Society of Korea.

Clark, Donald N. 1986. Christianity in Modern Korea. *Asian Agenda Report,* no. 5. Lanham, MD: University Press of America; New York: Asia Society.

Clifford, James. 1986. On Ethnographic Allegory. In *Writing Culture: The Politics and Poetics of Ethnography,* ed. James Clifford and George E. Marcus, 98–121. Berkeley, CA: University of California Press.

Cohen, A. P. 1985. *The Symbolic Construction of Community.* London: Tavistock.

Cohn, Bernard S. 1987. The Census, Social Structure, and Objectification in

South Asia. In *An Anthropologist among the Historians and Other Essays,* ed. Bernard S. Cohn, 230–244. Delhi: Oxford University Press.

Cohn, Bernard S., and Nicholas Dirks. 1988. Beyond the Fringe: The Nation-State, Colonialism, and the Technologies of Power. *Journal of Historical Sociology* 1 (2): 224–229.

Cohn, Norman. 1961. *The Pursuit of the Millennium: Revolutionary Millenarians and Mystical Anarchists of the Middle Ages.* New York: Oxford University Press.

Comaroff, Jean. 1985. *Body of Power, Spirit of Resistance: The Culture and History of a South African People.* Chicago, IL: University of Chicago Press.

Committee for the Compilation of Materials on Damage Caused by the Atomic Bombs in Hiroshima and Nagasaki. 1981. *Hiroshima and Nagasaki: The Physical, Medical, and Social Effects of the Atomic Bombs,* trans. Eisei Ishikawa and David L. Swain. New York: Basic Books.

Connor, Walker. 1984. *The National Question in Marxist-Leninist Theory and Strategy.* Princeton, NJ: Princeton University Press.

Coriat, P. 1939. Gwek the Witch-doctor and the Pyramid of Dengkur. *Sudan Notes and Records* 22 (2): 221–238.

Crapanzano, Vincent, ed. 1977. *Case Studies in Spirit Possession.* New York: John Wiley & Sons.

Crouch, Harold. 1978. *The Army and Politics in Indonesia.* Ithaca, NY: Cornell University Press.

Daily News. 1988. 4, 11, and 18 February (in Thai).

Dao Siam. 1988. 16 March (in Thai).

Davis, Natalie Z. 1975. *Society and Culture in Early Modern France: Eight Essays.* Stanford, CA: Stanford University Press.

Davis, Winston. 1980. *Dojo: Magic and Exorcism in Modern Japan.* Stanford, CA: Stanford University Press.

Dean, Kenneth. 1986. Field Notes on Two Taoist *jiao* Observed in Zhangzhou in December 1985. *Cahiers d'Extrême-Asie* 2:191–209.

DeBernardi, Jean. 1984. The Hungry Ghosts Festival: A Convergence of Religion and Politics in the Chinese Community of Penang, Malaysia. *Southeast Asian Journal of Social Science* 12 (1): 25–34.

———. 1986. Heaven, Earth and Man: A Study of Chinese Spirit Mediums. Ph.D. dissertation, University of Chicago.

———. 1987a. The God of War and the Vagabond Buddha. *Modern China* 13 (3): 310–332.

———. 1987b. On a Chinese Rhetoric of Politeness and Persuasion. Ms.

———. 1992. Space and Time in Chinese Religious Culture. *History of Religions* 31 (3): 247–268.

———. Forthcoming. The Way That Lives in the Heart: Text and Performance in Chinese Religious Culture. In *Sourcebook in Chinese Religion,* ed. Donald L. Lopez. Princeton, NJ: Princeton University Press.

DeGroot, J. J. M. 1977 [1886]. *Les fêtes annuellement célébres à Emoui (Amoy): Études concernant la religion populaire des chinois.* San Francisco, CA: Chinese Materials Center.

Deleuze, Gilles, and Felix Guattari. 1987. *A Thousand Plateaus: Capitalism and Schizophrenia*. Minneapolis, MN: University of Minnesota Press.

Deuchler, Martina. 1977. The Tradition: Women during the Yi Dynasty. In *Virtues in Conflict: Tradition and the Korean Woman Today*, ed. S. Mattialli, 1–48. Seoul: Royal Asiatic Society Press.

———. 1980. Neo-Confucianism: The Impulse for Social Action in Early Yi Korea. *Journal of Korean Studies* 2:71–112.

———. 1987. Neo-Confucianism in Action: Agnation and Ancestor Worship in Early Yi Korea. In *Religion and Ritual in Korean Society*, ed. Laurel Kendall and Griffin Dix, 26–55. Korea Research Monograph, no. 12. Berkeley, CA: Institute of East Asian Studies, University of California.

DeVoss, David. 1980. Buddhism under the Red Flag. *Time*, 17 November: 90–92.

De Vries, Egbert. 1931. *Landbouw en Welvaart in het Regentschap Pasoeroean*. Wageningen, The Netherlands: Veenman & Zonen.

Dhofier, Zamakhysari. 1978. Santri-Abangan dalam Kehidupan Orang Jawa: Teropong Dari Pesantren. *Prisma* 7 (5): 48–63.

———. 1982. *Tradisi Pesantren: Studi Tentang Pandangan Kyai*. Jakarta: Lembaga Penelitian, Pendidikan, dan Penerangan Ekonomi dan Sosial (LP3ES).

Diamond, Norma. 1988. The Miao and Poison: Interactions on China's Southwest Frontier. *Ethnology* 27 (1): 1–25.

Dirks, Nicholas B. 1987. *The Hollow Crown: Ethnohistory of a Little Kingdom in South India*. Cambridge: Cambridge University Press.

Dirlik, Arif. 1982. Spiritual Solutions to Material Problems: The Socialist Education and Courtesy Month in China. *South Atlantic Quarterly* 81:472–501.

"Dogmakhua." 1988. *Choom Tang Khru* [Teachers' junction]. *Matichon*, 24 February (in Thai).

Domis, H. J. 1832. Aanteekeningen over Het Gebergte Tinger. *Verhandelingen van het Bataviaasch Genootschap van Kunsten en Wetenschappen* 13: 325–356.

Douglas, Mary. 1966. *Purity and Danger*. New York: Praeger.

Downie, Sue. 1989. Reluctant Ruler. *Asia Magazine*, 15–17 September. Reproduced in Joint Publications Research Service, *Southeast Asia Report*, JPRS-SEA-89-008-L, 7 December.

Dreyer, June Teufel. 1976. *China's Forty Million: Minority Nationalities and National Integration in the People's Republic of China*. Cambridge, MA: Harvard University Press.

———. 1982. The Islamic Community of China. *Central Asian Survey* 1 (2/3): 32–49.

Duara, Prasenjit. 1988. Superscribing Symbols: The Myth of Guandi, Chinese God of War. *Journal of Asian Studies* 47 (4): 778–795.

———. 1990. Knowledge and Power in the Discourse of Modernity: The Campaigns against Popular Religion in Early 20th-Century China. *Journal of Asian Studies* 50 (1): 67–83.

———. 1992. Writing Asian Histories and the Post-Structuralist Challenge.

Paper presented to the conference on Theory and Asian Studies, University of Oregon, Eugene, 15–16 May.

Duncan, John. n.d. The Decline of Traditional Confucian Social Values in the Face of Korea's Economic Development. Paper presented to the conference on Religion and Contemporary Society in Korea, University of California, Berkeley, 12 November 1988.

Durkheim, Emile. 1965 [1915]. *The Elementary Forms of the Religious Life,* trans. J. W. Swain. New York: Free Press.

Ea, Meng-Try. 1990. Recent Population Trends in Kampuchea. In *The Cambodian Agony,* ed. David A. Ablin and Marlowe Hood, 3–15. Armonk, NY, and London: M. E. Sharpe.

Ebihara, May. 1966. Interrelations between Buddhism and Social Systems in Cambodian Peasant Culture. In *Anthropological Studies in Theravāda Buddhism,* ed. Manning Nash et al., 175–196. Cultural Report Series, no. 13. New Haven, CT: Yale University Southeast Asian Studies.

———. 1968. Svay: A Khmer Village in Cambodia. Ph.D. dissertation, Columbia University.

———. 1987. Khmer Religion. In *The Encyclopedia of Religion,* ed. Mircea Eliade, 8:290–292. New York: Macmillan.

———. 1990. Revolution and Reformulation in Kampuchean Village Culture. In *The Cambodian Agony,* ed. David A. Ablin and Marlowe Hood, 16–61. Armonk, NY, and London: M. E. Sharpe.

Ecklund, Judith L. 1979. Tradition or Non-Tradition: Adat, Islam, and Local Control on Lombok. In *What Is Modern Indonesian Culture?,* ed. Gloria Davis, 249–267. Athens, OH: Center for International Studies.

Economist. 1989. Beijing's Copycat Scandal. 20 May.

Edwards, Walter. 1989. *Modern Japan through Its Weddings: Gender, Person, and Society in Ritual Portrayal.* Stanford, CA: Stanford University Press.

Eickelman, Dale F. 1982. The Study of Islam in Local Contexts. In *Islam in Local Contexts,* ed. Richard C. Martin, *Contributions to Asian Studies* 17: 1–16.

Nidhi Eiosriwong. 1988. Disunity and Dress. *Matichon,* 2 February (in Thai).

Ejima Shūsaku. 1977. "Genbaku taiken" ni kansuru shinborizumu no bunseki [An analysis of the symbolism related to the "atomic bomb experience"]. In Ejima Shūsaku, Kasuga Kōfu, and Aoki Hideo 1977, 7–35.

Ejima Shūsaku, Kasuga Kōfu, and Aoki Hideo. 1977. *Hiroshima-shi ni okeru "genbaku taiken" no shakai tōgō kinō o meguru ichi kenkyū* [A study of the function of the "atomic bomb experience" in the social integration of the city of Hiroshima]. Publication no. 15. Hiroshima: Hiroshima Shūdō Daigaku Shōgyō Keizai Kenkyūjohō.

Eley, Geoff. 1976. Defining Social Imperialism: Use and Abuse of an Idea. *Social History* 3:265–290.

Ellen, R. F. 1988. Social Theory, Ethnography, and the Understanding of Practical Islam in South-East Asia. In *Islam in South-East Asia,* ed. M. B. Hooker, 50–91. Leiden: E. J. Brill.

Ellwood, Robert S. 1987. New Religions: New Religions in Japan. In *The Ency-*

clopedia of Religion, ed. Mircea Eliade, 10:410–414. New York: Macmillan.

Elson, R. E. 1984. *Javanese Peasants and the Colonial Sugar Industry: Impact and Change in an East Java Residency, 1830–1940.* Singapore: Oxford University Press.

Emmerson, Donald K. 1978. The Bureaucracy in Political Context: Weakness in Strength. In *Political Power and Communications in Indonesia,* ed. Karl D. Jackson and Lucian W. Pye, 82–136. Berkeley, CA: University of California Press.

Erbaugh, Mary. n.d. Struggling to be Civil: China's Quest for Courteous Public Language. Ms.

Erwin, Cordelia. 1918. Transition: A Korean Christian Wedding. *Korean Mission Field* 14 (4): 73–76.

Evans-Pritchard, Edward E. 1956. *Nuer Religion.* Oxford: Clarendon Press.

———. 1962. The Divine Kingship of the Shilluk of the Nilotic Sudan: The Frazer Lecture, 1948. In Edward E. Evans-Pritchard, *Social Anthropology and Other Essays,* 192–212. New York: Free Press of Glencoe.

———. 1976. *Witchcraft, Oracles, and Magic among the Azande.* Abridged with an introduction by Eva Gillies. London: Clarendon Press.

Ewha Womans University Committee for the Compilation of the History of Korean Women [EWUCCHKW]. 1977. *Women of Korea: A History from Ancient Times to 1945.* Trans. and ed. Y. Kim. Seoul: Ewha Womans University Press.

Fabian, Johannes. 1983. *Time and the Other: How Anthropology Makes Its Object.* New York: Columbia University Press.

Fan Zuogang et al. 1987. *Nongcun jingshen wenming jianshe xintan* [New explorations into building rural spiritual civilization]. Beijing: Nongye Chubanshe.

Fang Xing et al. 1982 (reprinted 1984). *Pochu mixin wenda* [Questions and answers on eradicating superstition]. Xi'an: Zhongguo Qingnian Chubanshe.

Farouk, Omar. 1988. Malaysia's Islamic Awakening: Impact on Singapore and Thai Muslims. *Conflict* 8:157–168.

Federici, Silvia. n.d. "The Great Caliban: The Struggle Against the Rebel Body." Ms.

Federspiel, H. 1985. Islam and Development in the Nations of ASEAN. *Asian Survey* 25 (8): 805–821.

Fei, Xiaotong. 1981. Ethnic Identification in China. In Fei-Xiaotong, *Toward a People's Anthropology,* 60–78. Beijing: New World Press.

Fernandez, James. 1986. Persuasions and Performances: Of the Beast in Every Body and the Metaphors of Everyman. In James Fernandez *Persuasions and Performances: The Play of Tropes in Culture,* ed. 3–27. Bloomington, IN: Indiana University Press.

Feuchtwang, Stephan. 1974. Domestic and Communal Worship in Taiwan. In *Religion and Ritual in Chinese Society,* ed. Arthur P. Wolf, 105–129. Stanford, CA: Stanford University Press.

Field, Norma. 1991. *In the Realm of a Dying Emperor.* New York: Pantheon.

Fields, Karen E. 1985. *Revival and Rebellion in Colonial Central Africa*. Princeton, NJ: Princeton University Press.

Fischer, Michael M. J. 1986. Ethnicity and the Post-Modern Arts of Memory. In *Writing Culture: The Politics and Poetics of Ethnography,* ed. James Clifford and George E. Marcus, 194–233. Berkeley, CA: University of California Press.

Fletcher, Joseph, Mary Ellen Alonso, and Wasma'a K. Chorbachi. 1989. Arabic Calligraphy in Twentieth-Century China. Paper presented at the conference "The Legacy of Islam in China: An International Symposium in Memory of Joseph F. Fletcher," Harvard University, 14–16 April.

Foard, James H. 1982. The Boundaries of Compassion: Buddhism and National Tradition in Japanese Pilgrimage. *Journal of Asian Studies* 41 (2): 231–251.

———. n.d. Position paper prepared for the workshop "States of Change: Religion in East and Southeast Asia," Boston, 8 April 1987.

Forbes, Andrew D. W. 1987. The Role of the Hui Muslims (Tungans) in Republican Xinjiang. Paper presented at the Second European Seminar on Central Asian Studies, London School of Oriental and African Studies, 7–10 April.

Forest, Alain. 1980. *Le Cambodge et la colonisation française: histoire d'une colonisation sans heurts (1897–1920)*. Paris: Editions l'Harmattan.

Foucault, Michel. 1975. Film and Popular Memory. *Radical Philosophy* 11: 24–29.

———. 1977. Nietzsche, Genealogy, History. In *Language, Counter-Memory, Practice,* ed. Donald F. Bouchard, 139–164. Ithaca, NY: Cornell University Press.

Freedman, Maurice. 1966. *Chinese Lineage and Society: Fukien and Kwangtung*. London School of Economics Monographs in Social Anthropology, no. 33. London: Athlone.

———. 1967. Immigrants and Associations: Chinese in Nineteenth-Century Singapore. In *Immigrants and Associations,* ed. L. A. Fallers, 17–48. The Hague: Mouton.

———. 1969. Geomancy. *Proceedings of the Royal Anthropological Institute of Great Britain and Ireland for 1968,* 5–16.

Friedman, Edward. 1989. Democratization and Re-Stalinization in China. *Telos* 80:27–36.

Frieson, Kate. 1988. The Political Nature of Democratic Kampuchea. *Pacific Affairs* 61 (3): 405–427.

Fujian ribao [*Fujian Daily*]. 1982. 28 January (in Chinese).

———. 1982. 22 December.

———. 1983. 23 January.

———. 1983. 7 October.

Fujitani, Takeshi. 1993. Inventing, Forgetting, Remembering: Toward a Historical Ethnography of the Nation-State. In *Cultural Nationalism in East Asia: Representation and Identity,* ed. Harumi Befu, 77–106. Research Papers and Policy Studies, no. 39. Berkeley, CA: Institute of East Asian Studies, University of California.

Funston, John. 1980. *Malay Politics in Malaysia: A Study of UMNO and PAS.* Petaling Jaya, Malaysia: Heneimann.

———. 1981. Malaysia. In *The Politics of Islamic Reassertion,* ed. Mohammad Ayoob, 165–189. London: Croom Helm.

Gansu Provincial News Agency [Gansu Sheng Xinwenshe]. 1989. Lanzhou Muslims Riot over Publishing of Book. In Foreign Broadcast Information Service, *Daily Report—China,* FBIS-CHI-89-092, 15 May:59.

Gao Mingkai and Liu Zhengtan. 1987. *Xiandai hanyu wailaici yanjiu* [Research on foreign terms in modern Chinese]. Beijing: Wenzi Gaige Chubanshe.

Gates, Hill. 1987. Money for the Gods. *Modern China* 13:259–277.

Geertz, Clifford. 1960. *The Religion of Java.* New York: Free Press.

———. 1963a. The Integrative Revolution: Primordial Sentiments and Civil Politics in the New States. In *Old Societies and New States,* ed. Clifford Geertz, 105–157. New York: Free Press.

———. 1963b. *Agricultural Involution: The Processes of Ecological Change in Indonesia.* Berkeley, CA: University of California Press.

———. 1973a. "Internal Conversion" in Contemporary Bali. In Clifford Geertz, *The Interpretation of Cultures,* 170–192. New York: Basic Books.

———. 1973b. The Integrative Revolution: Primordial Sentiments and Civil Politics in the New States. In Clifford Geertz, *The Interpretation of Cultures,* 255–310. New York: Basic Books.

———. 1973c. *The Interpretation of Cultures.* New York: Basic Books.

———. 1980. *Negara: The Theatre State in Nineteenth-Century Bali.* Princeton, NJ: Princeton University Press.

Gellner, Ernest. 1983. *Nations and Nationalism.* Ithaca, NY: Cornell University Press.

Gerth, H. H., and C. Wright Mills, eds. 1976. *From Max Weber: Essays in Sociology.* New York: Oxford University Press.

Gimlette, Dr. John D. 1975 [1915]. *Malay Poisons and Charm Cures.* London: Oxford University Press.

Gladney, Dru C. 1987. Muslim Tombs and Ethnic Folklore: Charters for Hui Identity. *Journal of Asian Studies* 46 (3): 495–532.

———. 1988. Hui-Wei Guanxi: Hui-Uighur Relations and Ethnoreligious Identity in the Political Economy of Xinjiang. Paper presented at the Annual Meeting of the Association for Asian Studies, San Francisco, 25–27 March.

———. 1990a. The Ethnogenesis of the Uigur. *Central Asian Survey* 9 (1): 1–28.

———. 1990b. The Peoples of the People's Republic: Finally in the Vanguard? *Fletcher Forum for World Affairs* 14 (1): 62–77.

———. 1991. *Muslim Chinese: Ethnic Nationalism in the People's Republic.* Harvard East Asian Monographs, no. 149. Cambridge, MA: Council on East Asian Studies, Harvard University.

Glorious Qur'an, The. 1977. Trans. and commentary A. Yusuf Ali. U.S.A.: The Muslim Students' Association of the United States and Canada.

Gluckman, Max. 1959. *Custom and Conflict in Africa.* Glencoe, IL: Free Press.

———. 1963. The Magic of Despair. In Max Gluckman, *Order and Rebellion in Tribal Africa,* 137–145. New York: Free Press of Glencoe.

————. 1966. Les rites des passages. In *Essays on the Ritual of Social Relations,* ed. Max Gluckman, 1–52. New York: Humanities Press.

Goody, Jack. 1968. Introduction. In *Literacy in Traditional Societies,* ed. Jack Goody, 1–24. Cambridge: Cambridge University Press.

Gouldner, Alvin W. 1978. Stalinism: A Study of Internal Colonialism. *Telos* 34:5–48.

Gramsci, Antonio. 1957 [1970]. *The Modern Prince and Other Writings,* trans. L. Marks. New York: International Publishers.

Granet, Marcel. 1959 [1926]. *Danses et légendes de la Chine ancienne.* 2 vols. Paris: Presses Universitaires de France.

Gray, Dennis. 1992. Cambodia's Buddhist Revival. Associated Press (AP) wire service report, 27 March.

Grottanelli, Chrisiano. 1985. Archaic Forms of Rebellion and their Religious Background. In *Religion, Rebellion, and Revolution: An Interdisciplinary and Cross-Cultural Collection of Essays,* ed. Bruce Lincoln, 15–45. New York: St. Martin's Press.

Guha, Ranajit. 1988. The Prose of Counter-Insurgency. In *Selected Subaltern Studies,* ed. Ranajit Guha and Gayatri Spivak, 45–86. New York: Oxford University Press.

Gunn, G. 1986. Radical Islam in Southeast Asia: Rhetoric and Reality. *Journal of Contemporary Asia* 16 (1): 30–54.

Habermas, Jürgen. 1975. *Legitimation Crisis,* trans. Thomas McCarthy. Boston, MA: Beacon Press.

————. 1989 [1962]. *The Structural Transformation of the Public Sphere,* trans. Thomas Burger and Frederick Lawrence. Cambridge, MA: MIT Press.

Hackett, Rosalind. n.d. New Christian Identities in Africa: The Pentecostal/Charismatic Reenvisioning and Reordering of the World. Proposal for the Institute for the Advanced Study and Research in the African Humanities, Northwestern University.

Hall, Stuart, and Tony Jefferson. 1976. *Resistance through Rituals: Youth Subculture in Post-War Britain.* London: Hutchinson.

Hall, Stuart. 1981. Notes on Deconstructing "the Popular." In *People's History and Socialist Theory,* ed. R. Samuel, 227–240. London: Routledge and Kegan Paul.

Handler, Richard. 1984. On Sociocultural Discontinuity: Nationalism and Cultural Objectification in Quebec. *Current Anthropology* 25 (1): 55–71.

————. 1985. On Dialogue and Destructive Analysis: Problems in Narrating Nationalism and Ethnicity. *Journal of Anthropological Research* 41 (2): 171–182.

Hanks, William. 1984. Sanctification, Structure, and Experience. *Journal of American Folklore* 97 (384): 131–166.

Hansen, Chad. 1985. Punishment and Dignity in China. In *Individualism and Holism: Studies in Confucian and Taoist Values,* ed. Donald Munro, 359–382. Ann Arbor, MI: University of Michigan Press.

Hardacre, Helen. 1984. *Lay Buddhism in Contemporary Japan: Reiyūkai Kyōdan.* Princeton, NJ: Princeton University Press.

―――. 1986. *Kuruozumikyo and the New Religions of Japan.* Princeton, NJ: Princeton University Press.

―――. 1989. *Shinto and the State, 1868–1988.* Princeton, NJ: Princeton University Press.

Harding, Susan F. 1986. Convicted by the Holy Spirit: The Rhetoric of Fundamental Baptist Conversion. *American Ethnologist* 14 (1): 167–181.

―――. n.d. The Born-Again Telescandals. Paper read to the Department of Anthropology, University of Chicago, 13 February 1989.

Harlan, Rolvix. 1906. *John Alexander Dowie and His Christian Catholic Apostolic Church in Zion.* Evansville, WI: Press of R. M. Antes.

Harootunian, H. D., and Masao Miyoshi. 1988. Introduction. *South Atlantic Quarterly* 87 (3): 387–399.

Harrell, C. Stevan. 1974. When a Ghost Becomes a God. In *Religion and Ritual in Chinese Society,* ed. Arthur P. Wolf, 193–206. Stanford, CA: Stanford University Press.

―――. 1990. Ethnicity, Local Interests, and the State: Yi Communities in Southwest China. *Comparative Studies in Society and History* 32 (3): 515–548.

Harvey, Youngsook Kim. 1983. Minmyonuri: The Daughter-in-law Who Comes of Age in Her Mother-in-law's Household. In *Korean Women: A View from the Inner Room,* ed. Laurel Kendall and Mark Peterson, 45–61. New Haven, CT: East Rock Press.

―――. 1987. The Shaman and the Deaconess: Sisters in Different Guises. In *Religion and Ritual in Korean Society,* ed. Laurel Kendall and Griffin Dix, 149–170. Korea Research Monograph, no. 12. Berkeley, CA: Institute of East Asian Studies, University of California.

Hawk, David R. 1982. Cambodia: Precarious Recovery. *Christianity and Crisis,* 9 August, 240.

Hayashi Kyōko. 1984. The Empty Can, trans. Margaret Mitsutani. In *Atomic Aftermath: Short Stories about Hiroshima and Nagasaki,* ed. Ōe Kenzaburo, 135–151. Tokyo: Shueisha Press.

Hebdige, Dick. 1979. *Subculture: The Meaning of Style.* New York: Methuen.

Heberer, Thomas. 1989. *China and Its National Minorities: Autonomy or Assimilation?* Armonk, NY: M. E. Sharpe.

Hechter, Michael. 1975. *Internal Colonialism: The Celtic Fringe in British National Development, 1536–1966.* London: Routledge and Kegan Paul.

Hechter, Michael, and Margaret Levi. 1979. The Comparative Analysis of Ethnoregional Movements. *Ethnic and Racial Studies* 2 (3): 260–274.

Heder, Stephen P. 1979. Kampuchea's Armed Struggle: Origins of an Independent Revolution. *Bulletin of Concerned Asian Scholars* 11 (1): 2–24.

Hefner, Robert W. 1983. The Problem of Preference: Ritual and Economic Change in Highland Java. *Man* 18:669–689.

―――. 1985. *Hindu Javanese: Tengger Tradition and Islam.* Princeton, NJ: Princeton University Press.

―――. 1987. Islamizing Java? Religion and Politics in Rural East Java. *Journal of Asian Studies* 46 (3): 533–554.

―――. 1990. *The Political Economy of Mountain Java: An Interpretive History.* Berkeley, CA: University of California Press.

Herbert, Patricia. 1982. *The Hsaya San Rebellion (1930–1932) Reappraised.* Working Papers, no. 27. Melbourne, Australia: Monash University, Centre of Southeast Asian Studies.

Hering, B. B., and G. A. Wilis. 1973. *The Indonesian General Election of 1971.* Brussels: Centre d'Étude du Sud-Est Asiatique et de l'Extrême Orient.

Hiebert, Murray. 1989. Look, We're Buddhist. *Far Eastern Economic Review,* 3 August, 36–37.

Hildebrand, George, and Gareth Porter. 1976. *Cambodia: Starvation and Revolution.* New York: Monthly Review Press.

Hind, Robert J. 1984. The Internal Colonial Concept. *Comparative Studies in Society and History* 26:543–568.

Hinton, William. 1966. *Fanshen: A Documentary of Revolution in a Chinese Village.* New York: Vintage Books.

Hiroshima City. 1984. *Hiroshima Shinshi: Shakai-hen* [A new history of Hiroshima: Society volume]. Hiroshima: Hiroshima City.

Hiroshima Jōkōshi fuzoku Yamanaka Kōtō Jōgakkō genbaku shibotsusha tsuitōbunshū henshū iinkai, ed. 1985. *Hiroshima Jōshi Kōtō Shihan Gakkō fuzoku Yamanaka Kōtō Jōgakkō tsuitōki.* [Memorials for the Yamanaka Girls' High School of the Hiroshima Women's Higher Normal School]. Hiroshima: Hiroshima Jōshi Kōtō Shihan Gakkō fuzoku Yamanaka Kōtō Jōshi Gakkō genbaku shibotsusha tsuitōbunshū henshū iinkai [Editorial Committee for the Collected Memorials of the Atomic Bomb Dead from the Yamanaka Girls' High School of the Hiroshima Women's Higher Normal School].

Hiroshima Shiyakusho [Hiroshima Municipal Office]. 1971. *Genbaku sensai shi* [Record of the atomic bomb war damage]. 5 vols. Hiroshima: Hiroshima City.

Hobsbawm, Eric, and Terence Ranger, eds. 1983. *The Invention of Tradition.* Cambridge: Cambridge University Press.

Holquist, Michael. 1981. The Politics of Representation. In *Allegory and Representation,* ed. Stephen J. Greenblatt, 163–183. Baltimore, MD: Johns Hopkins University Press.

Horton, Robin. 1967. African Traditional Thought and Western Science. *Africa* 37 (1): 50–71; (2): 155–187.

———. 1971. African Conversion. *Africa* 41 (2): 85–108.

Hsieh, Shih-chung. 1989. Ethnic-Political Adaptation and Ethnic Change of the Sipsong Panna Dai: An Ethnohistorical Analysis. Ph.D. dissertation, University of Washington.

Hu Ping and Shengyou Zhang. 1987. Lishi chensilu [Historical reflections]. *Zhongguo zuojia* [*Chinese writer*], 1:128–163.

Hu Sheng. 1958. *Zhexue yanjiu* [philosophical research]. October.

Hu T'ai-li. 1986. *Shen, gui yu dutu: Dajia Le duxi fanying zhi minsu xinyang* [Gods, ghosts and gamblers: The influence of folk beliefs on the Everybody's Happy lottery]. Paper presented at the Second International Conference on Sinology, Academia Sinica, Taipei, 29–31 December.

Huang, Shu-min. 1989. *The Spiral Road: Change in a Chinese Village through the Eyes of a Communist Party Leader.* Boulder, CO: Westview.

Huaqiao ribao [Overseas Chinese daily]. 1989. San qian Musilin xuesheng Beijing youxing: ti yaoqiu yancheng Xing Fengsu zuozhe [Three thousand Beijing Muslim students protest: Request severe punishment of the author of *Sexual Customs*]. 13 May, 3.

Huntington, Richard, and Peter Metcalf. 1979. *Celebrations of Death: The Anthropology of Mortuary Ritual*. Cambridge: Cambridge University Press.

Hussain, Asaf. 1988. Islamic Awakening in the Twentieth Century: An Analysis and Selected Bibliography. *Third World Quarterly* 10 (2): 1005–1023.

Huters, Theodore. 1984. Blossoms in the Snow: Lu Xun and the Dilemma of Modern Chinese Literature. *Modern China* 10 (1): 49–78.

Ileto, R. C. 1979. *Pasyon and Revolution: Popular Movements in the Philippines, 1840–1910*. Manila: Ateneo de Manila University Press.

Indochina Chronology. Berkeley, CA: Institute of Asian Studies, University of California. 1984. July–September.

———. 1989. April–June.

Indochina Digest. Washington, D.C.: Indochina Project. 1992. 22 March.

———. 1992. 27 May.

Ishii, Yoneo. 1975. A Note on Buddhistic Millenarian Revolts in Northeastern Siam. *Journal of Southeast Asian Studies* 6 (2): 121–126.

Islamic Guidance Post. 1986. 4(43), June (in Thai).

———. 1987. 6(71), April (in Thai).

———. 1987. 6(79), October (in Thai).

Islamic Guidance Post: A Special Issue on Hijab. 1988. April (in Thai).

Jackson, Karl D., ed. 1989a. *Cambodia 1975–1978: Rendezvous with Death*. Princeton, NJ: Princeton University Press.

———. 1989b. The Ideology of Total Revolution. In *Cambodia 1975–1978: Rendezvous with Death*, ed. Karl D. Jackson, 37–78. Princeton, NJ: Princeton University Press.

Jackson, Peter. 1988. The Hupphaasawan Movement: Millenarian Buddhism among the Thai Political Elite. *Sojourn* 3 (2): 134–170.

Jackson, R. N. 1965. *Pickering: Protector of Chinese*. Kuala Lumpur: Oxford University Press.

Janelli, Roger L. 1986. The Origins of Korean Folklore Scholarship. *Journal of American Folklore* 99 (391): 24–49.

Jasper, J. E. 1926. *Tengger en de Tenggereezen*. Batavia: Druk van G. Kolff.

Jia Lusheng and Wa Lu. 1989. Bei shenpan de jinqian yu jinqian de shenpan [Money under trial and the trial by money]. In *Pian* [Scams], ed. Ren Qun, 1–61. Beijing: Guangming Ribao Chubanshe.

Jiang Renxiu. 1987. *Dajia Le Dubuo zhi Yanjiu* [Research into Everybody's Happy gambling]. Taichung, ROC: Taiwan Taizhong Difang Fayuan Jianchachu.

Jomo, Kwama Sundaram. 1986. *A Question of Class: Capital, the State, and Uneven Development in Malaya*. Singapore: Oxford University Press.

Jomo, K. S., and Ahmad Shabery Cheek. 1988. The Politics of Malaysia's Islamic Resurgence. *Third World Quarterly* 10 (2): 843–868.

Jones, Sidney. 1984. The Contraction and Expansion of the "Umat" and the Role of Nahdatul Ulama in Indonesia. *Indonesia* 38:1–20.

————. 1991. The Javanese *Pesantren:* Between Elite and Peasantry. In *Reshaping Local Worlds: Formal Education and Cultural Change in Rural Southeast Asia,* ed. Charles F. Keyes, 19–41. New Haven, CT: Yale University Southeast Asian Studies.

Jordan, David K. 1972. *Gods, Ghosts, and Ancestors: Folk Religion in a Taiwanese Village.* Berkeley, CA: University of California Press.

Jordan, David K., and Daniel L. Overmyer. 1986. *The Flying Phoenix: Aspects of Chinese Sectarianism in Taiwan.* Princeton, NJ: Princeton University Press.

Jorgensen, Joseph G. 1985. Religious Solutions and Native American Struggles: Ghost Dance, Sun Dance, and Beyond. In *Religion, Rebellion, and Revolution,* ed. Bruce Lincoln, 97–128. New York: St. Martin's Press.

Jorstad, Erling. 1981. *Evangelicals in the White House: The Cultural Maturation of Born Again Christianity, 1960–1981.* New York: Edwin Mellen Press.

Kalab, Milada. 1976. Monastic Education, Social Mobility, and Village Structure in Cambodia. In *Changing Identities in Modern Southeast Asia,* ed. D. J. Banks, 155–169. Paris: Mouton.

Kamezawa Miyuki. 1983. Hiroshima junrei [Hiroshima pilgrimage]. In *Nihon no genbaku bungaku* [The atomic bomb literature of Japan]. 15 vols. 11:417–457. Tokyo: Horupu Shuppan. Originally published in *Seito* 16 (1982).

Kapferer, Bruce. 1988. *Legends of People, Myths of State: Violence, Intolerance, and Political Culture in Sri Lanka and Australia.* Washington, D. C.: Smithsonian Institution Press.

Karklins, Rasma. 1986. *Ethnic Relations in the USSR: The Perspective from Below.* Boston, MA: Allen and Unwin.

Kartodirjo, Sartono. 1972. Agrarian Radicalism in Java: Its Setting and Development. In *Culture and Politics in Indonesia,* ed. Claire Holt, Benedict Anderson, and James Siegel, 70–125. Ithaca, NY: Cornell University Press.

Ke Lei and Sang Ya, eds. 1989. *Xing fengsu* [Sexual customs]. Shanghai: Shanghai Cultural Publishing Company.

Keeler, Ward. 1986. *Javanese Shadow Plays, Javanese Selves.* Princeton, NJ: Princeton University Press.

Kelly, John D., and Martha Kaplan. 1990. History, Structure, and Ritual. *Annual Reviews in Anthropology* 19:119–150.

Kendall, Laurel. 1985a. *Shamans, Housewives, and Other Restless Spirits: Women in Korean Ritual Life.* Honolulu, HI: University of Hawaii Press.

————. 1985b. Ritual Silks and Kowtow Money: The Bride as Daughter-in-law in Korean Wedding Ritual. *Ethnology* 24 (4): 253–267.

————. 1988. *The Life and Hard Times of a Korean Shaman: Of Tales and the Telling of Tales.* Honolulu, HI: University of Hawaii Press.

Kertas Perintah [White paper]. 1988. Toward Preserving National Security. Kuala Lumpur: House of Commons/Senate.

Kertzer, David. 1983. The Role of Ritual in Political Change. In *Political Anthro-*

pology, ed. Myron J. Aronoff, 53–74. Vol. 3. London: Transaction Books.

Kessler, Clive. 1980. Malaysia: Islamic Revivalism and Political Disaffection in a Divided Society. *Southeast Asia Chronicle* 75 (October): 3–11.

Keyes, Charles F. 1976. Toward a New Formulation of the Concept of Ethnic Groups. *Ethnicity* 3:202–213.

———. 1977. Millennialism, Theravāda Buddhism and Thai Society. *Journal of Asian Studies* 36 (11): 283–302.

———. 1983. Introduction: The Popular Ideas of Karma. In *Karma: An Anthropological Inquiry,* ed. Charles F. Keyes and E. Valentine Daniel, 1–24. Berkeley, CA: University of California Press.

———. 1987. *Thailand: Buddhist Kingdom as Modern Nation-State.* Boulder, CO: Westview.

———. 1989. Buddhist Politics and Their Revolutionary Origins in Thailand. In *Structure and History,* ed. S. N. Eisenstadt, 10 (2): 121–142. Special issue of the *International Political Science Review.*

———. 1990a. The Legacy of Angkor. *Cultural Survival Quarterly,* 14 (3): 56–59.

———. 1990b. Buddhism and Revolution in Cambodia. *Cultural Survival Quarterly* 14 (3): 60–63.

———. 1992. Buddhist Economics and Buddhist Fundamentalism in Burma and Thailand. In *Remaking the World: Fundamentalist Impact,* ed. Martin Marty and Scott Appleby, 367–409. Chicago, IL: University of Chicago Press.

Khien Theeravit. 1992. Thailand's Cultural Relations with Its Neighbors. Paper presented at the Conference on Regions and National Integration in Thailand (1892–1992), Passau, Germany, June.

Khieu Samphan. 1979. *Cambodia's Economy and Industrial Development.* Trans. Laura Summers. Data Paper, no. 111. Ithaca, NY: Cornell University, Southeast Asia Program.

Kiernan, Ben. 1980. Conflicts in the Cambodian Communist Movement. *Journal of Contemporary Asia* 10 (1–2): 7–74.

———. 1981. Origins of Khmer Communism. In *Southeast Asian Affairs 1981,* ed. Leo Suryadinata, 161–180. Singapore: Heinemann.

———. 1982. Kampuchea Stumbles to Its Feet. In *Peasants and Politics in Kampuchea, 1942–1981,* ed. Ben Kiernan and Chanthou Boua, 363–385. London: Zed Press; Armonk NY: M. E. Sharpe.

———. 1985. *How Pol Pot Came to Power: A History of Communism in Kampuchea, 1930–1975.* London: Verso.

———. 1990. The Genocide in Cambodia, 1975–79. *Bulletin of Concerned Asian Scholars* 22 (2): 35–40.

Kiernan, Ben, and Chanthou Boua, eds. 1982. *Peasants and Politics in Kampuchea, 1942–1981.* London: Zed Press; Armonk, NY: M. E. Sharpe.

Kim, Kwang-ok. 1988. Ritual Forms and Religious Experiences: Christians in Contemporary Korean Political Context. Paper presented at Conference of Religions in Contemporary Korea, Center for Korean Studies, University of California, Berkeley, 10–13 November.

————. 1989. Popular Culture Movement as Political Discourse in Contemporary Korea: *Madanggeuk*. Paper presented at the 88th Annual Meeting of the American Anthropological Association. Published in Korean in *Han'guk munhwa illyuhak* [Korean cultural anthropology] 21.

————. n.d. A Study on the Political Manipulation of Elite Culture. Paper presented to the 5th International Conference on Korean Studies, The Academy of Korean Studies, 30 June–3 July 1988.

Kim Kwang-ŏn, Yi Kwang-gyu, Yi Hyŏn-sun, and Ha Hyo-gil, eds. 1983. *Kŏnjŏnhan kajŏng ŭirye chunch'ik* [The wholesome family ritual code]. In *Kajŏng ŭirye taebaek'kwa* [Great compendium of family ritual], 338–354. Seoul: Hando Munhwa Sa.

Kim, Seong Nae. 1989. Chronicle of Violence, Ritual of Mourning: Cheju Shamanism in Korea. Ph.D. dissertation, University of Michigan.

Kim Sŏng-bae. 1983. *Naŭi sinhon sijŏl* [My newlywed season]. *Chŏnt'ong munhwa* (Traditional culture) 6:52–571.

Kim Taik-kyoo [Kim T'aek-kyu]. 1964. *Tongjok purak ŭi saenghwal kujo yŏn'gu* [A study of the structure of social life in a lineage village]. Seoul: Ch'onggu.

Kim Tu-hon. 1969 [1948]. *Han'guk kajok chedo yŏn'gu* [A study of the Korean family system]. Seoul: Ulyu.

Kim, Yong-choon. 1978. *The Ch'ŏndogyo Concept of Man: An Essence of Korean Thought*. Seoul: Pan Korea.

Kirsch, A. Thomas. 1973. Modernizing Implications of 19th-Century Reforms in the Thai Sangha. *Contributions to Asian Studies* 8:8–23.

Ko Chong-gi. 1982. *Algi swin kwanhonsangje* [Passage rites made easy]. Seoul: Huri Ch'ulp'an Sa.

Ko Misok. 1987. Kyŏrhonp'ungjo idaero chohŭnga (Marriage trends, is this the right way?), *Tonga Ilbo,* May 4:5 (in Korean).

Koentjaraningrat, R. M. 1985. *Javanese Culture*. Singapore: Oxford University Press.

Koh, Taiwon. 1959. *The Bitter Fruit of Kom-pawi*. New York: Holt, Rinehart & Winston.

Kumar, Ann. 1976. *Surapati: Man and Legend*. Leiden: E. J. Brill.

Kuntowijoyo. 1986. Islam and Politics: The Local Sarekat Islam Movements in Madura, 1913–20. In *Islam and Society in Southeast Asia,* ed. Taufik Abdullah and Sharon Siddique, 108–138. Singapore: Institute of Southeast Asian Studies.

Kurokawa Machiyo. 1982. *Genbaku no hi: Hiroshima no kokoro* [The atomic bomb monuments: The heart of Hiroshima]. Tokyo: Shin Nihon Shuppansha.

Kuroko Kazuo. 1983. *Genbaku to kotoba* [The atomic bomb and language]. Tokyo: San'ichi Shobō.

Labrousse, Pierre, and Farida Soemargono. 1985. De l'Islam comme morale du developpement: L'action des bureaux de progagation de la foi (Lembaga Dakwah) vue de Surabaya. In *Archipel: L'Islam en Indonesie,* ed. M. Bonneff, H. Chambert-Loir, Denys Lombard, and Christian Pelras, 2:219–228. Paris: Association Archipel.

Lan, David. 1985. *Guns and Rain: Guerrillas and Spirit Mediums in Zimbabwe.* London: James Currey.

Lasch, Christopher. 1984. The Politics of Nostalgia: Losing History in the Mists of Ideology. *Harper's* 269:65–70.

Laurie, Jim. 1985. Letter from Phnom Penh. *Far Eastern Economic Review,* 9 May.

Lawyers Committee for Human Rights. 1987. *Seeking Shelter: Cambodians in Thailand.* New York: Lawyers Committee for Human Rights.

Lay, Arthur H. 1913. Marriage Customs of Korea. *Transactions of the Korea Branch of the Royal Asiatic Society* 3/4:1–15.

Leach, Edmund R. 1968. Ritual. In *International Encyclopedia of the Social Sciences,* ed. David L. Sills, 3:520–526. New York: Macmillan.

Leclère, Adhémard. 1899. *Le Buddhisme au Cambodge.* Paris: Ernest Leroux.

———. 1917. *Cambodge: Fêtes civiles et réligieuses.* Annales du Musée Guimet, Bibliothèque du Vulgarisation, T. 42. Paris: Impr. Nationale.

Lee, R. M. 1988. Patterns of Religious Tension in Malaysia. *Asian Survey* 28 (4): 400–418.

Lefort, Claude. 1986a. The Image of the Body and Totalitarianism. In *The Political Forms of Modern Society: Bureaucracy, Democracy, Totalitarianism,* ed. John B. Thompson, 292–306. Cambridge, MA: MIT Press.

———. 1986b. *The Political Forms of Modern Society: Bureaucracy, Democracy and Totalitarianism.* ed. John B. Thompson. Cambridge, UK: Polity Press.

Lévi-Strauss, Claude. 1966. *The Savage Mind.* Chicago, IL: University of Chicago Press.

Lewis, Ioan M. 1971. *Ecstatic Religion: An Anthropological Study of Spirit Possession and Shamanism.* Harmondsworth, UK: Penguin.

Leys, Simon. 1977 [1971]. *The Chairman's New Clothes.* New York: St. Martin's Press.

Li Yih-yuan. 1988. Taiwan minjian zongjiao de xiandai qushi: Dui Peter Berger Jiaoshou Dongya fazhan wenhua yinsu lun de huiying [The modern tendencies of Taiwan's popular religion: A response to Professor Peter Berger's theory of cultural factors in East Asian development]. Ms.

Lian Shilun and Lian Huijin. 1985. *Shiba Wanggong de youlai (shang)* [The origins of the Eighteen Kings (vol. 1)]. Tanshui, ROC-Lian Shilun.

Liebman, Robert, and Robert Wuthnow, eds. 1983. *The New Christian Right: Mobilization and Legitimation.* Hawthorne, NY: Aldine.

Lifton, Robert Jay. 1967. *Death in Life: Survivors of Hiroshima.* New York: Basic Books.

Lipman, Jonathan N. 1989. Sufi Muslim Lineages and Elite Formation in Modern China: The Menhuan of the Northwest. Paper presented at the conference "The Legacy of Islam in China: An International Symposium in Memory of Joseph F. Fletcher," Harvard University, 14–16 April.

Lo Kuan-chung. 1976. *Three Kingdoms,* trans. and ed. Moss Roberts. New York: Pantheon Books.

Los Angeles Times. 1989. Chinese Muslims Protest "Sex Habits" Book. 13 May.

Löwenthal, Rudolf. 1940. The Mohammedan Press in China. In *The Religious Periodical Press in China*, with 7 Maps and 16 Charts, 2121–2149. Beijing: Synodal Committee on China.

Luo Zhufeng, ed. 1987. *Zhongguo shehui zhuyi shiqide zongjiao wenti* [The problem of religion in socialist China]. Shanghai: Shanghai Shehui Kexueyuan Chubanshe.

Lyon, Margo. 1979. The Dakwah Movement in Malaysia. *Review of Indonesian and Malaysian Affairs* 13 (2): 34–45.

———. 1980. The Hindu Revival in Java: Politics and Religious Identity. In *Indonesia: The Making of a Culture*, ed. James J. Fox, 205–220. Canberra, Australia: Research School of Pacific Studies.

Ma Shouqian. 1989. The Hui People's New Awakening at the End of the 19th Century and Beginning of the 20th Century. Paper presented at the conference "The Legacy of Islam in China: An International Symposium in Memory of Joseph F. Fletcher," Harvard University, 14–16 April.

McBeth, John. 1986. Thailand: A Long, Tough March Towards Total Security. *Far Eastern Economic Review* 17 April.

McCoy, Alfred W., ed. 1980. *Southeast Asia under Japanese Occupation*. Monograph Series no. 22. New Haven, CT: Yale University Southeast Asia Studies.

McFarland, H. Neill. 1967. *The Rush Hours of the Gods*. New York: Macmillan.

MacFarquhar, Roderick. 1989. The End of the Chinese Revolution. *New York Review of Books* 36 (12): 8–10.

MacGaffey, Wyatt. 1986. *Religion and Society in Central Africa: The Bakongo of Lower Zaire*. Chicago, IL: University of Chicago Press.

McGuire, Meredith. 1982. *Pentecostal Catholics*. Philadelphia, PA: Temple.

MacInnis, Donald E. 1972. *Religious Policy and Practice in Communist China*. New York: Macmillan.

———. 1989. *Religion in China Today: Policy and Practice*. Maryknoll, NY: Orbis Books.

McVey, Ruth. 1967. Taman Siswa and the Indonesian National Awakening. *Indonesia* 4:128–149.

Mak, Lau Fong. 1980. Rigidity of System Boundary among Major Chinese Dialect Groups in Nineteenth-Century Singapore: A Study of Inscription Data. *Modern Asian Studies* 14 (3): 465–487.

———. 1981. *The Sociology of Secret Societies: A Study of Chinese Secret Societies in Singapore and Peninsular Malaysia*. Kuala Lumpur: Oxford University Press.

Marr, David G. 1981. *Vietnamese Tradition on Trial, 1920–1945*. Berkeley, CA: University of California Press.

Marty, Martin A. 1988. Fundamentalism as a Social Phenomenon. *Bulletin of the American Academy of Arts and Sciences* 42:15–29.

Matichon. 1988. 23 February (in Thai).

Matory, James L. n.d. Vessels of Power: The Dialectical Symbolism of Power in Yoruba Religion and Polity. Master's thesis, Department of Anthropology, University of Chicago, 1986.

Mauzy, D. K. 1983. *Barisan Nasional: Coalition Government in Malaysia.* Kuala Lumpur: Marican.

Mauzy, D. K., and R. S. Milne. 1983–1984. The Mahathir Administration in Malaysia: Discipline through Islam. *Pacific Affairs* 56 (4): 617–648.

MCBCPP. *See* Ministry of Culture.

Means, G. P. 1970. *Malaysian Politics.* New York: New York University Press.

Merquior, J. G. 1979. *The Veil and the Mask.* London: Routledge and Kegan Paul.

Milne, R. S., and D. K. Mauzy. 1978. *Politics and Government in Malaysia.* Singapore: Federal Publications.

———. 1986. *Malaysia: Tradition, Modernity and Islam.* Boulder, CO: Westview.

Milner, Anthony. 1986. Rethinking Islamic Fundamentalism in Malaysia. *Review of Indonesian and Malaysian Affairs* 20 (2): 48–75.

Ministry of Culture and Information, Bureau of Cultural Properties Preservation [MCIBCPP]. 1969–. *Han'guk minsin chonghap chosa pogosŏ* [Report of the comprehensive investigation of Korean folk beliefs], cum. vols.

Mohanty, Chandra. 1989. Under Western Eyes: Feminist Scholarship and Colonial Discourse. *Feminist Review* 30:61–88.

Moose, Robert J. 1911. *Village Life in Korea.* Nashville, TN: Methodist Church, Smith and Lamar, agents.

Mortimer, Rex. 1974. *Indonesian Communism under Sukarno: Ideology and Politics, 1959–1965.* Ithaca, NY: Cornell University Press.

Mouer, Ross, and Yoshio Sugimoto. 1986. *Images of Japanese Society: A Study in the Structure of Social Reality.* London: KPI.

Muhammad Abu Bakar. 1973. *Mahasiswa Menggugat.* Kuala Lumpur: Pustaka Antara.

———. 1987. *Penghayatan sebuah ideal: Suatu tafsiran tentang Islam semasa.* Kuala Lumpur: Dewan Bahasa dan Pustaka.

Mullaney, Steven. 1983. Strange Things, Gross Terms, Curious Customs: The Rehearsal of Cultures in the Late Renaissance. *Representations* 3:40–67.

Mullings, Leith. 1984. *Therapy, Ideology, and Social Change: Mental Healing in Urban Ghana.* Berkeley, CA: University of California Press.

Munn, Nancy D. 1974. Symbolism in a Ritual Context: Aspects of Symbolic Action. In *Handbook of Social and Cultural Anthropology,* ed. J. J. Honigmann, 579–612. Chicago, IL: Rand McNally.

———. 1990. Constructing Regional Worlds in Experience: Kula Exchange, Witchcraft, and Gawan Local Events. *Man* 25 (1): 1–17.

Munro, Robin, ed. and trans. 1989. Special Issue on Syncretic Sects and Secret Societies: Revival in the 1980s. *Chinese Sociology and Anthropology* 21 (4): 3–103.

Murdoch, John B. 1974. The 1901–1902 "Holy Man's" Rebellion. *Journal of the Siam Society* 62 (1): 47–66.

Murray, Dian H., in collaboration with Qin Baoqi. 1993. *The Origins of the Tiandihui (Heaven and Earth Society).* Stanford, CA: Stanford University Press.

Muzaffar, Chandra. 1986. Islamic Resurgence: A Global View. In *Islam and*

Society in Southeast Asia, ed. Taufik Abdullah and Sharon Siddique, 5–39. Singapore: Institute of Southeast Asian Studies.

———. 1987. Islamic Resurgence in Malaysia. Petaling Jaya, Malaysia: Penerbit Fajar Bakti Sdn. Bhd.

Naemubu [Ministry of the Interior]. 1986. Uriŭi chŏnt'ong hollye [Our traditional wedding rite]. Seoul: Saemaul Kihwik Kwan [New Village Planning Commission].

Nagata, Judith. 1984. Reflowering of Malaysian Islam. Vancouver, Canada: University of British Columbia Press.

Nakamura, Mitsuo. 1983. The Crescent Arises over the Banyan Tree: A Study of the Muhammadiyah Movement in a Central Javanese Town. Yogyakarta, Indonesia: Gadjah Mada University Press.

Naquin, Susan. 1976. Millenarian Rebellion in China: The Eight Trigrams Uprising of 1813. New Haven, CT: Yale University Press.

Nash, M. 1984. Fundamentalist Islam: A Reservoir for Turbulence. Journal of African and Asian Studies 10 (1–2): 73–79.

The Nation (Bangkok).

Newborn, Jud. n.d. Rethinking the Nuer. Master's thesis, Department of Anthropology, University of Chicago, 1977.

New York Times. 1989. Muslim Students March in Beijing: 2,500 Protest a Book That They Say Blasphemes Islam. 13 May:A3.

Nguyen Tran Huan. 1971. Histoire d'une secte religieuse au Vietnam: le Caodaisme. In Tradition et Révolution au Vietnam. ed. Jean Chesneaux, Georges Boudarel, and Daniel Hemery, 189–214. Paris: Editions Anthropos.

Noer, Deliar. 1975. Islam in Indonesia and Malaysia: A Preliminary Study. Review of Indonesian and Malaysian Affairs, July–December, 51–70.

———. 1978. The Administration of Islam in Indonesia. Modern Indonesia Project, Monograph Series, no. 58. Ithaca, NY: Cornell University, Southeast Asia Program.

Nongmin ribao. 1986. 16 September (in Chinese).

———. 1986. 7 October.

———. 1987. 3 March.

———. 1987. 7 August.

———. 1987. 18 November.

Nora, Pierre. 1989. Between History and Memory: Les Lieux de Mémoire. Representations 26:7–25.

O'Donnell, G. A. 1973. Modernization and Bureaucratic Authoritarianism. Berkeley, CA: Institute of International Studies, University of California.

Ōe Kenzaburo. 1965. Hiroshima nōto [Hiroshima notes]. Tokyo: Iwanami Shoten.

Oliver, Victor L. 1976. Caodai Spiritism: A Study of Religion in Vietnamese Society. Leiden: E. J. Brill.

———. 1978. Caodaism: A Vietnamese Socio-Religious Movement. In Dynamic Religious Movements: Case Studies of Rapidly Growing Religious Movements around the World, ed. David J. Hesselgrave, 273–296. Grand Rapids, MI: Baker Book House.

O'Neil, Daniel J. 1980. Being Skeptical about "Internal Colonialism." *World View* 2 (6): 23ff.

O'Neil, Mary R. 1986. From "Popular" to "Local" Religion: Issues in Early Modern European Religious History. *Religious Studies Review* 12 (3–4): 222–226.

Ong, Aihwa. 1988. Colonialism and Modernity: Feminist Re-Presentations of Women in Non-Western Societies. *Inscriptions* 3–4:79–98.

Overmyer, Daniel L. 1976. *Folk Buddhist Religion: Dissenting Sects in Late Traditional China.* Cambridge, MA: Harvard University Press.

———. n.d. Attitudes toward Popular Religion in Ritual Texts of the Chinese State: The Collected Statutes of the Great Ming. Ms.

Owen, Stephen. 1986. *Remembrances: The Experience of the Past in Classical Chinese Literature.* Cambridge, MA: Harvard University Press.

Ownbey, David, and Mary Somers-Heidhues, eds. 1992. *"Secret Societies" Reconsidered: Studies in the Social History of Early Modern China and Southeast Asia.* Armonk, NY: M. E. Sharpe.

Pagadhamma. 1988. The Yala Case: Patipatha for Friends with Different Religious Persuasions. *Matichon,* 15 February (in Thai).

Pak In-bae. 1989. "Ideology saengsan hualdongron" kwa "hyonjang munhua woondongron" [A study on "ideology production theory" and "in-field cultural movement theory"]. In *P'alsip Nyondae Sahoe Woondong Nonjaeng* [Debates on Social Movements of the 1980s], ed. Hangilsa, 346–360. Seoul: Hangilsa Co.

Pak, Ki-hyuk, and Sidney D. Gamble. 1975. *The Changing Korean Village.* Seoul: Shin-hung.

Palmer, Spencer J., ed. 1967. The New Religions of Korea. (Special Issue) *Transactions of the Korea Branch of the Royal Asiatic Society* 43.

Pantup Danasin. 1988. A Letter. *Bangkok Post,* 4 March.

Parsons, Talcott. 1949. *The Structure of Social Action.* Glencoe, IL: Free Press.

Peacock, James L. 1968. *Rites of Modernization: Symbolic and Social Aspects of Indonesian Proletarian Drama.* Chicago, IL: University of Chicago Press.

Perry, Elizabeth. 1985. Rural Violence in Socialist China. *China Quarterly* 103:414–440.

Peterson, Mark. 1983. Women without Sons: A Measure of Social Change in Yi Dynasty Korea. In *Korean Women: View from the Inner Room,* ed. Laurel Kendall and Mark Peterson, 33–44. New Haven, CT: East Rock Press.

Pillai, M. G. G. 1987. The Question of Chinese Education in Malaysia. *Bangkok Post,* 12 November.

Pillsbury, Barbara L. K. 1978. Being Female in a Muslim Minority in China. In *Women in the Muslim World,* ed. Lois Beck and Nikki Keddie, 651–673. Cambridge, MA: Harvard University Press.

———. 1989. China's Muslims in 1989: Forty Years Under Communism. Paper presented at a conference on Muslim Minority/Majority Relations, City College of the City University of New York, New York, 24–26 October.

Piscatori, James P. 1986. *Islam in a World of Nation States.* Cambridge: Cambridge University Press.

Surin Pitsuwan. 1988. The Lotus and the Crescent: Clashes of Religious Symbolisms in Southern Thailand. In *Ethnic Conflict in Buddhist Societies: Sri Lanka, Thailand, and Burma,* ed. K. M. de Silva, Pensri Duke, Ellen S. Goldberg, and Nathan Katz, 187–201. London: Pinter; Boulder, CO: Westview.

Plath, David W. 1964. Where the Family of God Is the Family: The Role of the Dead in Japanese Households. *American Anthropologist* 66 (2): 300–317.

Polanyi, Karl. 1944. *The Great Transformation.* New York: Farrar and Rinehart.

Ponchaud, François. 1989. Social Change in the Vortex of Revolution. In *Cambodia 1975–1978: Rendezvous with Death,* ed. Karl D. Jackson, 151–178. Princeton, NJ: Princeton University Press.

Pongpet Mekloy. 1991. Rebuilding a National Religion. *The Nation* (Bangkok), 23 February.

Poole, Peter A. 1975. Communism and Ethnic Conflict in Cambodia, 1960–1975. In *Communism in Indochina: New Perspectives,* ed. Joseph J. Zasloff and MacAlister Brown, 249–258. Lexington, MA: Lexington Books.

Porée-Maspero, Eveline. 1962–1969. Étude sur les rites agraires des cambodgiens. 3 vols. Paris: Mouton.

Chavivun Prachuabmoh and Chaiwat Satha-Anand. 1985. Thailand: A Mosaic of Ethnic Tensions under Control. *Ethnic Studies Report* 3 (1): 22–31 (January).

Prakash, Gyan. 1989. Writing Post-Orientalist Histories of the Third World. Paper presented at conference on Colonialism and Culture, University of Michigan, 12–14 May.

Premasiri, P. D. 1988. Minorities in Buddhist Doctrine. In *Ethnic Conflict in Buddhist Societies: Sri Lanka, Thailand, and Burma,* ed. K. M. de Silva, Pensri Duke, Ellen S. Goldberg, and Nathan Katz, 42–58. London: Pinter; Boulder, CO: Westview.

Putra, Tunku Abdul Rahman, Tan Chee Khoon, Chandra Muzaffar, and Lim Kit Siang. 1984. *Contemporary Issues on Malaysian Religions.* Kuala Lumpur: Pelanduk Publications.

Pyun, Young-tai. 1926. *My Attitude toward Ancestor-worship.* Seoul: Christian Literature Society.

Qinghai Provincial News Agency [Qinghai Xinwenshe]. 1989. Qinghai Muslims Demand Author's Punishment. 15 May. In Foreign Broadcast Information Service, *Daily Report—China,* FBIS-CHI-89-093, 16 May:52.

Qu Haiyuan. 1987. *Dajia Le xianxiang zhi chengyin yu yingxiang zhi yanjiu* [Research into origins and influence of the phenomenon of Everybody's Happy]. Taipei: Xingzhengyuan Yanjiu Fazhan Kaohe Hui.

Qu Haiyuan and Yao Lixiang. 1986. Taiwan diqu zongjiao bianqian zhi tantao [Discussion of the religious changes in the Taiwan area]. *Bulletin of the Institute of Ethnology, Academia Sinica* 75:655–685.

Quinn, Kenneth M. 1989. Explaining the Terror. In *Cambodia 1975–1978: Rendezvous with Death,* ed. Karl D. Jackson, 215–240. Princeton, NJ: Princeton University Press.

Rachagan, Sothi. 1984. Ethnic Representation and the Electoral System. In *Ethnicity, Class, and Development in Malaysia,* ed. S. Husin Ali, 124–138. Kuala Lumpur: Malaysian Social Science Association.

Viroj Racharak. 1984–1985. Security Promotion in the Four Southernmost Provinces of Thailand. Individual research project in the field of Social Psychology, National Defense College.

Raillon, François. 1985. Islam et Ordre Nouveau ou l'imbroglio de la foi et de la politique. In *Archipel: L'Islam en Indonesie,* ed. M. Bonneff, H. Chambert-Loir, Denys Lombard, and Christian Pelras, 2:229–261. Paris: Association Archipel.

Chalardchai Ramitanon. 1988. Religion and Conflict. *Siam Rath,* 7–8 March (in Thai).

Ramsey, S. Robert. 1987. *The Languages of China.* Princeton, NJ: Princeton University Press.

Ranger, Terence. 1993. The Local and the Global in African Religion. In *Conversion to Christianity: Perspectives from History and Anthropology,* ed. Robert Hefner, 65–98. Berkeley, CA: University of California Press.

Redi Kyŏnghyang [Lady Capital and Country]. 1985. October 23 (in Korean).

Regan, D. 1989. Islam as a New Religous Movement in Malaysia. In *The Changing Face of Religion,* ed. James A. Beckford and T. Luckmann, 124–146. London: Sage.

Report from East Java. 1986. *Indonesia* 41:135–149.

Reynolds, Craig J. 1973. The Buddhist Monkhood in Nineteenth-Century Thailand. Ph.D. dissertation, Cornell University.

———. 1976. Buddhist Cosmography in Thai History, with Special Reference to Nineteenth-Century Culture Change. *Journal of Asian Studies* 35 (2): 203–220.

Reynolds, Frank E. 1972. The Two Wheels of Dhamma: A Study of Early Buddhism. In *The Two Wheels of Dhamma: Essays on the Theravāda Tradition in India and Ceylon,* ed. Bardwell L. Smith, 6–30. AAR Studies in Religion, no. 3. Chambersburg, PA: American Academy of Religion.

Reynolds, Frank E., and Regina T. Clifford. 1987. Theravāda. In *The Encyclopedia of Religion,* ed. Mircea Eliade, 14:469–479. New York: Macmillan.

Reynolds, Frank E., and Mani B. Reynolds, trans. with introduction and notes. 1982. *Three Worlds According to King Ruang: A Thai Buddhist Cosmology.* Berkeley Buddhist Studies Series, no. 4. Berkeley, CA: Group in Buddhist Studies, Center for South and Southeast Asian Studies, and Institute of Buddhist Studies, University of California.

Richards, Audrey. 1935. A Modern Movement of Witchfinders. *Africa* 8 (4): 448–461.

Richardson, Michael. 1981. Letter from Phnom Penh. *Far Eastern Economic Review,* 24 April, 104.

Ricklefs, M. C. 1979. Six Centuries of Islamization in Java. In *Conversion to Islam,* ed. N. Levtzion, 100–128. New York: Holmes and Meier.

———. 1981. *A History of Modern Indonesia.* Bloomington, IN: Indiana University Press.

Robinson, Michael E. 1988. *Cultural Nationalism in Colonial Korea, 1920–25.*

Seattle, WA: University of Washington Press.

————. 1991. Perceptions of Confucianism in Twentieth-Century Korea. In *The East Asian Region: Confucian Heritage and Its Modern Adaptation,* ed. G. Rozman, 204–225. Princeton, NJ: Princeton University Press.

Robson, S. O. 1981. Java at the Crossroads. *Bijdragen tot de Taal-, Land-, en Volkenkunde* 137:259–292.

Roff, William. 1967. *The Origins of Malay Nationalism.* Kuala Lumpur: University of Malaya Press.

————. 1985. Islam Obscured? Some Reflections on Studies of Islam and Society in Southeast Asia. *Archipel* 29:7–34.

Rogers, Mark. 1989. Wildness in Healing or Wildness in Ethnography? Performativity and Communication in Shamanic Ritual. *Chicago Anthropology Exchange* 18:81–93.

Rouffaer, G. P. 1921. Tenggereezen. In *Encyclopaedie van Nederlandsch-Indie,* 298–308. Leiden: E. J. Brill.

Rushdie, Salman. 1988. *The Satanic Verses.* London: Viking.

Rutt, Richard. 1964. *Korean Works and Days: Notes from the Diary of a Country Priest.* Seoul: Royal Asiatic Society, Korea Branch.

Sahlins, Marshall. 1976. *Culture and Practical Reason.* Chicago, IL: University of Chicago Press.

————. 1981. *Historical Metaphors and Mythical Realities: Structure in the Early History of the Sandwich Islands Kingdom.* Ann Arbor, MI: University of Michigan Press.

————. 1985. *Islands of History.* Chicago, IL: University of Chicago Press.

————. n.d. Social Science, or the Tragic Western Sense of Human Imperfection. Ms.

Said, Edward W. 1978. *Orientalism.* New York: Pantheon.

Saikal, Amin. 1987. Islam Resistance and Reassertion. *The World Today,* November, 191–194.

Narongrit Sakdanarong. 1988. An Article. *Matichon,* 29 January (in Thai).

Sam, Yang. 1987. *Khmer Buddhism and Politics, 1954–1984.* Newington, CT: Khmer Studies Institute.

————. 1990. Buddhism in Cambodia, 1795–1954, M.A. thesis, Cornell University.

Marvan Sama-oon. 1988. Hijab. *Matichon,* 10 February (in Thai).

Samson, Allan A. 1978. Conceptions of Politics, Power, and Ideology in Contemporary Indonesian Islam. In *Political Power and Communications in Indonesia,* ed. Karl D. Jackson and Lucian W. Pye, 196–226. Berkeley, CA: University of California Press.

Sangren, Steven P. 1987. *History and Power in a Chinese Community.* Stanford, CA: Stanford University Press.

Sanyaluck. 1986. 9, 10 June (in Thai).

Sarkisyanz, E. 1965. *Buddhist Backgrounds of the Burmese Revolution.* The Hague: Martinus Nijhoff.

Chaiwat Satha-Anand. 1987. *Islam and Violence: A Case Study of Violent Events in the Four Southern Provinces, Thailand, 1976–1981.* Tampa, FL: USF Monographs in Religions and Public Policy.

————. 1988a. A Letter. *Bangkok Post,* 26 May.

———. 1988b. Of Imagination and the State. In *Ethnic Conflict in Buddhist Societies: Sri Lanka, Thailand, and Burma,* ed. K. M. de Silva, K. M., Pensri Duke, Ellen S. Goldberg, and Nathan Katz, 27–41. London: Pinter; Boulder, CO: Westview.

Schattschneider, Ellen. n.d. Spirit Mediumship and Society in Modern Japan: A Proposal for Doctoral Research. Ms.

Schein, Louisa. n.d. "Beautiful Barbarians." Ms.

Schell, Orville. 1989. *Discos and Democracy: China in the Throes of Reform.* New York: Anchor.

Schipper, Kristofer. 1977. Neighborhood Cult Associations in Traditional Tainan. In *The City in Late Imperial China,* ed. G. William Skinner, 651–676. Stanford, CA: Stanford University Press.

Schlegel, G. 1956 [1866]. *Thian Ti Hwi, the Hung League or Heaven and Earth League: A Secret Society with the Chinese in China and India.* Singapore: Banfield.

Scott, James C. 1976. *The Moral Economy of the Peasant: Rebellion and Subsistence in South-east Asia.* New Haven, CT: Yale University Press.

———. 1977. Protest and Profanation: Agrarian Revolt and the Little Tradition. *Theory and Society* 5 (1): 1–38; (2): 211–246.

———. 1987. *Weapons of the Weak.* New Haven, CT: Yale University Press.

Scranton, Mrs. M. F. 1898. Grace's Wedding. *Korean Repository* 5:295–297.

Seaman, Gary. 1981. The Sexual Politics of Karmic Retribution. In *The Anthropology of Taiwanese Society,* ed. Emily Martin Ahern and Hill Gates, 381–396. Stanford, CA: Stanford University Press.

Shamsul A. B. 1983. A Revival in the Study of Islam in Malaysia (correspondence). *Man* 18 (2): 399–404.

———. 1989. From Urban to Rural: The "Migration" of the Islamic Resurgence Phenomenon in Malaysia. In *Urbanism in Islam: Proceedings of the International Conference on Urbanism in Islam.* 4:1–39. Tokyo: Institute of Oriental Culture, University of Tokyo.

Shanin, Teodor. 1989. Ethnicity in the Soviet Union: Analytical Perceptions and Political Strategies. *Comparative Studies in Society and History* 3:409–423.

Shapiro, Michael J. 1988. *The Politics of Representation: Writing Practices, Photography, and Policy Analysis.* Madison, WI: University of Wisconsin Press.

Shawcross, William. 1979. *Sideshow.* New York: Simon and Schuster.

Shichor, Yitzhak. 1989. *East Wind over Arabia: Origins and Implications of the Sino-Saudi Missile Deal.* China Research Monograph, no. 35. Berkeley, CA: Institute of East Asian Studies, University of California.

Shijie ribao. 1989. Zhongguo Xinwen Chubanzhe chajin Xing Fengsu yi shu: zeling Shanghai Wenhua Chubanshe tingye zhengdun [China News Publication Agency bans the book *Sexual Customs:* Instructs the Shanghai Cultural Publication Society to close down and reorganize]. 15 May, 6.

Shin, Susan. 1978–1979. The Tonghak Movement: From Enlightenment to Revolution. *Korean Studies Forum* 5:1–60.

Shue, Vivienne. 1988. *The Reach of the State.* Stanford, CA: Stanford University Press.

Siam Rath. 1987. 2 February (in Thai).

Siam Rath. 1988. 28 January (in Thai).

Siam Rath Weekly. 1988. 20–26 March, 10–11 (in Thai).

Silverstein, Michael. n.d. Metaforces of Power in Traditional Oratory. Lecture to the Department of Anthropology, Yale University, 1981.

Siu, Helen. 1989. Recycling Rituals: Politics and Popular Culture in Contemporary Rural China. In *Unofficial China: Popular Culture and Thought in the People's Republic,* ed. Perry Link, Richard Madsen, and Paul G. Pickowicz, 121–137. Boulder, CO: Westview.

Skinner, G. William. 1964. Marketing and Social Structure in Rural China, Part 1. *Journal of Asian Studies* 24 (1): 3–43.

Skinner, G. William, and Edward A. Winckler. 1969. Compliance Succession in Rural Communist China: A Cyclical Theory. In *A Sociological Reader on Complex Organization,* ed. Amitai Etzioni, 410–439. New York: Holt, Rinehart & Winston.

Slattery, Leighton B. 1988. A Letter. *Bangkok Post,* 4 June.

Smith, Anthony T. 1981. *The Ethnic Revival.* Cambridge: Cambridge University Press.

Smith, Frank. 1989. *Interpretive Accounts of the Khmer Rouge Years: Personal Experiences in Cambodian Peasant World View.* Wisconsin Papers on Southeast Asia. Madison, WI: University of Wisconsin-Madison, Center for Southeast Asian Studies.

Smith, Robert J. 1974. *Ancestor Worship in Contemporary Japan.* Stanford, CA: Stanford University Press.

Soedjatmoko. 1965. Cultural Motivations to Progress: The "Exterior" and "Interior" Views. In *Religion and Progress in Modern Asia,* ed. Robert N. Bellah, 1–14. New York: Free Press.

Solomon, Robert L. 1969. *Saya San and the Burmese Rebellion.* Rand Corporation Papers, P-4004. Santa Monica, CA: Rand Corporation.

Son Soubert et al. 1986. *Buddhism and the Future of Cambodia.* Rithisen, Cambodia: Khmer Buddhist Research Center.

Sophath Pak and Sara Colm. 1990. Up from the Ashes: Buddhism Rekindles in Socialist Cambodia. *Tenderloin Times* (San Francisco), 3 March.

Sorensen, Clark Wesley. 1981. Household, Family, and Economy in a Korean Mountain Village. Ph.D. dissertation, University of Washington.

———. n.d. Concubines, Wives, and the Struggle for Succession in Traditional Rural Korea. Typescript.

Southill, William Edward, and Lewis Hodous. 1935. *Hanying foxue da cidian* [The great dictionary of Chinese-English Buddhism]. London: Kegan Paul, Trench, Turbaum.

Spivak, Gayatri Chakravorty. 1989. Reading *The Satanic Verses. Public Culture* 2 (1): 79–99.

Stanton, W. 1899. The Triad Society or Heaven and Earth Association. *China Review* 21 and 22. Reprinted Hong Kong, 1900.

Stockwell, A. J. 1979. *British Policy and Malay Politics during the Malayan*

Union Experiment, 1942–1948. Kuala Lumpur: Malaysian Branch of the Royal Asiatic Society.

Stuart-Fox, Martin, and Bunhaeng Ung. 1986. *The Murderous Revolution.* Bangkok: Tamarind Press.

Su Xiaogang et al. 1988. *Heshang* [River elegy]. Taipei: Fengyun Shidai, Jinfeng Chuban Gongsi Lianhe Chuban.

Somboon Suksamran. 1982. *Buddhism and Politics in Thailand: A Study of Socio-Political Change and Political Activism of the Thai Sangha.* Singapore: Institute of Southeast Asian Studies.

Sun Meiyao, ed. 1988. *Xuanchuan gongzuo shiyong shouce* [A practical guide to propaganda work]. Beijing: Hongqi Chubanshe.

Sun Yat-sen. 1924. *The Three Principles of the People: San Min Chu I,* trans. Frank W. Price, Taipei: China Publishing Company.

Preecha Suwannathat. 1988. An Article. *Naewna,* 3 February.

Tamara, M. Nasir. 1985. *Islam as a Political Force in Indonesia: 1965–1985.* Occasional Paper, Center for International Affairs. Cambridge, MA: Harvard University Press.

Tambiah, S. J. 1970. *Buddhism and the Spirit Cults in North-east Thailand.* Cambridge Studies in Social Anthropology, no. 2. Cambridge: Cambridge University Press.

———. 1976. *World Conqueror and World Renouncer.* Cambridge: Cambridge University Press.

———. 1985. *Culture, Thought, and Social Action.* Cambridge, MA: Harvard University Press.

———. 1990. *Magic, Science, Religion, and the Scope of Rationality.* The Lewis Henry Morgan Lecture, 1984. Cambridge: Cambridge University Press.

Taussig, Michael T. 1980. *The Devil and Commodity Fetishism in South America.* Chapel Hill, NC: University of North Carolina Press.

———. 1987. *Shamanism, Colonialism, and the Wild Man: A Study in Terror and Healing.* Chicago, IL: University of Chicago Press.

Taylor, Charles. 1989. The Rushdie Controversy. *Public Culture* 2 (1): 118–122.

Thai Rath. 1988. 19 February (in Thai).

Thion, Serge. 1983a. The Cambodian Idea of Revolution. In *Revolution and Its Aftermath in Kampuchea: Eight Essays,* ed. David P. Chandler and Ben Kiernan, 10–33. Monograph Series, no. 25. New Haven, CT: Yale University Southeast Asia Studies.

———. 1983b. Chronology of Khmer Communism, 1940–1982. In *Revolution and Its Aftermath in Kampuchea: Eight Essays,* ed. David P. Chandler and Ben Kiernan, 291–319. Monograph Series, no. 25. New Haven, CT: Yale University Southeast Asia Studies.

Thompson, E. P. 1977. Folklore, Anthropology, and Social History. *Indian Historical Review* 3 (2): 247–266.

Tokyo Kyodo. 1989a. Muslim Students Demonstrate. In Foreign Broadcast Information Service, *Daily Report—China,* FBIS-CHI-89-091, May 12:23.

———. 1989b. Muslim Students Decry Sacrilege. In Foreign Broadcast Information Service, *Daily Report—China,* FBIS-CHI-89-092, May 15:52.

Tonga Ilbo (East Asia Daily News). 1987. May 4 (in Korean).

Tong Enzheng. 1989. Morgan's Model and the Study of Ancient Chinese Society. *Social Sciences in China,* Summer:182–205.

Trachtenberg, Stanley. 1985. Introduction. In *The Postmodern Moment: A Handbook of Contemporary Innovation in the Arts,* ed. Stanley Trachtenberg, 3–18. Westport, CT, and London: Greenwood Press.

Trocki, Carl A. 1990. *Opium and Empire: Chinese Society in Colonial Singapore, 1800–1910.* Ithaca, NY: Cornell University Press.

Tuggy, A. Leonard. 1978. Iglesia Ni Cristo: An Angel and His Church. In *Dynamic Religious Movements: Case Studies of Rapidly Growing Religious Movements around the World,* ed. David J. Hesselgrave, 85–101. Grand Rapids, MI: Baker Book House.

Turner, Victor W. 1967. *The Forest of Symbols.* Ithaca, NY: Cornell University Press.

———. 1969. *The Ritual Process: Structure and Anti-Structure.* The Henry Lewis Morgan Lecture, 1966. Ithaca, NY: Cornell University Press.

Ubuki Satoru. 1976. Hiroshima no hi o meguru shisōsei [The intellectual character of Hiroshima monuments]. *Heiwa kyōiku kenkyū* [Studies in peace education], 4:57–60.

ul Haq, Obaid. 1986. Islamic Resurgence: The Challenge of Change. In *Islam and Society in Southeast Asia,* ed. Taufik Abdullah and Sharon Siddique, 332–348. Singapore: Institute of Southeast Asian Studies.

Valeri, Valerio. 1990. Constitutive History: Genealogy and Narrative in the Legitimation of Hawaiian Kingship. In *Culture Through Time: Anthropological Approaches,* ed. Emiko Ohnuki-Tierney, 154–192. Stanford, CA: Stanford University Press.

van der Kroef, Justus M. 1979. Cambodia: From "Democratic Kampuchea" to "People's Republic." *Asian Survey* 19 (8): 731–750.

van der Veer, Peter. 1989. Satanic or Angelic? The Politics of Religious and Literary Inspiration. *Public Culture* 2 (1): 100–105.

Van Gennep, Arnold. 1960. *The Rites of Passage,* trans. M. B. Vizedom and G. L. Caffee. Chicago, IL: University of Chicago Press.

van Lerwerden, J. D. 1844. Aanteekeningen Nopens de Zeden en Gebruiken der Bevolking van het Tenggers Gebergte. *Verhandelingen van het Bataviaasch Genootschap van Kunsten en Wetenschappen* 20:60–93.

Verdery, Katherine. 1979. Internal Colonialism in Austria-Hungary. *Ethnic and Racial Studies* 2 (3): 378–399.

Verger, Pierre. 1981. *Orixas.* Salvador: Editoria Corrupio Comercio.

Vickery, Michael. 1984. *Cambodia: 1975–1982.* Boston, MA: South End Press.

———. 1986. *Kampuchea: Politics, Economics, and Society.* London: Pinter; Boulder, CO: Lynne Rienner.

———. 1988. How Many Died in Pol Pot's Kampuchea? *Bulletin of Concerned Asian Scholars* 20 (1): 70–73.

Volkman, Toby. 1985. *Feasts of Honor: Ritual and Change in the Toraja Highlands.* Illinois Studies in Anthropology, no. 16. Urbana, IL: University of Illinois Press.

von der Mehden, Fred. 1980. Islamic Resurgence in Malaysia. In *Islam and*

Development, ed. John Esposito, 163–180. Syracuse, NY: Syracuse University Press.

von Vorys, Karl. 1975. *Democracy without Consensus: Communalism and Political Stability in Malaysia.* Princeton, NJ: Princeton University Press.

Wach, Joachim. 1944. *Sociology of Religion.* Chicago, IL: University of Chicago Press.

Wagner, Edward W. 1983. Two Early Genealogies and Women's Status in Early Yi Dynasty Korea. In *Korean Women: View from the Inner Room,* ed. Laurel Kendall and Mark Peterson, 23–32. New Haven, CT: East Rock Press.

Wahid, Abdurraham. 1986. The Nahdatul Ulama and Islam in Present-Day Indonesia. In *Islam and Society in Southeast Asia,* ed. Taufik Abdullah and Sharon Siddique, 175–186. Singapore: Institute of Southeast Asian Studies.

Wakeman, Frederic, Jr. 1977. Rebellion and Revolution: The Study of Popular Movements in Chinese History. *Journal of Asian Studies* 36 (2): 201–238.

———. 1985. Revolutionary Rites: The Remains of Chiang Kai-shek and Mao Tse-tung. *Representations* 10:146–193.

Waldron, Arthur. 1993. Representing China: The Great Wall and Cultural Nationalism in the Twentieth Century. In *Cultural Nationalism in East Asia: Representation and Identity,* ed. Harumi Befu, 36–60. Research Papers and Policy Studies, no. 39. Berkeley, CA: Institute of East Asian Studies, University of California.

Ward, J. S. M., and W. G. Stirling. 1977 [1925]. *The Hung Society, or the Society of Heaven and Earth.* Vols. 1–3. Taipei: Southern Materials Center.

Ward, Ken. 1974. *The 1971 Election in Indonesia: An East Java Case Study.* Monash Papers on Southeast Asia, no. 2. Clayton, Australia: Monash University, Centre for Southeast Asian Studies.

Warner, William Lloyd. 1959. *The Living and the Dead: A Study in the Symbolic Life of Americans.* New Haven, CT: Yale University Press.

Watson, James. 1985. Standardizing the Gods: The Promotion of T'ian Hou (Empress of Heaven) along the South China Coast, 960–1960. In *Popular Culture in Late Imperial China,* ed. David Johnson, Andrew Nathan, and Evelyn Rawski, 292–324. Berkeley, CA: University of California Press.

Weber, Max. 1958 [1949]. *From Max Weber: Essays in Sociology.* H. H. Gerth and C. Wright Mills, trans. and ed. New York: Oxford University Press.

———. 1963. *The Sociology of Religion,* trans. Ephraim Fischoff. Boston, MA: Beacon Press.

———. 1978 [1956]. *Economy and Society,* ed. Guenther Roth and Claus Wittich. 2 vols. Berkeley, CA: University of California Press.

Weems, Benjamin B. 1964. *Reform, Rebellion, and the Heavenly Way.* Tuscon, AZ: University of Arizona Press.

Weller, Robert P. 1987a. *Unities and Diversities in Chinese Religion.* Seattle, WA: University of Washington Press.

———. 1987b. The Politics of Ritual Disguise: Repression and Response in Taiwanese Religion. *Modern China* 13:17–39.

Werblowsky, R. J. Zwi. 1976. *Beyond Tradition and Modernity: Changing Religions in a Changing World.* London: Athlone Press.

Werbner, Richard P. 1977. *Regional Cults*. Association of Social Anthropologists Monograph, no. 16. London: Academic Press.

Werner, Jayne Susan. 1981. *Peasant Politics and Religious Sectarianism: Peasant and Priest in the Cao Dai in Viet Nam*. Monograph Series, no. 23. New Haven, CT: Yale University Southeast Asia Studies.

Whitaker, Donald P., et al. 1973. *Area Handbook for the Khmer Republic (Cambodia)*. DA Pam 550–50. Washington, D.C.: U.S. Government Printing Office.

White, Christine Pelzer. 1992. Calling the Wandering Souls: A Plea for Deeper Understanding of the Missing in Action (MIA) Issue. *Indochina Newsletter* 74:2, 4–8.

Williams, Brackette. 1989. A Class Act: Anthropology and the Race to Nation across Ethnic Terrain. *Annual Review of Anthropology* 18:401–444.

Willmott, W. E. 1981. Analytical Errors of the Kampuchean Communist Party. *Pacific Affairs* 54 (2): 209–227.

Wilson, Constance M. 1970. State and Society in the Reign of Mongkut, 1851–1868: Thailand on the Eve of Modernization. Ph.D. dissertation, Cornell University.

Winn, R. A. 1921. The New Wife, a New Woman. *The Korea Mission Field* 17 (January): 21.

Winstedt, R. O. 1977 [1924]. Karamat: Sacred Places and Persons in Malaya. In *Malaysian Branch Royal Asiatic Society Reprint No. 4: A Centenary Volume*, ed. Tan Sri Datuk Mubin Sheppard, Singapore: Times Printers.

Wolf, Arthur P. 1974. Gods, Ghosts, and Ancestors. In *Religion and Ritual in Chinese Society*, ed. Arthur P. Wolf, 131–182. Stanford, CA: Stanford University Press.

Woodward, Mark R. 1988. The *Slametan*: Textual Knowledge and Ritual Performance in Central Javanese Islam. *History of Religions* 28 (1): 54–89.

———. 1989. *Islam in Java: Normative Piety and Mysticism in the Sultanate of Yogyakarta*. Association for Asian Studies Monograph, no. 45. Tucson, AZ: University of Arizona Press.

Wu Jing. 1982. *Pochu fengjian mixin wenda* [Questions and answers on eradicating feudal superstition]. Nanjing: Jiangsu Renmin Chubanshe.

Wynne, M. L. 1941. *Triad and Tabut: A Survey of the Origin and Diffusion of Chinese and Mohammedan Societies in the Malay Peninsula, 1800–1935*. Singapore: Government Printing Office.

Xu Hui et al., eds. 1988. Wenzhou: wenming yu yuweide fancha [Wenzhou: The contrast between civilization and ignorance]. In *Zhongguo guaixianxiang: xinwen qishilu* [Chinese strange phenomena: Revelations from the news media]. Shenyang: Shenyang Chubanshe.

Yagi, Shusuke. 1988. *Samnak Puu Sawan: Rise and Oppression of a New Religious Movement in Thailand*. Ph.D. dissertation, University of Washington.

Yang, C. K. 1961. *Religion in Chinese Society*. Berkeley, CA: University of California Press.

Yang, Mayfair Mei-Hui. 1989. The Gift Economy and State Power in China. *Comparative Studies in Society and History* 31 (1): 25–54.

Yeoh, Brenda S. A. 1991. The Control of "Sacred" Space: Conflicts over the Chinese Burial Grounds in Colonial Singapore, 1880–1930. *Journal of Southeast Asian Studies* 22 (2): 282–311.

Yi Kwang-gyu [Kwang Kyu Lee]. 1974. Kwanhonsangje [Weddings, funerals, and ancestor worship]. In *Han'guk minsokhak kaesŏl* [Introduction to Korean ethnology], ed. T. Yi, K. Yi, and C. Chang, 59–87. Seoul: Minjung Sŏgwan.

———. 1977. *Han'guk kajokŭi sajŏk yŏn'gu* [Historical study of the Korean family]. Seoul: Ilchisa.

———. 1983. Kwanhonsangje [Weddings, funerals, and ancestor worship]. In *Seoul Yukpaegnyŏn Sa* [A 600-year history of Seoul] 5:1272–1283.

Yi Nung-hwa. 1976 [1927]. *Chosŏn musok ko* [Reflections on Korean shamanism], trans. Yi Chae-gon. Seoul: Paengnŭk.

Young, Ernest. 1983. Politics in the Aftermath of Revolution: The Era of Yuan Shih-k'ai. In *Cambridge History of China,* ed. Dennis Twitchett and John K. Fairbank, 12:209–259. Cambridge; New York: Cambridge University Press.

Yu Guanghong. 1988. Making a Malefactor a Benefactor: Ghost Worship in Taiwan. Ms.

Zago, Marcello. 1976. Contemporary Khmer Buddhism. In *Buddhism in the Modern World,* ed. Heinrich Dumoulin, 109–119. New York: Collier Books.

Zhang, Yingjin. 1990. Ideology of the Body in *Red Sorghum:* National Allegory, National Roots, and Third Cinema. *East-West Film Journal* 4 (2): 39–53.

Zhang Zongrong. 1985. *Shiba Wanggong Chuanqi* [The strange tale of the Eighteen Kings]. Taipei: Yiqun Tushu.

Zhongguo Encyclopedia Committee. 1986. Minzu [Nationality]. In *Zhongguo dabaike quanshu* [The complete encyclopedia of China]. Minzu, 302–303. Beijing: China Complete Encyclopedia Publishing Society.

CONTRIBUTORS

Ann S. Anagnost is Assistant Professor of Anthropology at the University of Washington. Her current research looks at constructions of civility and modernity in post-Mao China and the discourse of population in Chinese political discourse.

Jean Comaroff is Professor of Anthropology at the University of Chicago. She has published widely on ritual and history, especially among the Tswana peoples of Southern Africa. Her most recent books are *Of Revelation and Revolution: Christianity, Colonialism, and Consciousness in South Africa* and *Ethnography and the Historical Imagination,* both with John L. Comaroff.

Jean DeBernardi is Assistant Professor of Anthropology at the University of Alberta. She received her education at Stanford University, Oxford University, and the University of Chicago and has done ethnographic fieldwork with Chinese communities in Malaysia and Taiwan. Her research interests include Chinese popular religious culture and sociolinguistics, and she is currently preparing a monograph based on her research in Malaysia.

Chaiwat Satha-Anand is Associate Professor of Political Science at Thammasat University in Bangkok. He works in the fields of violence/nonviolence, ethnicity, religions, and social theory. His English-language publications include *Islam and Violence* (University of South Florida, 1987) and his essay "The Nonviolent Crescent," which appears in *Arab Nonviolent Political Struggle in the Middle East* (Lynne Rienner, 1990) and has been translated into Arabic and Bahasa Indonesia. One of his most recent articles, "Toward a Peace Culture in Asia," appears in *Peace and Conflict Issues after the Cold War* (Paris: UNESCO, 1992). He is the convener of the Nonviolence Commission with the International Peace Research Association (IPRA).

James H. Foard is Associate Professor of Religious Studies at Arizona State University, specializing in Japanese religious history. His previous publications have concerned medieval Buddhism, Buddhism and literature, and popular pilgrimage. He is currently working on a book about Hiroshima.

Dru C. Gladney is Assistant Professor of Anthropology at the University of Southern California, Los Angeles. He has conducted field research on ethnic and religious nationalism in China, Central Asia, and Turkey. His publications

349

include *Muslim Chinese: Ethnic Nationalism in the People's Republic* (Harvard University Press, 1991), "The Ethnogenesis of the Uighur" (1990) and "Transnational Islam and Uighur National Identity" (1992; both in *Central Asian Survey*), and "Muslim Tombs and Ethnic Folklore: Charters for Hui Identity" (*Journal of Asian Studies*, 1987).

Helen Hardacre is Reischauer Institute Professor of Japanese Religions and Society in the Department of East Asian Languages and Civilizations at Harvard University. Her field is Japanese religious history, and she is the author of *Lay Buddhism in Contemporary Japan: Reiyukai Kyodan, Kurozumikyo, and the New Religions of Japan* (Princeton University Press, 1984) and *Shinto and the State, 1868–1988* (Princeton University Press, 1989).

Robert W. Hefner is Associate Professor of Anthropology and Associate Director of the Institute for the Study of Economic Culture at Boston University. He writes on religion, politics, and modernity and is currently preparing a book on Islam, nationalism, and capitalism in Southeast Asia. His most recent works include *The Political Economy of Mountain Java: An Interpretive History* (University of California Press, 1990) and *Conversion to Christianity: Historical and Anthropological Perspectives on a Great Transformation* (University of California Press, 1993).

Laurel Kendall is Associate Curator in Charge of Asian Ethnographic Collections at the American Museum of Natural History and Adjunct Associate Professor at Columbia University. She is the author of *Shamans, Housewives, and Other Restless Spirits: Women in Korean Ritual Life* (University of Hawaii Press, 1985) and *The Life and Hard Times of a Korean Shaman: Of Tales and the Telling of Tales* (University of Hawaii Press, 1988). She is currently working on a book about contemporary Korean weddings and a film about Korean shamans in the 1990s.

Charles F. Keyes is Professor of Anthropology and Director of Southeast Asian Studies at the University of Washington. He has written extensively on Buddhism and society and on relations among ethnic groups in Southeast Asia. Among his most recent works are *Thailand: Buddhist Kingdom as Modern Nation-State* (Westview Press, 1987) and an edited volume, *Reshaping Local Worlds: Formal Education and Cultural Change in Rural Southeast Asia* (Yale Southeast Asia Studies, 1991). He is currently working on a study of ethnicity and nationalism among Tai peoples of Southeast Asia.

Kwang-ok Kim is Professor and Chairperson of the Department of Anthropology at Seoul National University, South Korea. His interests are politics and rituals. His published books include *Political Aspects of the Traditional Way of Life in Korea, Elite Culture at Local Level Politics in Contemporary Korea, Religion and Social Structure of Taruko in Taiwan,* and *Affinal Ties and Inter-Village Relations in North China*. He has also written several articles. He has done fieldwork in Taiwan, Korea, and mainland China.

Shamsul A. B. is Professor of Social Anthropology at the National University of Malaysia, Bangi, Selangor, Malaysia. He has been researching Malaysian culture and political economy for the past twenty years and is the author of *From British to Bumiputera Rule* (Singapore, 1986) and numerous essays analyzing past and contemporary Malaysian society. He is currently finishing a book manuscript entitled "Malaysia—One State, Many Nations: Ethnicity and State Formation in Malaysia."

Robert P. Weller is Research Associate at the Institute for the Study of Economic Culture and Associate Professor of Anthropology at Boston University. He is the author of *Unities and Diversities in Chinese Religion* (University of Washington Press, 1987) and editor (with Scott Guggenheim) of *Power and Protest in the Countryside: Studies of Rural Unrest in Asia, Europe, and Latin America* (Duke University Press, 1982). He has a forthcoming book on resistance in China and is currently working on changing concepts of nature in Taiwan.

INDEX

353